The Peppers, Cracklings, and Knots of Wool Cookbook

The Peppers, Cracklings, and Knots of Wool Cookbook

The Global Migration of African Cuisine

Enjoy !

Diane M. Spivey

Diane M. Spivey

STATE UNIVERSITY OF NEW YORK PRESS

Production by Ruth Fisher
Marketing by Fran Keneston

Published by
State University of New York Press, Albany

For information, address the State University of New York Press,
State University Plaza, Albany, NY 12246

Library of Congress Cataloging-in-Publication Data
Spivey, Diane M., 1949–
    The peppers, cracklings, and knots of wool cookbook : the global
migration of African cuisine / Diane M. Spivey.
        p.   cm.
    Includes bibliographical references and index.
    ISBN 0-7914-4375-2
    1. Cookery, African.   I. Title.
TX725.A4S68   1999
    641.59′29073—dc21   99-26846
                                                          CIP

10 9 8 7 6 5 4 3 2 1

Dedication

To my husband, Donald, who gave only one response to my constant complaint that Africa had never been given its culinary due: "Don't *say* it, dear. *Write* it!" His neverending help and encouragement have been a beacon in my life as I sought to bring this project to completion.

I must also dedicate this work to the millions of African cooks at home and in the diaspora who deserve a culinary pedestal, the place where culinary artists belong who have helped to teach the world how to cook.

Racism, or as they say now, tradition, is passed down like recipes. The trick is, you got to know what to eat, and what to leave on the plate.

—From *Mississippi Masala*

Contents

Chapter Six
Without Rival, Anywhere: The Cultural Impact
of the African Cook in the Americas

Chapter Seven
Economics, War, and the Northern Migration
of the Southern Black Cook

Chapter Eight
Flapjacks and Blue Notes

Acknowledgments

The completion of this manuscript was made possible by a number of friends and colleagues who contributed hours, and in some cases days, out of their schedules to read and provide critical comment on the material, and to whom I owe an immeasurable debt of gratitude: the late Sylvia Boone, professor in the department of Art History and African-American Studies program at Yale University, who offered strong support and encouragement at the outset; Amii Omara-Otunnu, Director of the Center for Contemporary African Studies and professor in the department of history at the University of Connecticut; Vincent Bakpetu Thompson, professor in the department of history at Connecticut College; Robert M. Levine, Director of Latin American Studies and professor in the department of history at the University of Miami; and Donald Spivey, professor and chair of the department of history at the University of Miami. I would also like to thank Karen Kupperman, professor in the department of history at New York University, Professor Roger Buckley, Director of the Asian American Studies Institute at the University of Connecticut, and Edmund Abaka, a professor in the department of history at the University of Miami, for their guidance in helping me to locate particular sources. Additional thanks go to Whittington B. Johnson, professor in the department of history at the University of Miami, who has also been very supportive of my work.

I am indeed indebted to Mr. Thavro Phim of the Cambodian Genocide Project at Yale University, who provided me with translations of recipe titles in beautiful Cambodian script; Dr. Abigail

Kaun, a professor in the department of linguistics at Yale University, and her husband Mr. Shrikanth S. Narayanan, who found time in their schedules to translate some of my recipe titles into Tamil; Mrs. Betsy Criswell, proprietor of Guyana Market Place in Miami, Florida, who assisted me with information on the use of various Indian and Caribbean ingredients; Mrs. Lenny del Granado, secretary in the department of history at the University of Miami, who never hesitates to give her time and energy on behalf of myself and others; my artist-daughter Sahar Spivey, who provided sketches of Olmec heads and colonial cooks for this book; and especially to my editor, Ms. Zina Lawrence, and the staff at SUNY Press.

Invaluable to my research on this project are the vast and rich holdings of university, public, and private libraries, including the Library of Congress (with special thanks to reference librarian Judith Mistichelli); Yale Divinity School Library; Newberry Library in Chicago; Harvard University's Harvard-Yenching Library (with special thanks to Dr. Raymond Lum); University of Chicago Library's Department of Special Collections; Georgetown University Libraries; University of Miami's Richter Library; University of Maine libraries; University of Connecticut's Homer Babbidge Library; Connecticut State Library; University of Hartford's Mortensen Library; Trinity College library in Hartford; Tulane University's Amistad Research Collection; University of Baltimore library; University of Missouri's Elmer Ellis Library; Wright State University's library in Dayton, Ohio; Suffolk University's Mildred F. Sawyer Library in Boston, Massachusetts; the library of Washington & Lee University in Lexington, Virginia; Norwalk, Connecticut, Community College's Everett Baker Learning Resources Center; Mohegan Community College Library in Norwich, Connecticut; National College of Education, Mrs. John N. Crouse Library in Evanston, Illinois; Schomburg Center for Research in Black Culture in New York City; The State Historical Society of Missouri; Tantaquidgeon Indian Museum in Connecticut; Saint Joseph Museum in Missouri; Mystic Seaport Museum in Mystic, Connecticut; Hartford, Connecticut, Public Library; Philadelphia, Pennsylvania, Public Library; Windsor, Connecticut, Public Library; Dayton, Ohio, Public Library; Bridgeport, Connecticut, Public Library and the Harold Washington Branch of the Chicago, Illinois, Public Library.

Special thanks are also extended to the following embassies in Washington, D.C., all of which worked diligently to provide me with information on the customs and culinary backgrounds of their homelands: The Embassy of the Republic of Uganda, the Cultural Department of The Embassy of Peru, The Embassy of Madagascar, The Embassy of India and its Information Service, The Embassy of Guatemala, The Embassy of the Republic of Honduras, The Embassy of the Lao People's Democratic Republic, The Embassy of Ecuador, The Embassy of Mexico, The Embassy of Nigeria, and The Embassy of Malawi.

Lastly, my travels to Africa, especially Ghana, to Mexico, and to Caribbean ports of call such as Jamaica and the Bahamas, were turned into culinary adventures by the people I met with, talked with, ate with. The wonderful new acquaintances made during my stay at all of these places helped me hone my own culinary skills as well as gain a greater understanding of their cultures, past and present. For these precious gifts I am truly grateful.

Introduction

The battle for inclusion and multiculturalism has been joined in the realm of food. Africa has been a major contributor to world cuisine and this contribution has either been overlooked, trivialized, or denied. References to African cuisine as primitive, unsophisticated, and virtually nonexistent abound within the pseudo-studies of international and ethnic cooking. As far as the detractors are concerned, Africa has not influenced world cuisine because it had nothing worthy of emulating or of sharing with peoples and cultures outside or within the African continent.

To counteract such insensitivity and blatant misinformation, I embarked on what became a fifteen-year sojourn in and through libraries, archives, journals, private collections, oral sources, and intensive reading in the culinary arts, history, archaeology, anthropology, philology, paleontology, psychoanalysis, botany, agriculture, agronomy, biology, zoology, geography, cartography, theology, and music. Drawing also on the multiethnic heritage of my relatives and friends, from information gained in both conversation and their kitchens, I was able to grasp and document the unique transition and contribution of African cooking to cuisines throughout the world.

Travel abroad provided me with authentic honing of my perspective and understanding of the relationship between people of color, their culture, their food preparation, and helped to further refine my cooking and recipes.

I have been on a mission, and perhaps this mission began even earlier than I realized. I grew up in Chicago during the '50s and '60s. I remember that I could never get enough of cake. When I was in grammar school I could not wait for Sunday. The Sunday paper had numerous advertisements for cakes, both from scratch and mixes. The frostings came in many different colors and flavors. I cut them *all* out and pasted the pictures in a scrapbook. I ate "from scratch" cakes made by my maternal grandmother. She was always bringing cakes, ice creams, tea cakes, and apple pies to our house. Traveling on the 12th Street bus with ice cream packed in ice was no easy matter. It made her angelic to me. She, like my paternal grandmother, made cakes that were unique and tasted like no others. This was true of many of their recipes for other dishes. We had other relatives and family friends who created great culinary delights that were sure award winners.

The '60s were beautiful for other reasons as well. There were many voices of reason that would help destroy the myths of inferiority that contributed so greatly to African American self-hatred. Learning about your roots can be a hard and arduous task when you are an African American wading through discourse that demeans your very existence and denies your contributions. The '60s certainly challenged and helped me to become conscious and alive, spiritually. I am not talking about religion. I am talking about the spirit that motivates and sparks an inner hunger for knowledge and an accurate historical record. Over the years, however, that inner hunger for knowledge sparked a war that has emerged and taken center stage in my life.

During my attempt to break out of my mother's old habit of filling everyone's stomach, day after day, with chicken dishes, I borrowed cookbooks from the library. I have always enjoyed dishes from various cultures, but in this case I wanted to master those foods about which I already possessed some knowledge. I started out with texts on African, Mexican, and African American cuisine. The discourse contained in volumes on African cuisine, to my utter disgust, were usually consistent in their themes:

1. No food products were indigenous to Africa, thereby precluding Africans from being capable of developing any sort of cuisine prior to European intervention, and

2. Africans came into contact with ninety-nine percent of the foods they consumed only as a result of the slave trade, and

3. African culinary traditions vary from country to country and have absolutely nothing in common.

All of Mexico, and for that matter, South America were also savage and primitive culinary environments, according to these experts, until Europe descended upon them. The cuisines showcased for these areas today tend to celebrate what is considered to be the European influence. African Americans, whose heritage and legacy was for so long relegated to slavery, had their cuisine pigeonholed in the narrow, albeit important and tasty, categorization of "soul food," specifically chitlins, corn bread, fatback, greens, and the like.

I began to read and study other cookbooks written on various peoples of color throughout the world. I discovered many commonalities in ingredients and methods of food preparation shared between Africa and other so-called Third World countries. The countless recipes I recreated and served to family and friends had an unmistakable African imprint. It was disconcerting, however, to find that the cookbook authors usually failed to acknowledge an African connection or contribution. In a number of cases, Mexican cuisine and culture was allowed to align itself strictly with that of South America. India somehow reached out a culinary hand and touched Indonesia. Thailand and Burma had obviously worn Cambodia's apron. Why was there not one contribution from African kitchens to those of any other country on the planet? It was a personal affront and a call to intellectual arms.

I found myself at war, challenged to get the record straight about the African contribution to the world of food and cooking. Armed with my inner hunger and passion to learn more of the African culinary past, I rediscovered "Lucy" and East Africa, the cradle of humankind and civilization and therefore the cradle of the culinary arts (you will notice that my study begins with East Africa, but its cuisine is only one of many types characteristic of the continent). East African cuisine and culture migrated to every part of the continent, diversifying and establishing new concepts, while retaining basic aspects and characteristics of the old. Throughout the continent, prosperity arose out of superior agricultural environments and transcontinental trade and commerce in gold, iron, ivory, and agricultural and other goods. These factors became the foundation of Africa's fabulous cities and trading ports, as well as famous seats of learning.

Exploration and migration continued beyond African coasts to every corner of the globe, and from very ancient times through the end of the 1400s A.D., even greater prosperity was attained through intercontinental trade. East Coast cuisine and culture transplanted itself by means of explorers, merchants, travelers, and seamen bound for India, Indonesia, China, Southeast Asia, and Japan. The Dravidians of southern India and the Khmers of Southeast Asia, for example, are two of numerous ancient, Eastern civilizations that still bear many African imprints. Africa's East and West Coast cultures made their indelible marks through exploration, migration, and trade expeditions on the Olmecs and Mayans, the Chavin, Mound Builders, Caribs, and other cultures in the Americas. It was obvious to me that the twenty- and thirty-ton basalt heads revealing African features that were excavated in Mexico in the nineteenth and twentieth centuries had to be redefined as something far greater than slaves and mere baggage handlers, "who European explorers brought with them to the Americas." I reexamined and went beyond previous sources and interpretations that labeled Africans, found in residence in Colombia on Balboa's arrival, as nothing more than "shipwrecked Negro pirates from Ethiopia."

Such explanations must be classified as utter nonsense in light of the fact that Europe as well was the recipient of the fruits of African agricultural, mining, and intellectual labors. Conventional scholarship conveniently ignores that the Greeks and Romans, in ancient times, copied African medical, philosophical, political, and social systems and expertise. In a later era, when Europe emerged from the Dark Ages, the European economy came to be dependent upon West African gold. In addition, the Moors introduced Spain to rice, sugarcane, dates, ginger, cotton, lemons, and strawberries, as well as the silk industry. Agricultural techniques learned from the Moors would later enable the Portuguese to amass fortunes on sugarcane and coffee plantations in Brazil. It was precisely those plantation systems (or what is better known as the slave trade) established all over the Americas which also led to the rape and plunder and colonization of Africa and, for that matter, a sizeable chunk of the rest of the world. Africa's wealth and power, its social and economic order were demolished as a result, and all of Africa's contributions and expertise were quickly defined away from Africa and attributed solely to those who had either stolen or copied them. This was the beginning of the colonization of history and scholarship.

Africa's history was colonized in order to rationalize the European plundering of Africa. African culinary traditions, as part of that history, suffered the same fate. The "de-colonization" of African cuisine is the underlying theme in *Peppers, Cracklings, and Knots of Wool,* as it dispels the long-told lie that Africans have always been dirty, naked, human-flesh-eating little (and big) black savages, picking their toes, waiting in darkness for Europe to show them where the groceries were. *Peppers, Cracklings, and Knots of Wool* tells a story; a story of Africa's culinary and cultural contributions to ancient, magnificent civilizations, both at home and on numerous foreign shores, and how those contributions continue to mark our cuisine, culture, and society today.

In order to fully understand and appreciate those contributions and their impact on African cooking on the French, Portuguese, Spanish, and British colonies in Brazil, the Caribbean, and the United States, from slavery to contemporary times, one must look at historical records which examine Africans, uprooted from their homeland, forced to labor for the masters of the "New World," but who nevertheless survived and maintained their cultural heritage. Such heritage is noticeably demonstrated in their language, religion, folkways, traditions, and innovations in music, dance, and most certainly cuisine. The ability to be creative and produce new variations on old themes is the heart and soul of African culture and cooking and deserves full inclusion. The culinary creations of these artistic African women and men are countless, yet small credit, at best, has been given them. Perhaps with the exception of greens, corn bread, and let us not forget chitlins, Africans, let some people tell it, "had little influence in the cooking preferences of Europeans" and the rest of the world. We have been omitted from history on this front; this book serves to put us in.

As the African race has been virtually left out of culinary history, it is to me the same as being uprooted from our cultural and ancestral homes all over again. In the historical sense, we have been pushed into a small, unlit, insignificant corner; a corner that has defined our present and will seal our destiny if not challenged;

a corner, as Toni Morrison would say, that merely "hovers on the periphery of [culinary] imagination."

I have indeed brought challenge to this corner of history, as my study represents an entirely different approach to presenting culinary information. Throughout the book I have punctuated the story with ethnically rich, spicy, delicious recipes for main dishes, soups, breads, drinks, stews, casseroles, hors d'oeuvres, and desserts. Intertwined with serious social and historical content, food and recipes, are my own social, or idiosyncratic, commentaries. In order to ensure that the book would be reader friendly, I have chosen to omit footnotes, or the traditional scholarly format, which would usually run rampant throughout the pages of a presentation such as this one. Those wishing to follow up on sources and references used for this text will find complete bibliographic essays for each chapter in the rear of the book.

Regarding the recipes, I would like to make one or two points clear at the outset: African cooking has always been just as much a creative art form as it is a science. Precise measuring, typical of Western recipes, is not a tradition in the African culinary process because the cook prefers (which is demonstrative of her or his skill and resourcefulness) to manipulate the ingredients until the food comes out "just right." The recipes presented here are all entirely my own creations, except where otherwise noted, and have been standardized and modernized for ease of preparation. I have, however, tried to remain faithful to roots of ethnic tradition relating to ingredients and African contribution.

I offer a taste of Africa, by way of the pots and cauldrons of people of color from various parts of the globe. It is a culinary contribution that has always been present.

Feasting among the "Eastern Ethiopians"

⁂ ⁂ ⁂ ⁂

The African Element in Dravidian Cuisine

Septimus Severus, Emperor of Rome, was said to have re-tained all of the habits he acquired in his youth, especially his taste for African cooking. During his reign, from A.D. 193 to 211, he insisted that his table be constantly supplied with special foodstuffs, including fruits and vegetables, he had imported directly from Africa. Obviously, such shopping trips would have been unnecessary had these foods been available in Europe. The fact is Africa was a source of agricultural production and culinary fare like no other. The emperor's reign, to be sure, was not the first nor the last time in history that African foods were in demand and had to be transported to distant lands; lands far, far away from African shores. The continent's vast wealth attracted Roman emperors, Greek politicians and travelers, merchants and royalty from India and the Far East. African history is, in fact, the story of the migration and settlement, barter, and interaction with Africa's cuisines, material wealth, and cultures in other lands such as India, Southeast Asia, Mexico, South America, the Caribbean, Native America, to name a few.

Septimus Severus's love for Africa's victuals is understandable considering the continent's bounty of agricultural products and the wide array of cooking styles. In fact, the wealth of Africa's East

Coast centered around food. It was spices, used in the preparation of those foods, that enticed a ruthless, savage European invasion of the East Coast of the continent in 1501. Prior to that time, Africa's centuries-old control on the lucrative maritime trade in spices with India had made the East Coast societies famous as cities well supplied with vast arrays of food available to the average citizen. East African trading ports had become famous in many corners of the globe as "city empires" which not only oversaw their own tremendous internal and international trade network in iron, gold, and ivory but were also involved in an age-old development of cuisines; a bartering, between Africa and India, of numerous ways and preparations of different foods.

To term the development of cuisines in East Africa an age-old process is to put it mildly. As DNA studies on "Lucy," discovered in Ethiopia, and *Zinjanthropus Boisei*, excavated in Kenya, indicate, East Africa represents the birthplace of humankind and civilization. It is also the origin of cooking and cuisine.

Eight thousand years ago, while Europe was still chilling out in the Ice Age, the Sahara was a green fertile region supporting a large population. An abundant and reliable food supply provided by fertile soil and livestock such as sheep, goats, and cattle enabled a sedentary population to develop in the Saharan region. With numerous rivers flowing throughout the Sahara, fishing populations also flourished. There were a number of fruits and vegetables, some of which have been documented as existing in prehistoric times on Rusinga and Mfangano Islands. Mary, of the husband and wife team of Louis and Mary Leakey, did extensive research on these islands in the Lake Victoria area. She found many fossil seeds and fruits, some belonging to the cucumber family, and many having the same characteristics as their present-day counterparts.

From earliest to modern times, seeds from various flowers, fruits, and melons were also eaten as snacks in Africa. Pumpkin and sunflower seeds are two that could be toasted and eaten out of hand like peanuts. They were a favorite of children and adults alike. They were also used in various soups and stews as flavor enhancers and as thickeners. Seeds from the egusi melon are favored by many African cooks as an addition to meat and fish stews.

Olodowan Egusi Stew

3 Tbs. egusi seeds (see glossary), OR, 3 Tbs. pumpkin seeds (see glossary)

³/₄ tsp. cumin seeds (see glossary)

¹/₂ tsp. EACH coriander seeds, whole allspice, and yellow fenugreek seeds (see glossary)

¹/₄ tsp. EACH black fenugreek seeds and whole cloves (see glossary)

³/₄ inch piece cinnamon stick

3–4 Tbs. palm oil (see glossary) or peanut oil

Black pepper, to taste

1 large EACH onion and tomato, chopped

¹/₂ of a large red bell pepper, chopped

3 small "bird" chilies or malagueta pepper to taste, finely chopped (see glossary)

About ³/₄ to 1 pound beef stew meat, cut into bite-size chunks

3¹/₂ cups beef broth

1 cup water

³/₄ cup plus ²/₃ cup crushed tomatoes

2 Tbs. plus 2 tsp. light molasses

Salt and freshly ground black pepper, to taste

1 cup chopped collard greens

Toast melon seeds in a dry skillet by stirring over medium heat until lightly browned (some seeds may pop). Cool completely, then grind to a very fine meal. Toast the next 7 ingredients together in a dry skillet. Cool completely, then grind to a powder.

Heat oil in a pot. Add melon seeds, cooking and stirring for a minute, then ground spices and black pepper. Continue cooking and stirring for another minute or so. Add next 4 ingredients, then meat. Cook and stir for a couple of minutes. Stir in next 4 ingredients and mix well. Taste for needed salt and pepper. Bring to a boil, lower heat and simmer, covered, for 1 hour. Stir in collard greens and continue simmering for another 30 minutes. Add additional broth if you prefer a thinner stew. Taste for needed seasonings. Serve by itself or with rice.

East African civilization enriched the entire continent and beyond. Of the many trading ports and settlements on the eastern seaboard, sixty-five were located in Tanzania, twenty in Kenya, twenty-eight on Pemba Island, fourteen on the island of Zanzibar, and another fourteen in Somalia. One of the great commercial cities, Mombasa, was at the height of its development as an important seafood emporium. Bananas and fish and a fruit called *jammun* (which looked like an olive but was sweet to the taste) were said to be the primary staples of the diet of the inhabitants of Mombasa. In 1331, Ibn Battuta, who visited various East Coast cities, commented on eating habits and foods in Mombasa and Mogadishu. He observed rice cooked with butter, served on large wooden dishes. Side dishes included stews of chicken, meat, fish, and vegetables. Unripe bananas were sliced or mashed and cooked in fresh milk and served as a sauce. Curdled milk was placed in another vessel with peppercorns, vinegar, and saffron, green ginger, and mangoes, which, he said looked like apples but have a nut inside. Ripe mangoes were said to be very sweet and eaten like fruit; but unripe mangoes were as tart as lemons and were cooked in vinegar. Apparently the Mogadiscio (or Mogadishu) ate rice with these marinated mangoes, or pickles, as Ibn Battuta called them. In light of the present state of the people of Mogadishu in the 1990s, and the shortage of food there, Ibn Battuta's comments regarding the abundant amount of food available and consumed by the Mogadishu of the prosperous fourteenth century are most striking. He describes the people as being very fat and corpulent.

The captivating fragrance of the delicious patties that follow, and the accompanying recipe, Spicy Yellow Rice With Minted Peas, signify tasty dishes reminiscent of East African food stalls. Both can be successfully served for lunch or dinner.

⁂⁂⁂⁂⁂⁂⁂⁂⁂⁂⁂⁂⁂⁂⁂⁂⁂⁂⁂⁂⁂⁂⁂⁂⁂⁂⁂⁂⁂⁂⁂⁂⁂⁂⁂⁂⁂⁂⁂

Lamb and Beef Patties Stuffed with Vegetables

1/2 pound ground lamb
1/2 pound ground round
8 cardamom pods, toasted and ground (see glossary)
1 1/2 tsp. garam masala (see glossary)
1/2 tsp. (or to taste) freshly ground black pepper

Salt to taste
1 onion, chopped
⅓ cup shredded carrots
⅓ cup peeled potatoes, cut into very small, thin chunks
2 Tbs. masa harina (corn flour)
¼ tsp. EACH ground cumin and black pepper
⅛ tsp. salt
2 Tbs. COLD milk
⅔ cup COLD beef broth or bouillon
Peanut, sesame seed, or vegetable oil

Combine first 6 ingredients and mix thoroughly. Stir in onions, carrots, and potatoes. Divide mixture into 4 equal portions. Shape into round patties, flatten, and set aside. Combine masa harina, cumin, black pepper, and the ⅛ tsp. salt. Mix well. Coat both sides of patties with masa harina mixture. Reserve leftover mixture. Lightly grease a skillet. Brown patties on both sides. While patties are browning add milk and bouillon to reserved masa harina mixture and blend well. When patties have browned, pour harina-bouillon mixture into skillet (do not pour directly on patties). Cover and simmer for 15 to 20 minutes.

And as an accompaniment:

ℒℒℒℒ

Spicy Yellow Rice with Minted Peas

2 Tbs. butter or palm oil
¾ tsp. berbere seasoning (A) (see glossary)
½ tsp. turmeric
¼ tsp. EACH freshly ground cloves and cayenne powder
½ onion, finely chopped
½ tsp. minced malagueta chili pepper, or 1 or 2 "bird" chilies, finely chopped
½ cup uncooked long grain rice
2½ cups water
¼ tsp. salt
¼ tsp. or more (to taste) black pepper
2 cups fresh sugar snap peas (about .40 pound)
Water
2 tsp. lemon juice

1 mint leaf
1½ tsp. sugar
1 tsp. peanut or sesame seed oil
4 black peppercorns, crushed
2 allspice berries, crushed
½ cup raisins, fresh ones preferred (optional)

Melt butter in saucepan or skillet. Add berbere seasoning and cook
and stir for about a minute. Add turmeric, cloves, and cayenne,
continuing to cook and stir for another 30 seconds or so. Add onion
and chili(es) and cook and stir for a couple of minutes. Add rice and
cook and stir for a minute or two. Stir in water, salt, and pepper.
Reduce heat, cover and simmer for 20 to 25 minutes.

Cook peas in small amount of water with lemon juice and mint leaf
for about 12 minutes. Drain peas and discard leaf. Stir sugar into
peas. Heat oil in saucepan or skillet. Add crushed peppercorns and
allspice berries. Stir continuously for about a minute. Add peas and
cook and stir just enough to thoroughly coat with oil and spices.
Serve rice in a small platter, surrounded by peas and garnished
with (if you desire) raisins.

East Africa, as a result of its abundance of spices, fruits and
vegetables, and yields from numerous mining operations, became
part of a vast commercial network linking it with those countries
along the eastern coast as far north as Egypt and as far south as
South Africa. Southern Africa's role in building the East Coast
civilization and the establishing of Africa's intercontinental trade
network has been grossly misstated by the white inhabitants of
South Africa who claim that they imported from Europe the fruits
and vegetables that made, they contend, "the richest, most complex
and civilized" cuisine on the continent. They claim credit for bringing to the continent its first pickled fish, meat pies, skewered and
grilled meats, stews, as well as salads, condiments, baked goods,
and wines. Let them tell it, they even taught Africans how to barbecue. All of Africa, including the southern part, needed no lessons
on cuisine or food preparation from Europe.

According to the colonialists of southern Africa, it was they
who were the first to develop what we call jerky. In truth, Afri-

cans dried and preserved antelope and beef, which they cut into strips in the fashion later described as jerky. It was this jerky, or biltong, as the Europeans renamed it, that ironically became the very sustenance of the armies under Cecil Rhodes that plundered and massacred the agriculturalist and cattle-breeding communities of the Matabele and Zulu nations of Zimbabwe and the rest of southern Africa.

The agriculturalist and cattle-breeding communities were only two of southern Africa's specialized societies. The use of iron agricultural implements for the production of crops was common to most African communities, thus allowing villages to surround themselves with their own gardens and fields in which millet and other foods were grown. Preparation of various foods played a very important role in maintaining the stability of all of southern Africa's specialized societies. Women prepared snacks that were taken along and eaten during long hours in the fields while crops were being planted or harvested. Jerky was one such snack.

Rich in protein and quite filling, jerky was sometimes taken as a serious, wholesome meal for miners, cattle herders, as well as warriors who had taken on the task of defending African lands against invaders. Try the following recipe. The African jerky will enhance your stamina in addition to delivering a long-lasting taste delight.

Matabele Strike Hold Beef Jerky

Marinade:
½ tsp. very finely grated ginger root
1 tsp. EACH ground cayenne and salt
¼ cup EACH honey and palm (see glossary) or peanut oil
½ cup sherry or dark rum
Juice of 2 lemons
2 to 2½ pounds lean shoulder steak (or antelope)

Combine all marinade ingredients and mix thoroughly in large bowl or dish.

Cut steak into strips about six to eight inches long, two inches wide and ¼ inch thick. Remove any fat. Place strips in marinade. Toss and stir until strips are thoroughly coated. Cover and set aside for one hour.

Meanwhile, line the bottom of your oven with foil, then preheat at 175 degrees. Hang strips from top oven rack. Allow oven door to remain slightly open so that moisture is not retained. Depending on the leanness of the meat and surrounding moisture, 4 or 5 hours should do it. Strips must be very dry, but with flexibility that allows them to bend before breaking. After cooling, store covered, in a cool, dry environment.

Food production in Africa was not dependent upon iron, but Africa's skill in iron production made possible an industrial advancement that impacted on agriculture and cooking. Iron industries created new productions in mining tools and farming tools as well as household and kitchen utensils. Many of these cooking utensils would make easier the preparation of long simmering sauces and soups, both the essence of African cuisine. Pots made of such tough metals allowed faster and more efficient preparation of foods by means of frying, braising, and steaming. The roasting of meats and fish on skewers or by grilling would also become a less arduous task.

Widespread mining activity (there have been four thousand ancient mining sites discovered so far), together with the increasing influx of cattle-breeding communities, pushed agriculturalist communities to higher ground, literally, to the hills, where they developed a different type of farming and irrigation system. Yams and sweet potatoes, onions and eggplant, spinach (silver beets) and beans, cabbage and tomatoes, peppers and bananas, coconuts and rice, okra and various spice berries, were just a few of the crops farmed on every available hillside. Intensive terrace farming was the way of agricultural life in some parts of southern and eastern Africa. Mounds were constructed for this purpose where there were no hills.

Despite the Africans' own accomplishments in agriculture, animal husbandry, industry, trade, and food preparation, cookbooks such as *African Cooking,* by South African–born Laurens van der Post and the editors of Time-Life Books, state that Africans had not come in contact with fruits and vegetables, tobacco, tea, or coffee until the invasion by the Portuguese; and that the Portuguese were responsible for revolutionizing food and cooking on the African continent. According to the Time-Life book, the Portuguese should also be thanked for improving Africa's breeds of cattle, sheep, and goats. It is a wonder that Africans survived at all prior to the coming of Europeans, if we take these "studies" seriously.

Nevertheless the African population increased quite rapidly in the two thousand years before European arrival. Along with larger populations and urban settlement came various technical improvements and increased specialization of services, such as advances in an already elaborate art and architecture, examples being the great stone edifices in Zimbabwe, and the evolving of a highly complex political organization. Sophistication of African agricultural methods, with its tie to African skill in iron production, provided the catalyst for these advances.

Such sophistication was evident in Kilwa, one of numerous important trading ports, and considered to be the "city-empire" of Africa's East Coast. Throughout the town were orchards, fruit gardens, and many streams and channels of sweet water. Its inhabitants, the Zanj, were jet black in complexion. The Zanj controlled the gold and iron trade from the mines of Zimbabwe and Mozambique. Acting as brokers in foreign export-import transactions, which included trade with Arabia, India, Indonesia, China, and Southeast Asia, these East Coast peoples became extremely wealthy. The wealth that this trade generated built the city's stone and mortared houses and buildings, structured with windows and richly carved wooden doors. During centuries of commercial prosperity, native historians and poets wrote in Swahili *Mashairi,* lyric songs, and *tendi,* epic poems, of the magnificence and splendor of Kilwa's city life.

Much of this city life centered around food. Spicy aromas emanated from and permeated every corner of the city. Hot, yellow peppers, known as *mitmita,* as well as saffron, cloves, ginger, and other spices were favorite additions to several sauces that had meat as their prime ingredient. These meat sauces were sometimes ladled over various cooked vegetables such as potatoes and cabbage. They were also used as dips for numerous varieties of hot peppers. Added to soups and stews, they made a tasty seasoning.

This is one version of a wonderful meat sauce from Dar Es Salaam in Tanzania. Dar Es Salaam stands about 130 miles north of Kilwa. The ground chicken liver offers as much a flavoring to the sauce as do the spices. This meat sauce serves well as a mouth-watering dip for Ethiopian breads such as *injera,* the first and original pancake.

Lamb and Beef Sauce Dar Es Salaam

½ pound not too lean ground beef
½ pound lean ground lamb
1 cooked and ground chicken liver
½ of a large red bell pepper
1 large onion, chopped
2 small tomatoes, chopped
½ of a medium large peach, peeled and chopped
1 cup tomato sauce
½ cup sherry, divided in half
1 tsp. cayenne
1 tsp. freshly ground cardamom (see glossary), divided in half
2 tsp. garam masala (see glossary), divided in half
Salt to taste
½ tsp. freshly ground black pepper
8 sprigs fresh cilantro, chopped
1 mint leaf (stem removed), chopped
3 sprigs parsley (stems removed), chopped

Brown beef and lamb together in large pot. Stir in next 12 ingredients, including only half of sherry, half of cardamom, and half of garam masala. Simmer, *uncovered*, over low heat, stirring occasionally, for about 30 minutes. Add remaining sherry, cardamom, garam masala, cilantro, mint, and parsley. Taste for needed salt and pepper. Continue simmering for another 25 to 30 minutes.

Can be served inside of pita breads with rice and/or cooked spinach for a lovely and wonderfully delicious sandwich.

Africa's lucrative maritime trade network in spices and minerals generated enormous jealousy and rivalry on the part of Portuguese and other European explorers, who were looking to establish authority and decisive power over all of the trade markets that existed between Africa, India, and the Far East. Yes, Spices! Spices allowed lavish feasts on a magnificent scale to be produced. Hundreds of recipes were concocted and no two were exactly the same. Europeans did not have spices and therefore could not create the cuisines that spices helped to produce. Used everyday in the cookery of these continents, they had the added advantage of preserving many foods. They were an indispensable commodity which became desperately sought after by Europeans. Also, many spices are related to herbs and it was herbs that were used in medicines in First World countries. Europeans' knowledge of medicine lagged far behind that of older civilizations, such as Africa. Ancient Egypt had a school of pharmacology. Imhotep, engineer and designer of the pyramids, brain surgeon, and physician to the pharaoh, lived two thousand years before Hippocrates, whom the Greeks claimed was the father of medicine.

Europe would attempt to lay claim to everything of value that Africa had. The lucrative spice trade was the enticement for the Portuguese invasion of Africa's East Coast in 1501. In fact, the Portuguese were so hell bent on repositioning East Africa's wealth into Portuguese hands that they called upon God and the Church to help them do it (as did the rest of Europe). The rape and destruction of Kilwa, Mombasa, Zanzibar, Brava, Malindi, and other East Coast cities was carried out with the endorsement and full participation of the Catholic Church and the Christian faith. In the case of Kilwa, Franciscan priests and their head vicar came ashore singing church melodies and brandishing crosses. They all gathered at the palace of the Swahili king, planted their crosses and prayed. When they had satisfied their lust for religious incantation, they ran into the town and ravaged and plundered all of the town's supplies and merchandise. Among hundreds of items appropriated, of particular interest to the priests were ornate leather casks containing beers brewed with fresh ginger and cloves, and wines fermented from various fruits such as blackberries, bananas, and watermelon. Honey beer, palm wine, and drinks made with cinnamon and raisins and aniseed were just a few that were the prevalent beverages confiscated by the invaders. Well, the priests had a good time sopping up the fine liquors they stole from the houses. It is doubtful that any of the liquor made it back to Portugal.

The following is a highly refreshing drink that has a tendency to make you hungry, after a couple of glasses. It can be made with or without liquor. With liquor, it is guaranteed to shatter the fast of a Pope. And frankly speaking, I am sure it did.

Spiced Yansoon

2½ cups water
16 allspice berries
3 tsp. aniseeds
2 Tbs., plus ½ tsp., sugar

Combine all ingredients in a saucepan. Boil for 5 minutes. Pour through strainer into cups. Makes 2 cups.

For an alcoholic beverage:
Strain hot yansoon into a small pitcher or container and cool completely. Fill two glasses with crushed ice. Divide yansoon between the two ice-filled glasses. Add a couple of ounces of 151 proof rum or other preferred spirit to each glass. Stir well. Garnish each serving with a very light sprinkle of ground cloves.

Between the ninth and fifteenth centuries, the Indian Ocean trade among Africa, India, and the Far East consisted of bartering and trade of merchandise and foodstuffs. The trade was also a cultural exchange in the preparation of marvelous foods. The demand for ivory was very important to Africa's export trade with China and India. In China, carrying chairs of ivory were manufactured for kings and their military and civilian officers. There were ivory chairs for dining, as well as for other important events. Ivory from East Africa was manufactured in India as handles for daggers and as chess and other game pieces. In addition, ivory bangle bracelets were extremely important in marriage ceremonies in India. The bracelet given to the bride was hers alone to wear during her lifetime. When she died, it was cremated with her. The marriage ceremony was a lavish affair. Nothing was spared in the preparation of food, drink, and entertainment to make the wedding day unforgettable. Depending on the wealth of the families and the number of guests, a wedding feast may have consisted of six to twelve meat dishes, with equal numbers of rice and vegetable dishes, snacks, and desserts.

A decoration or garnish for special occasion or festive dishes is *vark,* an edible silver. Now, I know that the thought of your teeth grinding metal may come to mind and that it should not be on the menu; but vark is odorless and tasteless. It comes in small, thin sheets, and is meant to lend a touch of elegance to the dish. Besides, your friends will all think you must be terribly rich if you can afford to eat it. The silver that adorns the following dish may be odorless and tasteless, but I assure you that this concoction is very much the opposite. It is majestic in its appearance, magical in its flavors and aroma. Quite truly, it is fit for a king—for his wedding, or anybody else's.

Lambchops Braised in Saffron Milk

8 shoulder lamb chops
Berbere seasoning (A) or garam masala (see glossary), lightly sprinkled and massaged into each side of chop
Seasoned salt and paprika
Flour
4 Tbs. (or as needed) palm, peanut, or sesame seed oil
1³/₄ cups milk
¹/₄ cup coconut milk
¹/₄ heaping tsp. saffron threads (see glossary)
3 Tbs. butter
2 onions, chopped
8 sprigs of fresh parsley, chopped
2 slices of bread, crumbled
1 8-ounce can crushed pineapple
³/₄ tsp. berbere seasoning (A) (see glossary)
¹/₄ tsp. EACH garam masala (see glossary) and cayenne
¹/₈ tsp. EACH ground nutmeg and ginger
³/₄ to 1 tsp. salt

¹/₂ tsp. white pepper
¹/₄ tsp. whole black peppercorns, crushed
¹/₃ cup dark rum
A couple of sheets of vark (optional)

Season chops with berbere seasoning (or garam masala), seasoned salt, and paprika. Coat with flour and brown on both sides in hot oil (allowing about 2 Tbs. for every 4 chops) in a large pot. While chops are browning, heat milk. When very, very hot add saffron and remove from heat. Stir occasionally for at least 15 minutes. Remove chops to a platter or dish and cover. Drain excess oil from pot (do not remove browned particles). Melt butter in same pot. Add onions, parsley, and bread. Cook and stir for a couple of minutes. Add pineapple, berbere, garam masala, cayenne, nutmeg, ginger, salt, white pepper, and peppercorns. Cook and stir for a couple more minutes. Stir in rum and saffron milk. Add chops to skillet, coating each chop with sauce. Simmer, covered, on low heat for approximately 45 to 60 minutes, or until chops are tender. Serve over yellow rice and garnish the serving platter or each individual serving with strips of vark, if you wish.

Common to both Africa and India is the seasoning of all food with hot peppers and a variety of spice blends. Also common to both continents is the skinning and "scoring" of chicken in the preparation of certain recipes. The purpose of "scoring," or cutting slits, is to allow the flavors and juices of the marinade to permeate the meat. The following is one such dish. The heavenly aromas this dish creates would definitely have made the gods sit up straight. If Greek gods did feast among the "blameless Ethiopians," they must have eaten one of Ethiopia's national dishes:

Doro Wat (Chicken Cooked in Pepper Sauce)

4 whole chicken legs, cut into 8 serving pieces. Chicken should be completely skinned and slits made into pieces so that flavors can penetrate
¹/₂ cup EACH thick coconut milk and lemon juice
¹/₄ cup milk

2 Tbs. spiced oil (recipe to follow), or 2 Tbs. butter
2 large onions, chopped
1 very large tomato, chopped
2 tsp. finely chopped fresh ginger root
1/4 tsp. freshly ground black fenugreek seeds
2 tsp. berbere (B) (see glossary)
1/4 tsp. (or more to taste) cayenne
1/2 tsp. white pepper
1/2 tsp. (or to taste) salt
1 tsp. paprika
1/4 cup dark rum
1/4 cup (4 Tbs.) ground split pea powder (dhal)
1/2 tsp. (or to taste) salt
4 hard-boiled eggs, slits or fork holes made all over
Black pepper, preferably freshly ground

Combine coconut milk, lemon juice, and milk in a shallow pan. Mix well. Place chicken pieces one layer deep in milk mixture. Massage milk mixture into both sides of chicken for a couple of minutes. Set chicken aside to marinate for 1 hour.

In a large pot, add the spiced oil and allow it to heat (if using butter, allow it to melt and brown over medium heat). Add the onions, tomato, and ginger root and cook and stir for a couple of minutes. Stir in fenugreek, berbere, cayenne, white pepper, salt, and paprika. Cook and stir for a couple of minutes more. Remove chicken from marinade. Stir marinade into pot. Add rum and stir to blend well. Add chicken to pot, coating each piece well with the sauce as it is added. Simmer chicken, covered, for about 40 minutes. Remove about 1 cup of liquid from pot. Allow liquid to cool slightly. Stir ground split peas and salt into 1 cup of liquid and blend well. Stir ground split pea mixture into pot. Cover and continue simmering for another 15 to 20 minutes. Place eggs on top of chicken during last ten minutes of cooking time. Before serving, sprinkle chicken generously with black pepper.

ℐℐ ℐℐ ℐℐ ℐℐ

Ethiopian Spiced Oil

1 pound butter, sliced into small chunks
1/4 cup chopped onion

1½ tsp. finely chopped ginger root
1 tsp. turmeric
1 Tbs. finely chopped garlic
¼ tsp. ground cardamom
½ inch piece of cinnamon stick
¼ tsp. nutmeg, freshly grated if possible
1 clove

Melt butter in saucepan without letting it scorch. Bring butter to a boil and add remaining ingredients. Simmer on very low heat for 40 minutes, or until the oil on top is completely clear and solids on the bottom are brown.

Using a sieve lined with cheesecloth, strain off the clear oil into a bowl. Strain a second time if any solids appear in oil. Seasonings may be discarded. This recipe will yield about 1 cup.

Ethiopian spiced oil can be stored in covered jars for up to 3 months in the refrigerator.

〰〰〰〰〰〰〰〰〰〰〰〰〰〰〰〰〰〰〰〰〰〰〰〰〰〰〰〰〰〰〰〰〰〰〰〰〰

The close ties between the people of Africa and India and their cuisines have been historically and traditionally ignored although there are those who persist in assigning Dravidian origins to Egypt while denying Egypt's Africanism. In describing the cuisines of India, particularly southern India, so-called food experts have credited the regional specialties in this part of the world to English tradition, coupled with that of the Balkans and Middle Eastern favorites from Turkey, Iran, Iraq, Syria, Israel, Jordan, Greece, and Lebanon. Anything but African.

The English, as well as the rest of Europe, have never been part of a culinary tradition that included masalas and tandoori cooked meats and breads, yoghurts and chutneys, nor chapatis and curries. Their culinary tie with traditional Indian cuisine is nonexistent. What is indisputable is the strong linkage in cooking style and taste of Africans and Indians. Both Indians and Africans favor the use of spices and peppers to create sauces to complement a variety of meat preparations, such as Ethiopian Kitfo, as well as desserts. Fruits and vegetables are combined to flavor one another in dishes designed as appetizers and side dishes such as black mushroom pilaf from southern India.

That linkage in cooking style is also attributable to the close affinities in prehistoric times between plants and animals in Africa and India. Geological research suggests that the Indian Ocean was once a continuous stretch of dry land extending from Madagascar to the Malay Archipelago, connecting southern India with Africa and Australia. Owing to improvements in hunting, first man, and woman, migrated from East Africa across this land bridge, sometimes called Lemuria, into India. During centuries of maritime prosperity, inhabitants of ancient Ethiopia and Somalia and countries all along Africa's East Coast made voyages across the Arabian Sea and Indian Ocean to countries in the east. African sailors constantly manned ships that were part of diplomatic missions and trading expeditions carrying merchants from Ethiopia, Persides, and Axum to the markets of Sieladiba, or Simhaladvipa (Ceylon). Cinnamon was one important commodity bartered at the markets of Ceylon. A tangy, yet sweet condiment for fruit, the following recipe, usually prepared with a profusion of the aromatic spice, offers a pungent and brash sensation to the palate.

Lavangapattai Malai Chaaru (Cinnamon Cream Condiment)

½ cup plain yogurt
½ cup sour cream
1 tsp. ground cinnamon
8 tsp. dark brown sugar
⅛ tsp. salt

Combine all ingredients, mixing well. Keep refrigerated. Use as dressing for fruit and other salads.

Spices and metals, ivory, tortoise shell, and rhinoceros horn were but a few of the many commodities loaded aboard East African trading vessels. Egypt never traded with India directly; however, Egyptians brought cloth, papyrus, and glass, from a period beginning about 1000 B.C., to Yemen in Arabia, a great center of trade. Some East African merchants making voyages in this region exchanged goods and then sailed on to India. It is also believed that the alphabet of western India had come from Africa with the sailors, metallurgists, shell fishers, and merchants on board the same ships. The merchants of western India exchanged Indian goods on the Diocoridus Islands near the Somali coast and brought back an alphabet from this region in the seventh or eighth century B.C. for use in their commercial ventures. Part of this alphabet denoted a monetary system, because it was African currency—cowrie shells— that were in extensive use in marketplaces all along the Malabar Coast. This alphabet later became an integral part of the written language of Tamil.

Tamil today is spoken by eighteen million people in India and Ceylon and by Tamilian immigrants in Assam, Burma, and Malaysia. The exception in the north is in the country of Baluchistan, where the people physically resemble the Dravidians of South India and who speak several Dravidian tongues, such as Brahui, Villi, and Santal. Certainly the cultural affinities of these two regions account for the similarities in their cuisines, such as the use of hot chilies and peppers.

The peoples of Africa, Baluchistan, and South India enjoy many of the same vegetables, such as okra and greens; for that matter, African Americans have always had a fondness for both vegetables. Okra, stewed with tomatoes and corn, fried, gumboed, or as an ingredient in many versions of succotash, became quite a versatile staple in African American kitchens. Okra is the most favored of all of India's tropical vegetables:

§§§

Kiirai Vendakkai (Okra Stewed with Spinach)

½ pound whole baby okra, each piece cut into halves and thirds, depending on the size
3 Tbs. sesame seed or peanut oil
¼ tsp. EACH black mustard seeds, cumin seeds, coriander seeds, black peppercorns, all toasted and ground to a powder
1 whole clove, toasted and ground to a powder
4 small red "bird" chili peppers, finely chopped
1 medium onion, chopped
1 large tomato, chopped
3 tsp. sugar

¹/₄ cup hot water
10 ounces spinach
¹/₄ tsp. finely chopped ginger root
Salt to taste

Heat 1 Tbs. of the oil in a skillet and add okra. Cook and stir until pieces are lightly browned. Remove okra and set aside.

Heat remaining 2 Tbs. of oil in skillet. Add chili peppers. Cook and stir for about 30 seconds. Add ground mustard, cumin, coriander seeds, peppercorns, and clove. Cook and stir for a minute or two. Add onion and tomato and continue to cook and stir for a couple of minutes. Mix in sugar, then water. Add okra, spinach, ginger root, and salt. Bring to a boil. Cover, lower heat, and simmer for about 14 minutes.

~~~~~~

Mustard greens, an African and African American favorite, are literally considered the soul food of the Sikhs of the Punjab region of India. The Sikhs regard mustard greens as a delicacy and accompany them with (are you ready?) corn bread. Their corn bread is made from masa harina, a fine corn flour like that used in Africa, Mexico, and South America.

~~~~~~

Pureed Greens with Groundnuts

1¹/₂ cups water
³/₄ cup coconut milk
2 finely chopped red "bird" chili peppers, or ¹/₂ tsp. crushed red pepper
¹/₄ cup finely crushed peanuts or walnuts
¹/₄ of a large green bell pepper, seeded and chopped
³/₄ tsp. garlic salt with parsley
2 tsp. finely chopped fresh ginger
16 ounces chopped mustard greens
16 ounces cut leaf spinach
Salt and freshly ground black pepper, to taste
5 Tbs. Ethiopian spiced oil (see recipe, this chapter), or ghee, or butter (If using butter, add a little black pepper and garlic salt.)

¼ tsp. ground ginger
½ of a medium onion, chopped

Combine water and milk in large pot. Stir in chili peppers, nuts, bell peppers, garlic salt, and ginger. Bring to a boil and add mustards, spinach, then salt and pepper. Simmer, covered, for 20 minutes. Stir in 3 Tbs. of spiced oil and continue simmering for 10 minutes more. When cooled down, puree in food processor.

Melt the remaining 2 Tbs. of spiced oil in a skillet or saucepan. Add ginger (and pepper and garlic if using butter) and cook and stir over medium heat for a minute or two. Add onions and cook and stir until onions start to brown.

Pour puree into a serving bowl and pour spiced oil mixture over it. Take a knife and swirl oil through puree a few times, allowing a "marbling" effect of the puree and oil.

⧚⧚

    Although Tamil literature records much ancient Dravidian history, Dravidian historians and scholars were the Brahmans. Like the Griots of African societies, they relied on the power of their memories to store the historical record. The Brahmans believed that to maintain the mental acuity necessary for skilled memorization, certain foods were mandatory in the diet. As the history of the people was orally transmitted from one generation to another, so were the recipes. Ghee, or clarified butter, is an ingredient now principally used in north Indian preparations. Hindu Brahmans, as well as the Jains, are strict vegetarians. They believe that ghee is the primary source of nutrition. The Brahmans believe that the development of intelligence is attributable to it and that it is brain food, possessing supernatural powers. For this reason, Hindu children are still given a spoonful of ghee each day "to sharpen their intelligence." People of India still follow the Brahman ritual of feeding a spoon of this oil to babies who are only minutes old.
    The almond is also considered to be "brain food" by the Brahmans in North India. It, like the sesame seed, which is very rich in protein, is extensively used in soups, sauces, stuffings, pilafs, and candies. Vegetarians, particularly Brahmans and Jains of south and southwestern India, consider sesame seeds to be one of their primary foods

and sesame seed oil as an essential flavoring and cooking oil. Sesame seeds are an important ingredient in all Hindu Brahman rituals, one of which is the ritual of paying homage to the dead.

The only pepper used in food preparations for the feast to honor the dead is black pepper, according to many sources. In certain East African societies one special type of hot pepper was sometimes chosen to lace the dishes served at gatherings after a funeral ceremony. Perhaps you might want to try these for a funeral wake. They are spicy enough to make the deceased open one eye. However, any occasion would be appropriate to serve these delicious patties.

Sesame Yam Patties

1½ medium-small yams or sweet potatoes
2 Tbs. dhal (see glossary)
1 Tbs. brown sugar
½ tsp. cinnamon
1 Tbs. sesame seed oil
¼ tsp. black mustard seeds
1 green or 2 red "bird" chili peppers, finely chopped
½ of a small onion, chopped
¼ tsp. EACH salt and freshly ground black pepper, or more to taste
½ tsp. toasted sesame seeds
2 tsp. EACH masa harina and dhal
About 2 tsp. sesame seed or peanut oil

Cook yams or sweet potatoes in skins until tender. Cool, then refrigerate until thoroughly chilled. Peel and mash in a bowl. Mix in the 2 Tbs. of dhal, sugar, and cinnamon.

Heat sesame seed oil in skillet. Add mustard seeds and stir for about 20 seconds. Add chili pepper and onion and cook and stir until onion begins to brown. Pour onion-oil mixture into yams (sweet potatoes). Add salt and pepper (taste and add more, as needed).

In a bowl, combine sesame seeds, masa harina, and remaining 2 tsp. dhal. Mix well.

Divide mixture into 6 portions. Roll each portion in sesame-masa mixture. Heat sesame seed or peanut oil in skillet. Add portions, gently flattening into rounds. Brown on both sides.

Whether you were a vegetarian or not, for Dravidians, rice was part of the diet. Rice cultivation was the economic basis of the culture. Wild rice is still indigenous to many different areas of India. There are more than 350 cultivated varieties of Indian wild rice. The importance of this crop to South India cannot be overstated. Aside from eating it, rice served many other uses. Sour rice water was used for washing clothes, a custom still practiced in remote parts of India. Among the many additions to tasty rice dishes is coconut, a favorite ingredient. In Africa, coconut is grated and added to cooked rice and vegetable dishes or combined with pulverized cooked rice or beans, rolled into balls and deep fried. Before serving as a dessert, these balls are cooled and rolled in sesame seeds. When cooked with rice, coconut adds a nice texture to the following recipe, which serves as a great stand-alone side dish.

Thengai Saadam (Coconut Rice)

¼ tsp. black mustard seeds
2 Tbs. sesame seed or peanut oil
1 large onion, chopped
2 green chili peppers, finely chopped
2 tsp. finely chopped ginger root
½ tsp. EACH salt and white pepper
1 cup EACH uncooked rice and coconut milk
1½ cups water
½ cup sweetened, finely grated coconut (see glossary)

Place mustard seeds in saucepan over medium heat. Cover and shake until seeds finish popping. Set aside.

Over medium heat, add oil to skillet. Add onions, chili peppers, and ginger root. Cook and stir until onions start to brown. Add mustard seeds, salt, pepper, then rice. Cook and stir about a minute. Stir in milk, water, and coconut. Bring to a boil, reduce heat, and simmer, covered, for 20 minutes. Remove from heat. Allow to rest for another 5 minutes.

Food and cuisine are mirrors that reflect the civilizations and institutions of a people. These institutions are sometimes presented in that society's written language and literature. Dravidian literature, much of which is in the form of poetry, ballads, and songs (in much the same way that the Kikuyu of Kenya composed lullabies and songs laden with their history), is quite reflective. Love of children was one of the most common motifs of Dravidian poetry. A mother with a young child who needed calming while she shopped at the market and/or cooked the meals at home would naturally recite some verses of popular poetry, set to improvised music. Morality and the practical wisdom of adjusting oneself to prevailing conditions were other messages that abounded in these poems. Ballads and songs were concerned with weddings, harvest, work, religion, and heroic sacrifice. In both Africa and India, there were cradle songs, songs of the dawn, when farmers go to work, songs of love, songs of field laborers, songs of wine, songs of play, and songs of festivals.

Food and songs were indispensable characteristics of harvest time because there were harvest festivals devoted to feasting. Harvest festivals in southern India showcased rice dishes, just as harvest feasts in parts of Kenya and Mozambique presented a preponderance of dishes comprised of millet and sorghum. Harvest celebrations in India, as was the case in many African societies, were marked by the offering of food to a deity and to neighbors, much music making and dance, as well as many other activities.

Imagine the taste of ground meats combined with spiced beans simmered with rice and vegetables. This meat is served in a festive dish sure to make you and your guests sing with praise.

"Mississippi Masala" Rice

A masala, or spice blend, is to Indian cuisine as berbere seasoning is to the cuisine of many East Africans. I call this dish Mississippi Masala because it contains a spice blend sometimes used in South

Indian cooking but it also contains hot sausage. I am related to two highly skilled cooks from Mississippi who each have concocted six different recipes of homemade hot sausage, made with either duck, lamb, pork (oops!), or beef (double oops!).

1 pound ground lamb
½ cup cooked and mashed great northern or white beans
1¼ tsp. garam masala (see glossary)
¼ tsp. EACH freshly ground cloves and crushed red pepper
Salt and freshly ground black pepper, to taste
1½ tsp. berbere seasoning (See glossary—use D)
1 large onion, chopped
½ cup sliced, cooked mushrooms
½ cup shredded carrots
½ cup raw rice
1 cup chicken broth
1½ cups beef broth

Brown lamb in a large skillet. Drain off oil as it collects. Stir in remaining ingredients. Simmer, covered, on low heat for 20 minutes. Allow to rest, covered, 5 minutes.

Common in both Africa and India was the practice of composing songs and ballads for every conceivable activity. Cooking was one such activity. Food could inspire the creation of a song. Sometimes songs would be the inspiration for the preparation of wonderful meals. I can personally vouch for the importance of song to cooking. I could not figure out what was wrong with a dish I was preparing one day. It was missing something, something crucial. I often listen to oldies while I do any kind of housework, including cooking. When Booker T. & the MG's dropped onto the turntable, I had it! Green Onions! The green onions pump special life into the following dish.

Vellai Tugeelil Sigappu Rajma (Red Beans in a Sea of White)

3 Tbs. sesame seed or peanut oil
1 large onion, chopped

1 heaping Tbs. chopped ginger root
½ tsp. crushed red pepper
1½ tsp. garam masala
White part of 2 green onions
2 Tbs. dried shrimp, finely chopped or ground
1¾ cup plus 2 Tbs. chicken broth
1 cup plus 1 Tbs. coconut milk
1¾ cups cooked great northern or white beans, pureed
½ tsp. white pepper
½ tsp., or to taste, black pepper
1⅓ cups cooked red kidney beans
Chopped green onions, tops and bottoms, for garnish

Heat oil in a medium pot and add the large, chopped onion. Cook and stir for a couple of minutes. Add ginger root, red pepper, and masala. Cook and stir for another couple of minutes. Add green onions and shrimp and cook another minute or two. Stir in chicken broth. Bring to a boil. Reduce heat, cover, and simmer for 15 minutes. Stir in milk, then bean puree. Add white and black pepper and blend well. Stir in red beans. Bring to a boil, reduce heat, and cover. Simmer on low heat for 10 minutes. Garnish each serving with green onions.

As throughout Africa, music and poetry were showcased during festivals for the arts in southern India. These festivals were also occasions for great food. A vast array of dishes were served at such events. The foods ranged from chicken and fish kari dishes, vegetable kari dishes, and tomato and spinach salads made with yoghurt, to coconut desserts such as barfis and karanjias.

Festivals were an important part of the Dravidian social, academic, and economic environment. Expressions of love and community support were exchanged and reinforced. Scholars and students alike from every school came to these events to set up debates, exchange philosophies, and give lectures and conduct discussions on matters of religion and politics. Another customary activity was to watch performances by actresses, dancing girls, and songstresses who treated audiences to theatrical and musical productions. As poets and other townspeople entered the city on the day of a poetry festival, the excitement was overwhelming. The city was gay with flags presented to the king to commemorate brave deeds, and other flags could be seen waving over shops that sold what was called the "gladdening toddy." Balladeers and wandering minstrels were plentiful and the streets were broad rivers of people listening to their music or singing themselves.

Various nationalities of people bought and sold at the shops of the marketplace on these days. Foodshops laid in huge supplies for the occasion, including greens, eggplant, jackfruit, mangoes, sugar candies, various desserts, cooked foods such as rice and kabobed meats and vegetables. All the food was devoured by the end of the day.

There are similarities between Diwali and the Busk Festival, or Boosketau, a festival celebrated by ancient Native Americans, and between Africans and their ceremony of "purifying the flame." As with the two latter ceremonies, Diwali is celebrated at the beginning of the new year, when everyone should buy new clothes, settle past debts, heal old feuds and quarrels—a time when everyone should wish everyone else good fortune. What sweeter way to heal old quarrels, and maybe even settle past debts, than to give a gift that is not only pretty, but tastes good too. Preparation is not time consuming and it is a simple, yet elegant dessert.

Carrot and Groundnut Dessert

3 big cooked carrots
1 cup cooked rice
½ cup EACH coconut milk and regular milk (or all coconut)
1 tsp. EACH rose water and dhal (see glossary)
¼ cup brown sugar
¼ cup plus 1 Tbs. white sugar
½ tsp. EACH cardamom and cinnamon
¾ cup sweetened, finely grated coconut
A little salt
3 Tbs. ground peanuts
Rose petals, washed and dried, for garnish

Grind carrots and rice together in food processor until smooth. Transfer mixture to a bowl. Beat in remaining ingredients, except nuts and rose petals. Pour into a baking dish. Cover top with nuts.

Bake, uncovered, in a 350 degree oven for 30 minutes. Garnish servings with rose petals.

ᘓᘓ

Similar to the African tradition, Indian royalty and commoners alike made great preparations for festivals. Many of the homes in the city of Madura in southern India were storied mansions like those in east African trading towns. The homes would receive special preparation in honor of festivals. The gates to the royal residences in Madura were built high enough to enable elephants to pass through. During festivals these ornamental gates were smeared with a fresh coating of sesame and coconut oils for the occasion. A concoction of sesame and coconut oils and jasmine also furnished the pomade used on both the king's and queen's cornrowed and topknotted hair, as they prepared for a festival. Both of these hairstyles were favorites worn by men and women of a number of African societies throughout the continent. It is important to note that these hairstyles spread from Africa to many faraway lands, and were adopted as the fashion by royalty and so-called common folk alike.

You will particularly like the fragrance of this pomade. Frankly, I happen to love coconut cake, so the smell makes me quite hungry. I used to have a co-worker in the early 1970s who oiled her afro with coconut oil. Once in a while I'd walk past her desk just to get a whiff of her hair. If you can pull yourself away from Sulfur-8 and Royal Crown and Alberto V05, you will find this to be a delicious smelling change.

Thaidai Mudi Thailam (Queenie's Pomade)

½ cup EACH watermelon juice and coconut oil
2, 2 × 2 or 2 × 3 inch pieces watermelon rind
2 rose petals
16 drops rose water
1 tsp. coconut extract

In a saucepan bring juice to a boil. Stir in oil, then rind and petals. Simmer, uncovered, for 2 to 3 minutes. Discard petals and rind.

Stir in rose water and extract. Cool completely. Stir well. Apply to hair and scalp.

Various drinks were offered at these festivals. Many a delightful and refreshing concoction had, as its key ingredient, tamarind fruit. The tamarind is native to East Africa, but is also widely grown in India, Guyana, Cuba, and other islands in the Caribbean. Available in compressed cakes, tamarind has a tangy, sour taste. The combination of spices gives this refreshing drink a unique flavor, as you might expect, and will want to try.

⸺⸺⸺⸺⸺⸺⸺⸺⸺⸺⸺⸺⸺⸺⸺⸺⸺⸺⸺⸺⸺⸺⸺⸺⸺⸺⸺⸺⸺⸺⸺

Tittippu Pulittani (Sweet Tamarind Water)

$2\frac{1}{2}$ cups water
4 ounces tamarind pulp (with seeds and fibers)
4 Tbs. chopped, fresh ginger root (do not peel)
Water
$\frac{1}{4}$ tsp. EACH ground ginger and turmeric
$\frac{1}{2}$ tsp. cinnamon
1 tsp. freshly ground cardamom (toast pods before grinding)
$\frac{1}{8}$ tsp. black pepper
$\frac{1}{4}$ cup fresh lime juice
$1\frac{1}{4}$ cups dark brown sugar, packed
3 tsp. white sugar

Boil the $2\frac{1}{2}$ cups water. Pour into a glass bowl or container. *Immediately* add tamarind and ginger root and allow to sit for an hour. You can help the pulp to dissolve by occasionally stirring and mashing with a spoon. Strain through a sieve over a pot, lightly pressing the tamarind against the sieve. Place remaining pulp back into bowl and add 4 more cups of boiling water. Allow to sit for about 15 minutes. Strain pulp again into pot. Discard remaining seeds and fibers. Add additional water to pot to produce 10 cups tamarind liquid.

Stir into tamarind liquid the ginger, cinnamon, cardamom, turmeric, and black pepper. Bring liquid to a boil and simmer for a few minutes. Remove from heat and strain again. Add lime juice and sugars. Stir until sugar has completely dissolved. Chill thoroughly and serve in tall glasses over ice. Always stir before pouring.

Now, if you want to find wisdom, if it is tranquility that you seek, brew yourself two or three cups of this:

⑃ ⑃ ⑃ ⑃

"Gladdening Toddy"

4 cups water
Cannabis sativa (ganja)—whatever amount you feel comfortable using
1 cinnamon stick
4 cardamom pods, toasted and crushed
⅛ tsp. cayenne
1 tsp. honey
6 tsp. sugar
2 teabags, orange and spice or orange pekoe

Bring water to a boil. Add remaining ingredients, except tea bags. Boil for about 6 minutes. Add teabags, cover, and remove from heat. Allow to steep for 8 minutes. Bring just up to a boil again (but do not boil). Strain into cups and serve. If desired, sweeten with additional sugar or honey.

When festivals were not being held, love and community support were expressed in other areas of Dravidian life. Agriculture played an important part in the economic life of the Dravidians from the beginning of history. As with distortions written about Africa regarding its supposed backwardness in food production, similar theories concerning the lack of sophistication in Dravidian agricultural methods are assumed. It is generally supposed that the Aryans were the first to introduce agriculture into southern India. However, the earliest Dravidians were not primitive tribes, as many scholars maintain, but tilled the ground with brass and iron implements and raised crops of various kinds, such as rice and sesamum. The Dravidians had developed and established methods of cultivation and irrigation in their mighty kingdoms in the north and south thousands of years before Aryans transplanted themselves onto the continent. Cultivation of the soil and animal husbandry was the main source of national wealth. To encourage agriculture, land was cleared and distributed among the people for cultivation, which carried concessions in taxation and special facilities. Free from taxation, land was also distributed for religious purposes. The importance of agriculture for both religious and secular purposes meant that stiff punishments for theft of grain and agricultural utensils were enforced, ranging from repayment ten times the amount stolen to hands being cut off or hanging.

One other important aspect of land distribution for religious purposes was that the best quality foods possible were produced. The importance of religion made for a powerful incentive for farmers to grow the best grains, the best peppers, the best crop, period. Many special dishes were prepared with ingredients only from certain areas or specific farms known for producing a superior tasting onion or potato. Sesame seed and coconut oils were usually added to these dishes to impart a special taste and aroma.

Superior crops provided a larger collection of revenue on land and trade. The king was expected to spend this revenue for the benefit of the people by improving the prosperity of the realm. These ancient Dravidian kings realized that the great remedy against famine was irrigation. Extensive irrigation works were carried out by these rulers, who had at their disposal large treasuries and an immense amount of labor. Dams were erected across rivers and channels were run off from them. Where dams could not be built, tanks, along with proper maintenance, were provided.

As special farming techniques allowed African societies to prosper, proper irrigation saw to it that the rich culture of the Dravidians in pre-Aryan times took the form of settled communities of farmers and herdsmen who enjoyed many amenities. The farmers were organized into communities and villages, each having been assigned a certain area of land, according to local custom. The boundaries of these villages were strictly defined and each settlement was separated from its neighbors by large expanses of forest. A hierarchy of village officers was established to ensure that land was equally distributed. The village's sacred tree or grove, the village deity, and the village dance or festival symbolized the unity of the village settlement.

Through the *Tamil Kural,* which is more than 1,800 years old, we are told that the Dravidians were organized into a nation with ideas made material in the advantages of economic self-sufficiency by the production of clothing and food. According to this literary work, the ancient Dravidians had solved the problem of food shortage. To the ancient Dravidian there was nothing nobler than the yoke and the plough, which were to them true emblems of freedom, honor, and virtue. In spite of every hardship, husbandry was the chief industry. It was a matter of pride to be able to grow and harvest one's own food. However, husbandmen supported all those who, for physical or health reasons, had to engage in different occupations.

Stews were one of the most common dishes prepared and shared with neighbors and friends, especially if the neighbors and friends contributed one or two ingredients to the pot. Different types of meat are interchangeable in this stew. The pineapple imbues this dish with a surprising melody of thought-provoking tastes.

Baked Chicken and Eggplant Stew

5 pounds of chicken thighs and drumsticks**
1 cup plain yogurt
1/2 cup coconut milk
1 tsp. EACH lime and lemon juice
2 to 3 tsp. garam masala or tandoori masala
Garlic salt with parsley, black pepper, and curry powder
2 Tbs. peanut oil
1 tsp. garam masala
2 medium onions, chopped
2 large tomatoes, chopped
1 tsp. EACH turmeric and garlic salt with parsley
2 to 3 hot chilies, finely chopped, OR 1/2 tsp. crushed red pepper
Freshly ground black pepper
1 cup beef or chicken broth
1 1/2 cups shredded red cabbage
Almost 3/4 of a small eggplant, peeled and chopped

**The traditional way of preparing the chicken is to remove the skin and then "score" (cut slits all over) the meat. I love chicken skin and in this case refused to give it up. However, you may go the traditional route, if you prefer.

Salt and freshly ground black pepper
3 tsp. EACH yellow split pea powder and water
3 Tbs. sauce from baking pan
1 cup pineapple tidbits, well drained

Place chicken in baking pan large enough so that pieces do not overlap.

Combine next 4 ingredients and mix well. Pour mixture over chicken. Allow chicken to soak for 6–12 hours in refrigerator. Season chicken with next 4 ingredients (seasoning skin side up only is sufficient). Bake chicken, covered, in a preheated, 350 degree oven for 1³/₄ hours.

When chicken is almost done, heat oil in a skillet. Stir in masala and cook and stir for a minute or so. Add onions and continue cooking and stirring for a couple of minutes. Add tomatoes, continue cooking and stirring for a minute. Add turmeric, then garlic salt, then hot peppers and black pepper. Cook and stir for a minute. Stir in broth, cabbage, and eggplant. Taste for needed salt and pepper. Bring to a boil. Lower heat and simmer, covered, for 12 to 15 minutes. Combine split pea powder and water. Blend until smooth. Pour mixture into stew and mix well. Continue simmering for a minute or two. Taste again for needed salt and pepper. Remove from heat.

Skim *most* of oil from the top of sauce in baking pan (sauce will sit at bottom of pan). Stir sauce from baking pan and pineapple into stew.

To serve: Place steaming hot rice on the bottom of plate with stew ladled on top of rice, then nestle chicken in the stew. Spoon some of the sauce on top of the chicken.

Kikuyu societies understood that land and the foods cultivated on it were the foundation on which the societies' economies stood. Ancient Dravidian writers comprehended as well the need for fostering agriculture. In number 35 of the *Purananuru,* considered to be one of the greatest Dravidian literary works, the poet strongly urges the king to lighten the load of the cultivators of the earth.

The Dravidian philosophy of feeding its citizens made it clear that the role of farmers was extremely crucial. Among the Aryans, soldiers were next in importance and rank to the priests. Among the Dravidians the farmers were next in importance to the religious men, and the military class was below that of herdsmen and artisans. One reason for this was the belief that a special bond existed between farmers and the village goddess from whom came famine or a rich harvest. Therefore, the progress and development of the village was intertwined in the realm of food. Cooking up sumptuous repasts was not only a necessity, it was a way of life. For the fishing societies, the coastal waters, lakes, and backwater lagoons provided salt- and freshwater catch that was either baked, pickled, or presented in some gravied or sauce dish. Vegetables were sure to be added to such dishes. Fishing societies were known to grow, on a minute scale, a few vegetables. But to prepare hearty vegetarian meals or elaborate fish and vegetable combination menus, containing just the right spicing, their farmer-neighbors' produce was indispensable.

Fishing operations were planned according to the moon's phases and this, therefore, called for a devising of lunar computation of time. This computation of time was measured by a calendar that was completely solar. Ancient Egyptians, of course, led the way in terms of devising calendars. However, centuries ago astronomy was one of many fields of study for which the Dravidians built academies. Farmers also found it helpful to watch the movements of the sun and moon and the seasonal changes.

Much of the bounty yielded from these fishing expeditions was the basis for an innumerable array of fish recipes. The succulent recipes below are worthy examples of East African and "eastern Ethiopian" fare. Fish braised in coconut milk is a favorite tradition in parts of Mozambique and Tanzania. These offer a variety of possibilities as additions to your dinner menu.

�utututututututututututututututututututututututututututututututututututut

Thengai Paalil Kadarpatchi
(Scallops in Coconut Milk Sauce)

1 pound bay scallops, rinsed and drained
1¹/₂ tsp. garam masala (see glossary)

2 tsp. EACH masa harina and dhal (see glossary)
1½ Tbs. EACH sesame seed oil and peanut oil
1 medium onion, chopped
1 small tomato, chopped
2–3 "Bird" chili peppers, stems removed and finely chopped
½ tsp. dried shrimp
¼ tsp. EACH whole cloves and coriander seeds, both toasted and ground
½ tsp. yellow fenugreek seeds, toasted and ground
Freshly ground black pepper and salt, to taste
1 cup coconut milk
1 to 1½ tsp. EACH dark brown sugar (packed) and dhal
1 rounded Tbs. (packed) finely grated coconut
Lots of freshly ground black pepper and salt

Place scallops in a bowl. Stir in next 3 ingredients, coating scallops evenly.

Heat both oils in a skillet. Add next 4 ingredients. Cook and stir for a couple of minutes. Add next 5 ingredients. Continue cooking and stirring until onion becomes clear. Add scallops to skillet and cook and stir for a few minutes. Combine milk, sugar, dhal, coconut, and some more salt and pepper and blend well. Stir mixture into scallops. Bring to a boil, lower heat, and simmer, uncovered, on medium low heat for 2–3 minutes. Taste for salt and pepper. Serve over rice.

Crab can be particularly inviting for a light lunch or part of brunch when it is used as part of a seasoning for other seafood. Such is the practice of both Indian and African cooks who reside along coastal towns.

Sole Food

1¾ pounds of sole or sea bass fillets, rinsed and drained
4 Tbs. butter
1½ tsp. berbere seasoning (see below)

¹/₂ tsp. cayenne pepper
¹/₂ tsp. garam masala (See glossary)
1 onion, chopped
10 whole sprigs coriander, chopped
About ¹/₄ pound lump crabmeat, flaked
2 whole slices wheat bread, torn into very small pieces
2 egg yolks
3 tsp. lemon juice
¹/₂ tsp. salt
Freshly ground black pepper

𝄢 𝄢 𝄢 𝄢

The Sauce:

¹/₂ cup coconut milk
¹/₂ cup regular milk
¹/₂ tsp. garam masala
¹/₂ tsp. berbere seasoning*
¹/₄ to ¹/₂ tsp. crushed black peppercorns
Salt to taste

Place fillets one layer deep in baking pan.

Melt butter in saucepan or skillet. Stir in berbere, cayenne, and garam masala. Add onion and coriander and cook and stir for a minute or two. Remove from heat and stir in crabmeat and bread.

Combine eggs, lemon juice, and salt. Blend well. Stir into crabmeat mixture. Cover tops of fillets with equal portions of crabmeat mixture. Sprinkle black pepper over fillets.

Bake, covered, in a 375 degree oven for about 15 minutes.

While fillets are baking, immediately combine sauce ingredients in saucepan over medium heat. When mixture starts to smoke, reduce heat to low and leave it there, stirring occasionally. DO NOT LET IT BOIL. Mixture will thicken somewhat by the time fillets are done.

Spoon sauce over (or under) servings of Sole Food.

Berbere Seasoning:
¹/₄ tsp. EACH coriander seeds, fenugreek seeds (yellow), cardamom pods, allspice berries

a rounded ¼ tsp. whole cloves
a small piece cinnamon stick

Shake and stir all ingredients for several minutes in a dry skillet until cardamom pods brown somewhat (not burn) on the outside. Cool, then grind to a powder.

The symbol of a fish adorned all seals at the royal mansions and main palace of the Pandya Kingdom. The Pandya Kingdom of southern India, traditionally ruled by female sovereigns, was comprised of 365 villages. Some of these villages extended to the sea. The Pandyas were famous pearl fishermen whose fame brought them riches from shores as far off as Greece and Rome. Pandya queens were great patrons of literature and therefore believed in promoting learning and culture. One aspect of their culture that they promoted was the continued development of seafood cookery. The Didinga of the Sudan do not eat fish; however, female sovereigns of this and other areas in Africa saw the benefit of having seafood added to the diets of the people, especially their armies. Considered to be "vegetables of the sea," seafood was eaten regularly by people who lived along the coastal waters and inland streams and lakes.

The combination of seafood and sweet potatoes may seem an odd one; but then, I did not think people who let Wednesday's horoscope tell them what to do belonged in the White House, either.

Chakkaravalli Paalil Kadil Miin (Sea Bass in Sweet Potato Cream Sauce)

For the fish:
¼ tsp. EACH cumin and coriander seeds
1 allspice berry
2 whole cloves
2 Tbs. peanut or sesame seed oil
³⁄₄ of a medium-small onion, chopped
1 or 2 green chili peppers, finely chopped
¼ tsp. finely chopped fresh ginger root
¼ tsp. (or more, to taste) salt

$^1/_2$ tsp. freshly ground black pepper, or to taste
$1^1/_3$ pounds deboned bass or red snapper

Toast together in a dry skillet cumin, coriander, allspice, and cloves. Cool, then grind to a powder.

Heat oil in skillet. Add onion, chili and ginger root. Cook and stir for several seconds. Stir in ground spices, then salt and pepper. Cook and stir for another 15 seconds. Add fish, and cook for about 25 seconds. Turn fish over, coating with spice mixture. Turn fish again. Cook for another 25 seconds, then turn again. Cook and stir the onion and spices for a few seconds. Cover skillet and cook for about 10 to 15 minutes, or until fish is white and no longer translucent. At least twice during cooking time, gently loosen fish from bottom of skillet with a spatula, as fish may stick.

Carefully remove fish and cooked particles from skillet and set aside on a covered platter. DO NOT CLEAN SKILLET.

For the sauce:
$^1/_4$ tsp. EACH coriander and cumin
3 allspice berries
1 whole clove
1 Tbs. peanut or sesame seed oil
Remaining $^1/_4$ of a medium-small onion, chopped
1 or 2 green chili peppers, chopped
$^1/_2$ of a large tomato, chopped
$^1/_4$ tsp. finely chopped ginger root
$^3/_4$ to 1 tsp. salt
$^1/_2$ tsp. (or more, to taste) freshly ground black pepper
$^3/_4$ cup (packed) cooked sweet potato
$1^1/_4$ cups coconut milk (the $^1/_4$ cup can be regular milk)

Toast together in a dry, *covered* skillet the coriander, cumin, mustard seeds, allspice, and cloves. Shake skillet occasionally. When mustard seeds have stopped popping remove from heat. Cool, then grind to a powder.

Heat oil in same skillet in which fish was cooked. Add onion, chili, tomato, and ginger root. Cook and stir for a minute or two. Stir in ground spices, then salt and pepper. Cook and stir for about a minute. Remove from heat.

Combine sweet potatoes, coconut milk (or milks). Blend well, but mixture may stay slightly lumpy.

Return skillet to heat. Stir in sweet potato mixture and cooked particles from fish and bring to a boil. Lower heat and simmer for about 5–6 minutes, stirring frequently. Pour hot sauce over fish and serve immediately.

A seafood preparation as filling as this one can certainly be served as a rewarding main course.

Seafood with Vegetables Stew

¼ tsp. black mustard seeds
1 Tbs. EACH sesame seed and peanut oil
¾ cup EACH grated cabbage and carrots
1 medium-large onion, chopped
1 medium tomato, chopped
2 red or green chili peppers, finely chopped
1 Tbs. finely chopped ginger root
7 whole sprigs fresh dill, chopped
¼ of an eggplant, peeled and cubed
¼ tsp. EACH coriander seeds, cardamom pods, and cumin seeds, toasted and ground
¼ to ½ tsp. EACH freshly ground cinnamon and black pepper
¼ pound peeled and deveined shrimp
½ pound bay scallops
¾ cup coconut milk
½ cup milk
3 tsp. dhal
½ tsp. garam masala
Salt and freshly ground black pepper, to taste

Toast mustard seeds by heating in covered skillet. Shake skillet over medium heat until seeds stop popping. Add oils and heat. Add cabbage and carrots and cook and stir for a couple of minutes. Stir in onion, tomato, chilies, ginger root, dill, and eggplant. Cook and stir for another 2 or 3 minutes. Add coriander, cardamom, cumin, cinnamon, and some black pepper. Cook and stir for about a minute. Add shrimp and scallops. Continue cooking and stirring until shrimp loses translucence and scallops turn white.

Mix together both milks, dhal, and masala. Blend well, then stir into seafood mixture. Stir in salt and more black pepper. Bring to a boil. Lower heat and simmer, uncovered, for a few minutes. Serve over hot yellow, or white, rice.

Even though fish were sometimes called "vegetables of the sea," they were "vegetables" off-limits to certain segments of Indian society. The creed of Jainism mandates a strict vegetarianism and opposition to animal slaughter in general. Jainism was introduced into southern India in the third century B.C. Those laypersons who follow Jain doctrine cannot be farmers because in using the plough a farmer might cause injury to plants and animals, as well as to the earth itself. Certain occupations are off-limits to Jain followers because metal and wood "suffer excruciating pain as they are worked."

For a group who professed to care so much about living things, the Jains, it seems, came up with some funny ideas about humanity. The Digambara order, the principal Jains in central and south India refused to admit women on the grounds that women were not capable of attaining liberation; that it was impossible for them to receive full salvation. According to the Digambaras, for women to pursue full ascetic careers or be able to receive full salvation they had to await rebirth as males. It really makes you wonder if they were eating too many nuts and berries.

Not that I care, but I wonder if the Jains would disapprove of my using peanuts instead of almonds for this recipe, since the almond is considered by some to be brain food. Of course, if the Jains are going to talk to me about having to be reborn as a man, I know they could not possibly be eating brain food. The peanut, which is grown throughout South India, is considered by some to be "the poor man's nut" and a lesser substitute for the more lofty almond. Peanuts are also grown in various parts of Africa and commonly used in the cuisines of most African people. On the African continent, peanuts, or ground nuts, occupy a very important place in food preparation. By all means, use almonds if you dare. Try this salad "on the side" with baked or tandoori-style chicken, because I guess all veggies and no meat can eventually make you go OINK.

⁂⁂⁂⁂⁂⁂⁂⁂⁂⁂⁂⁂⁂⁂⁂⁂⁂⁂⁂⁂⁂⁂⁂⁂⁂⁂⁂⁂⁂⁂⁂

Jain Cabbage and Carrot Salad

2 cups shredded cabbage
2 carrots, cut into almost paper thin rounds
4 Tbs. lemon juice
2 Tbs. vinegar
6 tsp. sugar
4 Tbs. peanut or sesame seed oil
1 red bell pepper, chopped
2 small red chili peppers, finely chopped
1 tsp. sambaar podi (see glossary—use B)
1½ tsp. asafoetida (see glossary)
2 tsp. yellow ground split pea powder (dhal)—see glossary
1 to 2 tsp. finely chopped peanuts (optional)
Sprinkles of cinnamon, salt, and freshly ground black pepper

Combine cabbage and carrots in a large bowl. Stir in lemon juice, vinegar, 4 tsp. sugar, and mix well. Set aside for about an hour, stirring occasionally.

Heat oil in skillet and add bell pepper and chili. Cook and stir for a couple of minutes then stir in, one at a time, sambaar podi, 2 tsp. sugar, asafoetida, and dhal. Continue cooking and stirring for another minute or so (add a couple of tsp. of oil if mixture begins to stick). Stir in peanuts (if desired) and remove from heat. Fold hot dressing into cabbage mixture and blend well. Sprinkle with cinnamon, then salt and pepper, adjusted to taste. Serve at room temperature or chill and serve. Stir well before serving.

Two main ingredients in African food preparation were onions and tomatoes. Jain cuisine, however, does not include onions. Therefore, I know that this is blasphemy, and that I really should place this particular vegetarian dish in a different section. But after all, you really do not have to embrace Jainism to enjoy a good vegetable side dish.

Kaara Kattiri Carrot Kuuttu (Spiced Carrots and Eggplant in Tomato Sauce)

1 Tbs. tamarind pulp plus ¼ cup boiling water
3 Tbs. peanut or sesame seed oil
½ (rounded) tsp. EACH coriander and cumin seeds, toasted and ground to a powder
1 whole cinnamon stick, toasted and ground to a powder
2 cardamon pods, toasted and ground to a powder
2 medium onions, chopped
3 carrots, sliced in thin rounds
½ of an eggplant, peeled and chopped into cubes
2 serrano or "bird" chili peppers, finely chopped
½ of a large tomato, chopped
Salt and freshly ground black pepper, to taste
1 cup tomato sauce
1 (rounded) Tbs. brown sugar or jaggery

Pour boiling water over tamarind. Stir until pulp has dissolved. Allow to sit for 15–20 minutes. Strain, discarding seeds and fibers. In a saucepan, boil tamarind liquid for 15-20 seconds. Set aside, covered. Heat oil in skillet. Add ground coriander, cumin, cinnamon, and cardamon. Stir spices in oil for 15 seconds. Add onions, carrots, eggplant, and chilies. Cook and stir until onions become clear. Add tomato and some salt and pepper and continue cooking and stirring for a minute or so. Stir in tomato sauce and sugar (or jaggery). Cover and simmer over medium-low heat, stirring occasionally, until carrots are crisp-tender. Taste again for needed salt and pepper.

A communal way of thinking dictated policy and practice in many African societies. Making sure that everyone was fed and clothed was of the utmost importance. Likewise, Dravidian kings were always devoted to the dietary welfare of their people, some-times no matter whose side they were on, religious or otherwise. One literary work from the period of the First Sangam, titled *Pura Nanura,* praises a Chera monarch who actually supplied food to both of the contending armies in the Mahabharata War for all eighteen days of the fight. Wells for water were dug and fruit and nut-bearing trees and herb plants were planted all along roads which were used by soldiers traveling to and returning from the war.

Fighting men had particular interest in one of the fruits grown in India. This was the rare black Nelli, the black gooseberry, which was said to have the virtue of conferring immortality upon the eater. This berry was used by chiefs and kings as a hype in preparing warriors for battle. "Eat this and you shall live forever," was the royal proclamation. I think it goes without saying that the king's army indulged in many preparations of this black gooseberry.

If you drink this, you will not live forever, I am sorry to say; but the memory of the superb flavor of Blackberry Rose Water will be with you for a long time to come.

Blackberry Rose Water

1 cup (½ dry pint) blackberries
2 cups water
⅛ tsp. nutmeg
A small piece of cinnamon that fits into a ¼ teaspoon
¼ tsp. EACH freshly ground cardamom and whole cloves
1 Tbs. lime juice
2 Tbs. EACH honey and sugar
1½ tsp. rose water (see glossary)

Puree blackberries in blender or food processor. Transfer to sauce-pan. Add remaining ingredients, except sugar and rose water. Bring to a boil. Simmer for about 6 minutes. Remove from heat. Allow to cool slightly and add sugar and rose water. Stir until sugar is completely dissolved. When cool, strain into serving container. Chill thoroughly and serve over mounds of crushed ice in beverage glasses.

Signaling the advent of war was done by means of drum communication. No warrior could leave for battle, however, without first having his sweet tooth sweetened.

Fruits in Chilled Yogurt and Blackberry Puree

8 ounces of plain yogurt
³/₄ cup coconut milk
¹/₂ cup sour cream
2 tsp. rose water
¹/₃ cup plus 3 Tbs. sugar
¹/₂ tsp. freshly ground cardamom
¹/₄ plus ¹/₈ tsp. ground cinnamon
1 cup blackberries
¹/₂ cup sweetened, finely grated coconut (see glossary)
¹/₄ cup plus 2 Tbs. diced apple
¹/₄ to ¹/₃ cup *fresh* raisins (try a health food store)
Chopped peanuts for garnish (optional)

Combine first 7 ingredients and blend well. Puree blackberries. Stir puree into yogurt mixture. Stir in coconut, then apples and raisins. Chill thoroughly. Serve in small dessert glasses. Garnish each serving with chopped nuts, if desired.

The kings' armies were important in maintaining stability in the realm, but just as important were food supplies. Food staples from South India were important commodities in Dravidian commerce and trade. Various nuts, such as walnuts, pine nuts, pistachios, and cashews, and dried fruits, were items that were bartered. Okra, eggplant, mushrooms, legumes and lentils, rice (*arisi,* in its Tamilian form), and an array of other vegetables, were also part of their wealth in trade. The variety of spices available in the south seemed endless and included fennel, black mustard seed, carom, bay leaves, cardamom, mace, mango powder, cumin, and cloves, to name just a few. Sandal oil in golden jars, sandal, aloe, and teak woods, gold, jewels, and fine fabrics were all merchandise being internally exchanged in marketplaces all over India. These market-places, which used African cowries as currency in many transactions, displayed the products of villages whose inhabitants had carried their wares over clean roads, sprinkled with scented water. The roads were lined with huge shops on both sides. A few of the shops were, in modern-day terminology, taverns, where wines, liquors, and other local beverages were consumed.

Possessing coveted articles such as spices created wealthy maritime cities in the ancient south. South India was one of the most important maritime locations of the old world and was mistress of the eastern seas. Commodities specifically obtainable in the south such as gold, diamonds, iron (minerals purchased from Africa), pearls, and conch shells allowed South Indian trade to generate wealth for the entire country. Just as lucrative an export item was *pippali,* the Dravidian long pepper. Used daily in native cuisine, it attracted foreign traders whose purchase of these and many other commodities supplied wealth and prestige to the people of India.

The pippali is a cylindrical fruit, one inch long, which grows like spikes from the stem. They are dried to yield the pepper. It is a spicy black pepper and has a gingerlike taste and smell. It is usually ground and prepared in breads, pickles, and chutneys. The dried root of the pippali is also popular in herbal medicine. Believed to have miraculous healing power, it has had many medicinal uses in South India. It was also eaten during Diwali, in combination with the pepper root, usli ghee, ground nuts, and jaggery.

Pippali Pepper Rounds can be eaten alone for breakfast or lunch. They are a "must have" to accompany tomato, chicken, or vegetable soups. A delicious way to bring out the flavors in soups is to tear pippali rounds into pieces and place them in bowls. Ladle soup over the pieces. Witness the excitement.

Pippali Pepper Rounds

1 cup masa harina
$1/2$ tsp. whole pippali, toasted and ground
$3/4$ tsp. salt
$1/4$ tsp. (or more to taste) cayenne

2 Tbs. plus 2 to 3 tsp. of finely chopped peanuts or walnuts
½ cup cooked kernel corn
¾ cup milk
2 Tbs. sesame seed or peanut oil
Sesame seed or peanut oil for frying rounds

Combine first four ingredients in a bowl and mix well. Stir in nuts.

Puree corn with ¼ cup milk in food processor. Transfer mixture to a small bowl. Add remaining milk and oil and mix well. Add corn-milk mixture to dry ingredients and stir just until well blended.

Heat a few tsp. of oil in skillet. When hot, place spoonfuls of batter in skillet in circles, flattening batter with the back of the spoon as you do so. Cook until deep brown on both sides. Repeat process.

The pippali long pepper was only one commodity that made the seaport of Puhar a rich and prosperous emporium of trade on the eastern coast. It received ships from every corner of the then known world. Day and night these ships brought cargoes that were swiftly transferred to inland towns. Night cargoes were guided to Puhar and other Coromandel coast, or east coast, ports, by means of huge tower lighthouses, which were said to exhibit blazing lights at night. Puhar was a grand, urban city where streets were constantly the locales of neverending festivals. In the marketplace were vendors who sold betel leaves, spiced areca nuts, wines and intoxicating liquors imported into India from Africa and Asia. There were also fruit and vegetable stands, as well as shops where snacks and cooked meals were obtainable. Most of these snacks were made with beans and peas, fruits, and numerous vegetables.

Sit down in front of the television or stereo, take off your shoes, relax and treat yourself to an endless stash of these banana snacks/ desserts. Their goodness eases you into the comfort zone.

Coconut Bananas

¼ cup coconut milk
1 tsp. rose water

⅛ tsp. EACH cinnamon and ground cardamom
1 Tbs. EACH confectioners sugar and sweetened, finely grated coconut
2 "junior" bananas

Combine first 6 ingredients in a glass baking dish and mix well. Add bananas and marinate for 1 hour. Bake in 350 degree oven for 20 minutes. Serve warm or chilled with ice cream or whipped cream.

∯ ∯ ∯ ∯

Coconut Banana Fritters

¼ cup coconut milk
1 tsp. rose water
1 Tbs. plus 2 tsp. confectioners sugar
⅛ tsp. EACH cinnamon and ground cardamom
2 Tbs. masa harina
3 Tbs. sweetened, finely grated coconut
4 "junior" bananas, cut in half
3 Tbs. sesame or peanut oil

Combine first 7 ingredients and mix well. Coat bananas with mixture. Refrigerate for 2 hours. Brown on all sides in hot oil.

These potato snacks are eaten like potato chips and popcorn. Keep a supply on hand to take with you to the ball game or on long drives in the car or on airplane trips. If you are traveling with children, you will be glad you did. If you do plan to serve them to children, you may want to adjust the amount of or omit the cayenne pepper.

Flaming Matches

2 potatoes
¼ tsp. EACH black fenugreek (toasted and ground), cayenne, salt, sugar, and asafoetida (see glossary)
¾ tsp. dhal (see glossary)
½ tsp. EACH yellow fenugreek (toasted and ground) and turmeric

Freshly ground black pepper, to taste
Sesame seed or peanut oil

Peel potatoes and cut into thin strips. Place strips in a bowl. Combine seasoning ingredients and mix well. Sprinkle seasoning mixture over potatoes. Toss potatoes to coat evenly. Deep fry potatoes in oil over medium heat in a skillet or deep fryer until golden brown. Drain on paper towels. Place "matches" on a dish and sprinkle with additional sugar and cayenne, if desired.

In a land of neverending festivals, the prosperity of the land was sometimes shown by means of gifts to royalty in other countries. Asafoetida, the dried gum from the rhizome of the Ferula plant, was offered to Chinese royalty in the form of a gift. It is prepared in powder or a brownish-black lump form. When in powdered form, and exposed to heat, it releases a lingering onionlike aroma. It is therefore favored by strict vegetarians, such as Hindu Brahmans and Jains, who are prohibited from eating garlic and onions (vegetables that are used to flavor meats). Asafoetida was an article of tribute from the Dravidian Cholas to the Chinese in 1077 A.D. Chola commercial expeditions to China were many and included sending embassies there as early as 1015 A.D. Chola embassies received in China in 1033 and 1077 A.D. have been recorded in the History of the Sung Dynasty, or *Sung Shih*. The latter embassy contained seventy-two persons and was given 81,000 strings of copper cash, which amounted to about as many dollars. In return, articles of tribute included glassware, camphor, brocades, rhinoceros horns, ivory, incense, rosewater, puk chuk, asafoetida, borax, cloves, and other spices.

These potatoes are so tasty you can almost eat them as a snack. In fact, I have on occasion prepared them to be eaten for exactly that purpose. Try preparing this recipe as a side dish.

Kaara Urulai Kizhangu Varuval (Spicy Fried Potatoes in Skins)

1 Tbs. EACH sesame seed oil, peanut oil, and butter or ghee
½ tsp. EACH black mustard seeds and turmeric

³/₄ tsp. dhal
¹/₄ tsp. EACH cayenne and asafoetida
¹/₂ to 1 tsp. salt
About ¹/₂ tsp., or to taste, freshly ground black pepper
4 small potatoes, scrubbed clean and sliced into thin rounds
1 whole green onion (with at least 3 tops), chopped
1 green chili pepper, chopped

Heat oils and butter (or ghee) together in a skillet. When hot, add mustard seeds and cover skillet. Shake skillet for 30 seconds to a minute. When popping stops, stir in turmeric, dhal, cayenne, ¹/₂ tsp. salt, asafoetida, and black pepper. Cook and stir for a minute or so. Add potatoes, onions, and chili. Cook and fold potatoes, over medium heat, coating slices with spice mixture and onions. Cover. Cook for a few minutes. Remove cover and cook and fold potatoes for about a minute. Cover again. Repeat process for about 15 minutes, or until potatoes are soft and tender. Taste for needed salt.

In about the eleventh century A.D. the Chola kingdom dominated almost all of southern India. In fact, the Coromandel coast is named after the Cholas. They possessed a powerful navy and established supremacy over the Indian seas. During their reign twelve thousand islands were under their domain. As Dravidian commerce and maritime relations spread into western and Southeast Asia, so did its culture. One of the most important expansions made by the Dravidians was into Southeast Asia. Hundreds of years before the Christian era, Dravidians had already begun to migrate into Indochina from South India through Burma and its southern coasts by sea and had founded settlements and commercial stations.

As "eastern Ethiopian," or Dravidian culture spread out into Southeast Asia, marriages between the black race of India and the natives of Asia would naturally follow. Dynasties were established which exhibited many traditions from India. Some of these traditions, such as the Kaundinya, exist today in the Bali Islands. In Kamatch Katka, in the Northeast corner of Asia, a Dravidian dialect is still spoken by one of its societies. A cuisine reflecting a combination of African and Indian traditional methods of food preparation would also be transplanted to various parts of Asia.

The religious, architectural, literary, and socioeconomic culture of the "eastern Ethiopians," together with African-Dravidian culinary heritage, was also being planted amidst the civilizations of Indochina, particularly Kambujadesa, or Kampuchea (Cambodia), as it is called today. African-Dravidian cultural expansion into Kampuchea would result in the creation of an empire that would dominate Southeast Asia for almost seven hundred years. The culinary styles of the Khmers of Indochina would also rule the culture and the stomachs of its citizens.

Catfish, Harvest, and Celebration among the Sons and Daughters of Kambu

For almost seven centuries, from 800 to the mid-1400s A.D., the dominant cuisine and culture of Southeast Asia was a combination of African, Dravidian, Chinese, and Indonesian principles. Those principles were practiced by the Khmers, a people generally described as having tight, curly hair, and as being black. The Khmers intertwined their lives with many sumptuous feasts, ceremonies, and festivals in which food was the primary focus. Food was the focal point in their religion, economics, and art. It was the subject of myths and legends relating to ceremonies during their holiday, planting, and harvest seasons. It was even important in the death and burial rites of a loved one.

To sustain the living, the Khmers produced multiple crops during both wet and dry seasons by utilizing a complex irrigation system. They linked the irrigation system, crop production, food preparation, and their daily lives to religious symbolism and duty. This linkage brought order to their society and helped to sustain them culturally, spiritually, and materially. The Khmers flourished. They eventually occupied the low-lying plains and the Mekong delta, the south of Laos, and provinces of southeastern Thailand.

Khmer expansionism gave them more opportunities to connect with and to cultivate the African presence. The black racial element had long been present in the populations of South India and

Indochina as the result of African exploration, travel, and migration. Early Chinese history has recorded that the African type inhabited all of the south of the country, including the islands of Hai-Nan and Formosa. Several texts in classic Chinese history speak of diminutive inhabitants in the southwest with "woolly hair" and "black and oily skin." Chinese folklore also mentions Li, an empress of China and consort of Emperor Hsiao Wu Wen, who is said to have been black. In the area of cuisine the African contribution can even be found in the island of Liu-Kiu to the south of Japan and, to a lesser degree, in northwestern Japan itself. As in Africa, the inhabitants of these various regions lade their dishes with hot peppers and spices.

The African cuisine connection is strongly evident in Khmer food preparations. Africans and Dravidians used several "wet" paste and dry spice seasonings; the Khmers use pastes as well, prepared with chilies, spices, and fruit juices. Compared to Chinese stir-fry dishes, Khmers may sometimes stir-fry only a portion of the ingredients (with little to no oil), which are to be added to the rest of the ingredients that require different preparation. Africans, Indonesians, Khmers, and Dravidians often marinated meats, fruits, and vegetables before further cooking. All four peoples complement their creations with sauces.

It was easy to create mouth-watering dishes from crops produced on Khmer lands. Similar to most delta regions, Khmer territory was very fertile land. Khmer society, true to African traditionalism, believed that its people and the fertility of the land were very closely connected. Egyptians, for example, believed that the Nile River, which fertilized its delta region, in many ways gave life to their people. They, like the Khmers, believed that this fertility of the soil, its people and population expansion, and the economic stability of their villages were interdependent.

Economic stability and adequate crop production was maintained even though Khmer life was governed by a cycle of six months of rain and six months of dry weather. The average household planned menus around their wet and dry seasons. Many households cooked "dry" dishes during the rainy season that least reminded them of how wet it was outside. During the dry months many more soups and liquid-based meals were prepared. Others believed, however, that better crop yields occurred if meals were prepared in keeping with and complementing the season. This is identical to the beliefs of certain African societies such as the Luvedu of South Africa, located farther away from the Equator, who also experience one long rainy and one long dry season. Africans closest to the Equator, the Akamba of Kenya and the Lugbara of Uganda and the Congo for example, experience two rainy periods and two dry periods during the year. These societies also believe that prepared meals must coincide with the seasons in order to remain one with God and nature.

For some, in more ancient times, it was believed that multiple-year harvests and the rains that nurtured them were the results of religious ceremonies and rituals. The rituals that are still performed today are done so as games and are no longer seen as religiously important. African societies in the Sudan, Morocco, Ethiopia, Somalia, and Kenya, and others on the continent's west coast, performed rituals for the same purpose. These societies performed some of their rain-producing rituals as games, many of which were played with rubber balls. The games were seen as religious in purpose and content and were a communal affair. For the Khmers, when the rains came, the annual flooding of the Mekong fertilized the rice fields with a rich silt to ensure a brand new harvest. This rich silt produced different types of rice. The ancient Khmers were said to have had two hundred ways of describing rice at different stages of growth and preparation. One type grown was *oryza sativa*, a rice usually sown in flooded rice fields, although it could be harvested only after the water had been drained off the field. *Oryza fluitans*, or "floating rice," grows higher and higher as the level of the water rises. This is a rare species of rice, known by modern Southeast Asians as *srangne*. Located in the Battambang region of Cambodia, it grows so tall that it has to be harvested by boat. Once harvested, the rice was taken to the village and placed in houses built specifically to store these crops. The king and the local temple received a portion of each crop. In most African societies, tribute, in the form of a portion of each crop, was paid to their kings at the end of each harvest. African and Khmer kings owned granaries where their rice and other cereal stocks were kept and overseen by appointed officials.

Rice, in the recipe that follows, is sensationally flavored to be presented as part of the main course or as a topping for stews and soups. You will not need to perform any rituals to get your family to rain compliments upon you for this one.

ᔓᔓᔓᔓᔓᔓᔓᔓᔓᔓᔓᔓᔓᔓᔓᔓᔓᔓᔓᔓᔓᔓᔓᔓᔓᔓᔓᔓᔓᔓᔓᔓᔓᔓᔓᔓᔓᔓᔓ

Rice Patties
ផ្ទែនប៉ាយសរ

1¼ cups chicken broth
¾ cup water
½ tsp. nuoc mam [fish sauce] (see glossary)
1 cup uncooked rice
½ tsp. (or more to taste) salt
¼ tsp. (or more to taste) cayenne
½ tsp. turmeric
5 allspice berries, ground
½ tsp., or more, freshly ground black pepper
2 stalks lemon grass, each cut up into 4 or 5 pieces

Stir all ingredients together in a baking dish. Cover and bake in a preheated 350 degree oven for 50 minutes. Let stand for at least 10 minutes. Discard lemon grass pieces.

For the patties:
4 tsp. sesame seed oil
1 medium onion, chopped
The baked rice
½ tsp. black mustard seeds (see glossary)
A little salt and some black pepper
2 eggs, well beaten
4 Tbs. rice flour (see glossary)
4 tsp. peanut oil, or more as needed

Heat sesame seed oil in a skillet. Add onion and cook and stir until onion browns. Transfer onions to a large bowl. Stir in baked rice, mustard seeds, salt and pepper, eggs, and rice flour. Mix well.

Heat peanut oil in skillet. Place rounded spoonfuls of rice mixture in skillet, flattening them into patties with the back of the spoon or spatula. Brown on both sides. "Rice Patties" are also wonderful as appetizers and snacks.

ᘓᘓ

In Kenya, among the Abaluyia, a pot used for cooking rice
was ceremoniously broken by the grandson of the deceased prior
to burial. This symbolized the loss incurred through death. For
the Khmers, too, rice, fish, and food in general was not only a
part of their daily lives but also a common element included in
death for these ancients. Excavated bas reliefs showing a blend
of religion, economics, art, and food make this point. A bas relief
in Banteay Chhmar shows individuals who have gone to hell
being pounded in a rice mortar. Still other inscriptions depict
mortals who, while fishing, were swallowed whole by large catfish
and had to eat their way out by eating the entire fish. These
persons in turn became fish and swam away to consume other
mortals.

Such myths and legends became an ongoing part of festivals
and ceremonies that were associated with harvest and new planting seasons. The same was true of the Koma of Ethiopia, whose
planting, harvest, and "first fruits" celebrations were marked with
acting out numerous legends. In ancient Kampuchea, one such
ceremony was the Plowing of the Holy Furrow; it marked the beginning of rice planting in May. A square-shaped area with an altar
placed in each corner was sectioned off just outside the palace
courtyard. The king chose a "King of the Plow" from among palace
officials who guided the plow which was being pulled by two prize
oxen. Behind the plowman walked a girl who was scattering rice on
both sides of what was designated as the sacred furrow. Oxen were
then unhitched from their yoke and led to a row of bowls, some
empty, others filled with rice. A bountiful harvest was said to be
assured if the cattle chose those containing food. The outcome was
guaranteed; the oxen would without fail choose the bowls containing rice.

The Khmers harvested and ate an abundance of seafood. This
array included gudgeon, shad, giant catfish, silvery featherbacks,
and small sharks. In addition, there was an abundance of black
carp, "bastard" carp (the *ts'ao-yu*), "spitting" fish, eels, and congers.
The prawns from Ch'a-nan were said to have weighed more than
a pound. Bivalves, octopus, and crocodiles were also favored. The
crocodiles must have been extremely large, because one traveler of
the times was quoted as saying that the crocodiles were "as large
as ships." One has to assume, however, that this was a bit of an
exaggeration. Khmer tables were seen with some rather large fish,

comparable to certain catch of West African fisherfolk. West Africans living along the coastal waters of Ghana were known to baste and grill a single fish, large enough to feed eighty to ninety people. Sometimes they would marinate and roast one stuffed with a mixture of onions, tomatoes, and rice. One favorite Khmer presentation was a gutted whole fish, about five feet long (head left on), which had been fried crisp and filled with sauteed vegetables. Preparing this dish with a giant sea bass from the Siemreap River or around the Mekong delta, the dinner table did look as if it had a ship sitting upon it.

If your skillet is not big enough to accommodate frying a whole giant sea bass, a smaller, oven-baked version will suffice. Just remember, your mission, should you decide to accept it, is to prepare enough to answer any encore calls, as this creation is sure to be considered quite tasty.

Stuffed Sea Bass with Golden Milk and Honey Sauce
មច្ឆាត្រឡាច់គភ៌ ជាមួយសុរវណ្ណទឹកដោះគោនិងទឹកឃ្មុំ

The marinade/sauce:
2 cups ice cold milk
1½ tsp. nuoc mam (fish sauce)
1 tsp. EACH caramel sugar and turmeric
2 tsp. EACH honey and lime juice
½ tsp. EACH salt and rose water
6 tsp. rice flour
2 cardamom pods, toasted and ground
About an inch long piece of cinnamon stick, toasted and ground
2 whole sea bass (head and tail left on), about 1¼ to 1½ pounds each, thoroughly cleaned and scaled

Combine all ingredients except fish and blend until smooth. Place fish in a glass container (if possible). Pour milk mixture over fish. Soak bass, turning several times, for 1 to 1¼ hours. Transfer fish to a greased baking pan. Reserve milk mixture.

6 tsp. peanut oil
½ tsp. black mustard seeds
6 dried black mushrooms (that have been soaked in warm water for 3 hours), chopped

1 medium carrot, sliced into almost paper thin rounds
$1/2$ of a medium onion, chopped
1 whole green onion (with 3 green tops), chopped
5 whole sprigs (stems included) coriander, chopped fine
$3/4$ tsp. finely chopped ginger root
Salt and pepper to taste

Heat oil in a skillet. Add mustard seed and cook and stir for 40 to
50 seconds. Stir in mushrooms and cook and stir for a few minutes.
Add remaining ingredients, cooking and stirring until carrots break
easily when cut into. Remove from heat. Place 2 heaping tablespoons of vegetable mixture inside of each fish. Close and secure
each fish with toothpicks. Sprinkle fish with additional salt and
pepper. Cover baking pan with foil and bake in a preheated 375
degree oven for about 55 minutes.

Pour reserved milk mixture into remaining vegetables in skillet.
Over medium heat, and stirring constantly, bring to a boil. Lower
heat, simmer for about 8 minutes, stirring frequently.

Place fish on serving plates. Remove toothpicks. Pour sauce over fish.

More of the sea's bounty yields delicious samples to savor. One
of Africa's favorite ingredients—peanuts—provides a special touch
to the accompanying sauce. This one is sure to delight your special
guests. The peanuts lend a slight crunch to every mouthful.

Spicy Fish with Peanut Sauce
ត្រីហិលជាមួយបទឹកក្រុលរក់សារិណ្ណុកផ្ដិ

The fish:
$1/3$ cup rice flour
1 tsp. salt
$1/4$ to $1/2$ tsp. cayenne
1 tsp. finely chopped peanuts or walnuts
$1/2$ to 1 tsp. black pepper
1 tsp. paprika
1 or 2 cups peanut or vegetable oil
1 pound whiting fillets (or other boneless fish)

Combine all ingredients except oil and fish. Mix well. Heat oil in skillet. Coat fillets with rice flour mixture (be sure to use all of mixture). Brown fillets on both sides in hot oil. Drain on paper towels and cover with foil.

Drain oil from skillet except 2 Tbs. Scrape away crumbs left from fried fish.

The Sauce:
1 Tbs. sesame seed oil
$\frac{1}{2}$ tsp. dried lemongrass (that has been soaked in warm water for 3 hours), finely chopped (see glossary)
1 whole scallion (with 3 green tops), chopped
$\frac{1}{4}$ of a medium onion, chopped
2 to 3 green chili peppers, finely chopped
1 medium tomato, chopped
2 tsp. finely chopped fresh ginger root (see glossary)
$\frac{1}{4}$ cup finely chopped peanuts or walnuts
$\frac{1}{4}$ tsp. whole cloves, toasted and ground to a powder
$\frac{1}{2}$ tsp. yellow fenugreek seeds (methi), toasted and ground to a powder (see glossary)
$\frac{1}{4}$ tsp. cayenne
1 cup chicken broth
5 tsp. caramel sugar
$\frac{1}{2}$ tsp. nuoc mam (fish sauce) see glossary
3 tsp. rice flour
Freshly ground black pepper
$1\frac{1}{2}$ to 2 tsp. coconut milk
2 tsp. oyster sauce

Add sesame seed oil to oil in skillet and heat. Add lemongrass, scallion, onion, chili peppers, tomato, ginger root, and nuts. Cook and stir for a couple of minutes. Stir in cloves and fenugreek. Stir in cayenne. Cook and stir for another minute or so.

In a small bowl combine remaining ingredients. Blend until smooth. Pour mixture into skillet with vegetables, cooking and stirring as mixture thickens. Simmer on low heat, stirring frequently, for 8 to 10 minutes.

Ladle sauce on individual plates. Fish fillets should be served on top of sauce. If desired, garnish with chopped green onions and finely chopped nuts or sprigs of coriander. Accompany dish with rice noodles.

The fishing season was as crucial to African coastal societies as it was to Khmer community life. In Khmer society, the fishing harvest, which lasted for weeks, was just as vital as rice to the economy. The flooding Mekong overflowed into many inland pools and creeks. When the Mekong receded, these natural ponds were cut off from the main stream and could be easily fished. Sometime in November, when the Mekong began to recede and the waters flowed back down to Tonle Sap, thirty-thousand fishermen rushed to the lake. They quickly set up rattan dams and fish traps. Millions of fish spread over 770 square miles of water were squeezed down into an approximate one-hundred-mile area. Fish were so heavily concentrated in these waters that all you needed was a bucket. The harvest season catch totaled nearly 130,000,000 pounds, which was more than four times the saltwater fish catch by all boats operating in Cambodian waters in the Gulf of Siam.

Boatloads of fish that arrived in the cities and villages were met by an assembly line. The catch was first cut open and cleaned. A portion was salted (sometimes referred to as "corned" in West Africa) or dried in the sun, or both, but a substantial amount of the catch was speedily taken to the marketplaces. Shoppers purchasing fresh fish from these markets turned the river's bounty into the Khmer's most popular seasoning and sauce, *nuoc mam* and *nuoc cham*, respectively. Nuoc mam is used like salt in Western kitchens. Added to almost all preparations, it is made from fermented anchovies and salt, layered in wooden barrels. Fermentation begins annually during the fishing season, and, after five to six months, the sauce is ready. Nuoc cham, too, is used to season foods. It is generally a combination of nuoc mam, chili peppers, lime, and a few other ingredients, depending on what the individual cook decides is best for the dish he or she is preparing. Truly considered indispensable, it is served as a dipping sauce for the prepared food. It must be my African genes. Personally, I sometimes pour tons of it over the entire dish.

For your next seafood expedition, "Shrimp and Crab Salad" promises to be a delightful diversion you will want to try again and again. Shrimp combined with crab is another African favorite. It is a different and tasty offering guaranteed to linger in your thoughts well after the last morsel has disappeared.

Shrimp and Crab Salad
សាឡាត់ បង្គា និងសាច់ក្តាម

4 ounces cooked lump crabmeat, flaked
1/4 pound cooked shrimp with tails left on (remove shells)
1 whole green onion, finely chopped
1 tsp. ground peanuts or walnuts
1 Tbs. plus 1 tsp. chopped red bell pepper
3/4 to 1 tsp. finely chopped coriander
A few dashes of crushed red pepper
A little garlic salt with parsley
Freshly ground black pepper, and a little salt, to taste
1 Tbs. lime juice
2 tsp. EACH nuoc mam, caramel sugar, and peanut butter
2 to 3 tsp. coconut milk
1/2 tsp. honey
3/4 tsp. sugar
Lettuce and tomatoes

Combine first 10 ingredients and mix well. In a separate bowl combine remaining ingredients, except lettuce and tomatoes. Blend well. Pour over seafood and fold and stir until well mixed. Serve on lettuce, garnished with tomatoes.

During the Khmer's New Year celebration, which was one of fourteen major national holidays they celebrated, both boys and girls participated in a so-called "tug of war" based on the "Churning of the Sea" legend. It was a ritual intended to produce a heavy rainfall for newly planted crops. Rites performed in Africa for the same purpose were important in strengthening community consciousness and were educational opportunities for the young regarding social and spiritual matters.

As the legend unfolds in Khmer-land, Vishnu, in his incarnation as Kurma the tortoise, is seated on the ocean bed of the Sea of Milk while the Mandara mountain is using his shell as its base. The mountain acts to stir and churn the sea below. The stirring and churning begins as the gods and demons—the "stone generals" (fifty-four gigantic stone figures on each side of the bridge leading to the gateways of Angkor Thom)—tie a snake around the mountain. When the snake is pulled back and forth, the water is churned. If the churning movement is performed successfully, important lost objects are recovered by being thrown up out of the sea. The source of immortality is one lost object. Others include the cow of plenty, the goddess of good fortune, and the nymph of loveliness. Perseverance in churning is rewarded by "putting an end to the sufferings of fatigue." An end to fatigue and the legend itself are closely linked to irrigation. The recovered objects were, to the Khmers, a promise of prosperity. The promise was certain to be fulfilled with an annual yield of two or more harvests. Of course, the irrigation systems were responsible for such yields, but the Khmers believed that part of one of the irrigation systems had to be built under the bridge where the fifty-four giant stone figures were because these "generals" had to attend to their churning duties. The result, prosperity, was then carried to every rice field, which was turned into "oceans of ambrosia."

Another objective connected with acting out the "Churning of the Sea of Milk" legend was expansion of the population. The fertility of the Khmer people was just as important to the Khmers as the fertility of the soil. Weddings, therefore, were quite festive events. In some societies in Africa, the wedding ceremony lasted for days and was full of many rituals. In other African societies the groom, and those he chooses to aid him, must fight a symbolic fight with the bride's people, in order to win her. This provides great entertainment for the community and is followed by a huge feast at the groom's home. The Khmers held parties before and during their two-day wedding festival. Sometimes prenuptial parties were held for the bridegrooms. They were most assuredly, however, *not* comparable to modern bachelor parties held in the West. Priests were consulted in order to decide which days were favorable for marriage. There were also documented occurrences of Khmers consulting magic diagrams and horoscopes to select wedding dates.

Guests bearing gifts always began the wedding procession. The bride and groom wore clothing replicating the fashions of Khmer kings and queens of earlier eras. When the ceremony was completed, red silk thread was used to tie the couple's hands together. Just as rice is thrown at newlyweds in America, the ancient Khmers threw seeds over the bride and groom. They were then taken aside and given instructions on the duties of being husband and wife. In Africa, the bride and groom generally received their instructions regarding their individual duties, days before the wedding ceremony. After a Khmer wedding, as guests departed, they left money in a container next to the door for the newlyweds. These gifts also expressed the gratitude of the guests for being served many delicious and elaborate dishes during the wedding celebration.

In order to increase fertility in the bride and groom, the Khmers believed that certain seafood dishes should be consumed. Other special seafood preparations were meant to endow unborn children with greater beauty and intelligence. A number of East Coast African societies required expectant mothers to eat specific foods containing minerals they believed would strengthen the body of the child. African and Khmer societies prepared meals that were said to ensure good fortune and prosperity for the couple. For both peoples, ceremony was attached to each and every dish. It was like raising a toast with each mouthful, each swallow. Spicy and sweet, Shrimp and Spicy Rice was meant to fill the married couple's wish for a full and happy life. It is also meant to fill your wish for a satiated stomach.

Afro-Khmer Shrimp and Spicy Rice

1/4 of a medium onion
3 whole sprigs coriander, stems included
1 or 2 green chili peppers
2 Tbs. chicken or beef broth or water
2 tsp. peanut oil
1/2 cup uncooked rice
1/4 tsp. ground cumin
1/4 tsp. whole cloves, ground
1/8 tsp. chili powder

A few sprinkles of crushed red pepper
1/2 tsp., or to taste, freshly ground black pepper
1 cup water
1 tsp. honey
Salt

Combine the first four ingredients in a food processor or blender and grind.

Heat oil in a saucepan. Add rice and cook and stir until brown. Stir in ground onion mixture. Add cumin, cloves, chili powder, red pepper, and black pepper. Stir in water, then honey. Bring to a boil, lower heat, cover, and simmer on low heat for about 20 minutes. Remove from heat. Before serving, taste for needed salt.

Just before the rice has finished cooking, prepare the shrimp:

2 Tbs. peanut oil
1 pound shelled and deveined shrimp
1/2 to 1 tsp. coarsely ground garlic salt with parsley (available at most supermarkets)
2 tsp. EACH nuoc mam and caramel sugar
1/2 to 1 tsp. freshly ground black pepper
Salt to taste

Heat oil in skillet. Add shrimp and cook and stir for 30 seconds or so. Stir in remaining ingredients. Cook and stir shrimp for approximately another 4 or 5 minutes.

Serve rice topped with shrimp.

When marriage brought forth the birth of a child, it was a particularly festive event, highlighted by serving preparations such as bean curd simmered with vegetables and coconut milk. Because the Khmers believed in rebirth or reincarnation they believed that this new life was somehow linked with the death of someone who had lived earlier so that celebratory dishes were essential. Therefore, the rite of burial was still another festive event, accompanied by dishes such as chicken in coconut milk and shrimp cakes. Among some African societies there is belief of only partial reincarnation. Only "some" of the characteristics of the deceased person are said to be reborn in the baby.

The Khmers used four different types of funeral ceremonies. Burial by water, cremation, and placing the corpse underground are certainly familiar methods in the West. However, there was also the practice of "burial by birds." When the Khmers buried someone by birds, the body was taken to the countryside where the flesh was allowed to be consumed by birds. The interesting part is that the procession of mourners was led out of the city, singing and dancing all the way to the designated area. This portion of the funeral procession gave them much in common with Africans and with African American folks in New Orleans. Among the Ndebele of southern Africa, three months after interment, beer is brewed and the burial party assembles for the rite "to wash the hoes." Brewed beer is then used to wash all the implements used for the burial. After the burial itself the mourners return home to roast and eat, without salt, an ox (for a deceased man) or a goat (for a woman). The roasted animal symbolizes "the beast to accompany the deceased." Serving special foods at funeral receptions has always been a commonality of these cultures.

The last funeral reception I attended was held for a friend's nephew, Lawrence, who hated food. The experience will be emblazoned in my mind forever. Five feet, nine inches tall, Lawrence weighed around 120 pounds all of his life because very few things tasted good to this person. He especially hated chicken. Can you figure it? Well, for some strange reason, the wake was held on the same night as the reception, in the next room. People were filing back and forth between rooms, some carrying plates of food. Apparently, at least one food carrier got a little careless. As I was leaving, I took one last look at Lawrence. I suddenly noticed a strange object between his arm and chest, one that did not quite belong. His aunt, who was sitting a few feet away, got up and started coming toward me. Knowing how upset she would become, knowing we would all be subjected to one of her screaming-into-the-night tantrums if she saw this thing, I took my finger and quickly and discreetly manuevered it further down between the folds of his clothes. With his aunt and certain others constantly touching his clothes and hands, I wondered how long it would be hidden from view. I felt really bad because Lawrence always said he would never be caught dead with a chicken bone in his hand. Fortunately, it was a pig knuckle. All I could think about was the irony of him lying in the ground on top of one.

SSSSSSSSSSSSSSSSSSSSSSSSSSSSSSSSSSSSSSSSSSSSSSSSSSSSSSSSSSSSSSSSSSSSSSS

Chicken and Pineapple Ginger Sauce

ម៉ាន់ និង ពីកប្រលក់ម្ពាស់ ខ្ញី

1 Tbs. tamarind pulp
1 cup boiling water
1/8 tsp. EACH cloves, nutmeg, cinnamon, and ginger
1 tsp. nuoc mam (see glossary)
8 tsp. caramel sugar (see glossary)
3 tsp. rice wine or other white wine
1 tsp. lime juice
5 whole chicken legs (5½ pounds)
Black pepper, garlic salt mixed with parsley OR regular salt, dehydrated crushed cilantro leaves

For the sauce:
2 Tbs. peanut oil
2 whole green onions, chopped
2 tsp. finely chopped ginger root (see glossary)
2 serrano OR "bird" chili peppers, finely chopped
10 cardamom pods, toasted and ground
Freshly ground black pepper to taste
1/4 tsp. cayenne
1/2 cup crushed pineapple (do not drain)
1/3 cup unsweetened pineapple juice
1 tsp. nuoc mam
3 tsp. caramel sugar
1 Tbs. rice wine or other white wine
3/4 cup coconut milk
1 Tbs. rice flour
Salt to taste

Combine tamarind, water, cloves, nutmeg, cinnamon, and ginger. Stir until tamarind has dissolved. Allow to sit for approximately 15 or 20 minutes. Strain, discarding seeds and fibers.

Add nuoc mam, caramel sugar, wine, and lime juice to tamarind liquid. Mix well.

Place chicken one layer deep in a baking pan. Pour tamarind mixture over chicken. Marinate for 30 minutes at room temperature, turning chicken pieces twice. Place chicken, covered, in refrigerator and marinate for 4 hours, turning chicken pieces frequently. Remove from refrigerator and sprinkle chicken with black pepper, garlic salt mixed with parsley OR regular salt, and dehydrated crushed cilantro leaves. Bake, covered, in a preheated 350 degree oven for 55 minutes.

Just before chicken is done, heat peanut oil in a skillet. Add green onion, ginger root, and chili peppers. Cook and stir for a couple of minutes. Add cardamom, black pepper, and cayenne. Cook and stir for another minute or so. Add crushed pineapple, pineapple juice, nuoc mam, caramel sugar, and wine. Continue cooking and stirring frequently for a few minutes.

Combine coconut milk and rice flour. Blend until smooth. Stir mixture into skillet. Taste for needed salt. Simmer for about 1 to 2 minutes. Serve sauce over chicken pieces.

※※※

If you were reborn as a female during the eleventh through the fifteenth centuries, girls between the ages of seven and eleven participated in a special ceremony called the *ch'en-tan*. The ritual of the ch'en-tan was cause for celebration and was another of the many feast days of the year. Performed by Taoist priests for girls who had reached puberty, the ch'en-tan was practiced as "a rite of passage" in much the same way as the Gikuyu, Nandi, and Akamba peoples of Kenya performed the *irua* (clitoridectomy). Among the Akamba, girls go through the first stage of initiation rites when they are between 4 and 7 (Nandi rites begin when the girl is about ten) years old. After the operation is performed, there is public celebration which includes singing, dancing, eating various foods, drinking beer, and making food and drink offerings to the dead. Over the next few weeks, while their wounds are healing, relatives visit the girls and present them with gifts of money, chicken, sheep, and cattle. During the Khmer celebration, there were exchanges of gifts and other elaborate proceedings. Music could be heard everywhere, sometimes continuing far into the night. Different rice dishes, hot and spicy soups, and meat dishes and wines were offered.

Fragrant, spicy, and flavorful, keep this dish on hand. It is the answer to a prayer whenever folks drop over unexpectedly.

〰〰〰〰〰〰〰〰〰〰〰〰〰〰〰〰〰〰〰〰〰〰〰〰〰〰〰〰〰

Taoist (or Brahman) Priest's Soup
សម្ល្ររ្ពាហ្មណ៍

1 Tbs. EACH sesame seed oil and peanut oil
4 ounces soft bean curd [tofu] (half of an 8 ounce square)
1 medium onion, chopped
1 medium tomato, chopped
$^{1}/_{3}$ cup finely chopped walnuts
2 green chili peppers, finely chopped
$^{1}/_{2}$ tsp. cardamom pods, toasted and ground to a powder
6 allspice berries, toasted and ground to a powder
$1^{3}/_{4}$ cups EACH chicken and beef broth
1 medium yam or sweet potato, cooked and peeled
$3^{1}/_{2}$ Tbs. (approximately) creamy peanut butter
Freshly ground black pepper and salt, to taste
$^{1}/_{4}$ to $^{1}/_{2}$ tsp. cayenne
2 whole stalks lemon grass, each cut into 3 pieces (see glossary)
$^{1}/_{4}$ cup caramel sugar (see glossary)
A pinch of dried shrimp (see glossary)
$1^{1}/_{4}$ cups cooked green baby lima beans
$^{1}/_{2}$ cup coconut milk (see glossary)

Heat sesame and peanut oils in a pot. Add bean curd and brown on both sides. Transfer bean curd to saucer and set aside. Add onion and tomatoes to hot oil in same pot. Cook and stir for 1 minute or so. Add walnuts. Continue cooking and stirring for another minute. Add chili pepper, cardamom, and allspice. Cook and stir for 30 seconds to 1 minute. Stir in chicken and beef broths. Add sweet potato, breaking it up as it is stirred in. Over medium heat, stir in peanut butter. Bring to a boil, lower heat to simmer. Simmer for a minute or two and add black pepper, cayenne, lemon grass, and caramel sugar. Blend well and simmer for about 8 to 10 minutes. Add dried shrimp.

Slice bean curd into thin strips. Stir bean curd and lima beans into soup. Continue simmering for another 20 minutes. Add coconut milk. Bring to boil again and simmer on low heat for about 3 minutes. Discard 6 pieces of lemon grass before serving.

Every rite, every ritual was in some way preparation for Khmer females to bring their daughters into the "family business" at the marketplace. These very young girls could be seen, along with their mothers, displaying their eatables from 6 A.M. until midday. Known for their business acumen, it has been said that the Khmer economy depended on Khmer women. In Accra, Ghana, and other African cities as well, the open-air retail market was principally in the hands of women. African women, like their Khmer counterparts, handled the family resources and were economically independent as traders. Many Khmer stalls would also try to sell you stoves as well as pink earthenware in the form of dishes and some iron cooking pots and pans (no doubt obtained from Africa or India), in which to carry home the foods. Oil from coconuts, as well as beeswax, which the women frequently used as hairdressings, were also for sale in many stalls.

Another product from bees which Khmer women sold in stalls at the marketplace was honey. Khmers drank milk but they also drank four kinds of wine. Honey wine was one type, and it was made by mixing together half honey and half water. Fermentation was started by means of a drug. (Note that Africans were known to be expert beekeepers.) In addition to honey wine, Africans manufactured palm, grain, and other fruit and vegetable wines. The manufacture of honey wine could be quite delicate due to the nature of bees. One bas relief tells the story of how bees made large nests high up in trees or on rocks. The Khmers would light fires under these hives, thereby smoking out the occupants. After a few months the bees would seek new homes. The Khmers, however, studied each migration so that the process would start over again. There were at least three or four other types of wines manufactured and sold by the Khmers. One was rice wine, called *pao-leng-*

kio (*ranko*, in Khmer), which was made of raw rice or the remains of cooked rice. A second type, *p'ang-ya-ssu*, was made by macerating, or steeping in liquid, certain kinds of leaves from trees. Another was made from the sugarcane. The process is described as extracting juice from the cane stalk by means of a press consisting of two vertical grindstones, operated by a pair of elephants pulling on hawsers. In addition, along the tributaries of the rivers grew the plant called *chiao* (or *kiao*); its leaves were sometimes used as spoons and the liquid or juice from this plant could be fermented.

The following concoction is a mellow one, sure to please on those nights after work when you just want to relax with a good book in one hand and a satisfying drink in the other. AAAAAH! BUDDY, BUDDY!

Honey Wine Toddy

2 cups red wine
1 stick cinnamon, crushed
1 tsp. lime juice
6 tsp. honey
1/2–1 tsp. sugar
6 Tbs. 150 proof white rum

Bring wine, cinnamon, and lime juice to a rolling boil for 1 minute. Remove from heat and immediately strain into 2 cups. Stir 3 tsp. honey and about 1/2 tsp. sugar into each cup. Pour 3 Tbs. rum in each cup and immediately ignite. Allow flames to diminish and serve.

There was but one food stall my father would visit when the family went shopping for Christmas presents on Sundays down on Maxwell Street in Chicago. "Jimmy's," as it is still called, sold and still only sells Polish sausage, pork chops, hot dogs, and hamburgers. The only condiments they had for these sandwiches were raw and grilled onions and mustard. None of the stands sold pig ears or feet—pickled or otherwise. You had to go to a tavern or some little tiny grocery store in the black community to get you some pickled pig. There would be this huge jar sitting on the counter in this little tiny store. I hated the way the feet looked, all crushed up against each other. It made me itch. But the taste made up for thine eye being offended. This was "street food" at its finest.

Various "street food" was prepared and sold by women in the retail open-air marketplace in every African city. Marinated and slowly roasted, speared chunks of lamb or chicken were merely one delight. Likewise the individual stalls in which Khmer women displayed their eatables, included spring rolls, said to be served for every occasion in Khmer society, and pickled parts of the pig. Not a very popular item in African society, pork certainly became a staple in the African American community. Whether African American or Khmer, different cooks naturally flavored these parts according to individual tastes. Great as a snack or appetizer, they actually should be considered a delicacy.

⁊⁊⁊

Pig Feet Khmer Style

4 pig feet
Enough water to cover feet
3 tsp. EACH nuoc mam and white vinegar
4 stalks lemon grass, cut up
Freshly ground black pepper
4 to 6 red "bird" peppers or ½ tsp. crushed red pepper
4 Tbs. caramel sugar (see glossary)
8 tsp. white wine
4 tsp. white vinegar
2 tsp. EACH nuoc mam and lime juice
Freshly ground black pepper (generous amount)
½ tsp. EACH crushed red pepper and rice flour
Finely chopped coriander and "bird" peppers

Place feet in a pot. Cover with water. Stir in next 5 ingredients. Bring to a boil. Lower heat and simmer, covered, for about 2 hours and 10 minutes.

Transfer feet to a baking pan and cover tightly with foil. Combine remaining ingredients, except coriander and bird peppers. Mix well. Remove foil and brush feet with a few coats of sauce. Cover pan tightly and bake in a preheated 350 degree oven for 15 minutes.

Brush feet with sauce again. Garnish with coriander and bird peppers and serve with sauce.

Feet may also be soaked in sauce for 2 hours, then baked, covered, for 2 hours and 15 to 20 minutes, basting with sauce every 30 minutes. Bakes to a beautiful, brown skin.

Female vendors, operating numerous food stalls in Khmer markets, featured various versions of crunchy spring rolls filled with combinations of chopped shrimp, onions, carrots, cellophane noodles, lettuce, and pork. Another combination included ground nuts, cabbage, some type of ground meat, and mashed beans or peas. Just like Africans, African Americans, people of the Caribbean, and Central and South Americans, Southeast Asians were fond of black-eyed peas. It is not hard to figure out. In Khmer society, both the men and women wore their hair in cornrows, partied often and with vigor, and preferred their food on the hot and spicy side. I say folks of this persuasion would of course be partial to black-eyed peas.

African Americans are also partial to preparing black-eyed peas as part of a New Year's Day celebration dinner. As an addition or change to the menu, prepare them in the form of spring rolls. You can make the following recipe the day before, refrigerate overnight, and brown before serving. You would do well to serve these delectable morsels as an appetizer or snack.

Black-eyed Spring Rolls
ខ្ទែយ៉ សំពេញ្ញកអង្កុយ

Filling:

³/₄ cup cooked black-eyed peas, pureed smooth (Add 1 or 2 Tbs. of black-eyed pea liquid or beef broth, if necessary)

³/₄ cup grated carrots

³/₄ cup rice noodles (see instructions below)

3 tsp. ground walnuts or peanuts

³/₄ tsp. sesame seed

1 whole green onion, finely chopped

5 whole sprigs coriander, finely chopped

Approximately ³/₄ tsp. black pepper, or to taste
¹/₂ rounded tsp. crushed red pepper
10 allspice berries, ground
1¹/₂ tsp. garlic salt with parsley
1 tsp. nuoc mam (see glossary)
¹/₂ pound ground pork

For rice noodles:
Bring 2 cups of water to a rolling boil. Remove from heat. Immediately add a handful of rice noodles. Push and stir noodles until they are completely submerged in water. Set aside for about 15 minutes. Drain water. Cut up noodles and measure out ³/₄ cup. Cut noodles into smaller pieces in measuring cup.

Combine all ingredients except ground pork. Mix well.

Brown ground pork in a skillet. Break meat up into small crumbs. Stir pork crumbs into black-eyed pea mixture, mix well, and set aside.

Wrappers:
20 to 21 circular, 6 inch rice papers
1 egg, well beaten
2 or 3 cups (approximately) peanut or vegetable oil

Hold both sides of rice papers under a little running water to soften (if areas of paper remain stiff, brush with a little more water). Very gently shake off excess water. Lay papers on a flat surface and brush with beaten egg. Place about a rounded tablespoon of filling on edge of paper. Roll forward (away from you) until paper covers filling. Gently fold and tuck both sides of paper inward toward the center to enclose filling, and continue rolling until you reach the end. You should probably moisten no more than four papers at a time if you are working alone (the rice papers will harden again the longer they sit). Refrigerate rolls, covered, for 1¹/₂ to 2 hours, or overnight.

Add oil to skillet. Place spring rolls into COLD oil in skillet, one layer deep. When frying begins, continue cooking until rolls are golden brown on all sides. Serve with nuoc mam sauce for dipping.

After the last black-eyed spring roll was sold, after the last customer had been persuaded to purchase a fragrant pomade for their plaited coiffure, Khmer women closed their stall at the marketplace to attend to other duties. Along with controlling commerce and trade, they held other important roles in Khmer society. One of the ways that they helped to ensure financial stability was to engage in initiating new ways of employing different plants and other products that could be used as ingredients for items needed in daily life, as well as for foods and food production. Ancient Khmer women, as did ancient Egyptian females, manufactured perfume, which the Khmers called *tuk ap.* Similar to Egyptian compounds, tuk ap was composed of dried flowers, santal, and yellow cane sugar. Styrax, its main ingredient, came from North Indochina where twenty- to thirty-foot styrax trees grew. Yellow globules of sap drain for up to two months from the cut made in the trunk of the tree. In making the perfume, flowers are boiled and this mixture is infused with smoke from burning santal and styrax. When it was not being processed as food, sugarcane was also used in medications for the sick as well as for wounded soldiers. Soaps and paints that were compounded with sugarcane were sometimes used in ritual bathing by the female actors, musicians, and dancers (ballet included) before a performance at the palace or temple or participation in a royal procession. But of course its biggest use was in the preparation of entrees and desserts.

Male children helped cultivate the bounty of the land and surrounding waters. In addition to sugarcane, young boys learned to grow cereal grains, which were raised on the plains, and vegetables and fruit trees such as mangoes, peaches, bananas, pomegranate, taro, oranges, and little red lychees (called *kulen,* which the villagers harvested still on its branches and gathered into bunches to sell at the market) along river banks and in village gardens. In other individual gardens were grown onions, mustard, leeks, aubergines, watermelon and pumpkin, coconuts and pawpaws. Fruits and vegetables cultivated by the Khmers have been shown to have origins in other parts of the world, particularly Africa and the Americas. In both African and Khmer cuisine, some of these fruits and vegetables were sweetened and pureed and served as soups, dessert custards, or as "thickeners" in various dishes. Seasoned perfectly, these "thickeners" were actually the gravies or sauces that were prepared and presented as the signature component of African and Khmer meat and seafood soups, stews, and main dishes.

Many years ago, while I was attempting to perfect the "thickener" for a special pot roast dinner I was preparing, it was suggested to me that a small amount of seasoned, pureed apples or pears, stirred into the liquid, would enhance the flavor. I was amazed to find out how well it worked. Depending on the fruit or vegetable used, spices can be used to bring out or play down the flavor of the "thickener." In the home of one of my relatives, ham hocks and lima beans, with a touch of sweetened applesauce added, could not be avoided. It was THE meal prepared on Wednesdays because hocks went on sale on Wednesday. When I arrived on one of these ham hock nights, Marvelyn, my expectant cousin, was sitting in the kitchen engaged in an orgy with Oreos. She had already gained twenty pounds and she was only in her fifth month. I asked where the hocks were, because all of her pots were clean. She kept eating her Oreos and did not answer. I asked again. She finally told me that she had dinner before I got there. I asked her what she ate, because it was late and there was no indication that any cooking had taken place. She answered that she had eaten earlier than usual and that she had had ham hocks. I walked over to the garbage can and looked in. I said, "Marvelyn, where's the bones?" She said, "I tried to give 'em to the dogs." I told her I knew the dogs did not have them because the dogs look at her like she is crazy when she offers them bones she has been working on. "Girl, where's the bones?" I repeated. She said, "I rinsed them off and put them away." "Away, where?" I asked. "In the refrigerator!" it came back. Sure enough, I opened the refrigerator door and there was a bowl with twelve sucked-all-the-color-off ham hock bones sitting in it. When I inquired as to what she thought she might do with used bones she replied that she was going to make her some stew. I can only tell you that I did not eat dinner at her house for several weeks after that.

Try "Papaya and Ham Hock Soup." It is very delicious and said to be eaten by mothers for several weeks after giving birth. It better be, if you are planning on eating it for several weeks.

Papaya and Ham Hock Soup
សម្ពរល្ពៅ និង កន្លាក់ជើងជ្រូក

1 cup beef broth
1½ cups chicken broth
2½ cups water
2 smoked ham hocks (*just* over 1 pound), rinsed in cold water
Half of a 2½ pound ripe papaya (peeled, seeded, and fibers removed), pureed
1 tsp. peanut oil
½ of a medium onion, chopped
1 whole green onion, chopped
1½ or 2 serrano or "bird" chili peppers, chopped
½ of a medium tomato, chopped
3 sprigs coriander, chopped
2 tsp. EACH nuoc mam and caramel sugar
1 or 2 spinach leaves, shredded
Freshly ground black pepper and a little salt, to taste

Combine broths, water, and ham hocks in a medium sized pot. Bring to a boil, lower heat, cover and simmer for 1 hour and 40 to 45 minutes. Remove ham hocks and cool. Remove outer skin. Remove meat from bones and shred. Return meat to pot. Stir in pureed papaya.

In a skillet, heat oil. Add onion, green onion, chilies, tomato, and coriander. Cook and stir for a few minutes. Add onion mixture to pot. Stir in nuoc mam, caramel sugar, spinach, black pepper, and salt. Bring to a boil. Lower heat, cover and simmer for 15 to 20 minutes.

Expecting a baby can lead to any number of midnight dessert orgies. Tonight, leave the Oreos alone and consider a healthier alternative. Although the traditional Khmer dessert was fruit, dessert custards and puddings made of fruits, vegetables, as well as peas and beans were, as I have mentioned, an integral part of the African and Khmer culinary repertoire. Try this sweet take on Hoppin' John. It is a Khmer pudding made with (and I know you will not believe this) black-eyed peas and rice.

Sweet Black-Eyed Peas

½ cup cooked black-eyed peas
1 cup cooked rice (that has been cooked with lemon grass)
1½ cups coconut milk
½ cup EACH regular milk and finely grated coconut
12 Tbs. caramel sugar
1½ tsp. EACH vanilla and rose water
2 Tbs. sugar (white)
Sweetened coconut
Rose Petals (optional)

Puree black-eyed peas and rice together in food processor. In a non-stick or heavy gauge steel saucepan combine both milks, coconut, caramel sugar, vanilla, and rose water. Stir in black-eyed pea mixture. Cook and stir until mixture comes to a full boil. Continue cooking and stirring for about a minute. Immediately remove from heat. Pour mixture into a bowl (DO NOT SCRAPE BOTTOM OF PAN IF MIXTURE SCORCHES). Stir in white sugar and mix well. Cool completely. Refrigerate until thoroughly chilled. Serve in dessert dishes, topped generously with sweetened coconut and garnished with washed and dried rose petals (optional).

One's duty to the welfare of neighbors and the community in general was the overriding factor in how the Khmers responded to any situation. Southeast Asian tradition and culture engaged in, comparable to ancient African societies, ritual activities that were regarded as communal affairs. These traditions and activities had, as their base, religion and the continued solidarity and well-being of the community.

A more recent tradition and activity which symbolizes principles of unity and expressions of love and caring is the African

American seven-day celebration of Kwanzaa, derived from the Swahili phrase *matunda ya kwanzaa*, meaning "first fruits." There are seven principles, derived from ancient African beliefs, and referred to as *Nguzo Saba*, which are symbolized in the lighting of one candle each day of the seven-day period. Rain is of great significance here, as it is in African and Khmer societies which believe that God expresses his providence through rainfall. Rain is therefore believed to be the eternal and mystical link between past, present, and future generations. *Mazao* (crops), symbols of the harvest, is the first symbol of Kwanzaa. The other six are: *mkela* (map), symbol of tradition and history; *kinara* (the candle holder), symbol of roots and parents; *vibungi* (ears of corn), symbol of children and the future; *zawadi* (gifts), symbol of labor and the love of parents; *kikombe cha umuja* (unity cup), symbol of the principles of unity of the people; and *mishumaa saba* (the seven candles), symbol of Kwanzaa itself. In participating in Kwanzaa ceremonies, the symbols are placed on a table each night during the Kwanzaa celebration. One candle should be lit each night until all seven are burning. At that time an African feast should be served as well as an exchange of gifts of cultural and educational significance.

Ancient African beliefs that are the basis for the seven principles of Kwanzaa coincide with the symbols and principles that governed the production of food in the lives of ancient Southeast Asians as well. In both African and Southeast Asian societies, continued crop production on land their ancestors had occupied for many centuries, and which was regarded as sacred, determined the welfare of future generations.

The "Hill People" of Kambujadesa personified these beliefs. The Kuoy, one society of "Hill People" who had settled in the Dangrek Mountains, had continuous, long-standing communication with the Khmers of the plains. As a result, a few of their principles of food production, over time, began to coincide. However, other societies, such as the Phnongs, did not want their lives or their land changed in any way and so refused to ingest African-Dravidian culture as it spread during the first centuries A.D. They kept themselves somewhat isolated in the mountains and continued their old way of hunting, gathering fruits, and growing rice. They also continued their old way of preparing meals. They cultivated cardamom, the seeds of which were used as a spice in many dishes and in the production of some medicines. Here was one spice that the Phnongs and the plains Khmers had in common. Bas reliefs from this period show that the 102 hospitals in Angkor Wat and Angkor Thom and throughout Kambujadesa relied on supplies of cardamom as an ingredient in some curatives. Perhaps the Phnongs were not totally cut off from the rest of Kambujadesa. Maybe they engaged in a bit of cardamom trade and commerce (Indian cuisine is known to have made use of the whole and ground seeds, and the plant has been found growing in the ruins of ancient Khmer trading stations dated at around 1000 A.D.). Pepper was also grown in the forests where it twined around rattan like green grass. There was one with a blue-green color which was said to be the most bitter.

Despite the fact that Southeast Asians cultivated and/or traded with Africa and India various crops that were used to create a multitude of delicious meals, credit for the unique style and excellence of Southeast Asian cuisine has most certainly been given to the French. In fact, the most talked about and revered cuisine in the world is that of the French. No major city on this planet boasts of having "first rate" restaurants without having at least one that serves French food. Even restaurants serving "American" or "Continental" cuisine will sometimes do so, they will tell you, with a French flair or influence. It is really ironic when one looks squarely at the fact that wherever France has gone and imposed imperialism, be it Algeria, Angola, Saint Domingue (Haiti), or Vietnam, the cuisines of all the colonized countries became the cuisine of France. Ironic because in every non-European country where France has landed, the native cuisines of those countries are said either to be nonexistent or to have "improved" after contact with the French. The French occupation of Kambupuri or Kambujadesa, or as it is today called, Cambodia, allowed France to absorb many delicious recipes and methods of food preparation totally unknown to them before that contact.

Many of the indigenous people are well aware of their culinary influence on the French and other Europeans, and like indigenous peoples everywhere, Southeast Asians take pride in the fact that it is their land and their own ingenuity that provide them with the means to produce their varied creations. Unfortunately, in the early 1960s, John F. Kennedy instituted the "Hamlet Program" in Vietnam, which was designed to remove the people from their ancestral land and villages to "hamlets" or camps. The prevailing theory was that the move would make them invulnerable to spreading Vietcong doctrine. Thus, the United States took over the role of colonialist from the French who had occupied Vietnam since the 1800s.

The empire of the blacks of Southeast Asia fell in approximately the mid-fifteenth century. However, their methods of cooking and their tasty dishes were not to be forgotten. By the late fifteenth to early sixteenth century, Europe's imperialistic activity in Africa and the so-called New World would wrestle Africa's spice trade and wealth and power from its grip and change forever the stability with which the African continent fed its people. The colonization and slavery imposed on the Americas would bring Europeans into contact with architecture, religious practices, language, and other cultural traits, similar or identical in many ways to that of West Africans, Egyptians, and the Khmers. The colonizers would also be introduced to spices that were the trademarks of foods and cuisines which were previously not known to them. These were spices, foods, and methods of preparation that had already, for thousands of years, traveled back and forth between four continents.

Likewise, before the colonization of Mexico and Central America by the Spanish, aboriginal peoples and their cuisines flourished in these lands. The Mayans were one group who predated the Aztecs and whose eating habits dominated the area. Important to the origins of Mayan and Mexican cuisine is an ancient group of people whose contribution has been ignored or denied. The giant basalt and stone sculptures excavated in Mexico and Central America describing these ancients tell us that they were men and women from the continent of Africa.

Peppers, Cracklings, and
Knots of Wool

𝄢 𝄢 𝄢 𝄢

African Foods and Culinary Heritage
in Mexico and Central America

n 1950, it was written that a German physician named
Grafenberg "discovered" a certain zone, or spot, in the vagina.
His discovery was renamed after him. This zone, or Grafenberg
spot ("G spot" for short), was determined to be the center where, if
properly manipulated, orgasm would occur. So in 1950 a European
male lay claim to discovering even the woman's orgasm.

The discovery of the "G spot" can be likened and compared to
the discovery of America. Like the "G spot," America had been
there all the time and vast numbers of people, including Africans
and Asians, were already intimately familiar with its existence,
having explored and traveled there long before the arrival of Christopher Columbus and other Europeans. Columbus's fame as "dis-
coverer" of the Americas, and as the man responsible for bringing
groceries to Africa and the rest of the world is insulting and utter
nonsense. Migration and trade between the Americas and Africa
had made the exchange and transplanting of foodstuffs between
the two quite common. Columbus himself knew that Africans had
preceded him to the Americas, especially since he met many in
residence when he arrived. What was a "New World" to Columbus
and his followers was an old familiar one to African explorers and

merchants. Moreover, Columbus used African knowledge of the ocean routes to guide him. When he visited Ghana in 1480 his keen interest in sailing west to find the location of what he believed was the fabled land of spices resulted in Ghanaians showing him the logs of Bakary II. Research has shown that Columbus had access to Bakary II's meterological and cartographic records, and that both Bakary II and Columbus derived their knowledge of transatlantic travel from ancient African navigators who had engaged in extensive trade with civilizations in Mexico, Central America, Colombia, Ecuador, and Peru.

Many of these ancient African navigators were from West Africa, a region opulent in its material wealth and standards. Ghana's history, for example, reaches far back beyond known record. There were towns and trading centers flourishing before the 18th Dynasty in Egypt. West Africa was a region very similar in its advanced institutions to those of the Ethiopian empire in the east (Ethiopia and the Sudan were considered by the Egyptians to be the source of Egyptian civilization). But there were four principal trading empires in West Africa which flourished from very remote times down to the eighth through sixteenth centuries A.D. Trade and barter between Africa, the Americas, India, and Asia reached its pinnacle during this period, West Africa's Golden Age.

One of those trading empires was Ghana, which originated in the western Sudan and covered an area including the present-day nations of Guinea, Senegal, Mali, and Mauritania. Ghana's founders, the Soninkes, were divided into clans, each representing a division of labor that regulated various functions of government. The empire, known as the "Land of Gold," owed its extreme wealth not only to its rich soil, which produced numerous crops, and to its control of caravan trade routes to the north, the east, Ethiopia, and Egypt but also because it ruled the greatest source of gold bound for Europe and Asia. The empire's gold and iron mining and manufacturing could be traced back more than a thousand years.

Another gold manufacturing empire was Mali. Its roots, in fact, were in gold, and during the Middle Ages it controled the largest trading center in the world. That center was located in the city of Jenne, which had arms stretching to India and China. Foreign merchants who came to trade in the country were impressed at the prosperity enjoyed there and took note that even the common people were "not oppressed by poverty." Mali was the home of the Mandinka, or Mandingo, people and their capital was located on the Niger River. When the capital was moved to Niani, a massive program of agricultural expansion ensued. Agriculturally minded kings mandated that their soldiers also become farmers and raise cotton, peanuts, grains, and other staples. Many farms were also expert in the raising of poultry and cattle. An abundant food supply and lucrative commercial trading profits, particularly from control of the salt and gold trade previously in the hands of Ghana, guaranteed prosperity. The abundance and variety of food in Mali assured everyone of a good, balanced diet.

One plant that guaranteed food and other necessities was the multipurpose baobab tree *(adansonia digitata)*, which grew wild in savanna regions of Mali and other parts of Africa. Its bark was turned into rope. Medicines were made from an extracted liquid and from its dried leaves; the same leaves were also used to thicken stews. A meal for making bread was derived from this plant, as was a red dye. Its fruit contains a source of seed-rich oil and the pulp in which the seeds are embedded not only is an excellent source of vitamin C but has also been used to make refreshing drinks containing tartaric and other acids. In addition, the hollowed-out trunks were used to store water and other materials, as well as to inter the mummified remains of the dead.

Spinach salads can be excellent sources of vitamin C, particularly when the accompanying sauce, or dressing, is made with fruit juice. Whether your style is vegetarian, or you prefer the added touch of cooked shrimp or chicken, you will find this a flavorful and delicious prelude to any main course.

ᛋᛋᛋ

Savanna Spinach Salad

For four servings:
8 Tbs. palm oil (also called dende; see glossary), OR, 8 Tbs. vegetable or peanut oil
2 tsp. achiote seeds (see glossary)
4 Tbs. orange juice
8 tsp. rum
4 tsp. light molasses

$\frac{1}{2}$ tsp. EACH cinnamon and cumin
8 shakes crushed red pepper
8 to 10 ounces salad spinach
4 whole green onions
Red onion slices
Paper thin carrot slices
Cucumber slices
4 sliced plum tomatoes

Combine first 7 ingredients in a skillet. (If using vegetable or pea-nut oil and achiote seeds, first prepare the following: heat oil in skillet. Add achiote seeds and stir constantly in hot oil for 3 to 6 minutes, until oil turns a deep orange. CAUTION: Seeds may pop. If seeds begin to pop, cover skillet and continue process by shaking back and forth.) Bring to a boil and simmer, stirring frequently, for 2 minutes. Cool.

In a large bowl combine spinach, green and red onions, carrots, and cucumbers. Add dressing. Toss to coat evenly. Garnish servings with sliced tomatoes.

An abundance of food was only one of Mali's assets. Mali was also well known for its famous seats of learning at Walata, Gao, Jenne, and Timbuktu. It was in Walata, the traveler Ibn Batuta reported in the fourteenth century, that there were female physi-cians and teachers and women in other positions of authority, thus enjoying equal status with men. Timbuktu was reputed to hold no equal in the arena of scholarship, culture, and learning. The Songhay, whose empire rose from 1350 to 1600 A.D., settled along the shores of the Middle Niger, captured Timbuktu, and began an era of tremendous development. They built and staffed universities and other educational institutions throughout their principal cities to include courses in diction, elocution, astronomy, prosody, math-ematics, music, ethnography, rhetoric, philosophy, medicine, hy-giene, and logic. In 1473, they added to their domain the city of Jenne, in which stood attractive buildings designed to take advan-tage of the beauty of the surrounding landscape. Jenne was also the home of an advanced society and a well-known university, which employed thousands of teachers who prepared courses, gave lectures, and led research in numerous areas. Their medical school trained physicians and surgeons in many skills; one being the successful removal of cataracts from the human eye.

When West Africans were not using scalpels, they were making sculptures. The Nok culture of northern Nigeria, one of West Africa's producers of magnificent iron and bronze sculptures, is believed to have flourished as early as 1000 to 2000 B.C. Figurine specimens from archaeological material have yielded dates of approximately 900 B.C. However, many cultures from this region flourished during this time period and earlier. Many evolved into the importance of, for example, the Hausa states, whose principal cities became places where international trade routes converged. The Hausa states linked trade routes between states of the Sudan and the Mediterranean coast, attracting activity from other parts of the Sudan, Guinea, North Africa, and Egypt.

Ancient West Africa's commercial activities and the racial, linguistic, religious, and certainly culinary affinities between Africa and the Americas, justify conclusions of pre-Columbian African voyages to the Americas. Between 1200 and 100 B.C. the main food and cultural exchange centers in the Americas were agricultural ceremonial complexes headquartered in the areas of San Lorenzo, La Venta, and Tres Zapotes in the Gulf Coast area of Mexico. These centers came into being due to religious, economic, and technological factors. The centers provided a marketplace that attracted commercial trade, artists, and intellectuals, and offered specialized services. They were also, during this time, controled by agriculturally minded leaders, devoted to an intense campaign of crop production, combined with religious ceremony. Their intentions were well rewarded. These early folk, known as the Olmecs, or "the people who lived in the direction of the rising sun," were considered to be the "first great civilization in the Americas." Many scholars have written that the Olmecs were the "mother culture for all the fabled Indian empires that rose and fell in Mexico and Mesoamerica." Olmec civilization, which diffused into Peru and other parts of South America, prepared lavish, mouth-watering repasts. Maize and other ancient and domesticated plants and lush vegetation, such as chilies and spices, sweet potatoes, cacao, tomatoes, various beans, peanuts, avocados, pumpkins, and squash merged on

Mexican soil to create new foods and medicines that solidified an already progressive culinary and social environment. The preparation and presentation of every meal was an expression of numerous aspects of religious and social customs, language, architectural styles, and even the calendar, all of which had come together on the shores of Mexico long before the arrival of Europeans.

Unfortunately, the debate still rages regarding who the Olmecs were and to whom Olmec religious and social customs belong. Some scholars claim that the Olmecs were Chinese, others claim American Indian ancestry. Still others categorize them as a "Science Mystery" and cannot agree on which cultural groups Olmec language, architectural styles, and calendar can be attributed. Physically the Olmecs have been described as "baby faced," with "flat, rather infantile noses." The archaeological world was introduced to a stunning find in 1862 when a colossal basalt head was found in Tres Zapotes. Vera Cruz revealed the first of several in 1896. Five more were found during an expedition in the state of Tabasco in La Venta beginning in 1938. Still others were uncovered in 1946 in the San Lorenzo plateau in southeastern Vera Cruz. During the spring of 1967 Yale University led an expedition to San Lorenzo in southeast Mexico which yielded another giant stone head, as well as other artifacts such as altars and pyramids. The colossal heads were covered by close-fitting caps. These same style caps were worn by Egyptian priests as well as by the sultans of Mali when they held court. In addition, on the rear side of the colossal head found at Tres Zapotes is carved seven "Ethiopian-type braids . . . that taper off into rings and tassels," that is, the hairstyle common to many African societies—cornrows. In other words, every one of these colossal heads, standing five to nine feet in height and weighing between twenty and thirty tons each, have exhibited African facial and cosmetic features. In fact, hundreds of pieces of sculpture possessing "Ethiopian features," or the "typically African physiognomy" of thick lips and broad, flat noses, have been found all over Mexico from Campeche in the east to the southern coast of Guerrero, and from Chiapas, next to Guatamala's border, to the Panuco River north of Veracruz. Archaeological pieces representing Africans have also been found in Central America, Panama, Colombia, Ecuador, and Peru. One absurd explanation for the African presence in these areas is that they were "a cargo of captured blacks" whom Phoenician seamen had "turned into their servants" and brought with them to the Americas. However, there is compelling evidence that during the most remote periods in history Africans made transatlantic voyages to the Americas for the purpose of trade and exploration. Some records of pre-Columbian African trading expeditions have survived and shed light on the advanced and rich civilizations that flourished on Africa's west coast.

Archaeological evidence that further supports the African roots of the Olmecs is the common architectural style during this and later eras in Mexico of man-made mounds and step pyramids, identical in construction and intended purpose to those of Africa. Step pyramids were erected as early as three thousand years before Christ in Egypt. The Pyramid of Djoser at Saqqara, built around 2750 B.C., and the Pyramid of Medum, built for the Pharaoh Sneferu in 2700 B.C., are two such well-known structures. The first such structure in the Americas was erected at La Venta, the same area where colossal heads were unearthed. Like the Egyptian structures, it is "sun-star oriented and encircled by a precinct," and the religious function and the astronomical and spatial relationships are identical to those found in Egypt.

Sun-star orientation and astronomical relationships were important components of the Olmec calendar, considered "a masterpiece of mathematical and astronomical knowledge," and one of the most striking connections between Africa and Mexico. The Egyptian influence is highly plausible given that the Mexicans began to count their years on February 26, 747 B.C., a day "celebrated in the era of Nabonassar, which was fixed by the Egyptians 747 years before the Christian era; for the beginning of their month Toth corresponded with the meridian of the same day." In addition, the twelve lunar mansions in the Olmec calendar correspond to the twelve Egyptian gods, and the inclusion of the five useless or dateless festival days were Egyptian influenced. The symbols of the Mexican months are also similar to the Egyptian.

Symbols were important in other aspects of ancient Mexican culture, specifically burial methods, which were comparable to those in East and West Africa. Mummification was practiced by the Olmecs and cultures in Peru. Common funerary characteristics on both sides of the Atlantic took the form of metal objects or stones such as jade being placed into the mouths and nostrils of the deceased, as well as filling the place of interment with foods and clothing to accompany the deceased to the next world. Artificial beards worn by kings and high priests and the ritual use of purple as a royal and priestly color worn while presiding over important funeral, celebratory, or religious ceremonies were practices common to both African and Olmec culture.

Religious ceremonies were sometimes performed before, during, or after an important surgical procedure. One such procedure, known as trepanning, was used by the ancient Egyptians (the method was later picked up by Hippocrates) as well as in both ancient Mexico and Peru. Soldiers, having received blows on the skull, might undergo this treatment to relieve cranial pressure. Physicians performed the operation with success in most cases.

Religion took the form of sun, serpent, and feline worship and was practically identical to the worship of Egyptian and East and West African societies. It should be noted that many Mayan and Aztec gods are ancient Olmec dieties. Pictorial records show them with black skin, some with black skin and tightly curled hair; the most important of them are said to be gods of the traveling merchants. Those traveling merchants may indeed have been influential in bringing to the Americas plants such as the rubber tree, an item that flourishes on the west coast of Africa, particularly Liberia, and parts of Mexico. The name Olmec is derived from Olli, which means rubber; the term Olmec itself has been translated as meaning "Rubber People." Balls for games very similarly played in ancient Mexico and Africa were made of this rubber. The names connected with the games and some of the terms for how the games were played have been traced linguistically to African origins.

Language was one of the most important connections between Olmecs and Africans. One Harvard philologist, Leo Wiener, has argued in four volumes that words used in everyday life and for numerous foods and crops grown in Mexico and the Americas are of African origin. His four books on the African presence in and contribution to the ancient Americas philologically presents evidence of the African influence on Mexican, Native American, and Peruvian religion, their social, political, and economic organization, and their agriculture. A number of Mexican and other scholars have also written that archaeological evidence points to the African as the first inhabitant of Mexico.

This should come as no surprise. It is reasonable to conclude, based on the most compelling and current work in paleontology along with archaeological finds, including DNA evidence, that humankind originated in East Africa and migrated from there to every continent on the planet. The Americas were no exception. Along with the migration and development of culture and civilization comes the development and evolution of agriculture and food ways. Like a vast number of people in Africa, Olmec economy was based on agriculture, hunting, and fishing. They were quite active in increasing their agricultural activity, particularly in the area of maize production, in the fertile river lands throughout the Gulf and Pacific Coasts in Mexico. What the land or water did not provide, they acquired through a well-organized, sophisticated commercial network. In fact, every aspect of the Olmec cultural environment, even art and sculpture and the playing of ball games, were important tools in producing abundant amounts of food.

Playing games of ball was the most important means of ensuring abundant harvests in some African countries. Although these games were connected with other religious observances, their primary function was to obtain rain for crops. However, in certain regions ball games were played to, hopefully, end rains that had lasted too long. Thus, the games were played to obtain preferred changes in the weather "through the movements and changing fortune of the game." Africans who played for rain production contended that the ball was like a dark rain cloud that was sometimes hit about with ladles or sticks. This was essentially the forerunner to hockey. Both women and men engaged in these games. Some villages engaged in a type of football, which was played three different ways to produce three yearly harvests of the same crop. Among the Gulf Coast Olmec in Mexico, in addition to a game similar to the one just described, another game, played with two teams and a solid rubber ball, was played by launching the ball beyond the opponent's half of the court. The players had to ensure that the ball, which represented the sun in its path across the sky, did not fall, guaranteeing healthy, abundant crops. This had to be accomplished by hitting only with the player's hips, elbows, or knees.

For the Olmecs, it was particularly important that teenage boys and men, athletes of the games, consume seeds from various melons and nuts; although, as in Africa, Olmec children and adults alike loved snacking on fruits, seeds, and nuts between meals. Eaten in certain quantities or in certain culinary preparations, these foods gave the ball player added strength and skill.

Seeds from fruits and vegetables, such as watermelon, squash, and pumpkin, were ground to a paste and added to vegetable and meat dishes, as well as to drinks, in both ancient Africa and Mexico. Watermelon, ironically, is one food plant (the seeds from this plant have actually been excavated from ancient archaeological sites as far north as Arizona and New Mexico) that has been conceded as being of African origin. This, apparently, accounts for the "Moorish element" evident in Olmec blood when refreshing, cold drinks, now called *orchatas* or *horchatas*, are prepared. Orchatas are deliciously mild beverages, some made with rice, others with seeds from certain melons, and flavored with spices, fruit juices, and honey. Drunk before, during, and after a game, orchatas were, in essence, the ballplayers' Gatorade.

Watermelon Seed Orchata

¹/₄ cup watermelon seeds
¹/₂ inch stick canela (see glossary), or cinnamon stick
A heaping ¹/₄ cup fresh raisins (available at health food stores)
2 cups of water
1 tsp. lime juice
2 tsp. honey
2 tsp. sugar

Toast watermelon seeds and cinnamon in skillet. Grind to a powder.

In a saucepan bring water to a rolling boil. Add ground seeds, spices, and raisins. Simmer for 5 minutes. Remove from heat. Pour liquid through a cheesecloth-lined strainer into a bowl or pitcher, pressing against raisins with the back of a spoon. Stir in remaining ingredients. Chill overnight. Serve over ice.

As anyone knows, an athlete cannot live on Gatorade alone. Gifts and personal accolades from family and friends, particularly female friends, were very healthy inducements to the ballplayers in accomplishing the goals of the game. As I am about to present a recipe using pumpkin seeds and cracklings, a recipe reminiscent of the dishes eaten by ballplayers after a game (as soon as they had strength enough to eat), I felt that this would be the place to present a song. The following verses are lyrics to a Mexican song— a song of food and love. Notice that the person singing speaks of finding a girl with her hair done up in a knot. This reflects the popular hairstyle worn by many females of African descent. A favorite hairstyle of West African and other black women in ancient times was combing the hair high up on the head and knotting it at the top in a ball or braids. The reference to the hair's being in a knot of "wool" is indicative of African hair. Note, too, the reference to "dark one."

Las Calabazas (The Pumpkins)

Si te fueras a la Puebla, me traeras una poblana
No te la pido con trenzas, sino con chongo de lana.
Dame morena, de lo que comes, calabacitas con chicharrones,
Dame morena, de lo que comes, calabacitas con berenjenas.
Moreno pintan a Cristo, morena a la Magdalena,
Y tu para no ser menos, tambien te pintas morena.
Dame morena, de lo que cenas, calabacitas con camarones.
Dame morena, de lo que almuerzas, calabacitas con buenas
    fresas.
Dame morena, de lo que tragas, calabacitas con verdolagas,
Dame morena de lo que chupas, con calabazas unas chalupas.
Me gustan las calabazas
De las que produce el suelo,
Pues calabazas de amor
Ni me gustan ni las quiero.

Translation:
If thou wilt go to Puebla, bring me a little country girl,
I do not beg thee for one with braids, but with a knot of wool
    ["hair combed in style peculiar to the part of the country"].
Give me, dark one, what you eat, little pumpkins with cracklings
    ["the skin of pork or bacon with some meat fried"].

Give me, dark one, what you eat, little pumpkins with egg
plant.
Dark one, painted by Christ, dark one like Magdelena
And thou in order not to be less, also paint thyself, dark
one.
Give me, dark one, what you eat for supper, little pumpkins
with shrimp.
Give me, dark one, what you eat for breakfast, little pumpkins
with good strawberries.
Give me, dark one, what you devour, little pumpkins with
purslane,
Give me, dark one, what you sip, with pumpkins some
chalupas ["a kind of tortilla or enchilada fried"].
I like pumpkins
Of those that the ground produces.
But pumpkins of love
I do not like, I do not want.

> (Blanche and Edna V. McNeil, *First Foods of America*
> [Los Angeles: Suttonhouse Ltd., 1936], p.129)

Remember the tune "Love Potion Number Nine"? Hot, spicy, and ready for adoring fans, try this fare on someone close to your heart (athlete or not). The next love song you hear will be written for you.

$\mathscr{S\!S\!S\!S\!S\!S\!S\!S\!S\!S\!S\!S\!S\!S\!S\!S\!S\!S\!S\!S\!S\!S\!S\!S\!S\!S\!S\!S\!S\!S\!S\!S\!S\!S\!S\!S\!S\!S\!S\!S\!S\!S\!S}$

Pork Skins in Pumpkin Seed Sauce

$^{1}/_{4}$ cup shelled pumpkin seeds (see glossary)
$^{1}/_{4}$ tsp. EACH coriander seeds, whole cloves, and black peppercorns
$^{1}/_{2}$ tsp. cumin seed
1 cup plus 1 or 2 Tbs. beef broth
3 Tbs. butter
1 rounded Tbs. chopped, fresh coriander
2 serrano chilies
1 large onion, chopped
A heaping $^{1}/_{2}$ tsp. dried parsley flakes
1 large tomato, chopped
4 tomatillos, husks removed, rinsed, drained, and chopped

2 Tbs. crushed chicharrones (see glossary)
Salt to taste

Toast pumpkin seeds in a dry skillet over medium heat by stirring seeds frequently until they bloat (they will pop as they bloat so have a cover handy). Remove from heat and cool.

Toast coriander, cloves, peppercorns, and cumin in a dry skillet by stirring frequently until they brown a bit. Remove from heat and cool.

Combine toasted seeds and spices with ³⁄₄ cup of the broth in food processor or blender and grind thoroughly until smooth.

Melt butter in skillet. Add fresh coriander, chilies, onions, parsley, tomatoes, and tomatillos. Cook and stir for several minutes until onion starts to become clear. Stir in ground seeds and spice mixture. Cook and stir over medium low heat for 5 minutes. Stir in remaining broth, then crushed chicharrones. Taste for needed salt. Cook and stir for another 10 minutes.

Serve over broiled, grilled, or baked chicken, beef, or fish. Makes a lovely sauce or gravy for rice or corn.

❧❧

Pre-planting ceremonies were marked by the playing of ball games and the consumption of "water foods." Water foods were eaten to mark the beginning of the rainy season, during which ceremonies were conducted to ask the gods for adequate rain prior to planting the major corn crop. The water foods were either white, or transparent in color, or had a large water content, or all of the above. It was believed that when these preparations were consumed by the people, water was indirectly supplied to the newly planted seed in the ground. The consuming of these foods, therefore, brought a message of rain in a transformed culinary-agricultural code.

It is perfectly all right if your tears fall into the pot while you are cutting up the onions for this wonderfully rich, spicy lamb soup, especially since the preparation and consuming of water foods keeps you one with nature. My grandma used to prepare her meals outside on the covered porch in summer. If it was raining, no one would notice a little extra moisture in the pot.

Lamb Soup

2 Tbs. vegetable oil
1 tsp. achiote seeds (see glossary)
3 cups beef broth
1 cup chicken broth
³/₄ to 1 pound boneless lamb for stew
4 serrano chili peppers
1 inch wide strip poblano chili pepper
1 pasilla chili pepper, soaked in scalding hot water for 1 hour, seeds and ribs removed and finely chopped
2 tomatillos, husks removed, rinsed, drained, and chopped
1 large onion, chopped
A rounded ¹/₂ cup thinly sliced carrots
2 to 4 Tbs. chopped cilantro (coriander)
¹/₂ of a large tomato, chopped
1 small sweet potato, chopped
2 tsp. sugar
A rounded ¹/₄ tsp. whole cloves, ground
A rounded ¹/₄ tsp. ground canela (see glossary) or cinnamon
¹/₄ tsp. thyme
Freshly ground black pepper, to taste
Salt to taste

Heat 1 Tbs. oil in medium size pot. Add achiote and shake and stir around in pot for a couple of minutes to release orange color (achiote will pop; have cover for skillet handy). Remove achiote granules and reserve. Add broths, then lamb, to pot. Bring to a boil. Simmer, covered, on low heat for 1 hour and 15 minutes. In a skillet toast serrano and poblano chilies on all sides. Remove from skillet and cool. Heat remaining 1 Tbs. oil in skillet. Add reserved achiote and stir around again for a couple of minutes. Remove achiote granules and discard. Add pasilla chili, tomatillos, onions, carrots, and cilantro to skillet. Chop serrano and poblano chilies and stir into skillet. Cook and stir for a few minutes until onion is translucent. Add tomatillo mixture to lamb in pot. Add tomatoes, sweet potatoes, sugar, cloves, cinnamon, thyme, black pepper to pot. Bring to a boil, lower heat, and simmer, covered, for about 50 minutes. Taste for needed salt. Make 1 to 2 days ahead. It tastes even better after a couple of days.

⁂⁂

The consumption of water foods as part of the social, cultural, and religious order of the games was symbolized in Olmec villages and in the agricultural ceremonial complexes in the form of an ideographic language. Like that of Egypt and Ethiopia, the language was hieroglyphic in form and combined the jaguar, their symbol of earth itself, and the serpent, symbolizing water, to represent plant fertility. This earth-water-agriculture connection was an expression of plant life, food, and life itself.

Part of that life centered around the economy, which was based on hunting, fishing, farming, and the trading of goods and raw materials. The land was owned by the entire community and the population received equal portions of the harvest. Besides maize, part of the harvest included *annatto*, used for flavoring and coloring food; *chayote*, a squash-like fruit; hog plum, a fruit tree; *sapota* and starapple, both fruit trees; amaranth, a pot herb and grain; and yam bean, an edible tuber, to name just a few. There was usually a division of labor in the Olmec culture of Mexico and a complex social stratification similar to African societies. In the agricultural ceremonial centers, god-kings, or leaders, were responsible for the governing of the kingdom and took on such tasks as work organization. Other religious men held sway over the intellectual life of the community and taught the knowledge of the period, including astrology and divination. Likewise, in Africa societies were divided into a certain number of clans, each clan representing a division of labor that regulated the various functions of the government. Those functions included architecture, metal working, and the manufacture of clothing. Others were involved in animal husbandry, fishing, and agriculture. Most Africans, however, were farmers or cattle raisers. African farmers specialized in a staple crop such as yams, millet, rice, Guinea corn, or cassava. Beans and peas of many varieties grew between the rows of staple crops. Peanuts, squash, sesame seeds, and pumpkins were planted around the borders of the fields. Also in mass cultivation were sweet potatoes, hot peppers, eggplants, bush greens (which were varieties of spinach), maize, okra, onions, tomatoes, and cabbage. Such a larder produced a fabulous array of tempting dishes.

The signature of some of these tempting dishes was a garnish of sliced boiled eggs. Eggs as an ingredient and garnish help to complete the following Mexican-African inspired dish. Inspire your clan with this very rich and flavorful meat loaf.

Lodagaa Steak Loaf

3 to 4 eggs
2 Tbs. egusi seeds (see glossary)
1 pound ground steak
1 tsp. EACH cumin, garlic salt, and black pepper
1/2 tsp. salt
1/4 tsp. crushed red pepper
2 tsp. sugar
1 large ancho chili (soaked in scalding hot water for an hour, stem and seeds removed), finely chopped
1/2 cup cooked and chopped nopalitos (cactus)
1 medium-large onion, chopped
1/2 of a large green pepper, chopped
1 large tomato, chopped
Boiled egg slices (optional)

Place eggs in saucepan. Cover with cold water. Bring to a boil. Boil for 5 minutes. Remove from heat. Replace boiling water with ICE water. Keep water cold by adding ice from time to time for about 20 minutes. While eggs are chilling, toast seeds in a dry skillet over medium heat by stirring frequently until lightly browned. Cool completely, then finely crush. Combine crushed seeds with remaining ingredients, except egg slices, and mix well. Place half of mixture in a 9 inch loaf pan.

Peel eggs. Place eggs one behind the other, lengthwise, down center of meat mixture. Cover eggs, top and sides with remaining mixture.

Bake in 350 degree, preheated oven for 1 hour.

Garnish with sliced, boiled eggs (optional).

The Olmecs held a preference for manioc, also known as yuca (linguistic evidence has shown that manioc has been cultivated and eaten on the African continent long before European arrival and that there may have been an indigenous variety; furthermore, the method of planting this and other crops in the Americas was similar, if not identical, to the African method practiced in Unyamwezi and areas throughout Africa), chenopodium, and *jicama*, a tuber similar to the sweet potato that has a texture that is a cross between an apple and raw potato. Honey, cactus (used in salads and for making candy!), and agave leaves were natural products that were gathered. The *agave* genus, and its *maguey* species, is the source of tequila, pulque, and mescal. The Mayans, a descendant group of the Olmecs, pictured the agave plant in their manuscripts or picture stories, called *codices*, and frequently showed Africans crossing the ocean as merchants and bringing the art of extracting the juices from the agave plant, distilling it by fire, and becoming the gods of the traveling merchants.

Through Olmec merchants, the growth of trade helped to increase economic surplus. This enabled the village people to produce raw materials and handcrafts and to grow food that was not for immediate consumption. One of these foods that was part of intense trade activity was the cacao bean, the source of chocolate. Cacao cultivation has a very long and early history in the South Gulf Coast region. The word cacao itself has been traced back to Olmec culture. The cacao (*Theobroma cacao*) and the cola nut (*Cola acuminata*), a plant of African origin, are both caffeine rich and are of the same botanical family (*Sterculiaceae*). The Olmecs traded the cacao in other parts of Mexico and Guatemala, El Salvador, Belize, Honduras, Nicaragua, and Costa Rica. Not only was its high oil content popular and appreciated by groups who consumed large quantities of starch from foods such as maize but the cacao was also used as money.

If you are a chocoholic, the only thing standing between you and Valhalla is a clean skillet and a little of your time. If Cocoa Krispies for breakfast are not enough; if that cup of Swiss mocha cafe au lait did not get it; if that Hostess cupcake did not hit the spot, then what you need is a chocolate main dish. This recipe is a combination of an African meat and peanut sauce/stew and a Mexican *mole*. Lunching on an entree with rich, dark brown, chocolaty gravy will put this entire discussion into the proper perspective. Try it for dinner, too. It cries out to adorn baked lamb chops or steak. Mmmmmm good.

⚬⚬⚬

Chocolate Lamb and Beef Sauce

³/₄ pound ground lamb
¹/₂ pound ground beef
¹/₄ cup coarsely ground peanuts or walnuts
1 inch canela or cinnamon stick
¹/₄ tsp. black peppercorns
4 (9 inch) stalks of cilantro
1 onion, cut up
1 small ancho chili pepper, soaked in ¹/₂ cup scalding hot water for about an hour, drained, and stem removed
1 slice of bread
¹/₂ cup cooked calabash squash
2 tsp. raisins
1 tomatillo, cut up
1 or 2 Tbs. vegetable oil
1¹/₂ tsp. sugar
1¹/₂ ounces semi-sweet chocolate (you can use chips)
1¹/₂ ounces milk chocolate (you can use chips)
¹/₂ cup beef or chicken broth
Salt and freshly ground black pepper, to taste
Sesame seeds for garnish

Brown lamb and beef together in skillet. Drain oil. Break meat up into crumbs and transfer to a covered dish. Combine next 10 ingredients in food processor. Blend until very smooth paste. Heat oil in skillet. Empty contents of blender into skillet and cook and stir for a few minutes. Add sugar, then both chocolates. Stir until chocolate melts. Stir in broth, then salt and pepper. Simmer on low heat, uncovered, stirring frequently, for 10 to 15 minutes. Garnish servings with sesame seeds.

⚬⚬⚬

In the African tradition, food products were used as money. Their main source of wealth, actually, came from transcontinental trade. Caravan routes set up throughout the continent carried many different food products. Vast crops of cotton, millet, and sorghum were cultivated and traded. Wheat was brought in from North Africa. Sheep, cattle, and honey were imported from southern countries. Dried fruits, raisins, and other foods came from the east coast as well as from all points of the continent. Their most lucrative trade, however, was the salt and gold exchange with the northern Sahara. Trans-Saharan caravans linked all parts of the African continent. Salt was an indispensable item in the preparation of food, but it was also just as indispensable on the long trek of the caravans. On a caravan trip through desert countries, dehydration was a major problem. Salt, however, helped tremendously against dehydration and with food preservation; salt was so indispensable that travelers used it as currency.

Whether you are traveling by caravan or not, the following dish will give you something to look forward to at the end of your journey. The sauce is assured to make you travel across any desert to get to it, with or without your stash of salt.

Braised Rabbit in Chocolate and Cream

Marinade:
1 cup red wine vinegar
3 Tbs. corn or peanut oil
2 bay leaves
$^1/_4$ tsp. thyme
$^1/_2$ tsp. salt
$2^1/_2$ to $2^3/_4$ pounds rabbit meat
$2^1/_2$ Tbs. EACH masa harina (or yellow corn meal) and flour
3 Tbs. corn oil, OR peanut oil, OR rendered pork fat
Black pepper
1 medium onion, chopped
1 medium poblano chili, toasted, stem and seeds removed, and finely chopped
1 cup sliced mushrooms
$^1/_2$ tsp. ground cinnamon
$^1/_8$ tsp. dill weed
1 cup chicken broth
$^1/_2$ cup white wine

¼ cup semi-sweet chocolate chips
Freshly ground black pepper and salt, to taste
2 tsp. light molasses or maple sugar
2 Tbs. light whipping cream

Combine marinade ingredients in a large bowl and stir vigorously to mix well. Add rabbit and coat pieces well with mixture. Cover and refrigerate for 4 to 6 hours.

In a small bowl, combine corn meal and flour and mix well.

Heat oil in skillet. While oil is heating, remove rabbit one piece at a time from marinade and sprinkle with black pepper. Holding each piece over corn meal mixture, spoon corn meal mixture all over pieces, coating well but allowing excess mixture to fall back into bowl. Brown meat in hot oil on both sides. Transfer meat to a covered platter or container.

Add onions, poblano, and mushrooms to skillet (add 2 to 3 tsp. of oil to skillet, if necessary). DO NOT REMOVE COOKED PAR-TICLES. Cook and stir a few minutes, until onion becomes trans-lucent. Add cinnamon and dill weed and continue cooking and stirring for about 1 minute. Stir in chicken broth, then white wine. Bring to a boil. Add chocolate and stir until completely melted. Taste for needed black pepper and salt. Mix well. Return rabbit to simmering sauce. Simmer, covered, over low to medium-low heat for about 40 minutes.

Remove rabbit from sauce. Stir in molasses, then cream. Taste again for needed salt and pepper. Bring to a boil. Simmer for al-most a minute. Return rabbit to sauce, coating each piece with sauce. Simmer for another 2 minutes. Serve immediately.

In West Africa, lucrative commercial trading profits and a substantial food supply helped make possible a high quality of life. There were farmers who raised cotton, peanuts, grains, and other crops. There were also farms expert in the raising of cattle and poultry. In most kingdoms everything was abundant, particu-larly the food supply. The variety of foods assured a balanced diet to all inhabitants. Also, locally produced items, such as metal goods and cotton cloth, known as *chigguyiya*, were exchanged. Local blacksmiths produced weapons and tools of iron. Fine jewelry was fashioned of gold, bronze, silver, and copper. Shops of potters, sandal makers, and weavers of many kinds of cloth were also in abundance.

Similarly, the Olmecs ruled immense trade networks that stretched from Mexico's highlands into Guatemala. They brought jade and obsidian into the Gulf Coast area. Most of it was used for making jewelry, mirrors, tools, and their famous art objects. Noticeably, the agricultural ceremonial centers were strategically placed at trade control points where numerous access roads were in place to make travel easier. *Chamil* and *tonamil* were two of a number of crops that continued to be part of Olmec commerce and trade, as a massive program of agricultural expansion ensued, further advanced by terraced crop production and the use of irrigation canals.

Meats were part of the Olmec diet and important items in the commercial network. Dishes were prepared that included monkey, parrot, armadillo, jaguar, puma, otter, turkey, deer, and water fowl. Coconut milk and peppers were two ingredients frequently combined in African and Olmec meat preparations. With these ingredients in mind, one taste of this offering is sure to convince you that a generous helping will serve to balance your diet. The fragrances that will permeate your kitchen will entice others to balance theirs right alongside of you.

Masar Spicy Roasted Turkey

2 cups broth (about ⅔ cup chicken, the rest beef)
1 tsp. cumin seeds
½ tsp. anise seed
4 Tbs. chopped coriander (about six, 9 inch stalks)
4 chipotle chili peppers, soaked in scalding hot water about 1 hour and 20 minutes; stems, seeds, and inner ribs removed
½ tsp. black peppercorns
4 Tbs. sunflower seeds
2 Tbs. raisins
8½ pound turkey
½ cup butter or margarine

1 cup turkey pan drippings
4 Tbs. cognac
½ cup coconut milk
2 Tbs. milk
3 tsp. masa harina
Salt and pepper

Combine first eight ingredients in food processor and blend until smooth.

Baste turkey with some of the mixture. Place 1 stick butter or margarine inside turkey cavity. Bake in preheated 325 degree oven for about 2½ hours.

In skillet or saucepan combine remaining mixture, turkey pan drippings, cognac, and ½ cup milk. Simmer for about 1 minute or so. Combine 2 Tbs. milk and masa harina. Blend until smooth. Add masa harina mixture to skillet. Stir until thickened. Taste for needed salt and pepper. Spoon over servings of turkey.

"Exotic" meat dishes from the Olmec repertoire were composed of home-grown staples sold in market spaces set aside at the agricultural ceremonial centers. Deer meat was cut into strips and marinated in fruit juices and herbs. It was then cooked with eggplant, spinach, and onions.

The enchanting flavors of the following dish cast a spell, a spell that lifts only when the gods have had their share. Prepare one or two potato side dishes, so that the gods may dine royally.

Braised Venison with Garden Gravy

4 pound rump of venison

The marinade:
1 cup vinegar
2 tsp. EACH lemon, lime, and orange juice
2 bay leaves
½ tsp. EACH dried thyme and basil
4 Tbs. chicha or whiskey

2 juniper berries, crushed
Seasonings and Gravy:
Corn or peanut oil
Salt, black pepper, cayenne, paprika, and masa harina
¼ cup corn or peanut oil
½ tsp. achiote seeds
3 cups beef broth
2 EACH onions and tomatoes, chopped
2 sliced tomatillos (see glossary)
2 poblano chili peppers, toasted, stems removed, and chopped
Reserved marinade
⅓ cup chicha or rum
Salt and black pepper, to taste
¼ of a small eggplant, peeled and chopped
2 large spinach leaves, finely chopped

Place venison in glass bowl.

Combine marinade ingredients in a saucepan and bring to a boil. Simmer for 2 to 3 minutes. Cool completely. Pour marinade over venison. Marinate for 24 hours, turning several times.

Reserving marinade, remove venison. Generously baste with peanut oil. Generously coat with salt, pepper, cayenne, paprika, and masa harina.

Heat the ¼ cup of oil and add achiote seeds (have a lid ready as seeds will pop). Shake the pot back and forth until seeds turn very dark brown. Remove seeds and discard.

Brown venison on all sides in hot oil. Remove venison from pot. Stir into pot broth, onion, tomatoes, tomatillos, and chilies. Return venison to pot. Cover, simmer for 2½ hours.

Remove venison from pot and wrap tightly in foil. Stir in remaining ingredients. Cover and simmer over low heat for about 15–20 minutes. Spoon garden gravy over slices of venison.

African women also set up spaces or food stalls in the markets of their trading cities. One of the dishes they prepared was *Killishi*, roasted meat basted with oil, herbs, and spices. Some women sun-dried strips of the meat first and then marinated it for days in the oil and herbs before further cooking. At the stalls Africans sold *Atchia-Kara*, a fragrant soup. Two enormous pots would be set up; one containing beef, goat, and lamb, in the other a thick, green sauce cooked with yams, which is ladled over the cooked meats. *Enjibotchi*, rice with a delicious sauce, and *Ekoa*, a durra porridge, were favorites at the market. There were also chickens in many beautiful colors, and these exquisite birds were turned into magnificent dishes.

Talk about finger-licking good, you really will not need a knife to cut this chicken. It is so tender, it falls off the bone if you are not careful with it. Sauces and gravies have always been an integral part of African and Mexican cuisines and the gravy you make with this dish will help you to understand why that is the case. Tell the Colonel I said he does not have anything to compare with this good-to-the-last-drop recipe.

Chicken with Onions

18 chicken wings, seasoned with: ground cumin, garlic salt with parsley, salt, black pepper, and paprika
Flour and masa harina
Peanut oil
1 tsp. achiote seeds
3 onions, sliced into rings
1 cup chicken broth
1½ cups water
2 bouillon cubes
½ cup cognac
2 small tomatoes (such as plum), chopped
4 9-inch stalks coriander, chopped
¼ tsp. EACH cinnamon and nutmeg
2 serrano chili peppers, toasted in a greased skillet and finely chopped
1½ inch by 4 inch piece of poblano pepper, toasted in a greased skillet and finely chopped
1 cup cooked white beans, whipped until creamy
Salt and freshly ground black pepper

Season chicken wings with spices and coat with a little mixture of flour and masa harina. Heat oil in skillet. Add achiote and shake skillet over medium heat for a few minutes (have a cover ready as achiote will pop). Strain achiote granules out of skillet. Brown chicken on both sides in hot achiote oil. Transfer chicken to a large pot. Layer chicken generously with onion rings.

Combine chicken broth and 1 cup of water in a saucepan. Bring to a boil. Add bouillon cubes and dissolve in hot liquid. Remove from heat. Add cognac, tomatoes, coriander, cinnamon, nutmeg, serrano, and poblano pepper. Stir well to blend. Pour mixture over and around chicken in pot. Use remaining ½ cup of water to "wash" saucepan. Add "wash" liquid to pot. Bring pot to a boil. Reduce heat and simmer, covered, for 60 minutes. Remove chicken from pot (carefully, so as not to break wings) and transfer to a covered container. Stir whipped beans into simmering juices. Taste for needed salt. Add a little black pepper. Simmer for about 2 minutes, stirring frequently. Return chicken to pot, covering pieces with gravy. Return to a boil, lower heat, and simmer, covered, for 3 to 5 minutes. Serve immediately with potatoes and/or rice.

Also obtainable from the markets was bread. Breads were central to African diets. As mentioned earlier, one source of meal for bread making was the multipurpose baobab tree. Thin and crisp, spicy brown gingerbread-like cakes were made. *Kulli-kulli*, which was a preparation of oil, pepper, spices, and ground peanuts, was sold. *Karra*, or meal dumplings, and bean cakes were both cooked in hot oil. There were also oblong-shaped bean cakes called *Jenkaraga* and yam fritters, both seasoned with red peppers and steamed or fried in oil. Olmecs, too, prepared and sold breads and cakes made of beans and/or peanuts. *Charamusca* refers in modern times to a candy, but long ago the term identified a cake that was a type of gingerbread containing crushed nuts. Other bean breads and cakes were made with melon seeds and corn ground to a meal. They made tea buns and oblong "doughnuts" from pounded beans mixed with spices, which were baked or fried in hot oil.

Both Mexico and Africa have many recipes for bean cakes and breads. Different cooks offer their own, special rendition.

Butawa Bean Cake combines spices, wine, and fruit from both continents for a glorious treat. Experience this treat for breakfast under a little syrup with bacon or sausages on the side. They are also wonderful eaten plain, as a snack, washed down with cider or milk.

Butawa Bean Cake

1 cup masa harina
³/₄ tsp. salt
1¹/₂ tsp. baking powder
¹/₄ tsp. ground cinnamon
¹/₄ tsp. whole cloves, toasted and ground
¹/₂ tsp. cumin seeds, toasted and ground
¹/₂ cup great northern or white beans, beaten until creamy
1 egg
¹/₃ cup light molasses
¹/₄ cup EACH unsweetened applesauce, finely grated coconut (slightly packed), and peanut oil
³/₄ tsp. achiote seeds
¹/₄ cup cognac (or sherry)
Peanut oil

Combine first 6 ingredients, mix and set aside.

Place beans in a separate bowl. Beat in egg. Add molasses, applesauce, and coconut and mix well.

Heat ¹/₄ cup oil in skillet. Add achiote and shake skillet back and forth, covered, over medium heat for a few minutes (achiote will pop). Discard achiote granules and stir orange achiote oil into bean mixture.

Over medium heat, heat a skillet. Pour cognac (or sherry) into hot skillet and leave it there for several seconds. Pour hot cognac into bean mixture and mix well. Batter will be thick.

Immediately heat a couple of Tbs. of peanut oil in skillet. When hot, spoon batter into skillet in rounds (like pancakes). Add additional oil as needed.

Makes nine 3¹/₂-inch cakes. You can, of course, make them smaller or larger if you prefer. SERVE IMMEDIATELY. Cakes taste best the same day made.

The Olmec marketplace also provided the bounty of nearby rivers and lagoons. The Olmecs hunted animals in the woods and along the banks of the lakes and rivers. They used these waters to navigate raw materials back and forth, such as the giant basalt boulders for their sculptures and drainage canals and the rubber to make the balls for their games. Fish, however, were the prized bounty of the waterways. Various remains indicate that the Olmecs harvested the rivers and lagoons to their fullest potential. They consumed alligator, ray, shark, clams, sea and land snails, turtle, and reptiles. Turtle meat and soup dishes were eaten; but certain species of turtle abundant in some of their marshlands produced a substance that the Olmecs took as a hallucinogen. Olmecs caught small, white fish by the hundreds and dried them on rocks in the sun (the taste resembled that of sardines), as in Africa where the Niger River always provided West Africans with enormous quantities of fish that were dried or smoked to keep for long lengths of time and thus could be sold in markets well into the interior of the continent.

Another favorite was shellfish. Oysters, shrimp, and crab were boiled alone or (as African cooks did all the time) combined with garden vegetables, a potent liquor, and an assortment of peppers to create a fabulous appetizer or side dish. Sample, for example, the following delectable fare.

Crab Rice

2 Tbs. peanut oil
1 medium-small onion, chopped
¹/₄ of a large tomato or 1 large plum tomato, chopped
¹/₄ heaping tsp. black peppercorns, crushed
¹/₂ of a medium-small red bell pepper, chopped
1 small chipotle chili pepper, soaked in scalding hot water for 45

minutes, stems, seeds, and inner ribs removed and finely chopped
4 serrano chili peppers, toasted in a greased skillet and chopped
1 pasilla chili pepper, soaked in scalding hot water for 45 minutes,
stems, seeds, and inner ribs removed and finely chopped
1 Tbs. finely chopped cilantro
1 cup uncooked rice
1 cup EACH beef and chicken broth
$1/4$ cup cognac or dark rum
$1/2$ pound cooked and flaked crabmeat
Salt and black pepper, to taste

In a skillet heat peanut oil. Add onion, tomato, peppercorns, bell
pepper, chipotle, serrano, and pasilla chilies, and cilantro. Cook
and stir until onion becomes translucent. Stir in rice. Cook and stir
for 30 seconds to a minute. Stir in both broths, cognac, crabmeat,
and salt and pepper. Mix well. Transfer to a baking dish and cover.
Bake in a preheated 350 degree oven for 1 hour.

There were those Africans, considered masters of the art of fish
cookery, who took saltwater fish and stuffed it with spiced bananas,
roasted it and served it with a sauce of palm wine, fruit juices, and
rice. Fish was ground, mixed with palm oil and bread crumbs, eggs,
juices, and of course spices, and baked either inside a whole fish as
stuffing, or steamed in banana leaves as individual pâtes. Presentations included fish grilled over vine wrapped woods, imparting
delicate aromas and flavors into the flesh.

In addition to the masters of the art of fish cookery, in Africa there
were fisherfolk who were "masters of the water" and experts in catch-
ing fish. In both Africa and Mexico, fishing and most other activities
were carried out according to the seasons of the calendar year. The
Mexican calendar, with its twelve lunar mansions and five useless or
dateless festival days, stood as a striking characteristic of African-
Mexican contact. While the ancient solar year of East Africans consisted of twelve months of thirty days, they had a thirteenth month
of five days which was considered worthless and during which no
important tasks were performed. Even though these days were said
to be useless, they were still celebrated with great pomp. Different
types of porridge were eaten during this time for religious significance

and were considered a must. Certain East African societies ate pounded wheat boiled in water or barley cereal over which they poured oil, or cooked with milk, to which salt and butter were added. Eating porridge during a religious festival is a universal and ancient custom in western Sudan. The non-Islamic Bambaras, however, also consumed *dlo*, a maize beer, during their festivals.

Maize beer or chicha and porridges and soups were all common dishes served during religious festivals and ceremonies in ancient Mexico and Central America. Bread soups or porridges, particularly, were said by the ancients to be beneficial to persons suffering from numerous ills. As in Africa, many dishes in Mexico and Central America are served garnished with whole or sliced boiled eggs, sprinkled with nutmeg or cinnamon. But do not wait until you are feeling under the weather to savor the flavors of this one. Its healing powers lie in the fact that it is worthy of preparing on any of your most celebrated occasions.

〰〰〰〰〰〰〰〰〰〰〰〰〰〰〰〰〰〰〰〰〰〰〰〰〰〰〰〰

Bread Soup

1 small chipotle chili pepper (see glossary)
1 small ancho chili pepper (see glossary)
1 pasilla chili pepper (see glossary)
2 raw carrots
3 Tbs. soaking water from peppers
4 cups chicken broth
2 cups beef broth
1/2 cup tequila (such as Patron, which is 100 percent maguey), or cognac
2 raw carrots, sliced thin
1/4 tsp. ground canela or cinnamon
1/4 (rounded) tsp. whole cloves, toasted and ground
1/4 tsp. aniseed (fennel), toasted and ground
1 bay leaf
5 whole stalks coriander (9 inches long), chopped
2 Tbs. butter
1 1/2 onions, chopped
2 large plum tomatoes, chopped
Freshly ground black pepper, to taste

¼ cup butter
3 cups chopped, crusty bread
Sliced, boiled eggs (optional)
Cinnamon (optional)

Cover chipotle, ancho, and pasilla chili peppers with scalding hot water in a small bowl. Allow to soak for at least an hour (reserve soaking liquid). While chilies are soaking, cook 2 carrots in water for about 30 minutes. Drain. Remove stems from chilies. Remove seeds and inner ribs from chipotle and pasilla chilies. Combine all chilies and cooked carrots in food processor, adding 2 or 3 Tbs. of soaking liquid from chilies to help pureeing process. Cover puree and set aside.

In a pot combine chicken and beef broths, cognac, 2 sliced carrots, cinnamon, cloves, aniseed, bay leaf, and coriander. Bring to a boil, lower heat, and simmer, covered, for about 15 minutes. Remove from heat. Remove bay leaf.

In a skillet, melt 2 Tbs. butter. Add onions and tomatoes. Cook and stir until onions become translucent. Add chili-carrot puree to skillet, continuing to cook and stir frequently for a few minutes. Return broth mixture to heat. Stir chili-onion mixture into broth. Add a little freshly ground black pepper. Bring to a boil. Lower heat and simmer, covered, for about 10 minutes.

While soup is simmering melt ¼ cup butter in a clean skillet. Add bread, stirring quickly to coat pieces with butter. Continue to stir bread until butter has been absorbed and bread pieces are lightly browned and somewhat crispy.

Spoon bread into bowls. Ladle hot soup over bread. Garnish with slices of boiled egg and sprinkle with cinnamon (both optional).

The calendar, in ancient Africa and Mexico, was more like a map of celebration and ceremony. During the African New Year, as celebrated in Morocco, "the days of the old woman" are honored. It is a ceremony and belief connected with certain dates of the solar year, the weather, and especially with agriculture. At Fez, the New Year's Day and the day after are called *Haguza*, said to be represented by the appearance of an old and hideous female spirit. In the cities of Tangier, Rabat, and Fez, parents insist that their children eat as much as they can to fill their stomachs with the New Year's food, otherwise, so says the legend, Haguza will fill any empty spaces in their stomachs with straw. In some areas, Haguza is said to be unlucky for ploughing and other agricultural activities, so the people hunt and play ball instead. Likewise, the ancient Olmecs hunted and played ball on their New Year's Day; "filling one's stomach" on this occasion was certainly part of the fun.

Tasty as it is easy to prepare, filling your family's stomach with the following dish will definitely earn you a home run, goal, points, AND a touchdown. Because of the abundance and variety of fruit available in the African, Mexican, and Central American tropics, fruits were often combined with various meats to produce unique flavors such as this:

Chicken Cooked with Fruits

4 very large, whole chicken legs
½ cup EACH apple juice and orange juice
3 tsp. lime juice
1¼ inch piece cinnamon stick
½ tsp. EACH cumin seed and whole cloves
A rounded ¼ tsp. achiote seeds
Garlic salt with parsley, seasoned salt, black pepper, paprika, flour
Several Tbs. of peanut oil
½ of a ripe mango, peeled
½ of a ripe plantain, peeled
1 onion, chopped
A little salt
4 to 6 tsp. raisins (fresh—obtainable from a health food store)

Place chicken in a pan, skin side down, 1 layer deep. Combine apple, orange, and lime juices in a bowl.

Toast cinnamon, cumin, cloves, and achiote in a dry skillet for a couple of minutes. Cool. Grind to a powder. Add about 1 tsp. ground spices to juice mixture and blend well. Pour mixture over chicken in pan. Marinate chicken for 6 hours, spooning mixture over chicken frequently.

Remove chicken from juice mixture (reserve mixture) and season on both sides with garlic salt, seasoned salt, black pepper, and paprika. Coat with flour.

Heat several tablespoons of oil in a skillet. Stir ¼ tsp. of the ground spices into hot oil. Brown chicken on both sides in hot oil.

While chicken is browning, puree mango and plantain with a little of the reserved juice mixture (just enough to make a smooth puree).

Transfer chicken to a baking pan, placing the pieces one layer deep.

Drain all oil from skillet, except 1 or 2 Tbs. DO NOT REMOVE COOKED PARTICLES. Heat reserved oil and add onions. Cook and stir for a couple of minutes. Stir in half of spice mixture. Cook and stir for a minute or two. Add remaining spice mixture. Cook and stir for almost 1 minute. Add puree to skillet and cook and stir for a minute. Blend in remaining reserved juice mixture. Cook and stir for a minute or two. Taste for needed salt. Add raisins.

Pour sauce all over chicken pieces. Cover with foil and bake in a preheated 350 degree oven for 1 hour.

Holidays and celebrations created a crowded social calendar in Mexico and Central America and always included chicha (masticated and fermented mash) and pulque. These drinks were used in ceremonies connected to religious customs that were also practiced in Africa. Ancient Mexico's five intercalary days on their calendar were also considered useless, and as in Africa, the gorging of oneself with food was very crucial. It was important that people not quarrel on these days for fear of causing the entire year to be beset with dissension and hard times. They did whatever had to be done in order to bring about *nama*, or "grace, favor, prosperity, abundance." For the Mandes of West Africa it was the hope for *baraka* ("a blessing"), or that which would produce a return of fortune for the ensuing year. Good fortune was defined as an abundance of new births and an abundance of good crops.

Serve this delectable cactus cocktail to the most quarrelsome and argumentative persons you know. If you do not have to spar with them over whether or not they can have your share, you have brought about nama. Meaning, if they are through eating, they will now go home—content.

Cactus Cocktail

½ cup chopped, cooked cactus (see glossary)
8 ounces cooked lump crabmeat, shredded
1 medium red onion, chopped
3 whole stalks (about 9 inches long) coriander, chopped
4 tsp. finely chopped celery
Dressing:
¼ cup very thick coconut milk
¼ cup sour cream
5 toasted and finely chopped serrano chilies
1½ tsp. sugar
1¼ tsp. lime juice
½ tsp. Worcestershire sauce
¼ tsp. EACH dark rum and salt
Freshly ground black pepper to taste

Combine first 5 ingredients in a bowl. In a separate bowl combine dressing ingredients and blend well. Pour dressing ingredients into cactus mixture. Toss gently, making sure all of cactus mixture absorbs dressing. Refrigerate until well chilled. Stir a bit before serving. Can be served as an appetizer, as you would a shrimp cocktail, on leaves of lettuce, garnished with small tomato wedges.

Sometimes bringing about nama is an impossibility. That is why I always say, sweets for the sweet. But African yams and Mexican chicha combine in this light and fragrant dessert that will turn the head or heads (plural, if we are talking beast) of even the most grumpy mule of an individual.

Yam and Plantain Fruit Pudding

1/2 of a medium yam or sweet potato
1 large, very ripe plantain
1 cup water
1/4 tsp. ground canela or cinnamon
A generous shake of nutmeg AND ginger
1 tsp. honey
4 Tbs. ground piloncillo (see glossary), or dark brown sugar
2 Tbs. butter
1/4 cup EACH tequila (OR cognac OR white rum), apple juice, and orange juice
1 1/2 tsp. vanilla
A little salt
Sweetened, flake coconut

Peel and cut up yam and plantain into small pieces and place in a saucepan. Add about two-thirds of the water and stir in cinnamon, nutmeg, and ginger. Bring to a boil. Lower heat and simmer gently, uncovered, for 15 minutes, adding remaining water during cooking time. Potato should be tender. Remove from heat and add butter. Stir until butter melts. Add remaining ingredients, except coconut. Blend with electric mixer until fairly smooth.

Pour into a baking dish. Bake in a preheated 350 degree oven for 25 to 30 minutes. Serve in dessert dishes at room temperature or chilled, garnished generously with sweetened, flake coconut.

A baraka, or abundance of new births, was always welcomed by the Olmecs and they intended to explain the phenomenon of birth by their artistic symbolism. The jaguar, as one of their most important symbols, was considered the defender of the newborn. The child, once grown, would guarantee the continued health and life of the people throughout his or her adulthood.

"Life," or the birth of a child, was celebrated as a religious occasion and great feasting took place among the Olmecs. However, to bear or not to bear was sometimes the question. In the fields of ancient Central America there grew medicinal plants that could terminate a pregnancy or induce birth. To be sure, it was always a sign of prosperity whenever a woman became pregnant. The birth of the child was always treated with pomp; it was a thanksgiving celebration of sorts. In Africa, in ancient times, the blood of a lamb, goat, or cow was added to special foods for the occasion. Likewise, the Olmecs took the blood of a deer or jaguar and added it to a special porridge or other preparation that was passed among the guests at the celebration. Guests were also treated to a corn dumpling stew, similar to *Fotoli*, a Yoruba dish of corn dumplings and chicken soup.

This luscious, savory stew thickens nicely with masa harina and mashed yam. Take a whiff, then a spoonful. Your first taste will tell you why serving this dish is truly a "blessed event."

〰〰〰〰〰〰〰〰〰〰〰〰〰〰〰〰〰〰〰〰〰〰〰〰〰〰〰〰〰〰〰〰〰〰〰〰

Balimaya Pek Corn Dumpling Stew

The dumplings:
1½ cups masa harina
1¼ tsp. salt
½ tsp. freshly ground cumin
¾ tsp. ground cilantro
¼ tsp. cayenne powder
A little freshly ground black pepper
1 egg
¼ cup peanut oil
¾ cup water (or milk)
5 Tbs. creamed corn
Peanut or vegetable oil

Combine dry ingredients and mix well. In a separate bowl combine egg, ¼ cup peanut oil, and water. Blend well. Stir in creamed corn. Add egg mixture to dry ingredients and blend well.

Heat 1 cup or more peanut or vegetable oil in a large skillet. Spoon 12 equal portions of batter in hot oil, very slightly pressing each portion down with the back of the spoon to "round" them out a bit. Brown on both sides. Transfer dumplings to paper towel–lined aluminum foil and cover tightly.

The stew:
2¹/₄ pounds boneless, skinless chicken breast
4³/₄ cups chicken broth
2 chipotle chili peppers, soaked in scalding hot water for an hour or more
¹/₄ cup pumpkin seeds
¹/₄ (heaping) tsp. achiote seeds
1 inch piece of cinnamon stick
1 chicken bouillon cube dissolved in ¹/₂ cup boiling water
3 Tbs. peanut oil
4 stalks coriander (about 9 inches long), finely chopped
1 large tomato, chopped
1 large onion, chopped
³/₄ tsp. freshly ground cumin
Salt and freshly ground black pepper, to taste
1 small, mashed, cooked yam
6 Tbs. creamed corn
2 tsp. EACH masa harina and cold water

Simmer chicken in 3¹/₂ cups of chicken broth, covered, for about 10 minutes. Remove from heat. Remove chicken from broth and cover tightly. When cool enough to handle, chop chicken and return to pot.

Toast chilies in a dry skillet for a minute or two. Remove stems, seeds, and inner ribs from chilies. Place chilies in food processor.

Toast pumpkin seeds, achiote seeds, and cinnamon stick in dry skillet, one at a time (pumpkin seeds will pop and bloat; achiote will darken; cinnamon should darken just a bit). Cool and then transfer all three to food processor with chilies. Grind to granules, add the *cooled* bouillon water and then process to a fairly smooth liquid paste.

Heat the 3 Tbs. peanut oil and add coriander, tomato, and onion. Cook and stir for a few minutes. Add the cumin and continue cooking and stirring until onion becomes translucent. Add pumpkin seed mixture to skillet and cook and stir for a few minutes more. Transfer mixture to chicken and broth. Mix well. Stir in mashed yam and creamed corn and blend well.

Mix masa harina and water together to make a smooth paste. Stir paste into chicken stew. Bring to a boil, lower heat and simmer, covered, for approximately 20 minutes.

Ladle stew into serving dishes. Place 2 dumplings on top of each serving (I prefer placing them on the bottom, underneath the stew, but you have to be sure to tell your diners they are there). Note: These dumplings are marvelous eaten all by themselves.

☙☙

Early Eurocentric literature on West African folkways spoke incorrectly of the birth of twins as an evil omen. To the contrary, twins in the cultures of West Africa were considered sacred. There were special festival days for twins and a special mashed yam and egg dish was prepared for the occasion. A whole boiled egg had to be prepared for each twin because the sharing of the egg was considered to symbolize the splitting of the twins. In the old culture, presents to twins always had to be identical.

Special foods were served when families came together to name an infant. West Africans, in what is now Ghana, served one of these dishes—the traditional dish of mashed yam and eggs. For the ceremony, pieces of yam and eggs are boiled together in pots of iron and baked earth until both are cooked. The yams are removed and mashed. Salt and palm oil are then added to the smooth puree. The boiled eggs are then served with the yams. This dish is also served at the purification of the mother after she gives birth and during puberty ceremonies for adolescent females.

Other West African groups shaved the baby's head for the naming ceremony. The Olmecs too shaved their male children's heads as evidenced in much of their art and sculpture. When the West African baby reached one week of age, the father invited every living member of the family to his home for a feast, the purpose of which was to name the baby, an act performed by the oldest member of the family. Palm wine or *Ntunkum* (fresh palm wine, fermented palm wine); *ahai*, a grain beverage or wine; barley beer, pepper wine, and ginger wine are prepared for this occasion. One of the traditional dishes served at this special gathering is *Abenkwan* (Palmnut Soup). It is of particular importance for the mother to consume it in order to give her plenty of milk to nurse the baby. One delicious combination for Abenkwan calls for:

Ten cups of palmnuts, onions, tomatoes, meat, ginger, and other spices. The palmnuts are washed and boiled until the skin is tender. They are then pounded in a mortar until the kernels slip out. Place pounded nuts in a large bowl and add 10 cups of hot water. You have to squeeze the juice out and remove the kernels. The juice is then strained. Add the juice to the meat, which has been browned with the chopped onion. Add tomatoes and pepper. When tomatoes are tender, remove them, grind them up, and return to pot, adding ginger. Simmer gently for about 1 hour. Stir in ground onion. Serve with rice. This makes approximately six servings.

Smoked or fresh fish may be substituted for the meat in palmnut soup.

The Olmecs likewise punctuated birthdays and other significant occasions with a special food and drink menu. Part of that menu included a mild drink made out of maize dough called *atol*. The maize dough was cooked with water, salt, honey, and milk. This drink was primarily consumed by itself; however, a number of corn and bean dishes often contained a small amount of this and other potent liquors.

After digging through pages of ancient Mexican secret rites, I would like to offer a recipe that challenges the senses. Tequila, rum, or chicha can substitute for the atol. Whichever you choose, the aroma that will engulf every room in your house will put you in a trance. Be careful in consuming the tequila called for in this recipe, or you might stay in one.

Atol Ceremonial Corn and Black Bean Soup

1 cup plus 2 Tbs. uncooked black beans, picked and washed
1/2 of one epazote leaf (see glossary)
1/4 cup tequila or rum
2 to 3 chipotle chili peppers (that have been soaked in scalding water an hour, stems, seeds, and ribs removed)
1/2 tsp. whole allspice, toasted and ground
2 1/2 cups milk
1 Tbs. plus 2 tsp. sugar

Freshly ground black pepper and salt, to taste
2 to 3 tsp. rendered oil from bacon
1 onion, chopped
¼ of a small red bell pepper
1 jalapeño chili pepper, chopped, or ¼ tsp. crushed red pepper
¼ tsp. cumin
Freshly ground black pepper and salt
1 cup cooked, kernel corn
1 or 2 sprigs cilantro, finely chopped
Quail eggs (optional)
Tequila or rum
Chicharrones

Soak beans overnight in a saucepan. Drain and put in enough fresh water to cover beans. Add next four ingredients. Bring to a boil. Lower heat and simmer, covered, for about 2 hours (add water as needed). When cooled, transfer beans to food processor. Add some milk and puree until smooth. Transfer beans to a non-stick saucepan over low heat. Add remaining milk and sugar, mix well, and taste for needed salt and pepper.

Heat oil in a skillet. Add onion, bell pepper, and jalapeño. Cook and stir for a minute. Add cumin, salt, and pepper and continue cooking and stirring for a couple of minutes. Add corn and cilantro and cook and stir for a minute or two.

In a separate, well-greased skillet, break one quail egg for each serving and cook "sunny side up." (optional)

Ladle hot bean puree in a serving bowl. Place a quail egg in the center of beans. Spoon some corn mixture around center of egg. Garnish with 1 or 2 Tbs. tequila. Serve with chicharonnes.

〰〰〰〰〰〰〰〰〰〰〰〰〰〰〰〰〰〰〰〰〰〰〰〰〰〰〰〰〰〰

The cultivation and preparation of corn and other foods took on mammoth proportions in Olmec Mexico. Their considerable efforts in strengthening and increasing crop production were a major reason why the Americas are heralded as one of the four major agricultural food-producing centers in the world. The ideas and knowledge of their culinary culture were disseminated by their god-kings, who exerted influence by "colonizing through trade" and thus created linkages throughout Mexico and all of Central America. African crops were part of Olmec culinary culture. Sadly, maps concocted to show food crops and their place of origin usually list no food plants as indigenous to Africa.

An accurate historical record would naturally assign a more primary role to Africa in crop and food evolution. There may well have been many plants and animals thriving on the continent long ago that are now extinct. Plants, whether they are cultivated for food, the trapping of game, decor, ritual or celebration, or for medicinal purpose, have a cultural significance. Plants play roles in each cultural aspect of a society and even in the diffusion of that culture. For example, the stems and leaves of the cotton plant were used for something else before the "fruit" was spun into a fiber. Stems and leaves from some food plants were found to have been woven long ago into fishing nets. An increased catch by a well-strung net meant more food for the inhabitants. More food meant an increased population. An increased population meant that additional amounts of land were needed. The acquiring of more land made possible the further diffusion of the people and their culture.

That diffusion was worldwide on the part of African culture. Ever since Columbus's arrival in the so-called New World it has been contended that corn, and most other food crops, were later introduced into Africa by the Spanish and Portuguese. This is wrong. During the Golden Age of West Africa, for which records of its trading empires begin in the eighth century A.D., corn was such an everyday—yet important—part of the life of the Yoruba people at Ife that there were street pavements made of potsherds at Ife that bore maize impressions. All along the West African coast and in the immediate interior there was in some areas a dominance of soft-grained maizes, which were ground for flour. Pounded cassava roots added to ground maize was sometimes soaked in water for a full day. Natural gases formed from the fermented dough which leavened the dough in the same fashion as yeast. Pancakes, biscuits, and dumplings of various sizes were formed from the dough. Prior to cooking, they were first wrapped in banana leaves. The dough was cooked whole or thinly sliced, fried in palm or groundnut (peanut) oil or steamed in double boiler vessels.

Inhabitants of the Americas, during this same period in history, also wrapped foods before cooking in cornhusks and banana and other large-leafed plants, then steamed it in the same liquor they used to wash it down. Travelers in West Africa washed down many a delicious meal with famous beers at the marketplace. One of the beverages sold at the market and sought after by the *Diula* (merchants) was a drink called *Do*. It was aged for various lengths of time, sometimes a month, two years, some as long as ten years (I guess this one was equivalent to Chivas Regal). Appealing as an appetizer or snack, Beef Steamed in Beer Batter is quite spicy, great eating, and nicely accompanies white or red wine, tequila, beer or any of a number of other drinks from your bartender's catalogue.

§§

Beef Steamed in Beer Batter
(Mixiote de Carne de Tlaxcala)

About 22 cornhusks (they should fan out at least 9 inches
2 chipotle chilies
1 huge ancho chili, OR about 4 regular size ancho chilies
Approximately 1½ pounds ground beef
1 large onion
1 to 2 tsp. finely chopped coriander
¾ tsp. freshly ground cumin
Salt and black pepper, to taste

Soak cornhusks overnight in warm water to soften.

Soak chipotle and ancho chilies in scalding hot water for 1 hour or more.

Brown ground beef in skillet. Drain oil from skillet. Crumb ground beef.

Remove stems, inner ribs (chipotles will have inner ribs), and seeds from chilies. Place chilies, onion, and coriander in food processor. Using pulse method, process contents only until finely ground. Transfer mixture to ground beef and mix well. Stir in cumin, salt, and black pepper and, again, mix well. Cover until ready to use.

Beer Batter:
3 cups masa harina
2 tsp. salt
1¹/₂ tsp. ground coriander (commercial is okay)
1¹/₂ tsp. freshly ground cumin
A little freshly ground black pepper
2¹/₂ cups cold beer
2 Tbs. plus 2 tsp. peanut oil

Combine dry ingredients and mix well.

Combine oil and beer, stir to mix slightly, then pour into dry ingredients (batter will rise, then fall and become thick as it is stirred). Stir just until well mixed.

Rinse and dry cornhusks with paper towels. Divide batter and beef mixture among 22 cornhusks by placing approximately 2 to 3 Tbs. of batter in the center of each cornhusk, then spreading it out to about a 2 inch square. Spoon approximately 2 heaping tsp. of meat mixture on top of batter, patting it down slightly to center it longways on the batter. Fold over one side of cornhusk to cover meat and batter. Fold over the other side to enclose contents. Fold each end of cornhusk down, then under to completely close. Place husk packages in steamer basket or on rack, a couple of inches over rapidly boiling water. Cover (the ancients covered them with additional cornhusks) and steam the packages for 45 to 60 minutes, depending on how many you cook at one time (a 10¹/₄ inch diameter steamer basket can take as many as half of the packages). Be sure to add additional water as needed. Note: Steamed batter will be slightly firm.

As an everyday part of life in both Olmec Mexico and Africa, corn became associated with local folklore. Accidental verbal associations in African folklore have been misunderstood and used by Europeans to further promote the misconception that the first appearance of maize in Africa coincides with the coming of Europeans and their chains. West Africans compared white corn to the white skins of Europeans. An old saying of the Yoruba people explaining the similarities between the words for European and the words for maize stated that when the first Europeans arrived in the Gold Coast the women were grinding a grain and remarked that these men were as white as corn. The Yoruba did make quite an extensive use for *tubab-nyo (baba-nyo)* or, "maize of the white variety."

West Africans, such as the Wolof of the Senegal/Gambia region, were known to grind the corn kernels into a flour that was then added to oil and a liquid. This basic batter was baked "in the cinders." Imaginative variations on the basic batter would turn out cakes, breads, and dumplings. Soups and stews using corn as the main ingredient were plentiful. Palm wine was consumed in West Africa but in some regions both wine and beer brewed specifically from corn were the only types consumed.

Corn soups were an integral part of the main sustenance of Africans and of the early cultures of Mexico and Central America. In this recipe, whole kernel corn and corn ground to a fine powder combine with onions, tomatoes, and peppers, ingredients indispensable to African preparations, to produce a subtle yet powerful taste, enhanced by a little rum.

Hunabqu Omon Corn and Masa Soup

1³/₄ cups chicken broth
2 cups plus 1 Tbs. beef broth
¹/₂ of a leaf of epazote
¹/₄ cup masa harina
1 cup cold water
Freshly ground black pepper, to taste
4 Tbs. plus 2 tsp. butter
1 medium red onion, chopped
4 toasted serrano chili peppers, finely chopped
1 small tomato, finely chopped
1¹/₂ cups cooked corn kernels
1¹/₂ cups milk
Salt to taste
1 to 2 tsp. tequila, chicha, or white rum for each serving
1 slice of fried and crumbled bacon, to garnish each serving

Add both broths and epazote to medium size pot. Bring to a boil, lower heat, and simmer for 5 minutes.

Combine masa and 1 cup water. Blend until smooth. Stir into broths and add black pepper. Bring to a boil again, lower heat, and simmer for 10 minutes. Discard epazote.

Melt butter in a skillet. Add onions, serrano chilies, and tomatoes. Cook and stir until onions are clear. Add corn and continue cooking and stirring for a minute or two. Add onion-corn mixture to broth-masa mixture. Stir in milk. Mix well and taste for needed salt. Bring once again to boil, lower heat, and simmer for about 3 minutes.

Lace 1 to 2 tsp. of liquor over each serving. Garnish each serving with 1 slice of fried and crumbled bacon. Serve very hot.

This recipe is a versatile vegetable side dish. Vegetarians may feel it needs no accompaniment. Whether the casserole teams up with meat and potatoes or flies solo, it is the spices that make the dish so tasty.

Corn and Green Vegetable Casserole

Approximately 2½ Tbs. butter
1 medium onion, chopped
1 plum tomato, chopped
½ of a small green bell pepper, chopped
A rounded tsp. of finely chopped coriander
2 fresh mint leaves
⅛ to ¼ tsp. ground nutmeg
½ tsp. ground cumin
1 ancho chili pepper, soaked in scalding hot water for about 30 minutes, stems removed, drained, and finely chopped
1 cup corn kernels (if frozen, thaw completely and drain)
1½ cups cut up green beans (if frozen, thaw completely and drain)
1 cup cooked green lima beans
½ cup beef broth
¼ cup EACH coconut milk and regular milk
1 tsp. sugar
Salt and freshly ground black pepper, to taste

Melt butter in a skillet. Add onions, tomatoes, green pepper, coriander, mint, nutmeg, cumin, and ancho chili. Cook and stir until onion starts to become clear. Remove mint leaves. Add corn, green beans, limas, and broth. Cover and simmer for about 8 minutes. Combine both milks and sugar. Stir into vegetables. Add salt and pepper and continue cooking and stirring for another few minutes.

Corn was and still is an intercontinental favorite. Africans, Olmecs, and peoples in the Americas in general enjoyed numerous ways of preparing it, particularly in combination with beans. Spiced Corn with Beans is very easy to prepare. The dish can be frozen and later thawed and added to a pound or two of cooked ground beef, for a quick and satisfying main entree.

Spiced Corn with Beans

Soak 1 cup of white lima beans overnight.

Put enough fresh water in pot to cover beans. Add salt and black pepper to taste. Simmer, covered, over low heat. After 1 hour of cooking, add 1 cup of fresh cut or frozen (thawed and drained) corn and 1 tablespoon of finely chopped cilantro. Continue cooking for another 20 to 30 minutes, or until beans and corn are tender. Add additional water to beans as needed during cooking time.

While beans are cooking: In a skillet, cook and stir 1 chopped onion, a rounded ¼ tsp. freshly ground cinnamon, 1 finely chopped jalapeño chili pepper, and 1 medium chopped tomato in 2 Tbs. peanut oil. Cook and stir until onions start to brown.

Stir onion mixture into cooked beans and corn, bring to a boil and simmer a minute or two. Serve immediately.

The very least that one can suggest is that perhaps Africa grew species of corn different from those grown in the Americas. Whether they did or did not, if indeed corn was indigenous solely to the Americas, Africans must have sailed to the "New World" prior to Columbus and brought the corn back to Africa themselves.

Visits by Africans to the Americas left behind a number of indelible marks. The Olmecs were just the beginning. Those marks even now are visible on the diets, cultural habits, and racial identities of societies who were more secluded from Spanish invasion. Some of the oldest, most secluded groups in Mexico and Central America have African blood. The Lacandones, for example, considered to be the last descendants of the Mayans (who are descendants of the Olmecs), are one such group, and have been found in modern times to still have the presence of the sickle cell in their blood, a trait exclusive to people of African descent. It should also be noted that the origin of the term *Lacandon* is a plural Mayan form, which translates: *ah AKAN-tun-oob*. Ghana is the home of the Akan people.

Like the Herero of Africa and the Mound Builders of Native America, these Olmec descendants participated in the renewal of the flame ceremony, which was a major and complex celebration. The celebration required prolonged periods of abstinence and dietary fasts. But when eating was a part of the activities, many special foods were prepared, along with the consumption of large quantities of a drink called *balche*. In general, Lacandones were said to eat large bouquets of lavender morning glories, although flower consumption was certainly supplemented by crop production. Tobacco was grown as a commercial enterprise, planted between rows of corn. They also grew beans, squash, chili peppers, cassava, sweet potatoes, tomatoes, and an ample variety of other fruits and vegetables. Much of this was turned into preparations combined with rabbit, duck, monkey, and parrot. Very young parrots were preferred because the older ones were said to be tough.

Polly want a cracker?

Crackers would not be the appropriate accompaniment for this glorious feast. But any time is the right time to have duck (or rabbit or quail), especially when it is fabulously dressed with cassava and rum sauce.

Otabu Lacandone Duck

5 pound duck
Freshly ground allspice
Freshly ground black pepper
Garlic salt with parsley

For the sauce:
1 Tbs. butter
1 small onion, chopped
1 stalk coriander, finely chopped
½ tsp. freshly ground allspice
1¼ cups milk
1 Tbs. dark rum
3 tsp. cassava flour (see glossary)
2 Tbs. rendered duck fat
2 tsp. orange marmalade or pineapple preserves
Salt and freshly ground black pepper, to taste

Sprinkle duck all over, inside and out, with allspice, black pepper, and garlic salt.

Preheat oven to 450 degrees. Place duck, uncovered, in oven. Lower oven temperature immediately to 350 degrees. Roast 20 to 30 minutes to each pound.

For the sauce, melt butter in a skillet or saucepan. Add onion and coriander and cook and stir for a couple of minutes. Stir in allspice and continue cooking and stirring until onions are brown.

Combine milk, rum, and cassava flour and mix well. Stir in duck fat, marmalade (or pineapple preserves), salt, and pepper. Stir cassava mixture into saucepan with onions. Simmer over low heat, stirring often, for 2 to 3 minutes. Ladle sauce over servings of duck. Note: this sauce is also wonderful over mashed potatoes. If you favor more sauce, you can certainly double the recipe.

The Lacandones had much in common with the people of the West African city of Mokwa, a town north of the Niger River, in terms of the meats they ate and how they liked them prepared. Kola nuts or Guru nuts (which Arabs referred to as African coffee) were plentiful in Mokwa, as were the food dishes sold by Mokwa women. Many of these dishes contained pigeon, monkey, guinea fowl, duck, turkey, and stewed chicken. They also sold bowls of wheat porridge, mango plums, limes, pisangs, oranges, groundnut oil (peanut oil), and ghee (clarified butter). These bowls and other eating utensils, water jars, basins, and ewers were ornamented with some of the same carvings found on their architecture.

Chicken in Peanut Sauce is one version of peanut stew transplanted straight from Ghana and Nigeria. The Lacandones' use of peanuts, chilies, onions, and spices is akin to the poultry dishes of the women of Mokwa. A feast for the eyes as well as the palate, serve this chicken on a bed of mustard greens and spinach.

Chicken in Peanut Sauce

8 large serving size pieces of chicken
Seasoned salt, black pepper, paprika, flour
A few tablespoons of peanut oil, as needed
1 large onion, chopped
1 large tomato, chopped
3 tomatillos, chopped
3 or 4 serrano chili peppers, toasted and finely chopped
1 carrot, sliced thin
2 Tbs. coarsely ground peanuts
3/4 tsp. freshly ground cumin
1/2 tsp. freshly ground cinnamon
13/4 cups chicken broth
1/3 cup Chicha, Tequila, or other corn liquor
About 1/4 cup smooth peanut butter
Freshly ground black pepper and salt, to taste

Season chicken with seasoned salt, black pepper, and paprika. Coat with flour.

Heat oil in a medium-large pot. Brown chicken in hot oil on both sides. Transfer chicken to covered platter.

Add next 8 ingredients to pot (there should be at least, but no more

than, 3 or 4 Tbs. of oil in pot). DO NOT REMOVE COOKED PAR-
TICLES. Cook and stir until onion becomes clear. Stir in broth and
chicha. Add peanut butter and stir until well blended. Taste for
needed salt and pepper. Add chicken, spooning vegetables and sauce
over pieces as they are added. Bring to a boil, lower heat, and
simmer, covered, for about an hour. Taste again for needed salt and
pepper. Serve piping hot.

As the African characteristics in Olmec cuisine and civilization
diffused throughout Central America and across the Isthmus of
Panama, a sister culture, one contemporary with the Olmecs, was
playing the same pioneering role in the development of sophisticated culinary heritage and culture. With the rise of Olmec society,
long-range maritime commercial networks were established between
Mexico and Central America and Ecuador, Colombia, and Peru.
The importance of the universality of Olmec influence would be
expressed through that commercial network. As a result, the kitchens of the Chavin society of Peru would evolve into an important
culinary center for western South America.

Zancu, Sweet Potatoes, and Beer

⁄⁄ ⁄⁄ ⁄⁄ ⁄⁄

African Merchants and Peruvian Kitchens, from the Coast to the Highlands

With the rise and dominance of African-Olmec cuisine and culture, a long-range commercial network was established between the Pacific coasts of Mexico, Central America, and South America. As early as 1000 B.C., this network created a route by which aspects of Olmec maize cultivation, step pyramid architecture, stirrup spout ceramic styles, and feline worship in religious ideologies reached Peru. The coast, valleys, highlands and cloud forests of Peru had already set a dramatic stage and formed the setting for the beginning of Peruvian crop production in about 4500 B.C. By 900 B.C. this setting had evolved into a flourishing, complex agricultural society, organized by the Chavin, who are believed to have produced the original culture of Peru. It was during this period that there was a sharp increase in long-distance trade of food products and cooking methods and in the diffusion of merchandise and ideas throughout most of the country.

These new ideas, in part, centered around the diffusion, from Mexico, of the worship of the jaguar god in their religious dogma. Intertwining religion with everyday life brought about the hosting of new religious feasts, the invention of new recipes for communal events, and the creation of imaginative, special dishes for celebration and ritual, as well as for everyday meals. Most of the foods grown along the coast that were part of these wonderful new menus were introduced from other places, Africa and Mexico to name two, and included avocados, peppers, gourds, manioc, and squash, in addition to *achira, mashua, kiwicha, tarwi,* and a number of berries. These foods, some of which were forced into obscurity as a result of the Spanish conquest, were transported in massive amounts over an extensive system of roads and footpaths to highland and forest areas of Chavin territory. Foods grown at higher elevations, using terrace-field cultivation, an agricultural method practiced extensively in Africa and other parts of South America, produced an assortment of dishes from cooks skilled in preparing freeze-dried produce. As in African societies, the Chavins practiced this agricultural method and cultivated eighty to one hundred varieties of vegetables, some grown at an altitude of 12,000 feet, that would grace numerous celebratory occasions throughout Peru.

Terrace-field cultivation and irrigation was an age-old method, practiced by ancient, technologically advanced African societies that were located on the western shores of Lake Victoria in East Africa. One such society was the Chwezi. They produced iron and steel and were engaged in lucrative trade with other people throughout the continent. The primary focus of the Chwezi, however, was agriculture and crop production, which was accomplished by terrace-field cultivation. They were not alone. The Chima, Chach, Suri (note that these names have much in common with South American names), and other East African groups utilized the same agricultural methods.

The Chwezi can be compared to the Chavin society. The Chavin also share many basic religious and artistic concepts with the Olmecs. All three peoples practiced aspects of the Egyptian technique of mummification, and buried the deceased with foods such as peanuts and different fruits of African origin. Much of the art and architecture of the Chavin and Olmecs depicted, and was geared to, religious ceremony and rituals that were performed for the purpose of ensuring abundant crops. Agriculture and human fertility were focal points of most rituals. All three peoples worshipped sky, earth, and water deities, represented in images that were the gods ultimately responsible for food and sustenance. Through these religious and artistic concepts the Chavins brought maize horticulture to the level of a science and an art. Long before the Spanish invaded the Inca Empire, the Chavins came into distinct culinary and cultural prominence. Centuries of sophisticated knowledge and experience had allowed them to cultivate maize and other foods on steep hillsides, out-of-the-way canyon corners, and other places where difficult soil and altitude conditions prevailed.

Difficult soil conditions were a challenge, but not an insurmountable one. Since Andean civilization was based on intensive agriculture, the very efficient use of every natural setting was achieved by the Chavin as they domesticated plants and animals. Their domesticated plants and animals had to be adapted to a specific zone in order to sustain growth. Crops cultivated in Peru's early history included roots and tubers such as *ahipa, arracacha, maca, achira, yacon,* and *mauka;* grains such as *kaniwa, kiwicha,* and *quinoa; nunas* (popping beans), *basul,* and *tarwi* were on their list of legumes; and *capuli* cherries, *lucuma,* and the *cherimoya* are just a few of the many fruits that were prevalent in Chavin orchards. Of course, squash, beans, chili peppers, maize, yuca (or manioc), and potatoes, more familiar crops, were also abundant. The Chavin had figured out how to grow these and numerous varieties of vegetation along the coast, such as edible tubers related to the yuca and sweet potato. Two fruits cultivated in coastal areas included *zapote de perro* and *pacai,* or *pacay,* also known as "ice-cream beans," which are filled with flat seeds and white, frothy, delicious sweet pulp ready to be scooped out with your fingers. The pacai comes from the *algarrobo* tree, the wood from which figurines are carved. In addition, in the Chavin multiple environments, plants grew in rainless deserts. In certain desert regions, plants were protected by *medanos,* or large sand dunes in symmetrical, half-moon shapes. They were formed by winds and their convex side turns toward the wind force, allowing cover for vegetation.

Like Africans, the Chavin were quite creative in their use of natural settings. The Chavin's most important use of a natural setting was in the continued development of the irrigation canals. From the beginning, absolute genius went into their construction. They were truly hydraulic engineers. The irrigation canals evolved as the principal method of environmental control. For crop cultivation, the combination of the canals and terraces reduced the impact of extreme moisture and temperatures and maintained soil fertility. One hundred different vegetables, various types of fruit trees, spices, as well as cotton were consistently supported by means of the irrigation canals. They carried water mainly from November through May, representing the rainy season in the highlands.

This dish has the distinction of offering everything to East Africans, who thrived in what is now Somalia. They had a great deal in common with the Chavin, as both peoples were known as artisans, smiths, farmers, masons, road builders, and terracing and irrigation specialists. As busy as both peoples kept themselves, I believe they would have appreciated a dish that not only has two of their favorite garnishes, sweet potatoes and hard boiled eggs, but also comes complete with bread. It is truly a meat and potatoes entree that promises fond memories of a delicious lunch or dinner.

Atalpa Uchu

8½ slices wheat bread, somewhat shredded
1½ cups evaporated milk, undiluted
½ cup milk
2 to 2½ Tbs. butter
1 Tbs. peanut oil
2 medium large onions, chopped
3 nine-inch stalks of coriander, chopped fine
¾ tsp. EACH cumin seeds and coriander seeds, toasted and ground
6 cups chicken broth
1 or 2 6½-inch guajillo chili peppers (see glossary), stems and seeds removed
2¼ pounds lamb stew meat, cut into small pieces
3 medium red potatoes, scrubbed clean and chopped into small chunks, DO NOT PEEL
Freshly ground black pepper, to taste
Salt, to taste
Boiled or baked, sliced sweet potatoes
Sliced boiled eggs

Pour milk into a bowl. Add bread to milk, stirring to soak all pieces.

In a large pot, heat butter and oil and add onions and fresh coriander. Cook and stir for a few minutes. Add ground cumin and coriander. Cook and stir for a few more minutes. Add broth and remove from heat. Squeeze excess milk from bread and reserve. Shred again, and stir into pot. Add reserved milk to pot. Return to heat. Stir in guajillo chili, lamb, and potatoes. Cover and simmer on medium-low heat, stirring frequently, for 5 to 10 minutes. Taste for needed salt and pepper. Continue to simmer, covered, stirring frequently, for 45 to 50 minutes. Remove chili pepper.

Garnish servings with sliced sweet potatoes and hard boiled egg slices.

Some natural settings provided self-irrigation. Special terracing was accomplished in certain coastal areas of Peru that allowed cultivation for some crops at higher altitudes because the fog at these heights produced moisture that gave these crops enough water to prolong the life of the plants. The main vegetable that could survive these conditions was maize. At even higher altitudes, the sacred grain quinoa was grown. For the Chavin, quinoa was a major source of protein of such high quality that it could often take the place of meat in the diet. The grains were traditionally toasted or ground into flour. They were boiled, added to soups, and even fermented into beer. Mixing quinoa with corn or other vegetables produced a nutritious meal.

Maize, or corn, and squash were favorite vegetables among the Turmu and Zilmamu of East Africa. They were just as popular among Chavin. *Zambo*, an ancient and lesser-known squash, was imported into Peruvian and Ecuadorian kitchens via Mexico. Its white meat and black seeds were cooked and served as dessert in a sweet, syrupy liquid. Serve the following vegetables as the Turmu and Chavin did, with other side dishes, such as mashed or seasoned boiled potatoes. You will also see how well the dish complements veal and lamb. In addition, baked chicken and grilled steaks have been favorably served in style accompanied by this dish. Tempt your taste buds with this center stage production.

Braised Squash and Cabbage with Corn

2 Tbs. peanut oil
3 Peruvian aji or serrano chili peppers, toasted and finely chopped
3 nine-inch stalks coriander, chopped
½ of a very small green bell pepper, chopped

³/₄ pound calabash squash, peeled, seeded, and chopped into somewhat thin pieces
³/₄ pound green cabbage (the outer, darker leaves should be removed before weighing), sliced into almost "julienne" strips
Freshly ground black pepper, to taste
Salt, to taste
¹/₂ cup beef broth
2 tsp. light molasses
¹/₄ to ¹/₃ cup *hot*, cooked kernel corn
Chopped poblano chili peppers (optional)

Heat oil in a medium size pot. Add serrano peppers, coriander, bell pepper, and squash. Cook and stir for a minute or so. Add cabbage, salt, and pepper and continue to cook and stir until cabbage is limp.

Combine broth and molasses. Mix well, then stir into vegetables. Cook over medium heat, stirring frequently, for about 5 minutes. Stir in hot corn.

Garnish servings with chopped poblano chili peppers (optional).

As in highland Chavin communities, African crops had to be cultivated at higher altitudes when the cities were built on steep hills. This was the case with old civilizations in South and Southeast Africa, such as the city of Engaruka, located three hundred miles from the coast on the Kenyan-Tanzanian border, and a three thousand square mile area occupied and farmed by the Penhalonga and Niekerk of the southeastern Zimbabwe highlands. The latter territory included hillside terraces climbing to forts, houses, pits, and storage buildings built into steep cliffsides. These settlements were built on hillsides rising from the coastal plain and continuing all the way up to the central plateau in Zimbabwe. The inhabitants were master engineers whose dams changed the direction of mountain streams and brought water to their hillside terraces. The terraces and dams were built without cement; rather, they used stones and boulders sometimes weighing a ton. Their water conduits ran for several miles, and the gradients were superior to the work of modern engineers at the turn of the twentieth century.

In Peru, cement-less irrigation canals were responsible for feeding large populations as well. There were about fifty brook-size rivers that trickled down from the Andes and supplied the ancient irrigation canals. Along the perimeters of these canals, flowers bloomed and crops yielded in abundance all year. During Chavin prominence, these great irrigation canals produced food that supported dense populations in the coastal and highland areas of Peru. In the highlands, the irrigation was achieved by means of terracing, which extended the cultivable area and resisted erosion.

It was also during ancient times in Peru that *escabeche* became a method of cooking originally intended to preserve foods. West African mothers taught their daughters the same method by extracting the juices from the oil palm tree. These juices were made into vinegars, which were used to pickle different varieties of fish. Escabeche has completely assimilated into the food customs of South America. The technique used in its preparation has remained unchanged for more than two thousand years. Colombia, Chile, Ecuador, and Peru, as well as other countries in South America, now consider escabeche a typical everyday dish. There are meat, fish, and vegetable escabeches, all of which require good-quality vinegars (either red or white) as main ingredients. Hot and sweet peppers, fresh herbs and spices, dried fruits such as figs, dates, prunes, or raisins, all combine to give escabeche its myriad stimulating, sweet and sour flavors. In Peru and other areas of South America, the meats and other ingredients are cooked together and the escabeche is served cold and pickled. Another method is to cook the meats separate from the vegetables and sauce and serve it warm or at room temperature.

One vegetable escabeche is made with okra. Okra is a vegetable well known to and prepared in numerous ways by Ghanaians, Nigerians, and other West Africans. Egyptians sometimes prepare it with lamb. African Americans braise, fry, and stew okra regularly as a culinary tradition. Okra Escabeche is a lovely side dish destined to hamper the departure of your dinner guests.

Okra Escabeche

1 pound okra, stems trimmed, pods uncut
4 tsp. peanut oil

1 small onion, chopped
½ cup sliced carrots (sliced almost paper thin)
4 Peruvian aji or serrano chili peppers, toasted and chopped
1 tsp. finely chopped ginger root
Salt and freshly ground black pepper
2 Tbs. vinegar
1 cup white wine

Blanch okra in salted, boiling water for 4 minutes. Drain.

Heat oil in skillet. Add onions, carrot, chilies, ginger root, salt, and black pepper. Cook and stir for a few minutes. Add okra and cook, stirring, for a few minutes more. Stir in vinegar and wine. Bring to a boil. Simmer, uncovered, on medium-low heat, for 4–6 minutes. Stir, cover, and simmer for 3 minutes more. Cool to room temperature and serve.

One of the groups in aboriginal Colombia who prepared very early versions of escabeche were known as the Chibcha or Muisca nation, and had the most advanced culture in the region. They too considered themselves "people of the jaguar" and believed the jaguar to be their tribal ancestor. The Chibcha practiced terraced agriculture with irrigation similar to that of Africans, in particular, the Bachwa of the Congo and the Bachwezi of Bigo, in western Uganda. The principal foods grown by the Chibcha were maize and potatoes, cubio tubers, quinoa, sweet manioc, arracacha, varieties of beans, squash, tomatoes, sweet potatoes, various vegetables, fruits, tobacco, coca, and cotton. Both men and women shared the agricultural duties. They also engaged in fishing and hunting. Their crafts included work in gold and copper and they were extensively involved in foreign trade.

Close to their own terrain the Chibcha were involved in trade with the Chavin who, as early as 3000 B.C., were already gardening the coastal site called Huaca Prieta in the Chicama Valley in Peru. These Peruvians cultivated cotton for weaving clothing and fishnets, as well as gourds and calabash (in which they also stored water), beans, chili peppers, yuca, potatoes, squash, and other edibles. Ancient Peruvians perfected crop cultivation. As among the Chwezi in East Africa, the Azanians of Somalia, and the Penhalonga and Niekerk of the southeastern Zimbabwe highlands, terraced-field cultivation, along with irrigation, was in practice and essential to a bountiful harvest of a multiplicity of crops.

These ancients originally timed their planting season by the blooming of a certain variety of cactus. Coastal inhabitants planted crops using bird guano, fish heads, and on occasion, llama dung, as fertilizer. Llama dung was primarily used in highland regions. The guano, a very potent fertilizer, accumulated in glacier-like blocks, 160 feet tall in some areas, on islets off the coast. They were reachable only by boats. The soil of the valleys was richly refertilized, like the Nile Valley, by silt overlay brought down by rivers. Two to three annual harvests of maize was normal, for the mild and temperate weather allowed constant growing seasons. It was certainly possible to experiment and develop cultivated plants from any wild varieties under these conditions.

It was also possible to develop myriad varieties of vegetable main and side dish recipes as a result of these experiments. Allow this excellent dish to become the main attraction at dinner tonight. Plan your dinner well in advance to give yourself enough time to practice taking your bows.

〰〰〰〰〰〰〰〰〰〰〰〰〰〰〰〰〰〰〰〰〰〰〰〰〰〰〰〰〰〰〰〰〰〰〰

Garden Patties with Onion and Cassava Cream Gravy

1 cup cooked Great Northern beans
³/₄ cup cooked calabash squash
2 thin cooked carrots, about 7¹/₂ inches long before cooking
2 whole stalks coriander (about 9 inches long), broken up
1 Tbs. raisins (fresh, from a health food store)
2 serrano chili peppers, toasted
¹/₂ tsp. sugar
2 Tbs. ground walnuts or peanuts
2 slices wheat bread, shredded
¹/₂ tsp. coriander seed, toasted and ground
¹/₄ tsp. EACH cumin seed and fennel (aniseed), both toasted and ground
Salt and freshly ground black pepper, to taste
3 to 4 Tbs. butter

Puree the first six ingredients together in food processor until smooth. Transfer mixture to a bowl. Stir in sugar, nuts, bread, coriander, cumin, fennel, salt, and black pepper.

Melt 2 Tbs. of butter in skillet. Place heaping tablespoons of mixture in hot butter, very slightly patting mixture to flatten a bit. Fry in hot butter until brown on the bottoms. Very carefully, and using a spatula, turn patties over (they will be very soft). Fry until brown on bottoms. Carefully transfer patties to a large plate or platter.

Repeat process with remaining butter and mixture. Keep patties covered while preparing gravy. Makes 8 patties.

For the gravy:
1 Tbs. butter
1 medium small onion, chopped
½ of a 9-inch stalk coriander, finely chopped
1 cup plus 1 Tbs. milk or light cream
1 Tbs. sherry
1 Tbs. cassava flour (see glossary)
A little salt, to taste

Using the same skillet (DO NOT REMOVE CRUMBS), melt butter. Add onion and coriander. Cook and stir until onions are brown. Mix together milk, sherry, and cassava flour in a small bowl. Add milk mixture to onions in skillet. Stir in salt. Cook and stir over low heat for about 2 minutes. Serve patties, doused with gravy, immediately.

Preparing the fields for planting was labor often turned into festival, complete with abundant food, instrumental music, and singing. Ground breaking began in the middle of the dry season, sometime in August, during the planting of the first corn. Great religious festivals were held in special fields, ceremonial-agricultural complexes such as Chavin de Huantar, the Chavin's main place of pilgrimage, just preceding this first ground breaking. Their ceremonies were similar to those of the Ngombe of the Congo, who sang religious songs during their planting festivals to acknowledge their dependence on God, and during their harvest celebrations in order to attribute successful productivity to Him. Historians and orators were a crucial part of ground breaking and other important festivals throughout the year (about one a month), which included theatrical productions in both comedy and drama. These productions depicted current cultural and social, but also historical, aspects of the peoples' lives. In both African and Peruvian societies, history was passed down to succeeding generations by its societies' orators and historians, who were specifically chosen for these lofty positions. There were also recitals by poets and storytellers, narrating myths and legends. Both meat and vegetable soups and chicha played a significant role in Peruvian myths.

While the story telling and theatrical productions ensued, popcorn *(quersu)* was one of the snacks eaten and enjoyed. A special flat ceramic with a narrow circular opening was invented in which to pop the corn. *Chicharron*, skin or rind of the guinea pig, fried in oil, was another Peruvian snack very popular in Mexico, Central America, and the West Indies. Better known in modern times as pork cracklings, African Americans are quite fond of them as well. A more substantial snack, the *tamal*, was similar to the Mexican tamale. Ground maize, mixed with oil, peanuts, peppers, and slices of cooked guinea pig were wrapped in a plantain, banana, or maize leaf and steamed, simmered in hot water, or sometimes grilled.

Chavin snacks included candies that were made from fruits, such as limes, and vegetables, such as sweet potatoes. The vegetables were usually ground to a paste and then colored and artificially flavored. Candied green walnuts, a favorite, were considered a delicacy. One version of *Kulikuli*, Nigerian peanut brittle, calls for one whole pint of sorghum (molasses) mixed with just a few cups of peanuts. For variety, the sorghum and peanuts were also combined with grated coconut or chopped fruit. The following candied nuts are somewhat less sweet than Kulikuli but are nonetheless a tasty treat for dessert or snack time.

Caramel Peanuts

2 Tbs. butter
6 tsp. water
½ tsp. cinnamon
1 cup ground piloncillo or light brown sugar
3 tsp. mild molasses
2 sprinkles of salt

1 cup finely grated coconut

2 cups chopped peanuts or walnuts

Line 12 cupcake "wells" with paper baking cups.

Melt butter in saucepan. Add water, then cinnamon and sugar. Over medium heat, stir until sugar has melted. Add molasses and salt. Cook and stir as mixture comes to a full bubbling boil. Stir constantly and vigorously for 4 minutes. Remove from heat and IMMEDIATELY stir in coconut and nuts and mix well. IMMEDIATELY divide mixture among the 12 baking cups (mixture hardens quickly).

Like the sun-worshipping societies in Africa, Peruvians held principal feasts and banquets to worship the sun and its relation to crop growth. The Galla society of Ethiopia understood the sun's importance. The Galla tell the story that God came to earth only once, one purpose of which was to oversee an adequate harvest for all of the people. The story continues that God expects the people to continue what has to be done to ensure abundance and now only looks at earth through the sun, which they believe to be His eye. Similarly, since the Peruvians believed that Higher Powers were constantly watching, since there was no question as to the importance of hard work, feasts were also held to offer gratitude for the standard of living Peruvian societies enjoyed. As far as their standard of living was concerned, no one was allowed to go hungry or unclothed. The land and food were equally distributed, just as in African societies. The Chavins and the Chimu (a later society, which dominated northern Peru from approximately 1000 A.D. until the Incas took control) had sense enough to know that if even *one* person was starving then it meant that the whole nation was poor, because that nation was not feeding all of its people.

No one could go hungry when the women from many nearby provinces came together for the feast of *Raymi*, or *Intip-Raymi*. It was a summer celebration for the sun, which, arriving at the farthest point of meridional career, returns on course to the north. In short, Peruvians engaged in astronomy, particularly, if not exclusively, for agricultural purposes. The women came together to prepare *zancu*, which was a bread made of boiled corn. Zancu was made of a type of corn grown for and eaten only at solemn feasts.

Another bread, also prepared with boiled corn, was made with the addition of berries and/or other fruits.

My mother, like many African Americans, would take a big slab of corn bread, put it in a bowl and pour buttermilk all over it. I hated seeing her mess up a well-made piece of corn bread like that. I prefer my breads dry. I prefer my cakes dry; that is to say, the ice cream must be placed in a separate dish. Anyway, some Peruvians prefer zancu swimming in a lake of milk; however, the camp is divided between buttermilk and sweetened, condensed milk. Try it all three ways, if you like.

〰〰

Zancu

2 cups milk
²/₃ cup corn kernels (if using frozen, thaw and drain)
1½ cups masa harina
1 tsp. salt
3 Tbs. peanut oil
1 small onion, chopped
½ tsp. allspice berries, toasted and ground
¼ cup packed light brown sugar or ground piloncillo
2 eggs
Butter
2½ to 3 tsp. ground peanuts or walnuts
Milk, or coconut milk, or buttermilk, or cream (optional)

In a saucepan combine corn and milk. Simmer over medium heat for 3–4 minutes. Set aside to cool slightly (skim off film that forms on the top after it cools).

Combine masa harina and salt and mix well.

Heat oil and add onions. Cook and stir for a couple of minutes. Add allspice and continue cooking and stirring until onions are browned. Remove from heat.

Puree corn and milk in food processor. Transfer puree to large bowl. Add sugar and mix well. Beat in eggs, then oil-onion mixture. Gradually stir masa harina mixture into corn-milk mixture. Blend well. Butter a 9-inch square or round baking pan. Sprinkle 2 tsp. ground peanuts on bottom of pan. Pour batter into pan. Bake in preheated, 350 degree oven for 25 minutes. Serve plain with stews and soups, or meat dishes, or drenched in milk.

The Chavin held celebrations such as the *Chuñu* (or *Chuño*) feast. In the highlands, harvested potatoes were preserved by spreading them out and leaving them overnight, exposed in the freezing air. The next day men, women, and children would thaw them by exposing them to the sun, and then walk over the partly withered tubers, squeezing out the water released by the freezing. The same process was repeated for several nights until the potatoes were completely dehydrated and were ready to be stored. This is called *chuñu*. The resulting product, made mostly from potatoes, was long-term insurance against crop failure. Thousands of rock-walled storage centers were constructed in the central highlands that were filled with chuñu and dried and salted meat called *charqui*. Chuñu feasts were occasions to showcase charqui, or jerked meat, chicha, soups, and cakes made from maize meal and the whole seed of the quinoa, as well as breads and cakes made from carob beans. A soup made of *oca* always appeared on the menu and was considered to be one of the staple meals. In addition, *chupe*, often prepared in the form of chowder, and meats, including ducks, were served. Stews, combining two or more kinds of potatoes, were prevalent. I have added oxtails to this one. Oxtails are a "seasoning" ingredient that some African cooks prefer to use to accompany dishes that include okra and tomatoes. A list of meats prepared in Chavin kitchens would include, but not be restricted to vicuña, llama, pigeon, deer, dog, rabbit, viscacha, hognosed skunk, tinamou, and guinea pig. The flesh and eggs of the iguana were also eaten. If you prefer, you may substitute another meat for the oxtails (as long as it's not iguana, or skunk, for that matter). No matter what meat you decide to add, the end result will be a wholesome, healthy, and soul satisfying repast.

Huacachupa Huchu (Peruvian Oxtail Stew)

5 cups of beef broth
1 bay leaf
1 very large onion, chopped

½ of a very large green pepper, chopped
2 oxtails, weighing a little over a pound
1 large ancho chili, soaked in scalding hot water 1 hour, stems and seeds removed, and chopped fine
2 small chipotle chilies, soaked in scalding hot water 1 hour, stems, seeds, and inner ribs removed, and chopped fine
1 medium sweet potato or yam, cooked and mashed
2 Tbs. chopped cilantro
1 inch piece cinnamon stick, toasted and ground
¾ tsp. cumin seeds, toasted and ground
½ tsp. coriander seeds, toasted and ground
1 cup crushed tomatoes
¾ cup chopped spinach or collard greens
¾ tsp. dried shrimp
2 Tbs. smooth peanut butter
1 Tbs. ground peanuts or walnuts
Approximately 2 Tbs. light brown sugar
3½ cups beef broth
Salt and freshly ground black pepper, to taste
1 cup kernel corn
14 whole okra, each cut into 3 pieces
1 large white potato cut into tiny cubes

Combine 5 cups of broth, bay leaf, onions, green pepper, and oxtails in a pot. Bring to a boil. Lower heat and simmer, covered, on medium-low heat for 2 hours. Stir in next 16 ingredients. Continue simmering, covered, for 40 minutes. Add remaining 3 ingredients and simmer, covered, stirring occasionally, for another 35 minutes. Remove oxtails and, using a fork (or with your hands when cool enough to handle), break meat away from bones and stir back into stew. Taste again for needed salt and black pepper.

The Ewe of Togo and Dahomey held ceremonies and festivals in the morning to initiate or ordain the community's new religious leader. His duties were primarily religious, but because religion and other aspects of life were inseparable, he would naturally be called upon to lend spiritual sustenance at all other ceremonies and feasts, particularly those dealing with food production. Peruvian festival banquets were, likewise, usually held in the morning because the principal meal of the day was breakfast. *Chupe* was a favorite breakfast dish. For its preparation, and there were two or three varieties depending on the reason for the festival, a wide assortment of rather "exotic" ingredients were needed: deer meat, sweet potatoes, (guinea pig) salt pork, (guinea) pigs' feet, bananas, peas or beans, maize, salt, and hot peppers. Hot peppers were always one of the essential, predominant ingredients in all of the cooking. One recipe requires that the ingredients are covered with water in a pot and simmered for five hours. It is then served as a stew. Other dishes served included *puchero* and *picantes*, which were made in great varieties. Preparation of and ingredients used in picantes, served year round at feasts and festivals, varied from the coast to the highlands, depending on the staples grown and traded. But it is a dish dependent on sauces, and those sauces were always hot and spicy. Hot and spicy was the same requirement prevalent in most African sauces. One picante, *carapulca*, was made with meat (deer, vicuña, llama) and potatoes, either white or sweet or both, pounded into meal. *Lagua* was composed of maize meal and guinea pig. *Adoba* included chunks of the pig alone in a very thick sauce. *Picanterias*, small shops or stalls that sell the different varieties, are still found today in parts of Peru.

The venison entree that follows is served with a tart blackberry sauce that you may wish to sweeten to your liking. No matter how tart or sweet you decide to make the sauce, you will bask in the glory of having served it over a tender and flavorfully prepared cut of meat.

Venison Steaks with Mora Sauce

4 venison steaks, cut from the round

Marinade:
¼ cup EACH peanut oil and vinegar
⅓ cup cream sherry
1½ tsp. salt
½ tsp. marjoram leaves
½ tsp. ground cloves

Paprika
Flour
A few Tbs. peanut oil

Place steaks in a glass dish. Combine marinade ingredients and blend well. Pour mixture over steaks and allow to soak for 6 hours in the refrigerator.

Generously sprinkle both sides of steaks with paprika and coat well with flour.

Heat oil in skillet. Brown steaks on both sides. Transfer to greased baking pan.

Cover and bake in preheated 350 degree oven for about 2 hours.

For the Sauce:
3 to 4 tsp. arrowroot
2¹/₂ Tbs. water
About ¹/₄ of a 14 ounce package of Mora (Andean blackberry) pulp, defrosted
²/₃ cup water
1 tsp. EACH lemon and lime juice
2 to 3 tsp. sugar, or to taste
¹/₈ tsp. EACH cayenne and allspice
About ¹/₈ tsp., or to taste, EACH salt and black pepper
1 Tbs. butter
1 Tbs. plus 2 tsp. rum or sherry

Combine arrowroot and 2¹/₂ Tbs. water. Mix well and set aside. Combine next 9 ingredients in a saucepan. Bring to a boil. Stir arrowroot mixture into mora mixture. Cook and stir until thickened. Remove from heat and stir in sherry and butter. Continue stirring until butter melts. Taste for needed salt and pepper.

Serve sauce over steaks with wild rice and whole, stewed tomatoes.

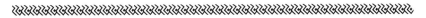

Festival banquets would not be complete without fish dishes. Fish was served fresh from coastal waters, but it was also salted and dried before further preparation. For highland communities in Peru, drying and salting fish was necessary pre-preparation to "keep" the fish as it made its way along the trade network. In West Africa, shrimp, cod, pike, flounder, gilthead, sole, lobster, crab, prawn, sprat, carp, eel, mackerel, alligator, and other varieties could be obtained from the oceans, rivers, and lagoons in great abundance. Africans, too, dried and salted fish and some of their favorite methods of preparation were serving it raw, smoking, frying, boiling, pickling, and what we would call gumboing.

Fish was sometimes obtained in Peru by using the cormorant bird. These birds were trained to dive into shallow waters to capture fish. There were also sun-dried mollusks and other shellfish that were stored as surplus and sold along the trade network. From seaweed the Peruvians obtained iodine, an important element in their diet. Seaweed was so essential to their diets that a bridge was constructed to connect with the *cunti-suyu* (linguistically, an African word) road leading to the coast. The bridge was called *chaquill-chaca* (seaweed bridge).

Dried shrimp was one of the types of shellfish frequently used in sauces in Peru. Sometimes rice or potatoes were layered in a baking dish with a sauce containing dried shrimp. West African societies, too, use a great deal of dried shrimp in stews and sauces and combine fish with coconut milk and other ingredients. Other Peruvian presentations included shrimp and other shellfish cooked with vegetables and milk, obvious forerunners to chowders made in Europe and America. The delectable and palate-challenging combination that follows creates a sauce fundamental to garnishing a variety of fish, meats, and vegetables. It can also be stirred into stews and thus used as a zesty seasoning.

Shrimp Sauce Over Fish and Sweet Potatoes

Two 1¹/₃ pound whole sea bass, scaled and cleaned, but heads and tails left on
2 cups beer
2 Tbs. peanut oil
5 or 6 tsp. chopped cilantro
1 medium onion, chopped
2 ancho chilies, soaked in scalding hot water 1 hour, stems and seeds removed, and finely chopped
2 serrano chilies

¼ tsp. EACH freshly ground ginger, nutmeg, cinnamon, and cumin
½ tsp. dried shrimp
4 Tbs. beer
1 cup plus 4 Tbs. milk
4 tsp. light molasses
Salt and freshly ground black pepper
Peeled, sliced, and cooked sweet potatoes and hard boiled egg slices, for garnish

Soak fish in beer for 30 minutes, turning once. Bake, covered with foil, in preheated, 375 degree oven for 35–38 minutes.

Heat oil in skillet. Add cilantro, onion, ancho and serrano chilies. Cook and stir a minute. Add ginger, nutmeg, cinnamon, and cumin. Cook and stir constantly another few minutes (mixture may stick a bit), scraping bottom of skillet as you cook and stir. Stir in shrimp, 4 Tbs. beer, ½ cup of the milk. Simmer on low heat until mixture thickens. Continue to cook and stir for 5–6 minutes. Add another ½ cup milk and continue to simmer on low for another 8–9 minutes, stirring frequently. Add remaining milk, molasses, and salt and pepper to taste. Spoon over servings of fish and sweet potato garnish. Garnish with hard boiled egg slices (optional).

Scoicha is made of fish or crab, potatoes, and bread dough soaked in the juice of the bitter orange, heavily spiced with pepper and salt. This sounds like a fish and dumpling stew. The Ashanti of the Ivory Coast and Ghana have very similar versions. One of their stews consists of shrimp, okra, onions, bush greens (about four different types of spinach), dried malagueta pepper, and salt simmered with corn meal dumplings. Other fish used in Peruvian scoicha and other fish dishes included mussels, clams, sea urchins, and starfish. The mussels used were the deep water variety. Land snails were steamed and eaten from very early times; in fact, modern Peruvians still steam snails for eating. Other sea creatures eaten included seal, dolphin, silverfish, sea shadow, flounder, ray, eel, sea perch, swordfish, tuna, sea lion, shark, and some varieties referred to as anchovies. One interesting method of "cooking" fish was done by marinating it in lemon and/or lime juices. Fish *ceviche*, as this dish is called, is one of Peru's national dishes and was always on the menu for celebrations and festivals.

I first had what was supposed to be a version of fish ceviche quite by accident during one of my trips to New York several years ago. I ordered a number of items on the menu, including a cebiche entree, as a take-out order at a certain "authentic cuisine" restaurant, which shall remain nameless. Now, I adore spicy food, which is why I went there in the first place. I noticed when I opened the packages that everything looked dry and colorless. To my enormous disappointment, upon sampling each dish, I found everything virtually tasteless, devoid of any type of spice or condiment, including salt. I was already back at the hotel, so I called the manager of the restaurant and asked what had happened. He responded in essence that since I had required an English-speaking waiter to place my order in English, it was obvious that I would not be partial to their more authentic fare. Well, I found out a little later that what I got was as authentic as this restaurant could make it. My second and last trip to this eatery was to return the chef's cooked-strictly-for-gringos goods. The authentic version of ceviche that I offer here is, I assure you, not without spice and condiment. This dish is a palate-waking experience. Feel comfortable in placing it on your lunch or dinner menu.

§§

Cebiche de Pescado (Fish Ceviche)

$^1/_2$ pound boned tuna, cut into thin cubes
$^1/_2$ pound flounder, sole, or cod, cut into thin cubes
$^1/_2$ cup EACH lemon and lime juice
$1^1/_4$ tsp. crushed cinnamon stick
4 serrano or 2 jalapeño chilies, seeds removed and finely chopped
$2^1/_2$ tsp. coarse salt
$^1/_2$ tsp. white pepper (or black pepper)
$^1/_2$ EACH of a small red and white onion, sliced into rings
$1^1/_2$ Tbs. finely chopped cilantro
2 Tbs. chicha, or white wine, or rum
$^1/_2$ EACH of a small green and red bell pepper, chopped
1 EACH sliced, cooked yam or sweet potato, and white potato
Lettuce

Place fish in a glass bowl.

Combine juices, cinnamon, chilies, salt, white (or black) pepper, and onions and mix well. Pour mixture over fish and stir gently. Refrigerate, covered, for 2 hours. Add cilantro, chicha, and bell peppers to fish. Mix gently. Refrigerate for another 4 hours or overnight, stirring mixture now and then.

Place a leaf of lettuce on each serving dish. Spoon a serving of cebiche on each leaf. Garnish with 1 slice each of yam and white potato.

﷯

Festival and banquet recipes may have varied regionally in West Africa and western South America, but feasts always turned out treats showcasing the tremendous variety of fruits that were cultivated in these areas. Africans ate an abundance of fig bananas. They were so sweet that when they were prepared in desserts, no sugar was needed. They also turned custard and cormantyn apples into fruit sauces, soups, and puddings by boiling them with palm wine, sugar, and cinnamon. The goldenberry, known to the Chavin as *uchuba, cuchuva,* and *topotopo,* and as *jamu* and *habwa* to the people of Malawi and the Sudan, respectively, was eaten by both Peruvians and Africans as a fresh dessert. It was also mashed, sweetened, and combined with guava or peaches and presented in the form of jams or preserves. Goldenberries were also used to lend intriguing flavors to sauces and glazes for meats, seafood, and vegetables. In Peru, cucumbers, guavas, cassia, avocados, *caimitos*, pineapple, soursop, *pepino* (it is not that sweet, but served mainly as a fresh dessert), and lucumas (the pulp of which tastes and smells like maple syrup), to name just a few, were turned into fruit salads, stews with fruits, fruit soups, tasty drinks, and desserts.

While goldenberries were also forced into obscurity due to "botanical colonialism" (as a result of the Spanish conquest), other fruits remained the object of elegant, yet simple, desserts. One such treat is Dazed Pears, a pleasingly rich, multipurpose offering. It serves well alone as a dessert or as a garnish for ice cream, cold or hot fruit soups, or as dressing for fruit salads.

Dazed Pears

6 tsp. dark rum or sherry
3 ripe pears, peeled, core removed, and quartered lengthwise
2 Tbs. water
½ tsp. freshly ground cinnamon
3 Tbs. ground piloncillo or light brown sugar
1 Tbs. light molasses
1 tsp. dark rum or sherry

Combine 6 tsp. rum or sherry and pears. Allow pears to soak, turning them frequently, for at least 2 hours.

Pour water into skillet. Stir in cinnamon, sugar, molasses, and rum. Bring to a boil, then add pears. Lower heat and simmer, uncovered, on medium-low heat for 8–10 minutes. Baste fruit frequently with syrup. Serve warm or cold.

Honoring the dead was another important reason for the Chavin to hold ceremonial feasts. Feasting, however, was not relegated to the souls of the living. Since the living believed it to be important to provide the dead with all of the comforts for the afterlife, graves yield valuable information. Among the foods found in the mummified remains in the graves at Ancon were African plants, such as sweet potatoes, yams, and manioc. Other plants shared between African and Peruvian societies included bananas and peanuts; these were also found in the Ancon graves. According to some opinions, many of these graves are no older than the sixteenth century. But one cannot judge the age of the graves by the presence of these foods. Nor can one judge the length of time these foods have been present on the continent by their appearance in these graves. Both Africans and Peruvians disinterred bodies, or mummy packs, regularly. The disinterred remains would then be dressed in new clothing or mummy wrappings. In addition, old food would be removed and fresh foods would be substituted. The bodies would then be reinterred according to ancient rites and burial customs. Ancient graves would sometimes house the remains of family members who had died at different times or even in different eras. Foods found in relatively recent tombs may have a relatively old appearance or origin in that area. But there is something else to consider. In determining the origin of a plant, it should be recognized that as different groups of people moved into different regions, for whatever reason and from whatever location, they brought with them different foods and plants. If the new environment was like the old, they could produce the same plant. New species also developed when old seeds mixed with new ones in the new soil, giving rise to hybrids.

The similarity of both the soil and climate of Africa and tropical America made it easy for crops from one continent to become domesticated and flourish on the other. Agricultural interaction and exchange between Africa and the Americas meant that varieties of the same plant could be "submerged" or change over time on both shores. If two regions have been growing varieties of the same plant and that plant changes or dies out only in one region, what you have in the other region is a secondary center of origin, or, center of survival. In Edgar Anderson's *Plants, Man and Life*, there is a discussion of the possibility that the ancient agricultural centers (such as the Americas), where it has been assumed agriculture was first developed and crops originally domesticated, were in fact "out-of-the-way corners in which the persistence of ancient agricultural methods has allowed ancient crop diversities to survive."

Cultural and agricultural interaction was one reason why the trade networks were large scale and successful. The trade networks and commercial routes ultimately connected the areas in Peru where Africans had already settled or where African influence had left its distinct mark. Some of the oldest routes between the coast and the sierras were located in northern Peru. One ancient route to the north joined coastal Tumbes to what is now Ecuador. A second very important trade route was the Serran-Huanca bamba-Jaen. It followed the upper Rio Piura and climbed the Andes by means of a stone-laid stairway road. It was thirty-seven miles in length and could be walked in three days time while loaded down with goods.

A list of these goods includes, but was not relegated to, gourds, cotton, sweet potatoes, possibly plantains, peanuts, and coconut. The sweet potato grows in the coastal areas of Peru, where the climate is ideal for the plant. Since traders from Africa would have first landed on the coasts, importation of these crops from Africa was most likely.

The Chavin had no problem adapting peanuts, alligator pears, warty squash, and manioc to every aspect of their cuisine. Peanuts have certainly proven to be a most versatile staple in both African and Peruvian culinary traditions. Nuts were used in Africa to flavor main courses, salads, soups, and desserts such as rice pudding. One recipe required that the nuts, broken into pieces, be soaked in water, then squeezed through a cloth. The liquid was then boiled with rice, sugar, cinnamon, and oil. In serving the following dessert to kids and adults alike, you really cannot go wrong. Because of the cereal (cassava and farina) and milk content, Africans and Peruvians enjoyed the pudding even for breakfast. It is a great dish for any time of day.

Peanut Pudding

2 tsp. farina
1 Tbs. plus 1 tsp. cassava flour
¼ cup plus 2 Tbs. light brown sugar or ground piloncillo
2 cups milk
¼ cup smooth peanut butter
¼ cup finely chopped peanuts or walnuts
½ tsp. EACH brandy, coconut, and vanilla extracts
Sweetened, finely grated, or sweetened flake coconut for garnish

Combine and mix together farina, cassava flour, and sugar. Pour milk in a medium saucepan. Gradually add farina mixture to milk, a little at a time, stirring constantly. Add peanut butter. Over medium heat, cook and stir constantly until mixture comes to a full boil. Continue cooking and stirring constantly for about 3 minutes. Quickly stir in nuts. Continue cooking and stirring constantly for another minute or so. Remove from heat and stir in extracts. Transfer to a serving dish and cool completely. Refrigerate. Serve cold. Garnish each serving with coconut.

Hot and sweet complement one another in this side dish. It can be presented as a most pleasing appetizer or as part of a baked chicken or sliced ham feast, ready to be savored over and over again.

Ocopa Arequipena
(Sweet Potatoes with Peanut and Chili Sauce)

2 Tbs. butter, melted
½ tsp. whole cloves, finely crushed
½ cup crushed pineapple
1 tsp. salt
4 whole stalks coriander, finely chopped
3 tsp. ground peanuts or walnuts
2 whole green onions, chopped
Freshly ground black pepper, to taste
2–4 Peruvian aji or serrano chili peppers, finely chopped
2 Tbs. dark rum or sherry
½ cup light cream
1½ tsp. *fresh* black raisins (try health food stores)
3–4 small sweet potatoes, peeled and sliced into rounds
Lettuce and sliced, boiled eggs

Combine first 12 ingredients in a bowl and mix well. Add sweet potatoes, folding and turning until they are well coated with mixture. Transfer to a baking dish. Cover with foil and bake in a preheated 350 degree oven for about 68 minutes. Serve as a side dish hot from the oven, or, as an appetizer, spoon servings of potatoes on lettuce leaves, garnished with slices of boiled egg.

Right behind peanuts and sweet potatoes in abundance were the three species of *oca*, two of *ullucu*, and one of white potato. These foods were traded extensively in the Peruvian highlands. They were also present in the pre-ceramic age in the Ancon-Chillon region. This presence underscores how well developed the trade networks were because these foods could not be grown on the coast.

Other commodities traded included different types of shells used for ornaments, turquoise, lapis lazuli for jewelry and various art objects, gold dust, and the *pototo*, the trumpet shell which the Yunca society obtained through barter with the people of Manta and Tumaco. It should be noted here that shells played an extremely important role in the Americas and Africa, beside that of ornamentation. In Africa, the blue cowrie shell served as money for centuries; the value of the cowrie was placed on its accessibility. Cultures from Peru exchanged agricultural products for blue and white shell money off the coast of Nicaragua and Darien, Colombia. These same, exact shells were found near the shores of Lower California and Central America and in graves at Trujillo and Ancon.

Another item of exchange was the coca plant (cocaine). It was grown in valleys on the eastern slope of the Andes. Chewing coca leaves while sucking on a lime was a common pastime between planting and harvesting. The cacao bean (chocolate) was also bartered. This was one of the items that connected Mexico with the trade network. Along with tobacco, many different species of beans, peas, and flavors of wine, especially chicha, and other goods, some already mentioned, formed the basis of barter between Africa and the Americas. From the bartering of *frijol canarios* (yellow canary beans), red kidney beans, and even dried white beans, bean puddings, garnished with sesame seeds and served from a *poto* (dry gourd) were produced. Other main dish bean combinations found their way onto Peruvian menus.

In this version of beans and rice, hot sausage is added for texture, but particularly for the delicious flavor it imparts to the dish. It is not too expensive and most of the time devoted to this dish is allowing it to simmer as the flavors meld.

Lima Beans and Rice with Sausage

1 pound roll of hot sausage, browned and crumbled
3 slices bacon, fried crisp and crumbled
Rendered fat from bacon
¼ of a very large green pepper, chopped
1 medium onion, chopped
½ of a large tomato, chopped
3 Peruvian aji or serrano chilies, toasted and chopped
1 Tbs. chopped cilantro

¼ heaping tsp. EACH cumin seeds and whole cloves, toasted and ground
¾ cup uncooked rice
1¾ cups chicken broth
1 tsp. EACH lemon and lime juices
About ¾ cup, plus 2 Tbs. cooked lima beans
A generous sprinkle of black mustard seeds
Salt and freshly ground black pepper, to taste
Chopped chicharrones

Brown and, when cool enough to handle, crumble sausage. Set aside, covered.

Fry bacon until crisp. Crumble and set aside, covered.

Heat rendered fat from bacon. Add green pepper, onion, tomato, chilies, and cilantro. Cook and stir for a minute. Add cumin and cloves and continue cooking and stirring until onion becomes translucent. Stir in rice and blend well. Add broth, lemon and lime juices, and lima beans. Stir in mustard seeds, salt, and pepper and mix well. Bring to a boil. Lower heat and simmer, covered, over medium-low heat for about 25 minutes, stirring frequently. Sprinkle each serving with 1 or 2 tsp. of chopped chicharrones, if desired.

One very hot and spicy West African sauce was composed of malagueta peppers, salt, onions, lemon and lime juice, melon seeds, nuts, oils, and other spices. Very often it was served in a separate bowl as a dipping sauce for meats, breads, and vegetables. Or, depending on how it was to be used later, it was sometimes combined with meat stocks, milk, or pureed vegetables and served as a gravy with other vegetables. White potatoes get the nod here, but they are only one vegetable that warrants the honor of tasting this good under this type of cover treatment.

Spiced Lima Bean Sauce
with White Potatoes and Rice

4 medium-large potatoes, peeled and sliced into rounds
1 cup cooked lima beans

½ cup coconut milk
2 Tbs. peanut oil
1½ small onions, chopped
½ cup chopped green pepper
2 serrano chilies, stems removed and finely chopped
½ tsp. black mustard seeds
¼ tsp. EACH cumin seeds and whole cloves, toasted and ground
½ inch piece cinnamon stick, toasted and ground
2 Tbs. finely chopped cilantro
1 to 1¼ cups milk
1 tsp. lime juice
½ cup cooked rice
Salt, freshly ground black pepper, and white pepper, to taste
Chopped red onion and chopped parsley or cilantro (optional)

Cook sliced potatoes in salted water for about 40 minutes. Drain. Return potatoes to pot and cover.

Puree beans and coconut milk in food processor.

Heat oil. Add onions, green pepper, and chilies. Cook and stir for a few minutes. Add mustard seeds, cumin, cloves, cinnamon, and cilantro. Cook and stir until onion browns. Stir in lima bean puree, then milk and lime juice. Stir in rice. Add salt, black and white peppers. Fold in potatoes. Taste again for needed salt and pepper. Heat through. Serve immediately.

Garnish with a little chopped red onion and a bit of chopped parsley or cilantro (optional).

The traveling medicine man, referred to in Titicaca as the *callahuaya*, with his packages of caffeine-rich herbs, tubes of snuffs, and other tablets, was but one of many traveling salesmen to journey the trade networks in Peru and the Americas. There were also the smoke vendors, who sold tobacco, as well as the wine merchants, who traded in various intoxicating liquors.

A liquor with the generic name of *pombe* was made in many countries in Africa. It was made from many different types of foods and food plants. In the Swahili language, pombe refers to an intoxicating native beer made from many kinds of grains and some fruits, such as bananas. In Angola, *mbombo* is fermented manioc from which *fuba* is made. People in the Congo favored malted liquors made from maize, cassava, or manioc. In East African countries such as Mozambique, liquors made from millet were said to provide the people with greater strength. *Malafu ma tombe* was considered, by West Africans, to be the best palm wine. In making it, a hole was made in the top of the palm tree, and a milklike liquid was collected that is said to be sweet for the first few days. It then becomes bitter and changes to a vinegar appropriate for use in salads and for pickling foods. After its preparation as wine, it is reported to be very nourishing and an efficient diuretic. The Hausa of Nigeria made palm wine, which they called *bumbo*, *bam*, and *bummi*. The liquid is first extracted by draining the stems of the palm tree. Once extracted, the liquid begins to ferment on the second or third day. West Africans also made wines from corn, sugarcane, and pineapple. Grains from corn milhio (millet) were used in brewing beer that was said to be the only beverage consumed by many Gold Coast residents.

A blackberry mixed drink with a blackberry chaser? You do not have to tell me that this is far out. There were several fruits and vegetables that Africans and Peruvians alike fermented to make wonderfully refreshing, tantalizing wines and intoxicating drinks. These drinks were sometimes "administered" to "cure" or "soothe" those suffering from a variety of physical ailments. The following is a modern version of an ancient remedy suggested for persons suffering with sore feet. I cannot testify as to whether or not it works because after consuming two or three of these drinks, I cannot remember where my feet are. Besides being unique, the taste is sensational.

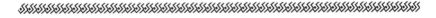

Mora Piggyback

7 ounces of mora (Andean blackberry) pulp,** defrosted (reserve ¼ cup for the chaser)
⅓ cup plus 1 Tbs. creme de banana liqueur
2 tsp. lime juice

෴ ෴ ෴ ෴ ෴ ෴ ෴

**Mora (Andean blackberry) pulp is available frozen at larger and specialty grocery stores in 14-ounce packages.

³/₄ cup orange juice
¹/₄ cup dark rum
¹/₃ cup sugar
2 cups crushed ice

The Chaser:
The reserved ¹/₄ cup mora
¹/₂ cup vermouth
1 Tbs. plus 2 tsp. sugar

Combine first 7 ingredients in food processor or blender and process for 2 to 3 minutes. The mixture will have a very thick, pink head on it. Transfer to a bowl.

Combine chaser ingredients and mix well.

To serve: Fill 9¹/₂ to 10 ounce glasses with crushed ice. Spoon 2 Tbs. of chaser into glass. Ladle about ¹/₂ cup of iced mora mix on top.

Liquor salesmen or wine merchants in Africa were called *pombeiros* by the Portuguese. In Peru the same African pombeiros were very active. These liquor agents, and the smoke vendors as well, had become residents of the West Indies, Panama, and South America long before Europeans stumbled into the "New World." Their various drinks, together with the high quality native maize beer, or chicha, and another beer made from cabuya juice, offered quite an assortment from which to choose. Chicha, made in Nicaragua, is said to have been quite strong, and resembled chicken broth with one or two egg yolks mixed in it. It was drunk from small saucer- or platelike calabashes. In modern times, when the chicha reaches a particular stage in fermentation, brown sugar is added. In pre-Columbian times, a meal made from ground, toasted sweet corn was added "to increase the sugar content and give the chicha its extra kick." Those Peruvians who brew by the book still grow this special sweet corn to use in brewing chicha. Traveling northward along the Andes, in areas that have retained many of their native customs, various ancient drinks are still made. All use the special ground, toasted corn as a sugar source in making drinks, both fermented and unfermented.

The following drink is referred to as a "blow dart" because if you make it strong enough, it should knock you out—suddenly.

⟫⟫⟫

Yugeno (Blow Dart—A Peruvian Cocktail)

3 ounces* chicha
3 ounces* pisco (Peruvian brandy)
2 tsp. lemon juice
2 tsp. lime juice
3 ounces* orange juice
1½ tsp. sugar
1 Tbs. egg white
Ice cubes
Lemon, lime, and orange peels

Combine all ingredients in a glass. Place shaker on top and vigorously shake several times. Strain into a chilled, ice filled, serving glass. Garnish with a twist of lemon or lime or orange peel, or all three.

⟩⟩⟩

Culinary and cultural traditions of the Chavin society point to its direct contact with the African elements of Mexico, Central America, and particularly Africa itself. The large-scale and sophisticated system of trade, connecting ancient societies of North, Central, and South America, embraced African participants and was primarily responsible for the transfer of foods and culinary traditions, language, art, and other cultural characteristics among one another.

African foods, cooking, and cuisine were integral components in the development of the culinary history and culture of the Americas from an early age. African participation in this development did

𝄃𝄃𝄃𝄃𝄃𝄃𝄃

*The proportions of the chicha and brandy and orange juice are definitely dependent upon how strong or weak you prefer your drink to be.

not end with Europe's unrelenting search in the Americas for gold, riches, and new lands to conquer. Native populations, forced into slavery as a result of this unrelenting search, were dwindling. The proposed solution to maintaining the appropriate numbers in the workforce came from the Christian Church. Black men, women, and children from the African continent, it was suggested, could and would be forced here, in chains, and made to provide that necessary labor. The coming of Africans to the Americas on this occasion would not be by choice. As slaves for the masters of the "New World," a total dependence on African ingenuity and creativity in the kitchen would result.

Africans would take cooking and cuisine to new and different heights, evolving them into a culinary art force that would influence virtually every aspect of life in the Americas ranging from art, music, and dance to economics and war. African cooks would help to form the basis for a new standard of living for Europeans, a catalyst for a European and "New World" social and economic revolution.

Body and Soul

≶≶ ≶≶ ≶≶ ≶≶

The Miscegenation of Cuisine
and Culture in Brazil and Cuba

For more than three hundred years, from the mid and late 1500s to 1888 in Brazil and 1868 in Cuba, the African female as slave dominated the plantation kitchen, enriching it with a variety of new flavors. These new flavors permeated the whole of Brazilian and Cuban cuisines. The African female cooks not only elevated the heretofore drab diets of the colonists in Brazil and Cuba but also helped Africanize the dress, language, music, religion, and folklore of these two countries and others in Latin America and the Caribbean. Brazil and Cuba were forged from a mixed racial and cultural heritage. The two societies were rooted deeply in the cane fields and coffee groves dependent upon African slaves. The African in general, and the African female as domestic and cook in particular, not only enriched the lifestyle of the Portuguese and Spanish in Brazil and Cuba, but also helped to produce enormous wealth for their mother countries.

The tremendous wealth produced by the establishment and expansion of Brazil's and Cuba's cane fields and coffee groves was built by an economic system based on skilled African agricultural and domestic labor. All African societies providing that domestic labor brought with them their diverse cooking talents, which became characteristic of the entire colony and not centrally defined to one specific area. In the pursuit of riches, most of the agricultural activity was cultivation for sugar, coffee, and other cash crops, which made the importation of food products essential for the growth and nourishment of the Brazilian population. The horsebean, from southern Africa and Guinea, wild rice, obtained from swampy soils near rivers in Central Africa, ginger from São Tome, as well as yams and taros, banana trees, sorghum, sesame, fruits, and vegetables were all imported into Brazil from Africa. African date trees were brought to Brazil in the sixteenth century. In addition, the first cows, along with the squash plant, arrived in Bahia, Pernambuco, and Rio de Janeiro from their home in Guinea. The earlier Portuguese invasion of Africa had allowed them to come into possession of a varied array of tropical fruits, vegetables, and spices, such as the coco tree, the *jaqueira* (tree of the breadfruit genus), mango, cinnamon and other spices, the breadfruit tree, couscous, as well as sweetmeats and different animals; some of them not adaptable to Europe, but all products of opulent and ancient African and Asian civilizations. As Brazilian imports, these products were placed in the hands of the African cook, a commodity as valuable as any of those cultivated from the soil. Already familiar with these foodstuffs, her skills allowed her to prepare wholesome, nourishing, and delicious meals for the owners of the huge sugarcane *fazendas*, or plantations.

There is nothing like steak cooked on the grill, and in Africa some of the most delicious cookouts took place as part of very solemn proceedings. For the funeral of a monarch, at least one hundred head of cattle were prepared. In this case, however, a two-pound grilled sirloin will do, and topped with a spicy, and I might add, appetizing, cooked fruit sauce, you will bear witness to nonstop eating.

§§

Grilled Steak with Mango "Dressing"

2 pounds boneless sirloin steak
Season to taste
About 2 tsp. dendê (see glossary), or peanut, or vegetable oil
½ of a ripe mango, peeled, cored, and sliced thin
¼ tsp. whole cloves, finely crushed
2 Tbs. dark rum

About 2 Tbs. dendê, or peanut, or vegetable oil
1 large plum tomato, sliced thin
½ inch slice (round) of a large red onion, chopped
¼ of a very small red bell pepper, chopped
Minced malagueta chili pepper, to taste
¼ tsp. EACH crushed red pepper and ground cumin
½ cup beef bouillon
Freshly ground black pepper, to taste
Salt, to taste
Chopped coriander, for garnish

Season steak to taste and grill to desired tenderness. Just before steak is done:

In a skillet, heat the 2 tsp. of oil. Add mango. Cook and stir for a minute or two. Stir cloves into mango. Continue cooking and stirring until mango is soft and can be mashed with a fork (mango may stick somewhat to skillet. DO scrape brown particles into mango as you cook). Continue to mash mango as it becomes soft until it is the consistency of pulp. Transfer mango to a bowl. Add rum to mango and mix well.

In the same skillet (DO NOT CLEAN SKILLET), heat the 2 Tbs. of oil over medium heat. Add tomato, onion, and bell pepper. Cook and stir for a minute. Add malagueta, red pepper, cumin, and black pepper. Continue cooking and stirring until onion becomes clear. Add bouillon. Lower heat, and cook and stir for a minute or two. Taste for needed salt and black pepper.

Spread a thin layer of "dressing" over top of steak and slice. Garnish with chopped coriander. It is also especially good with duck and chicken.

There is no shortage of sweet treats on Brazil's dessert menus. The following rice dessert, reminiscent of rice pudding, is colored with saffron, spiced with cloves, and sweetened most generously with sugar. My mother used to serve a much simpler version of this dish (rice mixed with milk and sugar) many years ago. Try this one after dinner tonight for a splendid end to the day's events.

⟨⟨

Sweet Saffron Rice

2 cups milk
1 cup sugar
Almost ½ tsp. saffron threads
¼ rounded tsp. whole cloves, finely crushed
½ cup coconut milk
3 cups cooked rice
4 tsp. cassava flour
½ tsp. EACH vanilla and coconut extract
Coconut milk (optional)

Combine milk and sugar in a saucepan over medium heat. When hot add saffron. Lower heat. Cook and occasionally stir over low heat for 20–25 minutes. DO NOT LET MILK BOIL. Add cloves and continue cooking and occasionally stirring for 15–20 minutes, WITHOUT ALLOWING MIXTURE TO BOIL. Add coconut milk. Stir in rice. Sprinkle cassava flour over mixture and stir to mix well. Over medium heat, bring to a full boil. Lower heat and simmer, stirring frequently, for 2–3 minutes. Remove from heat. Let stand for about 3–5 minutes. Stir in extracts. Cool. Serve warm or cold in dessert dishes alone or surrounded by a little coconut milk (note: canned coconut milk left in the back of the refrigerator for a few days has the consistency of whipped cream).

⟨⟨

Brazil's vast fazendas and cane fields began as a string of sugar plantations along the coasts of Pernambuco and São Vicente, and although São Vicente plantations quickly failed, they were Portugal's first "New World" settlements in the 1530s and 1540s. Prior to this, and indeed until Portugal became wealthy by way of its overseas empire in South America, the Portuguese had been a badly undernourished nation. The deficiency of meat (about 3.3 pounds per month per inhabitant), milk, and vegetables, and the preponderance of dried sardines and acorn bread (most of the time filled with dirt) in their diets had extremely negative effects on Portuguese health. It did not take long for culinary traditions of indigenous Brazilians to become firmly rooted into Portuguese diets. From manioc flour, native Brazilians made several varieties of *beiju* cakes, some containing crushed cashews and turtle fat, and *carima* cakes, a favorite with children. Native fish and turtle dishes were numerous and many of these preparations were considered delicacies. *Abuna*, or smoked turtle eggs; *mujangue*, manioc flour mixed with turtle egg yolks; and *paxica*, a ragout made with turtle's liver, peppers, salt, and lemon were just a few of the dishes adopted by European settlers. The Amazon, known for its huge fish, produced the *pirarucu*, *tucunare*, and the *tambaqui*, which, like various meats, could be slowly roasted in fat and then preserved by sealing in jars. However, the importation of black people for agricultural and domestic labor Africanized many of the native dishes, as well as those seen on Portuguese tables. Although indigenous Brazilians did make use of spices, peppers, and the banana plant and employed the cornhusk for cooking foods, African preparations made extensive use of the leaf of the banana for wrapping and cooking foods and created new and different dishes by creative spicing. The abundance of sugar also helped to create a new repertoire of sweet dishes.

Beginning in the 1550s, and throughout the entire seventeenth century, northeastern Brazil, principally Pernambuco and Bahia, cornered the market as specialists in and centers of Brazilian and world sugar production. Bahia had eighteen sugar mills. Pernambuco had twenty-three, worked by oxen or water, producing in 1576 fifty to seventy thousand *arrobas* of sugar (twenty-five arrobas was equal to more than six-hundred pounds). Each mill was worked by fifty Africans. With sugar in abundance, Brazil expanded its repertoire of pastries and confections. Sugar's sweet embrace with coconut, coconut milk, and eggs produced myriad puddings. The puddings often included peanuts or cashews and mashed fruits or vegetables, such as pumpkin or yam. African cooks in Bahia and other northeastern regions of Brazil prepared such dishes sprinkled with cinnamon or ginger and cooked in banana leaves. Sugar was added to fresh dough, from which various cakes or breads were made. All were accompaniments to an array of new foods introduced by Africans to the Portuguese. As the demand for sugar grew, so did the numbers of imported Africans.

Constant gratification of the palate was only partly responsible for the intense increase in African importation into Brazil and Cuba. Around the time of the settlement expedition of Diego Valazquez in 1511, through 1762, when Havana was captured by the British during the Seven Years War, there were only a few thousand African captives in Cuba. The slave revolution in Saint Domingue (Haiti) in 1791 destroyed the world's leading producer of sugar and coffee, which more than doubled sugar prices overnight. Spanish merchants residing in Havana, seizing the moment, took over the Cuban slave trade, and by the end of the eighteenth century and on into the nineteenth, tens of thousands of Africans, as well as thousands of Mayans from the Yucatan, were to enter Cuba as slaves as the sugar economy skyrocketed. In 1840, Cuba led the world in sugar production, processing more than 160,000 metric tons. Sugar far exceeded coffee, tobacco, and cotton in the rigors of cultivation both in Brazil and Cuba; "breathless haste" and "brute strength" was the requirement on the sugar plantation. As this was an operation that generated riches, the planters saw any slowdown in the work process as drastically affecting the quality and therefore quantity of the sugar. African workers constantly received physical punishment in connection with the planters' desire to maintain a factory-like rhythm of labor. Among Cuban and Brazilian planters, the rule prevailed that it was easier and cheaper to work field slaves to death in five to seven years and buy new ones than to invest in their long-term maintenance and reproduction. Working Africans to death was indeed the norm. About one-third of Cuba's Africans performed back-breaking labor on sugar plantations in 1840. By the end of every cane harvest as many as forty percent of the workers were in "sick bay" as the result of mistreatment, infection, disease, or serious accident. The death rate was so high and had become so well known on distant shores that planters in the antebellum southern United States, as a form of discipline, threatened Africans there with exportation to Cuba. The famous saying on Cuban plantations was, "Con sangre se hace azucar"—"Sugar is made with blood."

Blood spilled by Africans in slavery was often experienced and eloquently expressed by Juan Francisco Manzano, a house slave who learned to read and write and achieved literary prominence, and later freedom, in nineteenth-century Cuba. The influence of black writers had been evident in Cuba as early as 1608; however, with the exception of Manzano, most books in nineteenth-century Cuba were the products of white Creole intellectuals. Manzano's poems and autobiography discuss the brutal treatment of the Africans, including murders, and the continued application of the lash that he and other slaves endured on a sugar plantation. He wrote that he believed that a person's life was cut out for something other than becoming someone's "lap-dog," as he refers to himself, or cutting cane and planting corn. His autobiography also relates how domestic service was preferably saved for the lightest-skinned slaves, particularly females.

Light-skinned or not, plantation cooks in Cuba were always expected to outdo themselves at mealtime, even if it was in the preparation of something light, such as a salad. A combination of corn, rice, and a little spice is fully capable of beckoning you to intense gastronomic pleasure. Allow this salad to show you how easy it can be.

Corn Salad Manzano

1½ cups cooked corn kernels
1 cup cooked rice
2 whole green onions, chopped (white and green parts)
¼ of a medium-large red bell pepper, chopped
¼ rounded tsp. black mustard seeds
Finely minced malagueta chili pepper, to taste
Salt and freshly ground black pepper
2 tsp. EACH lemon juice, lime juice, dark rum, dendê (palm oil) OR peanut OR vegetable oil
1 tsp. "Hot Shot" (see recipe, this chapter)
¼ tsp. ground cumin
1 allspice berry, finely crushed

Combine first 8 ingredients in a bowl. Fold to mix well. Combine remaining ingredients in a separate bowl. Stir to blend well. Pour juice mixture into corn mixture, folding and turning to coat corn mixture well. Taste for needed salt and pepper. Serve hot as a side dish, or chilled on salad spinach leaves, each serving garnished with chopped cilantro.

Sugar was indeed made with blood in Brazil, which accounts for another saying coined during the first century of slavery there: "Brazil is sugar and sugar is the Negro." The "Negro's" involvement with sugar reaches back to Portugal, where Moors settled on the Iberian

Peninsula, adhered to culinary traditions that included dishes rich in sugar, fats, and oil. During their interaction with the Portuguese, Moors also introduced them to oranges, lemons, tangerines, and the process of preserving and putting up "dried fruits." Portuguese matrons of the sixteenth century brought a little of this knowledge to Brazil and quickly acquired a fondness for sugar added to their intake of fruit. The technical skills that aided the Portuguese in their success in the production and economic utilization of sugarcane had been furnished to them by the Moors. An important labor force in Portugal, Moorish agricultural systems conditioned the economic and social evolution of the Portuguese colony in Brazil. The Moors introduced to Portugal the mechanism for drawing water from wells and the device for raising water. They introduced the water mill, the ancestor of the colonial device used for grinding cane through the power of water falling over a large wooden wheel. In addition, Brazilian architecture was greatly influenced by the Moors with their preference for waterspouts, glazed tiles, and fountains. Through Moorish agricultural science, the utilization, and therefore value, of vineyards and olive and fruit trees increased.

Fruit dishes, sweets, and other "culinary" concoctions sometimes took on obscene forms in Portuguese cuisine. Certain confections were fashioned in "semi-phallic" shapes. Dressings or garnishes were said to have been given aphrodisiac seasonings to arouse "erotic vibrancy," or "the procreative tension." The horrors endured by Africans from the bestial rigors of sugar production were of no concern to the Portuguese, who brought this same predisposition for sexual stimuli and obscenity to the Brazilian colonial dining table:

> At the supper hour it was announced that there was a surprise in store for the guests. This surprise was nothing other than the substitution of toilet paper for plates at the table, and upon each bit of paper there lay a slender dark-brown sweet, cut up into small portions.
>
> (Gilberto Freyre, *The Masters and the Slaves* [New York: Alfred A. Knopf, 1946], 261.)

Sexual inuendo in the realm of food was not restricted to plantation kitchens. Cakes and sweets made by nuns in convents were given names with an aphrodisiac or sometimes obscene intent. Nun's belly, angel's titbits (often shortened to angel's tits), and nuns' sighs (but the preferred name was nuns' thighs) were just a few of the cakes and sweets that made the sisters' male friends "sigh at the convent doors." Since the sisters were unable to fulfill the fantasies of their admirers, they gave them candy and cakes instead; consequently, these sweet substitutes became sexually symbolic. Complaints were made that the abbesses and nuns of Portuguese convents spent more time making such delicacies as "little kisses," "weaned sucklings," "raise-the-old-man," "maiden's tongue," "married couples," and "love's caresses" than with service to God.

I remember the day when we moved across town in Chicago. I was five years old and my mother had the nerve to try to enroll me in a Catholic grammar school. We had been there only three minutes when we saw one of the nuns in a stance like Willie Mays. She was beating the hell out of one of the female students with a yardstick. I think this quelled my mother's desire to see me wearing a plaid uniform on a daily basis. My school days thereafter were spent in a more secular environment. You know, the nuns should have taken a page from the book of Ifa, a Yoruba oracle who understood heated behavior in women and natural feminine violence. Ifa would have explained to them that what the nuns needed was a little shea butter and some snails, ritual food of the Yoruba god Obatala. Shea butter (an oily paste made from the kernel of the shea tree—*Butyrospermum parkii*—throughout West Africa), snails, and some palm oil too, Ifa says, are good for calming down persons overwhelmed by primal terrors and vortical depression because these foods perform the act of libidinal transfusion. Maybe the nuns' service should have been to Obatala because his ritual snails contain quintessential semen. As all Yoruba gods know, "to give snail liquid to a hot female force is symbolically to impregnate her."

To soften quickly the temperament of those persons prone to "incendiary vaginas," one can use canned snails and mushroom caps for this taste-pleasing repast.

Desperate Virgins

2 Tbs. EACH dendê and butter or peanut oil
3/4 tsp. cayenne pepper (decrease amount of cayenne, if you are not that desperate)
1 clove garlic, crushed

12 large mushroom caps
1 tsp. EACH lime and lemon juice
¼ cup rum
Depending on the size, one or more snails for each cap
2 or 3 Tbs. finely chopped fresh cilantro
Black pepper, to taste

Heat dende and butter in a large skillet. Add cayenne and garlic. Cook and stir garlic over medium-low heat for a few minutes. Add mushrooms and continue cooking and stirring for a couple of minutes more until mushrooms are thoroughly coated with oil. Remove mushrooms from skillet. Add lime and lemon juices and rum to skillet. Stir in snails. Cook and stir until snails are thoroughly heated. Discard garlic.

When snails are assembled on mushroom caps, sprinkle with chopped cilantro and desired amount of black pepper.

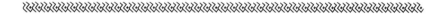

I would now like to offer something sweet. Perhaps a sweet might lend a hand. Indulge. Look upon this confection as a remedy against numerous ills, and not just those that afflict the female species, either. Men, no doubt, would be tempted to accomplish a cure of their own with this one.

"Incendiary Vaginas"

½ cup EACH coconut milk and sugar
2 Tbs. red wine
4 whole cloves, finely crushed
2 tsp. cassava flour
About 1 cup EACH finely grated coconut and chopped dates
½ tsp. vanilla extract
12 Maraschino cherry halves

In a saucepan over medium heat, combine milk and sugar. Stir until sugar has dissolved. Add wine, then cloves and cassava. Bring to a boil. Lower heat and simmer, stirring constantly, for 5 minutes. Remove from heat. Stir in coconut, vanilla, and mix well. Transfer to a small baking dish and place in 350 degree preheated oven for

29 minutes. Cool completely. Transfer mixture from baking dish to a plastic bag. Allow to rest for several hours or chill. Roll spoonfuls of coconut mixture in dates to form balls. Stuff balls in 12 paper or foil mini muffin cups and top with cherry halves. Keep Refrigerated.

In Brazil, the Church paid its service to God with the labor of African slaves. In fact, the Jesuits, or Society of Jesus, which entered Brazil with the founders of the royal government in 1549, became Brazil's largest landowner and greatest slave master. There were five Jesuit plantations in Bahia and every sugar-producing captaincy contained one or more. Together with sugar-producing plantations, the Jesuits owned extensive horse and cattle ranches. Their most prized possession, however, was the monopoly of the spice trade in the Amazon region. Equated with gold and diamonds in the Middle Ages, spices and the possession of salt mines were considered the foundation of economic power. The Jesuits obviously subscribed to the Yoruba belief that "no one who would enjoy life would oppose God, just as no one willingly eats an unsalted meal." The Jesuits controlled enormous quantities of cacao (chocolate), cloves, cinnamon, and sarsaparilla, which were harvested each year along the Amazon's major tributaries. To be sure, the Society of Jesus exploited both Africans and the natives of Brazil for their domestic labor and their agricultural labor in the cultivation of spice crops. Even though the society pretended to champion the rights of the indigenous Brazilians, the exploitation of both groups forged a close relationship between Africans and indigenous Brazilians, which brought about adoption by the indigenes of numerous aspects of African culture and the African-Brazilian religion, *Candomblé*. *Caboclos*, or *Mestizos* (persons of part Indian and part European descent), took part in their own Candomblé festivals, in which drinks were prepared with an infusion of spices, honey, herbs, alcohol, and parts of various plant species with hallucinogenic properties such as the genera Mimosa, Acacia, and Pithecelobium. One of the drinks, *jurema*, is reddish in color and made with the root or bark of certain plants; these plants were also mixed with tobacco and smoked. During the climax of a caboclo festival mangos, papayas, pineapples, passion fruit, bananas, custard-apples, watermelons, cantaloupes, sugarcane, apples, oranges, corn, peanuts, star fruit, and jack-fruit were distributed to the guests and formed the conclusion to the formal proceedings. Later, grilled meats were prepared on a huge spit outdoors. The caboclo festival is supposed to have originated in the Congo-Angola branch of Candomblé, and it incorporates the invocation of native Brazilian spirits, African gods, and Catholic saints. The Jesuits used their prejudice against African-based religion to justify exploitation of these groups. However, exploitation of human labor was of no consequence where money and profits were to be made. The Jesuits staunchly defended their rights and privileges, which included sanction from the home government for complete exemption from all customs duties in Portugal and Brazil for sale of their agricultural goods.

Whether or not the agricultural goods were grown on a Jesuit plantation or some other large or small fazenda, everything produced on the land was the product of the work of African males and females. Considered literally "the hands and feet" of the Portuguese, Africans built every house, all of the roads, most of the machines at the mills, channeled all of the water, and raised all of the livestock needed on the plantation. In addition to raising livestock and producing coffee, they cultivated various food crops. Although these crops were considered subsidiary, the rigorous production of cash crops demanded abundant, nutritious food for the laborers. Cashews and peanuts, with their high protein content, made their appearance in pastries, sweets, breads, stews, and other dishes, by way of African cooks. Rich in calcium, wild spinach was often tamed in eggplant or other vegetable casseroles; in addition, sauces laden with palm oil and hot peppers infused with vitamins A and C imparted incendiary flavors to the lackluster soups and roasted meats of European settlers.

This magnificent offering is anything but lackluster. Try this one out tonight.

﷽﷽﷽﷽﷽﷽﷽﷽﷽﷽﷽﷽﷽﷽﷽﷽﷽﷽﷽﷽﷽﷽﷽﷽﷽﷽

Leitão Assado Com Molho de Amoras (Baked Sirloin Pork Roast with Red Raspberry Glaze and Red Raspberry "Dressing")

1 sirloin pork roast, approximately 4 pounds
Seasonings to sprinkle all over roast (All are to taste, but be generous, especially with the paprika): garlic salt with parsley, sea-

soned salt, powdered cloves, pumpkin pie spice, black pepper, "Hot, Mexican style" chili powder, white pepper, parsley flakes, paprika
Flour
A few tablespoons of dendê or vegetable or peanut oil
4 Tbs. red raspberry preserves
1/2 cup of sour cream
1 cup plus 2 Tbs. commercial white simmer sauce
1/4 tsp. EACH powdered cloves, pumpkin pie spice, and finely chopped malagueta chili pepper
1/2 tsp., or more, EACH white pepper and black pepper

Season roast with spices. Coat with flour and brown all over in hot oil.

Bake, covered, in a preheated 350 degree oven for about 2 hours. Transfer all drippings, including any crusty particles, from baking pan to skillet in which meat was browned. Over low heat stir in 2 Tbs. (2 ounces) of red raspberry preserves. Stir until preserves have melted and mixture is fairly smooth. Spoon mixture over roast in baking pan, allowing it to coat top, sides, and both ends. Cover tightly with foil.

Add remaining 2 Tbs. (2 ounces) of preserves and remaining ingredients in the same skillet over medium-low heat. Stir to melt preserves and blend ingredients. Remove foil from meat and drain a tablespoon or two of the coating juices that have accumulated in bottom of baking pan. Add coating juices to mixture in skillet. When mixture begins to boil, lower heat and simmer for a couple of minutes.

Spoon "dressing" over slices of roast.

Through their own initiative, Africans supplemented their meager diets with many more fruits, vegetables, game, and fish than were seen on the masters' tables. As Brazil's economy rested squarely on African shoulders, the okra and fish stews consumed by Africans were important in maintaining their stamina for their roles in the economy.

Gold and other minerals, as well as rubber and cotton were export and cash crops for which African labor was exploited. Requests from

Europeans in eighteenth-century Brazil for mining technicians from Hungary and Saxony went unanswered. It was Africans, many from Benin, who were familiar with the mining of metals and who taught white owners principles of metallurgy, and who came to be specifically selected for these skills.

Mining areas were very dependent upon beef for food. Before mining became a major industry, northeastern cities developed markets for the sale of cattle and products such as beef jerky, which could be abundantly produced because of the presence of natural salt deposits. Minas Gerais and other mining territories were usually able to acquire supplies of beef intended for other regions. As major consumers of jerked and other preparations of beef, quadruple profits were made from sales in these areas due to the scarcity of meat. It became profitable to grow food for miners at Minas Gerais. Early settlers there grew maize, pumpkins, beans, and occasionally potatoes. By 1703, they were raising pigs and chickens, which they sold to travelers at very high prices.

African cooks, usually male, also came to be specifically selected for their skill in adding beans and wild onions or other wild vegetables to a pot of dried beef or fish and turning it into a delicious meal. A creative cook was essential since gold and other minerals contributed to the quadrupling of Portugal's foreign trade even as Brazil's sugar industry drifted into decline. African labor supplied one-half to two-thirds of the products that contributed to the expansion of Portugal's commerce. One of those products was *Coffea arabica*, or, coffee, which, together with African technology and labor, came to play an even bigger part in laying Brazilian infrastructural foundations.

Since coffee would not be cultivated for the benefit of Africans, it is ironic that such an important plant in African Brazilian culinary, social, and economic history is of African origin. *Coffea arabica*, or the coffee bean, originated in and is indigenous to Ethiopia. The Ethiopian town of Kaffa may have given coffee its name. The richest, most aromatic and robust coffee grown, *Coffea arabica* is the species of coffee that has traditionally provided the world its supply of the product. It also thrives in Equatorial Africa and is grown in other countries such as Arabia, India, Java, Sumatra, Pacific Islands, the West Indies, and Latin America. *Coffea robusta (Coffea canephora)*, first found growing wild in Zaire, has more and more become an important species, as it began to be grown commercially around the turn of the twentieth century. The use of coffee in solid form dates back to prehistory. All parts of the coffee plant were prepared as food by Africans from time immemorial. They consumed the leaves, fruits, and seeds from the various forest trees, bushes, and shrubs belonging to the *Coffea* genus. African societies obtained the sweet pulp by crushing the ripe red cherries from wild trees, mixed them with animal fat, and then shaped the mixture into round balls. Raw coffee's high protein content, which dissipates when prepared as a beverage, combined with fat, provided concentrated nourishment. The caffeine content was a helpful stimulant during hunting and trading expeditions. Camel drivers and traders took parts of the coffee plant prepared in pressed cakes on caravan trips and ate them with dates. Taken on hunting expeditions these cakes proved able to supply adequate nutrients and energy for a person for one day. These were not unusual staples, for they were perfect as a refreshment over long trails for heavily laden foot carriers loaded down with payload and weapons to fend off wild and dangerous animals. Benefitting from a lighter load, expeditions carried these rations in place of bulky and fresh foods.

It is interesting that fruit from Arabica trees do not appear for five years; while it takes from two to three years after planting a Robusta. Peaberry coffee, which is grown in Tanzania, the Republic of Cameroon, Burundi, Ethiopia (Harrar), Zaire (Kivu), Indonesia, Venezuela, and Colombia, is available in gourmet coffee shops, tagged Tanzania Peaberry. When the maturing cherries from a coffee tree contain only one stone, that stone is usually round and is referred to as the peaberry or male berry. It is possible to find them anywhere on the tree. Peaberry coffee is very reminiscent of the type made from home roasted coffee beans. In comparison to the length of time and trouble one must go through to produce coffee trees, try the following taste treat for ease of preparation. Even though I have suggested the use of Peaberry, any regular coffee will suffice.

⁄⁊⁊⁊

Mango Under Mocha

2 Tbs. plus 2 tsp. dark rum
2 tsp. sugar
1 whole ripe mango, peeled, seeded, and cut into bite size pieces

1½ ounces sweet chocolate, or ¼ cup milk chocolate chips
¼ cup plus 1 Tbs. Peaberry, or Kenya AA, or regular black coffee
⅛ tsp. cinnamon
½ tsp. cassava flour
3 tsp. coconut milk
Sweetened, finely grated coconut and whipped cream

Combine sugar and rum in a bowl. Stir until sugar dissolves. Add mango, folding and turning to thoroughly coat slices. Allow to sit for about 40 minutes, folding and turning occasionally. Arrange equal amounts of mango and marinade in 4 dessert dishes.

Combine coffee and chocolate over medium-low heat. Stir until chocolate melts. Stir in cinnamon, then cassava flour. Bring to boil over medium heat. Cook and stir for 1 or 2 minutes. Cool. Stir in coconut milk. Chill. Ladle mocha sauce over mango. Garnish with coconut and/or whipped cream.

Kenya AA, or Arabica coffee, is an excellent choice for those persons who seriously enjoy good coffee. Believe it or not, it reheats extremely well. It also combines well with other ingredients to produce heavenly creations. One forkful of this soufflé and your reaction will range from exhilaration to ecstasy.

Mocha Soufflé

½ cup cold, black coffee, preferably Kenya AA (Arabica)
1 cup milk
½ cup sugar
2 Tbs. butter
¼ cup milk chocolate chips, or 1½ ounces sweet chocolate
⅛ tsp. EACH cinnamon and nutmeg
4 whole cloves, finely crushed
4 tsp. cassava flour
⅓ cup plus 1 Tbs. finely grated coconut
¾ cup cooked rice
2 egg yolks (room temperature)

3 egg whites (room temperature)
¼ tsp. salt
2 Tbs. sugar

Combine coffee, milk, and sugar in a saucepan over medium heat. Stirring constantly, heat until mixture is scalding hot. DO NOT BOIL. Add butter and chocolate and remove from heat. Stir until chocolate has completely melted. Add cinnamon, nutmeg, and cloves and mix well. Sprinkle cassava flour over mixture, then stir in to blend well. Stir in coconut, then rice. Add egg yolks one at a time, beating well after each addition. Transfer mixture to a 1½ quart baking dish.

Beat egg whites until stiff peaks form, gradually adding salt and sugar during the process. Fold egg whites into coffee mixture.

Bake in a 350 degree, preheated oven for about 50–55 minutes.

୧୧

While tales were being spun in Europe around the magical hot brew, changes were being made in Africa in its preparation that greatly improved the taste. Beans, ground to a powder, were steeped in water for a day, allowing half the liquor to boil down, and then stored in containers to be heated and served as needed. The *ibrik*, or coffee boiler, helped to speed preparation time; powdered coffee, cinnamon, cloves, amber, and sugar were boiled together and the brew served in very small cups.

Arabica coffee trees had been brought to Dutch Guiana, or Surinam, in 1718. Earlier, cultivation had been attempted in Cayenne, French Guiana, but without success. Five years later, the plant was introduced to the Brazilian city of Belem do Pará. In 1727, seeds were planted in the southernmost part of Pará, followed in 1731 by an offer from the Portuguese crown. Portugal's government, seeking to increase the production of both cinnamon and coffee, exempted planters engaged in the cultivation of these two items from all customs duties for twelve years. The government's offer was taken seriously and by 1749 17,000 coffee trees were growing in Pará. In 1770, coffee was planted up the Amazon River near Manáos, where it blossomed. Rio de Janeiro and Bahia were next, and by 1797 it had reached São Paulo, the area of its most reknown and significant cultivation. It was in the drier climate of São Paulo that between two and three billion coffee trees found a thriving setting.

Such massive cultivation in Brazil resulted in a downward shift in Cuba's coffee production. Local consumption of the brew continued, as rural inhabitants drank large amounts with their two daily meals. On the large plantations and in urban areas, fruit drinks and alcoholic beverages (usually made from sugarcane) were also the norm. Juice from limes and sugar mixed with guavas or bananas were forerunners to the banana daiquiri and other popular drinks. Mango and pineapple refreshers were made from boiling water poured over the fresh fruit and outer skins, with ginger, cloves, and/or nutmeg stirred in. Watermelon juice and coconut milk mixed with Cuban rums and sprinkled with spices took center stage as the drinks of choice with many plantation meals. In the early 1840s coffee plantations outnumbered sugar plantations in Cuba; but with the rising cost of slave labor, United States tariff policies, the drop in coffee prices, and competition in the coffee market with Brazil, Cuban production was on the decline. African cooks on Cuban plantations, however, suffered no decline in their creative uses of either coffee or sugar with fruit and alcoholic beverages. Some of the same ingredients brought blissfully together for cocktails and drinks also merged in salads, desserts, and entrees. Spiced, mashed mango and diced pineapple, marinated in Cuban beer or liqueurs and topped with fresh, grated coconut was the sweet ending to dinner on numerous occasions. Often used to make flavorful punches, the strained juice from the passion fruit was also combined with honey, spices, and herbs to make light dressings for fruit or vegetable salads. Fresh fish received its crowning touch from sauces of tomato puree, rum, sweetened coffee, and coconut milk. In the culinary arena, African cooks in Cuba could draw many comparisons with those in Brazil. Sweetened coffee, *cachaca* (a very strong alcohol, 200 percent proof sugarcane rum to be exact), and coconut milk (an African Brazilian culinary staple) conspired to dress up gravies for chicken and beef; or, combined with chopped peppers, onions, bread crumbs, and shrimp or lobster, changed their plots to become lovely appetizers. While there may have been no real competition in the kitchen between the two societies, there were aspects of the coffee business in which competition with Brazil was most evident in 1800s São Paulo, particularly after 1850, where accelerated growth in coffee cultivation initiated a process of economic and demographic growth. Coffee had now, in fact, replaced sugar as the country's most important export. By the mid-1800s São Paulo's coffee plantations imported about four times as many Africans as did sugar plantations. The Portuguese believed that only the African, who had come from an agricultural environment that was used to so many different food plants for medicinal use and consumption, as well as a culinary environment that produced such a varied and nutritious array of dishes, was cut out for the strenuous plantation life that was to be faced in Brazil. The continued large-scale African importation for agricultural and domestic purposes thus reinforced the Africanization of the Brazilian kitchen. The 1860s saw São Paulo's agricultural production based entirely on coffee, which of course was based entirely on African labor. Half of the world's coffee supply came from Brazil in 1850; by 1900 half of the world's supply came exclusively from São Paulo, with an additional twenty-five percent from other towns in Brazil.

I have never really believed in being dictatorial when it comes to the amount of liquor added to someone else's drink. An individual cocktail usually calls for between one and a half and two ounces of liquor. If that is enough for you, then it is enough for me. On second thought, if that is enough for you, that is your business. However, if today is one of those days when you need a serious drink, one that does not play, then try on one of these coolers for size. Remember, making a drink is like listening to the radio—you can turn the volume up as well as down.

〽〽〽

São Paulo Midnight Express

½ cup EACH cold, black Kenya AA coffee and black cherry cola
2 Tbs. dark rum
2 Tbs. plus 1 tsp. coffee flavored brandy
Crushed ice
Combine all ingredients in a shaker and shake vigorously to mix well. Divide mixture between 2 brandy glasses and serve.

⚬ ⚬ ⚬ ⚬

Havana (Good Morning) Kiss

½ cup cold black Kenya AA coffee
4 Tbs. banana liqueur or brandy
1 Tbs. EACH coffee brandy and light cream
2 Tbs. dark rum
2 tsp. Kokomo fruit juice*

Combine all ingredients in a shaker and shake vigorously to mix well. Serve over ice in old-fashioned glasses.

The mass production of coffee in the 1800s meant only one thing: as coffee cultivation expanded throughout São Paulo, so did slavery. By 1811, Africans and African Brazilians comprised twenty-three percent of the population. That population doubled between 1811 and 1836, from 38,542 to 78,858; by 1872 it doubled again to 156,612. If the truth be told, a census is never correct; especially one that pretends to record accurate figures for the slave trade. Hundreds of thousands of Africans were brought into the country who were never officially counted. Whatever the actual number, São Paulo became home to the third-largest African population by the 1870s, exceeded only by Minas Gerais and Rio de Janeiro, which had also become an important source of African workers for expanding coffee planta-tions. When Brazil's economy moved to the south, African labor moved with it. Coffee-growing areas in Pernambuco were renamed "land of the Kaffirs." Maranhão was dubbed the "new coast of Africa."

Wherever Africans moved, so followed every aspect of African culture. It was particularly fitting that some Africans residing in coffee-producing regions came from areas in Africa that performed "blood brother" religious ceremonies. *Buni* and other solid prepara-tions of coffee were a special part of "blood brother" religious cer-emonies in Africa. According to tradition, the blood of the two

⚬ ⚬ ⚬ ⚬ ⚬ ⚬ ⚬

*Kokomo juice is a delicious blend of pure fruit juices, one of which is the passion fruit. It is available under the brand name "Summer Song" on your grocer's shelf.

pledging parties is mixed and placed between the seeds of a coffee fruit, then the whole fruit is either consumed or sometimes placed in a burial chamber. At other times, the seeds and blood drops are beaten together then eaten in a ceremony. In addition, midwives and barren women took part in fertility rituals where coffee grains were an essential component. Apart from religious duties, coffee played a fundamental role in African Brazilian so-called sexual magic. Coffee into which a "spell" had been cast, or what was called "witches coffee," was supposedly prepared with a great deal of sugar and "a few clots of the menstrual fluid of the sorceress herself." The blood of a woman of mixed heritage (a mulatta) and a large portion of sugar added to a cup of coffee was considered as a regular love potion. Preparing other love potions could be complex. Instructions include straining coffee through the lower portion of a nightgown in which a woman has slept for two consecutive nights. The same coffee must be divided in half and served to the target at breakfast and again at dinner. In Cuba, frogs and salamanders might hop and slither their way into concoctions intended for the lovelorn.

I agree with 007. If you give me a choice, I prefer my drinks shaken (I actually do not mind stirred), but never strained through a nightgown. I have presented Innocent Bahian Passion without "spirits," although you have the right to disagree. I simply felt that "innocent" means just that. However, If you prefer your drinks with more passion and less innocence, then by all means add a few ounces of rum and/or vodka, and make sure that you do not forget the finishing touch. If your wife catches you in her lingerie drawer and wants to know what gives, tell her you were just trying to get in touch with your feminine side.

SSSSSSSSSSSSSSSSSSSSSSSSSSSSSSSSSSSSSSSSSSSSSSSSSSSSSSSSSSSSSSSSS

Paixão Bahiana (Innocent Bahian Passion)

For each serving you will need:
½ cup cold passion fruit juice or Kokomo fruit juice*

SS SS SS SS SS SS SS

*Kokomo juice is a delicious blend of pure fruit juices, one of which is the passion fruit. It is available under the brand name "Summer Song" on your grocer's shelf.

2 Tbs. EACH cold cranberry juice and apple juice
4 Tbs. cold, black Kenya AA, Peaberry, or regular coffee
Ice
Cinnamon and nutmeg for garnish

Combine all juices and coffee. Stir vigorously to blend well. Pour mixture into a glass. Add ice. Sprinkle with cinnamon and nutmeg. Stir a bit and serve.

The role of African females on plantations, however, went way beyond making coffee and love potions. Culinary activity on a grand scale took place in the plantation kitchen. Okra, tomatoes, ground beef, or pork were kissed with cloves and found simmering in beef or chicken broth. Green and red bell peppers sauteed with onions and served over lime-flavored rice was a tasty accompaniment to roasted fish and plantains. Grilled sea bass with mango sauce and almonds often shacked up with fried yuca or pumpkin and *boniato* (white sweet potato) puree. Those African females who were not members of the kitchen crew toiled long hours in the fields. Cuban planters considered African women to be "made of iron" and sometimes utilized them in the cane fields right alongside of males.

Africans who were not working the fields for the sugar and coffee trade were involved in personal and domestic service. For their households masters and mistresses needed male slaves as body servants, butlers, porters, gardeners, postilions, and liverymen; females were employed as cooks, washerwomen, wet nurses, maids, and concubines (also considered an occupation). It was this total dependence on the African on the part of plantation owners, and particularly dependence on the African female in personal and domestic service, that brought about the Africanization of both Cuban and Brazilian cuisine and culture. At the core lay the fact that in Cuba and parts of Brazil, Africans outnumbered whites. The constant importation of large numbers of Africans allowed the colonists to benefit from the best of African culture. That culture was transferred to every aspect of the life and environment of the colonist child and adult through duties performed such as companion, accomplice, housemaid, empiric healer, cook, teller of tales, guide, and "housegirl."

As a teller of tales, the African female's linguistic influence on Brazilian Portuguese has never been acknowledged. African languages influenced the word formation, the structure and compounding, the inflections and vocabulary of Brazilian Portuguese. When African wet nurses told Portuguese tales to children the articulation and expression of ideas of these tales were changed. Gilberto Freyre, in his *The Masters and the Slaves*, describes the influence of the African nurse on spoken language in Brazil. He relates how the language of young children grew softer through contact with the African nurse. Words, considered harsh or sharp sounding when pronounced by the Portuguese, became much smoother when used in Brazil, due to African influence. Freyre describes the African nurse who gave the Portuguese child its first taste of *pirão com carne* and *molho de ferrugem*, both soft meat dishes, as presenting words exactly as she presents food; mashed, with the bones removed to take away the hard and brittle parts, leaving them "as soft and pleasing syllables in the mouth of the white child." The language of young Brazilians and Portuguese children, and adults too, for that matter, with its African "flavor," is said to be one of the most melodious forms of speech to be found.

The same "flavor" infused the language used in African stories, and they were added to the collection of Portuguese tales. During the first two centuries following colonization in Brazil, literary creation continued in the form of folklore, ensuring a vital and permanent African influence. Narrators spoke of the *aroken* or *akpalo* of Nigeria; but there were also griots of other areas, who specialized in oral traditions, divination, tales, verses, sayings, word puzzles, and satire, and recalled heroes and religious myths. Most legends of the *orishas* (deities) in the Cuban tradition of *Santeria* can be traced to Yoruba sources, but some are purely Cuban in origin. One legend, involving orishas Chango (considered quite powerful and the symbol of fire, thunder, lightning and one of the greatest warriors of the Yoruba orishas), Obba (Chango's wife and patron of the home and family life and of the Niger River), and Oshun (the symbol of love, gold, marriage, and the patron of river waters and of the arts), was a tale of food, love, and jealousy. Oshun had convinced Obba that the way to regain her husband's heart was through his stomach. After all, Chango adored food and would not hesitate to stay close to her if a good meal was waiting every night. Obba, who was not a good cook, took Oshun's advice and prepared a most unusual entree containing Obba's own ears. Well, I guess it was not a good night to try a new dish, because Chango brought guests for dinner. You know what they say: Never serve some dish to guests that you have never tried before. When he saw his wife's head all wrapped up and ears floating in the soup, Obba had to peel him off the ceiling. He wound up leaving Obba for Oshun, which had been Oshun's plan all along.

There was a very interesting rhythm and blues tune, popular in the 1970s, called "Smiling Faces Sometimes":

> Smiling faces, sometimes, pretend to be your friend,
> Smiling faces, show no traces, of the evil
> that lurks within . . .

Poor Obba. Someone should have told her that the recipe for giving your all to your man does not include body parts.

Well, I could have added pig ears to this dish, but frankly that would have been obscene. Salmon steaks will do nicely, thank you, and in combination with various vegetables, herbs, and spices, the flavor is superb. Enchant your husband with a plateful. Trust me, your marriage will be secured.

Salmon Steaks with Cabbage and Rice in Coconut Milk

2 big salmon steaks, seasoned with garlic salt (blended with parsley), white pepper, black pepper, and seasoned salt
3 Tbs. dendê (palm oil) or peanut oil or vegetable oil
¼ HEAPING tsp. EACH cumin seed and coriander seed, both toasted and finely crushed
¼ HEAPING tsp. EACH dried shrimp and dill weed
⅛ tsp. cinnamon
¼ tsp. crushed red pepper, or finely chopped malagueta chili pepper
About ¼ to ½ tsp. sugar
¾ of a medium-small onion, chopped
¼ cup chopped red bell pepper
¼ of a very small cabbage, chopped

¼ tsp. salt
Freshly ground black pepper
1¼ cups coconut milk
1½ tsp. EACH lime and lemon juice
1 tsp. cassava flour
¾ cup cooked rice
Salt and freshly ground black pepper

Place steaks in a baking dish. Season steaks with garlic salt, white and black pepper, and seasoned salt. Cover with foil and bake in preheated 375 degree oven for 25–30 minutes.

While fish is baking, heat oil in skillet. Add the next 8 ingredients. Over medium heat, cook and stir for about 2 minutes. Add bell pepper and cabbage. Cook and stir for another 5 minutes. Add about ¼ tsp. salt and some freshly ground black pepper, to taste. Continue cooking and stirring for another 13–15 minutes. Add coconut milk, then lime and lemon juices, and mix well. Sprinkle cassava flour over mixture, then stir it in to mix well. Add rice. Taste for needed salt and pepper. Bring to a boil. Lower heat and simmer, stirring frequently, for 2 to 3 minutes. Taste again for needed salt and pepper. Sauce should have thickened and reduced a bit.

Divide sauce between 2 serving plates. Place baked salmon steaks in center of sauce. Serve immediately.

꧁꧁

Myths were always a part of African music and dance. For example, numerous dances performed in Senegal were accompanied by the eating of cakes of cornmeal, which, when blessed by the religious leaders of the community, were said to bring good luck. Brazil's *macumbas, jongos*, and *batuques* certainly have their origins in West Africa and the Congo. In addition, the tango and samba, the *reisados*, which were popular dramatic dances originally celebrating the Epiphany, and the *congadas*, dances originally celebrating the coronation of a Congolese monarch, are all Brazilian versions of the types performed on the African continent. Some Brazilian versions of cakes eaten while these dances are performed are *akara*, fritters of bean flour mixed with chopped

shrimps and pimento, fried in palm oil, and served rolled in banana leaf, and *acarajé*, another fritter made of bean flour, salt,
onions, and dried shrimp fried in palm oil. One of Candomblé's
deities, Omolu-Obaluae (Sumbu in Angola), the orisha of disease
and healing, performs dances through one or more of its members
at Candomblé feasts and enjoys through all of its worshippers
aberem, (corn roasted in banana palm leaves), he-goats, roosters,
and popcorn. Candomblé, practiced by many African Brazilians,
encompasses numerous influences never absent from African religion; however, celebrations and festivals associated with African
gods were originally "non-official" counterparts of the feasts of the
Church. In Candomblé every orisha corresponds to a Christian saint
and is celebrated with feasting and dancing on a date nearest to
the saint's day. Candomblé foods such as *caruru*, a stew of leafy
greens and smoked fish; *farofa*, roasted manioc flour; *feijoada*, boiled
black beans cooked with dried beef onto which farofa was poured;
also boiled chicken, fried bananas, almonds, and peanuts, millet
cooked with coconut milk and sugar, hardboiled eggs, *abara, vatapá*,
and very heavily sweetened black coffee are among the items consumed by its worshippers. Many of the dishes are very reminiscent
of their African progenitors because they are considered foods of
the gods. One of the gods (or orishas), Iansa, is the Female Warrior.
Iansa (Matamba is her Angolan name) relishes *acarajé* and she-
goat. Oxossi, Lord of the Forests, protects those who live by hunting. He is quite fond of wild game, black and brown beans with
meat giblets, pigs, roosters, and corn. Then there is Ogun, divinity
of metal, especially iron, who is identified with toolmaking and
weapons. He serves as patron of soldiers, farmers, and smiths and
is very fond of, culinarily speaking, red cockerels and dogs. A rash
of road fatalities several years ago was said to place a temporary
ban on the sale of numerous foods, such as roasted yam and red
palm oil, items sold along city streets. The accidents were blamed
on Ogun's craving for foods that everyone else but he consumed.
Ogun was considered not only the god of war but also the god of
revolution. In more contemporary times in Cuba it has been felt
that the "Batista regime in Cuba . . . should have worried less about
Karl Marx than about Ogun, the rediscovered deity of revolution."
It is this loyalty or cohesion to aspects of the motherland, considered dangerous to colonial rule, that made Candomblé temples in

Brazil mandatorily registered with the police. This rule was revoked only in Bahia in 1976. Much literature dealing with Candomblé, such as Jorge Amado's novel *Jubiaba*, presents Candomblé in such terms as to remove it from the realm of religion altogether, leaving it "a wild emotional manifestation of primitive sensuality and eroticism."

It seems to me that one can get tired of red cockerels and dog. So it is too bad that we cannot make the following two offerings to Ogun. After one bite of either dish, I think he would consider giving up the pooch.

Yam Patties with Chilled "Dressing"

1 large yam or sweet potato, cooked and peeled
1 large carrot, peeled and very thinly grated
Finely minced malagueta chili pepper, to taste, OR 2 "bird" chilies, chopped
¼ tsp. ground ginger
2 Tbs. EACH light cream and light molasses
Salt and freshly ground black pepper, to taste
1 whole green onion, with at least 3 tops included, chopped
Fine bread crumbs
3 Tbs. dendê oil, or butter (about 1½ Tbs. for every 4 or 5 patties)

Combine all ingredients, except bread crumbs and butter. Mix well.

Heat 1½ Tbs. of dendê or butter in skillet over medium heat.

While butter is heating, pour out a small, but thick layer of bread crumbs on a sheet of waxed paper. Place spoonfuls (preferably one at a time) of mixture on bread crumbs, shaping with the spoon into circle or oval patties as you do so. Generously coat top of patty with more crumbs. With spoon or spatula transfer coated patty to hot skillet (you may need to reshape patty at this time). Repeat procedure with 3 or 4 more spoonfuls. Deeply brown patties on both sides. (Using a 9-inch skillet, cook patties in two batches. Wipe out skillet with paper towels between batches) Makes about 9 patties. Serve very hot.

Note: Mixture can be refrigerated and chilled before coating and browning.

ℒℒ ℒℒ ℒℒ ℒℒ

Chilled "Dressing"

1 packed Tbs. cooked yam or sweet potato
3 Tbs. light cream
½ tsp. EACH light molasses and dark rum
A little salt, freshly ground black pepper, and white pepper, to taste
A couple of shakes of ground ginger

Combine all ingredients* and mix until fairly smooth. Chill. Serve as a "dressing" for hot Yam Patties above.

Now for a main dish that is sure to tempt the gods, as well as their subjects.

ℒℒ ℒℒ ℒℒ ℒℒ

Beef Cooked with Rice and Spinach

Two 2½-pound boneless pot roasts
Garlic salt, seasoned salt, black pepper, paprika, and flour
4 Tbs. dendê, or peanut or vegetable oil
2 large red bell peppers, cut in half, then sliced
2 medium onions, cut in half, then sliced
½ tsp. EACH crushed red pepper (or chopped malagueta chili pepper), cinnamon, curry powder, and dried shrimp
¼ heaping tsp. whole cloves, finely crushed
1 tsp. parsley flakes
1 cup beef broth
¼ cup EACH dark rum and orange juice
1 tsp. sugar
Freshly ground black pepper
¾ cup uncooked rice
About 5 ounces chopped spinach
2 Tbs. finely chopped cilantro
½ cup coconut milk
Salt and black pepper, to taste

Season meat on both sides with garlic and seasoned salts, black pepper, and paprika. Coat with flour.

ℒℒ ℒℒ ℒℒ ℒℒ ℒℒ ℒℒ ℒℒ

*Feel free to double ingredients if you desire.

Heat oil in a large pot. Brown meat on both sides. Combine next 14 ingredients. Pour mixture over meat in pot. Bring to a boil, lower heat, and simmer, covered, for about 1½ hours. Transfer meat to a platter. Stir rice, spinach, cilantro, coconut milk, and additional salt and pepper (to taste) into simmering mixture. Return meat to pot. Continue simmering, covered, for another 25–30 minutes. Serve immediately.

Always the victim of this perverse obsession with primitive eroticism and sexuality is the African Brazilian female (in Brazil, the "mulatta" woman is very often specified). In addition to the perception that her place "is in the kitchen," racist stereotyping has universally portrayed her as a loose woman, concubine, prostitute, or "the object of any man's pleasure"; as opposed to intellectual, mother, wife, hard worker, or leader of her community. In more recent days the publication of the life of Carolina Maria de Jesus exemplifies the plight of the African Brazilian woman. Carolina chose not to marry for the same reasons that many Brazilian women, even those who, like Carolina, had children, did not marry. These women realized that they "would have lost too much." Under Catholic law, the female comes under complete authority and control of her husband, and the state, too, for that matter. It is interesting to note that the tenets of Candomblé are in absolute conflict with these beliefs. The African Brazilian female has been characterized as "a danger to established matrimony." As a slave, it was she, according to the most staunch supporters of the sexual exploitation of slave women, who "corrupted the sexual life of Brazilian society by precociously initiating the sons of the [plantation] family into physical love." Despite her condition as slave she has been termed "co-colonizer" of Brazil (along with African men), particularly with reference to the large proportion of the population that is African through miscegenation, and thus had considerable influence over the native Brazilian population. She is, therefore, seen as instigator/partner, not only in her own exploitation, but also in the systematic extermination of indigenous Brazilians. I would define her as a sexual suspect.

In both Cuba and Brazil, the offspring resulting from miscegenation were thought to be a tool to improve the African race, to advance it through whitening. It was, in Cuba as elsewhere, a reflection of the exploitative sexual behavior on the part of white males and the vulnerability and defenselessness of African females. To make the point, Cubans coined the phrase, "There is no sweet tamarind fruit, nor a virgin mulatto girl." Like Brazil, Cuba feigned a relative harmony, a racial democracy, even during the days of slavery, based on accepted European behavior of sexual relations between white males and black females. Today, particularly in Brazil, miscegenation is seen by many as a tool of genocide because it represents the whitening process, a process that makes it possible to deny the African and native Brazilian their contributions to Brazil.

The contributions of indigenous Brazilians and Africans were enormous. In fact, some Brazilian aristocrats could agree on one thing, that "Brazil owed its civilization to Africa" in that "the African provided the leisure for the aristocracy to pursue the arts and to govern." Obviously, only the aristocracy experienced leisure time because the 4 A.M. to 11 P.M. workday for Africans allowed them only short breaks for an early lunch, snacks, coffee, cachaca, and an evening meal. Around these breaks Africans were brutalized and depersonalized through grueling work and harsh treatment. Planters would tell you in a minute that there was nothing wrong with abusing Africans because they were inferior and because they were, after all, "by nature the enemy of all regular work." Africans contributed a great deal to the needs of the country and were considered one of the three pillars on which the physical and cultural life of Brazil stood (sugar and coffee were the other two). They were responsible for Brazilian agricultural and mineral development not only in terms of physical labor but also because their knowledge, experience, and expertise gained in Africa in agricultural methods and in the mining of metals molded a superior quality of life for others.

To be sure, it was a quality of life that they could not, as slaves, share in either Cuba or Brazil. Revolt and resistance were the inevitable consequences. The African female cook, always sexually suspect, took on the task of insurrection in the plantation household. Ground glass or poison stirred into the food of plantation owners was one of the most common forms of rebellion or insurrection in Cuba. Pedro Domech, coffee baron, had his cook and a supposed accomplice shot for allegedly preparing to serve him his very last supper. They never found any poison though. In 1844, six-hundred pounds of arsenic, enough to poison the entire white population, were discovered in the houses of some free Blacks. A bakery that supplied bread to an eight-thousand-man garrison employed all African cooks, who were said to have poisoned the entire supply. The deed was discovered just before the bread was sent to the barracks. Another family had their soup so heavily laced with arsenic that the very first mouthful made one family member quite ill. One arrested and tortured slave confessed that there would be plots to poison whites because poison was "better than war." A rash of poisonings did stir up such fear in plantation households that "in many good houses in this country, people live solely on eggs, which they eat from the shell," instead of eating the Africans' preparations. It was during 1844, or *el Ano del Cuero* (the Year of the Lash), as it is known in Cuba, that so many whispers were heard about blacks planning to poison whites that an attempt was made to give less opportunity for that end. Blacks were whipped mercilessly, most times to death, to gain confessions regarding plots to revolt. So as to not take any chances, whites forbade their employment in drug shops, nor were they allowed to prepare prescriptions of any kind. The prospect of a hot toddy served laced with arsenic also banned the sale of liquor in the countryside.

It almost seems as though fear was invented during the days of slavery. Even in Jamaica, African women were put to death just for the "possibility" that they might intend to poison the slaveholder. With the wide claim of African expertise in the properties of herbs, terror was kept alive and well in the hearts and minds of slaveholders. African women there, too, prepared powdered glass and poisonous herbs for deadly embellishments to late suppers and morning libations.

Well, perhaps one has to go without the evening cocktail and the afternoon cooler. But just try getting along without a nourishing, hot bowl of Rosemary Soup. It is guaranteed to soothe your nerves while exciting your spirits, as long as the person who prepares it is not holding a grudge against you.

❧❧

Puree of Great Northern and Rosemary Soup

3 Tbs. dendê oil
1 Tbs. peanut oil
2 big onions, chopped

1 tsp. dried shrimp
The "needles" from 3 sprigs of fresh rosemary, very finely chopped
6 to 7 sprigs dill, chopped
¼ heaping tsp. EACH dried basil leaves, thyme, and cayenne
1 very heaping tsp. EACH celery seed and parsley flakes
Black pepper, freshly ground, to taste
1 tsp., or more to taste, white pepper
⅓ cup uncooked rice
3½ cups chicken broth
½ cup coconut milk
¼ tsp. paprika
4½ cups cooked Great Northern beans, pureed smooth

Heat both oils in a pot. Add onions. Cook and stir until they become clear. Add next 10 ingredients. Cook and stir for a couple of minutes. Stir in rice and cook and stir for a few minutes more, allowing rice to brown a little. Blend in ³/₄ of the broth, coconut milk, then paprika. Bring to a boil. Lower heat and simmer, covered, for 20 minutes, stirring occasionally. Stir in remaining broth and bean puree. Taste for needed salt and pepper. Bring to a boil over low heat. Simmer for a couple of minutes, stirring often.

Those slaves who did not view successful insurrection merely in terms of poison added to limeade, mango punch, medicine, or a bowl of coconut soup plotted and carried out armed revolts or escaped and formed their own communities. As Carlos Franqui, a one-time member of Fidel Castro's 26th of July movement, wrote, "Revolution in Cuba means burning sugar cane . . ." and coffee groves, and that is exactly what frequently occurred, especially around 1840 in the province of Cardenas. Planters there finally concluded that they could quell the problem by providing better food and specific areas where Africans could raise their own pigs and livestock. Uprisings had also occurred in 1798 and 1799, and many more were recorded in the period between 1813 and 1839. Throughout Cuban colonial history there were those who escaped and formed *cimarrone* or "maroon communities" called *palenques*. Palenques were communities usually consisting of seven or more runaways; however, some had hundreds of members, while one or two had more than a thousand. The authorities viewed these villages as a threat to planter communities because they were said to be friends of and worked with the buccaneers, pirates, and freebooters who roamed the Caribbean, all enemies of Spain. This may account for palenque inhabitants having been defined as highway robbers, makers of mutinies, seditions, and rebellions. The city of Havana used much of its resources and money for expeditions against the palenques, as well as erecting a prison to house those recaptured. Women and men, shackled and tagged around the neck, could be seen "breaking rock" on a chain gang team, as recaptured cimarrones or runaways were put to work in Havana.

Runaway slaves had very often been former members of African Cuban brotherhoods called *cabildos*. One such cabildo, Lucumi Eyo, rose up in revolt just outside the city of Havana. Cabildos began in sixteenth-century Cuba (they were said to be very much like Moorish societies in sixteenth-century Seville) and served as an instrument of cohesion for members of the various African societies imported into Cuba through the slave trade. They calmed rivalries between ethnic groups by supporting their differences. They eased communication between Africans and Spaniards and helped to acclimate newly enslaved Africans to their current station in life. Free and slave joined cabildos, each one usually consisting of people of similar ancestry. Food preparation for members and for the worship of their deities was often an expression of similar ancestry. The orishas were kept spiritually alive and well, fed with their favorite foods in Cuba. Olokun, said to be an androgynous deity and "the owner of the ocean," represents symbols of prosperity, happiness, and fertility. Doves, coconuts, white fowl, and goats, Olokun's culinary preferences, were the main ingredients in many dishes consumed during cabildo religious celebrations. Cabildos were essentially the key to the survival of Yoruba religion in Cuba, thus becoming a shelter for African ways of life and for the supervision of the spiritual and social needs of the African Cuban community. Such needs were expressed and celebrated as communal reaffirmation of their African past during the many festival days, particularly January 6th, which coincided with traditional African celebrations of the winter solstice. During such celebrations, crabmeat and eggplant stews, grilled meats lathered with fruit sauces, pancakes pouting with shrimp or chicken, and fresh green bean salads lying in wait under papaya or cilantro salad dressing were main features. Known to strengthen differences between African Cuban and Hispanic Cuban cultures, cabildos were housed in the "colored" section of town with branches that had arms stretching to plantations, to Africans in slavery, who nevertheless kept the orishas happy with culinary offerings.

Many of those offerings were in the form of fresh fruits and vegetables. Prepare both of these for delicious alternative side dishes.

⁘⁘⁘⁘⁘⁘⁘⁘⁘⁘⁘⁘⁘⁘⁘⁘⁘⁘⁘⁘⁘⁘⁘⁘⁘⁘⁘⁘⁘⁘⁘⁘⁘⁘⁘

Green Bean Salad

Salad:
2 cups cooked, cut up green beans
Approximately 2 Tbs. grated carrots
1 whole green onion, chopped (white and green parts)
¼ to ⅓ cup finely chopped red onion
¼ of a medium-large red bell pepper, chopped
Minced malagueta chili pepper, to taste
¾ tsp. sesame seed

Dressing:
2 tsp. EACH lemon juice and dendê (palm oil) OR peanut OR vegetable oil
4 tsp. "Hot Shot" (see recipe to follow)
½ rounded tsp. sugar
¼ tsp. ground ginger
Salt and freshly ground black pepper
Chopped cilantro (coriander)

Toss green beans with remaining salad ingredients.

For dressing, mix all ingredients together, blending well. Pour over green bean mixture, folding and turning to thoroughly coat beans. Taste for needed salt and pepper. Serve hot or cold, garnished with chopped cilantro.

And now, for that hot time you have all been searching for:

§§ §§ §§ §§

Molho de Pimenta ("Hot Shot")

1½ cups dark rum or sherry
8 bird or 4 jalapeño chili peppers, each slit down the front, lengthwise, and 4–5 slits across (do not cut through to other side)
6 whole cloves
½ inch of cinnamon stick (preferably canela), broken up

Combine all ingredients in a closed, glass container and store for 7 days. Shake container occasionally and before each use. Sprinkle on vegetables and meats. Add to soups, stews, and sauces.

§§ §§ §§ §§

Baked Eggplant

¼ cup plus 1 Tbs. coconut milk
¼ cup light cream
⅛ tsp. ground cinnamon
¼ tsp. EACH salt and crushed red pepper flakes
Freshly ground black pepper, to taste
¾ tsp. cassava flour
½ tsp. sugar
7 allspice berries, finely crushed
1 Tbs. melted butter or dendê (palm oil)
1 small eggplant, peeled and sliced into rounds
1 whole green onion, chopped
1 slice bread, finely crumbed

In a large bowl combine all ingredients except eggplant, onions, and bread. Blend well. Add eggplant slices to mixture. Fold and turn to thoroughly coat eggplant. Transfer coated eggplant to a shallow baking dish, arranging slices so that they slightly overlap one another. Combine onions and bread crumbs. Mix well. Sprinkle over eggplant.

Bake, covered, in a preheated 350 degree oven for about 25–30 minutes.

The Catholic Church did not intend to help keep the orishas alive and well fed, nor did it engage in protecting the rights of slaves or free Africans or "coloreds"; however, the cabildos of Cuba were believed to have drawn less repression from the Catholic Church than that heaped upon African religious groups in Brazil. In African based Candomblé, it is believed that individual power resides in one's own head. Orishas or deities help individuals overcome daily problems but by "serving the head," by worshipping one's own head by ritual anointing with coconut, coconut milk, white or red kolanuts, and blood from a pigeon or hen, one's head will curse or bless one's actions. This ceremony was performed annually during the Benin society's Igue Festival. The sacrificed hens were generally cooked the day after the ritual and all participants would share in eating the meat. The constant attack on this and other aspects of African culture by secular and religious authorities, as well as the savage conditions of slavery, inspired many revolts in Brazil as well. One of the reasons for the consistent repression of Candomblé was that African religious communities were often sources of growth and mediums for the development of resistance. Many revolts were led by the Nigerian Hausas. As adherents to Islam, they united with the Yoruba in a "Muslim revolt" in 1809. With a common African culture, language, and religion, the incentive to organize and revolt was ever present. Another such uprising, in 1835, was composed of rebels who could read and write in what were thought to be characters "like the Arabic." The community-based ethics of African culture were constantly setting revolutionary struggles in motion. These rebellions, whether in Brazil, Cuba, Puerto Rico, Guyana, or Jamaica, challenged the world economic order. Entire countries were dependent upon the African as slave for that order to be maintained and could not tolerate maroon communities. One community-based African tradition was the recognized position of women in their society, which the maroons reproduced in their rebel environment. Women played very important roles in the lives of bush rebels; one such role was the production of crops, providing the sustenance of life through intense agricultural activity. While the men fought off attackers and hunted meat and game in the woods, women sowed the seeds and cultivated the same crops available to them in the plots of land allotted to them on plantations.

One Jamaican guerrilla warrior, Juan Lubola, was the leader of a maroon group that shared two hundred acres of cultivated crops near his headquarters at Lluidas Vale. It was reported to be the largest food supply in Jamaica during the early years of England's invasion. Lubola turned over his army and food supply to the English in 1660, enabling them to completely overpower the Spanish. In 1732, Nanny Town was captured in the Blue Mountains in Jamaica, but the rebels "great plantain walk" was spared destruction. Maroon females had warned that they *would* recapture their town and their crops, because, according to them, "it was better to be killed by the hands of the white man than die in the woods for want of provisions."

Provisions were often plentiful in Nanny Town, which was named after Nanny, an Ashanti chieftainess, who was considered to be one of the most outstanding "New World" civic and military leaders and the first national heroine of the Jamaican people. Nanny survived the end of the first Maroon War in 1740 and received a grant of five-hundred acres of land from the government of Jamaica. Plantains grown on this land often became irresistible morsels in the hands of the women of Nanny Town. The versatile plantain, whether roasted plain, made into a casserole, appetizer (such as Puerto Rican *mofongo*), sauteed or baked in butter, or combined with milk to produce creamy puddings, is as much a favorite side dish and dessert menu item in the Caribbean islands now as it was in Nanny Town.

Baked Plantains in Cream

2 ripe plantains, peeled and sliced into rounds
2 Tbs. butter, melted, or dendê
1 cup coconut milk
2 Tbs. dark sherry
1/8 tsp. EACH whole cloves (finely ground), cinnamon, and nutmeg
1/4 cup sugar
1/3 cup (slightly packed) finely grated coconut
1 1/2 tsp. cassava flour
Additional coconut and coconut milk (optional)

Arrange plantains in a baking dish.

Combine butter with next 8 ingredients, blending well. Pour mixture over plantains. Cover and bake in a preheated 350 degree oven for 20 minutes. Serve warm in parfait glasses or bowls garnished with additional coconut and coconut milk.

❦❦❦

Quilombos, as maroon societies were called in Brazil, tended to be the creation of African-born blacks. The social organization prevalent in quilombos most resembled that of African states at that time. Palmares, the most famous quilombo, was established in 1631 by Africans who escaped from various plantations. They chose a leader and set up a *republica*, based on a political system derived from several African models, in the interior of Alagoas. The settlement assumed an almost socialist way of life. The inhabitants made a genuine attempt to be independent as they brought to Palmares their expertise in agricultural activities. Their agricultural techniques were forerunners of diversification of crops, in contrast to the predominant monoculture of white planters. They combined the proceeds of their work in clearing land, setting up ranches, mills, and a marketplace, and in the distribution of food supplies among the inhabitants. Africans of Palmares, or, Blacks of the Palm Forests (most of the forest had actually been cut down by the time the republic was established), became settled cultivators like the black Seminoles and produced fruits, maize and other vegetables, which they stored in community granaries; domesticated animals; and engaged in fishing and hunting. Many became traders in gold and animal skins, others became artisans and blacksmiths.

Palmares also carried the reputation of being the first state to rise up against plantations. They raided Portuguese and Dutch homes and plantations for food and other supplies in order to sustain their capital, a fortified stronghold in a palm grove. As the population of Palmares grew, several Brazilian districts combined the resources of the plantation owners and the authorities to carry out countless attacks against the African "state." After seventy-six years of existence, Palmares was finally taken. Many Africans committed suicide rather than allow themselves to return as slaves.

The willingness of Africans to die for freedom was the single greatest fear of the planters. Revolution in Saint Domingue (Haiti) had "Africanized," in the most absolute terms, one country in the Caribbean. The Portuguese and Spanish in Brazil and Cuba, mindful that their countries' culinary, economic, and cultural development had been attained in the same manner as that of the French in Haiti, were fearful of the possibility of this same Africanization by slave revolution. It was for this reason that Brazil put out a call to Europe, began a program, you might say, for European immigration. This was a very serious issue because the purpose was to de-Africanize the country in every way imaginable. Just how serious can be measured by the fact that between 1808 and 1822 Rio de Janeiro alone imported seventeen French cooks and ten French bakers. In 1850, it was noted that the upper classes of Bahia and Pernambuco had modified their cuisine, serving fewer stews, bean and pork dishes, and the clincher—less pepper. I think they were serious.

De-Africanization of Brazilian cuisine attempted to take root in nineteenth-century cities in shops serving ice cream, cakes, cookies, shrimp patties, spongecakes, and Italian and French sweetmeats. However, if the truth be told, France, having by this time absorbed the knowledge of their African cooks in Haiti, could in no way help de-Africanize anybody's cuisine. The only thing the French could do was to help reintroduce it. While food prepared by Europeans for Europeans was being heralded as high brow and prestigious, the fact remained that the prestige of the African cooks of the "Big Houses" remained unchallenged and near-sacred. Advertisements continued to run in nineteenth-century newspapers, calling for black cooks:

> A very young slave girl, with a beautiful figure is for sale. She knows how to cook and starch and iron clothes. She is a perfect dressmaker, ideal for any seamstress . . .

What also remained unchallenged were the sought-after foods of the African street vendors. The culinary street vendor of Bahia, Recife, Rio de Janeiro, and Minas Gerais, in her Muslim-influenced African clothes, sold rice puddings and *alua*, a refreshing drink made in northern areas of rice flour or toasted corn with water and fermented with sugar in clay vessels. In Minas Gerais, it was made in the same manner and included pineapple rind. On Recife streets she sold fish delicacies, such as crab fritters, and meats cooked in brown gravies. Urban slaves, who had earned money on their own, could visit the markets and purchase the flavorful and inexpensive dishes cooked and sold by other Africans. Sweets, vegetables, candies, cakes, bread, and fruits were carried on these vendors heads or displayed in kiosks. The Bahian street vendor, or Baiana, offered the favorite dishes of the orixa (orishas), the Yoruba gods.

One of those favorite dishes is *Caruru*, reported to be one of the oldest African dishes still prepared in Brazil. The dish was a long way from its Nigerian homeland when the Portuguese began to sing its praises in the 1600s. Made with a variety of native African ingredients, numerous Brazilian versions have emerged; however, most, if not all, remain true to the essentials: okra, dried fish or shrimp, dendê oil, peanuts, and hot pepper.

The Baiana offered beans in various forms. For cakes and fritters, beans were grated, then mixed with onions, malagueta peppers, ground nuts, coconut, and coconut milk, then deep fried in dendê (palm) oil. The following bean concoction is a dessert made with African favorites: coconut, beans, and cassava, a favored combination among Africans in Brazil as well. Black Muslims in contemporary America showcase a version of this dessert in their eateries in Chicago and New York. Preparing a pie crust for the filling I offer below is not essential, as it bakes nicely alone in a buttered pie plate, spring form pan, or other baking dish. In this case, however, I found the combination of pie crust with the richly flavored ingredients irresistible, not to mention elegant. I know you will, too.

Pudim de Feijao (Bean Pudding Pie)

One 9-inch unbaked pie crust
1½ cups Great Northern beans, creamed (pureed smooth)
½ cup cooked and pureed cassava (yuca) (see glossary)
¼ cup plus 2 Tbs. coconut milk
½ cup dark brown sugar
½ cup plus 4 Tbs. white sugar
1 egg
4 Tbs. melted butter
¼ cup dark rum or sherry

2 Tbs. gari (cassava flour) (see glossary)
1 tsp. salt
2¼ tsp. vanilla extract
1¼ tsp. coconut extract
½ cup slightly packed, finely grated coconut
5 Tbs. chopped walnuts or pecans

Fit pie crust into a 9-inch, deep dish pie plate. Prick bottom of crust all over with fork tines.

Combine remaining ingredients, except nuts. Blend well by beating with an electric mixer on medium speed for a few minutes. Scrape down sides of bowl and continue beating for another couple of minutes. Pour filling into crust. Garnish filling with chopped nuts. Bake in a preheated 350 degree oven for 50 minutes. Cool completely before cutting.

The lyrics to Ary Barroso's "No Tabuleiro da Baiana" ("On the Baiana's Tray") are part of a song recorded in 1936 by Carmen Miranda. The lyrics praise the seductive power of some of the Baiana's trademark foods, such as vatapá, caruru, and *mungunza*; and as Zeca Ligiero points out in his article, "Candomblé Is Religion Life-Art," the lyrics associate African Brazilian religion, Candomblé, with deception and danger. Ligiero states that "African elements are absorbed, but their origins are stigmatized."

Without question, there is always stigma attached to African religion. It is just as clear, however, that in the case of this song it is the African female who is stigmatized. It is the African female who is stereotyped, down to her chicken stew and dendê oil, as a seductress and loose woman. According to the lyrics, the Baiana has filled her tray with enticing foods that she also offers to her gods, gods who will answer her prayers by giving her "Massa's love." The Baiana knows she will not be the recipient of true love; the only true love is saved for "Missy." *She and her culinary goods* are the objects of temporary pleasure, to be later forgotten by those who have sampled her. Sexual suspect personified.

Fish patties, sweets, vegetables, cakes, bread, and fruits, you see, were not the only commodities displayed by urban slaves on city streets. European mistresses suffered no slack in their coffers nor degradation of their virtue as long as they could exploit the African female street vendor and the African female streetwalker. Forcing these women into both occupations (sometimes they had to perform double duty), white mistresses and masters alike always pocketed their earnings, minus a small percentage; however, in numerous cases, the money made by these women was the sole income of the master or mistress of the household. Portuguese culture in Brazil, often intertwining the concepts of food and sex, can be seen in Brazilian fathers giving their sons, who are old enough "to know a woman," "money to buy a cake," meaning, they are acquainting them with "cake" other than that made of corn or flour.

Those that *were* made of corn or flour received top billing from the street vendor. The sounds of the "traywoman," the Baiana, vending her African delicacies, echo the cries from the cane fields and coffee groves, and very eloquently express the neverending sweat and labor of African women stirring pots in their own meager huts after toiling all day in plantation big house kitchens. The heart of Brazilian cuisine and culture rests on such toil. It is, after all, a cuisine and culture that "has its body in America and its soul in Africa."

> At ten o'clock at night
> In the lonesome street
> A black woman hawks
> Sounding this lament
>   Ee-Eh abara!
>   Here is abara!
> In her bowl
> There is fragrant sauce,
> Spices of Africa,
>   And acaraje!
>   O acaraje eco olalai o!
> Come, see for yourselves, it is piping-hot!
> All the world loves acaraje!
> All the world loves acaraje!
> But the trouble it takes to make!
> All the world loves abara!

But no one cares to know the trouble it takes!
At ten o'clock at night
In the lonesome street
The farther off the sound
The sadder its lament.
O acaraje eco olalai o!

(Song, translated from the Portuguese of Dorival Caymmi.
Cited in Ruth Landes, *The City of Women.*
[Albuquerque: University of New Mexico Press;
Macmillan Company, 1947], 111–112.)

The number of African females increased in urban areas (their number exceeded those still residing on plantations) after 1850 in Brazil, and a great many found employment as cooks. African females continued to work as cooks in Brazilian kitchens well beyond abolition in 1888. Their ability to create festive feasts from ordinary fare increased the value of these cooks in Brazil, Cuba, and the rest of the Caribbean, and in the colonies of the southern United States. The presence of African cooks on these plantations and in urban areas generated riches not merely in monetary terms, but also with regard to the diverse cuisine these cooks provided. That diversity was partly due to Africa's age, which has allowed it to be the home of numerous culinary "firsts."

Africans' culinary contributions took numerous geographical twists and turns as it journeyed to different colonies in the Americas. Part of that journey made several stops in the islands of the Caribbean and in the southern colonies and along the eastern seaboard of the United States. The plantation kitchens of the Caribbean and of the United States of America were turned into stages where Africans in bondage gave more performances than there were seats in the theater; stages where each new act outshone the last; stages that were set with unforgettable sights, sounds, smells, and tastes.

Without Rival, Anywhere

§§ §§ §§ §§

The Cultural Impact of the African Cook
in the Americas

African hands would make sugarcane and cotton king and white mistresses in every colony queens at their dinner tables. Without the African as slave, colonies in the so-called New World could not have survived. Neither would the colonists have dined so well. African cooks enhanced the culinary worlds of the French, British, Spanish, and Portuguese colonials. By as early as 1540, ten thousand Africans were shipped annually to the "New World," bringing with them the varied cuisines and culinary styles of West, Southwest and Central Africa. During the early stages of development in mainland America, these culinary styles would evolve from becoming permanent fixtures in colonial taverns and on battlefields during the Revolutionary War to turning southern plantations into the culinary heart of America and controlling the city of Philadelphia through its stomach. African cuisines would also take precedence in the Caribbean and help make Saint Domingue (Haiti) the jewel of the French colonies.

Before France obtained its economic salvation by way of Haitian slave labor, Haiti was visited by Christopher Columbus in his unrelenting search for gold and riches. As soon as he and his party arrived, they forceably took control of the island and renamed it Hispaniola. The Spanish produced artificial famine by deliberately destroying crops to starve out those natives who offered resistance.

After reducing the native population from roughly a million to 60,000 in fifteen years, the colonizers found it necessary to import laborers from elsewhere. Slavery was their answer. It was Bartolome de las Casas, a Catholic bishop, who proposed in 1517 that Africans be imported to replace the natives. After all, the Church never questioned the validity or immorality of enslaving Africans, especially since the Church itself was a large-scale slave owner. The king of Spain soon had four-thousand Africans imported annually into Hispaniola, Jamaica, and Cuba.

The Spanish, French, and British slaughtered one another for years on the island of Tortuga over possession of the Caribbean islands. By 1659, Tortuga was inhabited by fortune seekers, escaped galley slaves, debtors unable to pay bills, and fugitives from justice guilty of all sorts of crimes. Consequently, the French, now in control of the island, moved their headquarters to Haiti, which they renamed Saint Domingue, and established a colony there. Cocoa, indigo, cotton, and sugarcane were cultivated on the island, and, in order to continue to reap profits from these crops, more laborers were needed. The importation of Africans, therefore, was increased by thousands every year.

The continuous influx of Africans into the islands of the West Indies required overseers to impose a system of "breaking in," or "seasoning," the newly arrived Africans. As many as thirty percent of the arrivals would die within the seasoning period of three to four years. Constant whippings and lack of sufficient food caused Africans to refuse to work. A famous investigation in the 1790s revealed that Africans in slavery on the island of Barbados were issued nine pints of corn and one pound of salt meat per week; they were reportedly better fed than those on other islands. Africans who would not submit to slavery escaped and hid out in the mountains and formed their own groups, called maroons. By 1751 there were an estimated three-thousand maroons. A creative diet rich in fruits and vegetables greatly contributed to their survival. They also thrived on beans, meats, and fish, which they sometimes obtained by raiding plantations.

Now for you urban warriors, whose fights are settled in the boardroom or the classroom, only a great big helping of a satiating dish of beans will do. But do not stop there. Ladle these spiced legumes over slices of marinated and broiled shoulder steak. Please note: If heads did not roll during your earlier disputes, there are four below that might substitute.

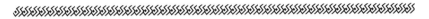

Maroon Four Fish Head Stew

2 cups black beans, OR 1 cup EACH kidney and Great Northern
About 2½ pounds chuck shoulder steak (London broil)
1 cup of beer
1 Tbs. molasses
½ tsp. EACH salt and ginger
1 Tbs. Worcestershire sauce
3 Tbs. rendered pork fat
1 onion, chopped
2 tomatoes, chopped
3 small red "bird" chili peppers, stems removed and finely chopped
¼ tsp. nutmeg
Salt and freshly ground black pepper, to taste
½ tsp. EACH parsley flakes and celery seed
4 fish heads
¼ ounce (half of a package) dion-dion (also spelled djon-djon), which are dried black mushrooms
1 cup uncooked rice
2 sprigs of cilantro, finely chopped

Wash beans. Place beans in a pot. Add enough water to cover by about 4–6 inches. Cover and allow to soak overnight.

Place steak in glass or steel dish. Combine beer, molasses, salt, ginger, and Worcestershire sauce. Mix well and pour over steak. Allow to soak for 4–6 hours or overnight in refrigerator. Steak should be turned several times during process.

Drain beans. Add enough fresh water to cover beans. Add next 9 ingredients. Mix well. Add heads and more water to cover. Bring to a boil. Lower heat and simmer, covered, for about 2 hours, adding water as needed.

While beans are cooking remove steak from marinade and broil or bake steak until tender (about 1¾ hours). Stir remaining marinade into simmering beans.

While steak is broiling and beans are simmering, add dion-dion to 2 cups boiling water. Simmer for 8 to 10 minutes. Strain and discard mushroom residue. Bring mushroom liquid and enough water to make 2¼ cups to a boil. Add 1 cup of rice. Simmer, covered, on low heat, 20 minutes.

When beans are soft, discard heads. Stir in cilantro. Taste beans for needed salt and pepper. Serve over slices of steak and a pile of rice.

Note: Fish heads can be simmered with beans for a while, then removed, prior to adding remaining ingredients.

Maroon settlements, composed of the Akan, Yoruba, Herero, and other African societies, were no longer growing fruits and vegetables on the sacred soils of their homeland. Nor were they preparing foods using the iron utensils and cooking pots for steaming, stewing, and frying the variety of foods that had been available to them in Africa. They refused to be cut off, however, from their religious beliefs, which extolled the link between religion and all life, including plant and animal life. Sheep, goats, and cattle were still used for religious ceremonies. Cattle were eaten by the Herero only when offered as a religious sacrifice.

As you will see, if there is a sacrifice you must make, it will not be in taste; nor will you have to follow the religious codes of the Herero by waiting for a special occasion before preparing this delicious dish.

Beef Baked with Papaya and Citrus Juices

¼ cup EACH lemon, lime, and orange juice
3 tsp. brown sugar
¼ tsp. crushed red pepper
Freshly ground black pepper and a little salt
About a 4 pound pot roast
Parsley flakes, paprika, and flour
2 Tbs. dendê (see glossary) or peanut oil

1 tsp. EACH garlic salt, brown sugar, and parsley flakes
Lots of black pepper and salt
3 to 4 "bird" chili peppers
4 Tbs. dark rum
4 to 6 tsp. cassava flour
½ tsp. finely chopped ginger
¾ of a papaya, peeled, seeded, and chopped
1 EACH large tomato and large onion, both chopped
2 sprigs of chopped coriander

Combine juices, sugar, salt, and chili pepper. Place beef in glass dish or bowl. Pour juice mixture over meat. Let beef soak for 5½ to 6 hours, turning a few times.

Reserving marinade, season meat with parsley flakes and paprika. Coat both sides with flour. Heat oil and quickly brown meat on both sides. Transfer meat to baking pan.

Combine remaining ingredients, except onion and coriander. Mix well. Place onion rings all around meat in the pan, and on top of meat. Pour mixture ALL AROUND meat, AVOIDING TOP OF MEAT. Cover with aluminum foil. Bake in preheated, 350 degree oven for 1½ hours, or until meat is tender. Stir coriander into sauce and serve.

The increase in maroon population was understandable when you consider that the murder of Africans, cooks or otherwise, carried no consequence in Haiti. The European opinion of "property" dictated that the torture, mutilation, or murder of a slave could always be justified. The colonialists considered Africa's West Coast "a good mother," a land that to them offered an unending supply of slave labor for the fields and the kitchen.

Enslaved Africans were always the ones who were planning the meals and doing the cooking. The kitchen was the center of much activity, or, better stated, much creativity. With such an abundance of fresh ingredients to work with such as the *carambola* (star fruit) and *cherimoyas* (custard apples), red snapper and conch, callaloo (dasheen or taro leaves) and *chayote*, colonialists enjoyed sumptuous repasts at every meal, day in and day out. Sweet potatoes were seasoned with ginger and cloves and served with roasted lamb; rice was simmered with the juice of oranges or sometimes dried black mushrooms (*djon-djon*) and presented with shrimp cakes. Tonight, why not present Baked Red Snapper Dressed in Capers and Cream. It is not necessary to wait for a balmy, tropical evening to indulge in such a tropics-oriented dish. Just make sure that the fish is fresh. This flavorful taste combination is enough, all by itself, to whisk you away to paradise.

Baked Red Snapper Dressed in Capers and Cream

Two 1-pound red snapper fillets (try to get "tail" fillets; the central bones can be easily removed by your seafood market)
Garlic salt (mixed with parsley), seasoned salt, and black pepper
2 tsp. lime juice
4 Tbs. "Hot Shot" (see index)
1 cup coconut milk
1/2 cup light cream
1/4 tsp. cinnamon
1 tsp. sugar
Freshly ground black pepper and salt
2 Tbs. EACH vegetable oil and butter
2 small onions, chopped
1 small red bell pepper, chopped
2 ROUNDED Tbs. capers
1 1/2 tsp. cassava flour

Place both snapper fillets one layer deep in a large baking pan (do not allow them to overlap one another). Season fillets with a little garlic salt, seasoned salt, and black pepper. Cover with foil. Bake in preheated 375 degree oven for about 30 minutes.

While fillets are baking, combine next 8 ingredients in a bowl. Mix well.

Combine oil and butter in a skillet over medium heat. When butter melts, add next 3 ingredients. Add a little salt and pepper. Cook and stir until onion lightly browns. Stir coconut milk/cream mixture into skillet and blend well. Taste for needed salt and pepper. Sprinkle cassava flour over mixture. Stir in to thoroughly blend.

Simmer over medium-low heat, stirring frequently, for a few minutes until sauce thickens. Transfer fillets to a serving platter. Cover fillets with sauce and serve immediately.

᯽᯽

Half of the 250,000 Africans in the Caribbean's French colonies were cooking, cleaning, and raising sugarcane in Haiti's cesspool by 1740. Haiti was also by this time the premier island, the jewel of the Caribbean. Not only was it the colony producing the most sugar, as well as being on its way to becoming the world's largest producer of coffee, it was also dazzling its colonists with a fabulous array of fruits. While the French in Europe were experiencing the wonders of coffee, dark and hot, French planters in Haiti were getting used to a host of interesting drinks such as rums and orange liqueurs, tropical preparations made with sorrel leaves, star apples, soursop, coconut milk, or pineapple. And if that was not enough, many a planter's fancy was delighted by sweet preserves or jellies made with green coconuts, guava (which is botanically related to the clove), or papaya; light desserts made with star apples, mangoes, or plantains, all laced with vanilla and cinnamon. By the late 1780s the island now held the largest slave population (460,000, which, again, was almost half of the one million in the Caribbean colonies) and planters there were recognized as the most efficient and productive sugar producers in the world; meaning, slave labor in the kitchen and in the fields had catapulted French culinary society and the economy to unparalleled heights. Exports from Haiti represented two-thirds of the total value of all exports from the Caribbean's French colonies and by itself exceeded the combined exports from the Caribbean's British and Spanish colonies. More than six hundred ships per year left Haitian ports, carrying a number of agricultural goods, such as sugar, coffee, cacao, indigo, and cotton to European cities.

Some of these same foods bound for European consumers were sharply curtailed from the French-controlled islands of Martinique and Guadeloupe during the 1790s. The Haitian Revolution created such unrest during this period that total production was dramatically reduced. However, food preparation on the islands continued to showcase staple ingredients common to all islands of the Caribbean. Crushed, hot peppers, lime juice (which performed double duty as a marinade for seafood), tomatoes, and onions were turned into sauces and garnishes for seafood and poultry.

Seafood, as one might expect, suffered no neglect in African hands in the English colonies of the Bahamas and Barbados. Conch, a Bahamas favorite, was ground and added to peppery batter and deep fried to produce fritters, or sauteed with herbs and spices and simmered with rice to yield a stew. Conch salad, made with pineapple chunks and chopped sweet red and green peppers, made a succulent gastronomic statement that no hungry diner was willing to suppress. Lobster and crabmeat, seasoned with nutmeg and various peppers, could be found swimming in a sea of rum-laced coconut milk soups duty-bound for lunch or dinner in Barbados. The most densely populated region in the Americas by the end of the seventeenth century, Barbados reigned supreme in the preparation of such dishes as *callaloo*, a very spicy stew combining crab, callaloo (a green leafy vegetable), okra and, sometimes salt pork. The island had at this time an African population of 50,000, and by way of its slave labor could boast its position as England's wealthiest colony. Part of that wealth was realized in the cultivation of transplanted African crops, which European planters wasted no time in adopting to their own palates. Sorghum (also called guinea corn), an African grain, had become the major staple in Barbados before the end of the seventeenth century. In addition, okra and other vegetables of African origin were regularly consumed by the island's population.

Jamaica replaced Barbados in the 1730s as a major sugar producer, supplying wealth for English dinner tables and English pockets. More than 3,600 Africans per year began arriving in the island in the 1680s. By the 1740s, the average plantation acreage was over two hundred with close to one hundred African laborers. Cassava, banana, and coconut breads studded with minced dried fruits, baked papayas filled with gingered beef and hot peppers, along with chicken and small game dishes dusted with Jamaica pepper (allspice), served as sustenance to plantation households. During the last quarter of the eighteenth century, the slave population was well over 167,000, giving the average estate 204 laborers. The domestic segment of this labor force was successful in breathing new culinary life into the drab dishes of the English.

When my husband and I were vacationing in Ocho Rios at the Jamaica Hilton Hotel we took delight in one of the chef's daily specials, which was called "Stop the Bus Chicken." Browned first in oil, then roasted, it was topped with a very spicy sauce and garnished with *benne* (sesame) seeds. According to our server, the dish received its name as the result of an incident that had occurred on a bus traveling from Ocho Rios to Montego Bay. It seems that a gentleman had purchased some barbecued chicken from a local street vendor in Ocho Rios before boarding. The cook had a penchant for preparing her grilled and roasted meats with fiery hot seasonings and sauces which the gentleman apparently had never before sampled. Unfortunately, his desire to experiment with local cuisine on the day of the bus trip was ill timed, because when the bus was about half way to Montego Bay he jumped from his seat screaming, "Stop the bus! Stop the bus! Stop the bus!" Snatching a newspaper from the hands of another passenger, he made his way to the front of the bus. He shouted at the driver to stop and let him off. The driver pulled off the road, the man got off and ran toward the bushes. The driver was understanding, so he waited. When the man came out of the bushes and returned to the bus, he apologized to everyone, extending his hand to the driver and to the passenger whose paper he had taken. Everyone smiled and expressed their concern, but it was noticeable that neither person whom he extended his hand toward extended theirs back.

Anyway, I am prepared to titillate you with the following. Add excitement to any roasted or grilled meat with "Stop the Bus Sauce." Do not worry about having to make any sudden stops along the road, although the taste is sensational and well worth the risk. I have tempered the required amount of pepper for those who are less adventurous. However, for persons whose temperatures fluctuate, my advice is, "Season to taste."

Stop the Bus Sauce

2 Tbs. mora (Andean blackberry) pulp (Available frozen in 14 ounce packages in larger and specialty grocery stores)
1 Tbs. light brown sugar
1 Tbs. plus 1 tsp. dark rum
1/2 tsp. lime juice
1/3 cup mashed mango
1/4 tsp. EACH ground ginger and crushed red pepper

$1/8$ tsp. "hot, Mexican style" chili powder
2 allspice berries, very finely crushed
1 small, finely chopped jalapeño chili pepper, stem and seeds removed
(optional)
$1/2$ cup beef broth
Freshly ground black pepper and a little salt, to taste
1 tsp. arrowroot

Combine all ingredients, except 1 tsp. rum. Simmer on low heat for 3 minutes. Add remaining rum. Simmer for 1 minute more.

Pour sauce into a gravy bowl or sauceboat and serve with poultry or game, or spoon over grilled or roasted meats 15 to 20 minutes before end of cooking time.

A new culinary life would eventually rule the island of Puerto Rico. There had been only a few Africans brought onto the island of Puerto Rico after its initial conquest in the sixteenth century. Arawakan slave labor was used at this time to mine gold. Twenty years after the revolution in Haiti, Puerto Rico became a new center of sugar production, more than doubling its sugar output from 1791 to 1805 to meet the demands of an expanding market and rising prices. Its plantation system differed somewhat from the rest of the Caribbean. The average size of each farm was about sixty acres and slave labor in the fields was supplemented with free wage labor. As small as these haciendas were compared to other Caribbean plantations, productivity was high. The slave population continued to expand, as new laborers were brought in, and by 1834, 42,000 Africans were in bondage there. That African presence is evident in such steamed concoctions as *pasteles*, a plantain leaf enveloping a mixture of pumpkin, mashed plantains, green bananas, and beef, pork, or chicken; and *sofrito*, a basic sauce loaded with onions, tomatoes, peppers, herbs, spices, and meat. One of the common characteristics of sofrito is the use of achiote, or annatto seeds, to give the sauce its red-orange color. By the late 1800s Puerto Rico had begun to produce a cane-based rum, which added tantalizing flavors to main dish chicken and beef recipes, puddings made from *sapodillas* (naseberries) and mammey and flan type desserts, such as *tembleque*, as well as sauces.

A viable African presence was quite evident on the small, beautiful, and fertile eastern Caribbean island of St. Vincent. The natives, sometimes referred to as Island Caribs and who were said to have had roots in Africa because of their dark skin, shared St. Vincent with numerous runaway slaves from other islands, many of whom intermarried with the natives. Runaway slaves came to be known as the Black Caribs of St. Vincent and together with their native hosts divided their agricultural and domestic duties between the women, who tended the fields and gardens and collected shellfish near the shores, and the men, who cleared the land and hunted and fished. Fishing was usually carried out with lines and nets made of silkgrass; however, the Black Caribs added the use of pineapple leaves for this purpose. A well-strung net determined the destination of the catch of the day. On many occasions it was seafood pepper pot, a stew that was kept simmering for hours and hours with fish heads, hot peppers, leafy greens, herbs, onions, and spices. Near the end of the desired cooking time, the heads are removed and chunks of fish and more leafy greens were added.

In addition to making sure that hearth and home were well endowed with marine life, Island and Black Carib men also performed technical household and agricultural duties such as making basketry items and special equipment needed to extract poisonous juice from bitter manioc (cassava) to process it for consumption. Bitter manioc contains prussic acid in its juices. Cooking can remove it, however, the root contains so great a quantity that if it is eaten raw or improperly cooked, it could kill you. The other variety, sweet manioc, tastes very similar to the white potato when boiled and can be used in much the same way. Usually, it was seasoned with salt, pepper, and lime juice and served with various meats. Made into bread, it was the mainstay of Caribbean peoples.

The following dessert exemplifies the variety of island sweet treats. Made with cassava (the sweet variety, of course), white yam *(ñame)*, and three different fruits, this rich pudding, with its intriguing flavors, promises to take its place among your most favored finales.

Cassava Cream Pudding

2 cups cooked and mashed cassava (see glossary)
³/₄ cup cooked and mashed white yam (ñame) (see glossary)
1 cup coconut milk
2 eggs
2 tsp. vanilla
1 cup sugar
6 allspice berries, very finely crushed
5 whole cloves, very finely crushed
³/₄ tsp. salt
3 Tbs. gari (cassava meal) (see glossary)
1 cup plus 1 rounded Tbs. finely grated coconut
1 cup crushed pineapple, together with all its juices
3 rounded (or 4) Tbs. diced fresh mango

Whip together cassava, ñame, and coconut milk. Beat in eggs, one at a time, then vanilla. Blend in sugar, allspice, cloves, salt, and gari. Beat in coconut, then pineapple. Beat mixture for 2 to 4 minutes, scraping down sides of bowl once or twice. By hand, stir in mango. Pour into a buttered 9x13 inch pan. Bake in preheated, 350 degree oven for 40 minutes.

When the last loaf of bread had been baked, Black and Island Carib women tended the fields and gardens, in which they continued to increase the number and variety of cultivated crops. One crop in particular, hot peppers, was important to their cuisine. It grew in abundance and variety and provided the fiery, yet flavorful, characteristics of many sauces, soups, and stews. *Coui*, a concoction of hot peppers and cassava juice, was used in place of salt to season meats and vegetables. Whether heated in vinegar over a low flame or marinated in one of the local rums, peppers were an indispensable culinary flavor principle that no cook was caught dead without.

The trade savvy and agricultural skills possessed by the Caribs required use of an efficient food storage system. The storage system helped to facilitate the use of food in various contexts, including religious rituals, secular celebrations, and everyday nourishment. Frequent feasts were held at which pineapple and cassava wine were the drinks of choice. Trinidad, Tobago, Grenada, St. Lucia, and for that matter all of the islands are known for their tropical punches, beers, and other alcoholic beverages. Trinidadians are quite fond of their ginger beer and sorrel drinks. Tobago and Grenada favor punches as well as drinks that punch, made with star apples and local rums. Guava, mango, and watermelon pulp provide the flavors for a number of refreshing libations just waiting to win you over. Do not linger a moment longer. Get your blender ready. Fill your glass with ice. The proof is in the marvelous taste.

Tropical Dream Team

³/₄ ounce of dried sorrel**
2 Tbs. fresh ginger, peeled and chopped
6 cups boiling water
7 ounces unsweetened guava pulp**
1¹/₃-pound piece of seedless watermelon, rind discarded
About half of a small, fresh mango, or its equivalent in unsweetened pulp
2 tsp. lime juice
1¹/₄ cups creme de banana liqueur
¹/₂ cup rum
Ice filled glasses
For every 1 cup of punch: 4 tsp. sugar (or to taste) and 1¹/₂ tsp. grenadine

Place sorrel and ginger in a large bowl. Add boiling water. Wait a minute, then stir a bit. Cover bowl with foil and allow to sit for 4 hours, stirring at least twice during this time period. Strain (discarding solids) into a tall pitcher.

⚜ ⚜ ⚜ ⚜ ⚜ ⚜ ⚜
**Sorrel is available in ¹/₂ ounce packages at Caribbean grocery stores. Guava and mango pulp are available frozen in 14 ounce packages at some larger and specialty grocery stores. They do not require defrosting before use.

Pour a cup of sorrel water into blender or food processor. Add guava, watermelon, and mango. Process until liquified and smooth (if mango solids resist, remove and process separately with a little of the fruit liquid). Transfer fruit mix to pitcher. Add lime juice, banana liqueur, and rum and mix well.

Pour one cup of fruit mix into each ice filled glass. To each glass add sugar and grenadine. Mix well.

≶≶

The growth of a sense of identity and community among Africans in the Caribbean was essential for their survival as a people. Minor cultural differences and variations in food preparation did not diminish one fact: their status as slaves. That sense of identity was, therefore, not "seasoned" out of the labor force brought onto mainland America from the islands. On mainland America, Africans were no longer the dominant population but they were still dominant in the kitchen. The cuisine and culinary skills that traveled to mainland America with the Akan, Yoruba, Hausa, Igbo, Ewe, Herero, Ashanti, Mende, Fulani, and others, stood right alongside those of Native America and laid the foundation for "American" recipes and helped to develop kitchen and appliance technology widely copied by people everywhere.

These culinary strides, studies tell us, are due totally to the "American" woman. Unfortunately, these histories have rarely been honest enough to include the "American" women who were actually in the kitchen. Mention in these histories of the AFRICAN and NATIVE American woman's contribution has been slight to none. Throughout every stage in the development of this country, it was African women and men in the kitchens creating and preparing the meals that have been widely copied by people everywhere. As slaves, there was no freedom of movement or expression; African hands were bound in chains in this country, but not while they were in the kitchen. In the kitchen, African ingenuity was never thwarted. Whites privately recognized and appreciated African artistry in cuisine. Black cooks were celebrated in one or two local histories for their cakes, gingerbreads, and pastries. Native American cooking methods and foodstuffs saved the lives of European colonials and, together with African culinary tradition, dining tables were developed, here in America, without rival anywhere.

African culinary tradition and the War for Independence worked hand in hand during colonial days. The war was fought intellectually in the taverns and eating establishments as well as physically on the battlefield. Although George Washington was thoroughly opposed to Africans fighting in the Revolutionary Army, he had no such qualms about them cooking for him and his troops. It is interesting, or should I say ironic, that out of all the places in the world for the Sons of Liberty and other revolutionary patriots to meet, eat, and plan their moves, they should choose Fraunces's Tavern, particularly when you consider that all the while the number of newly arrived Africans bound in chains was on the steady increase. Fraunces's Tavern became the "haunt" of the revolutionaries of the period. It has been said that no one served the cause of the colonists better than "Black Sam" Fraunces, an African from the West Indies, who was also the owner of the establishment. Fraunces migrated to New York where he purchased the Delancy mansion on Broad and Pearl Streets in 1762. Fraunces opened Delancy as a tavern which was to make him both a noted patriot and the leading restauranteur of his day. In a newspaper advertisement in New York in 1761, he announced himself as a caterer of delicacies, but he had a reputation as an innkeeper dating from 1755. However, it was at Fraunces's Tavern, then called the Queen's Head, where Fraunces and his many delicacies became famous. Excellent food was undoubtedly the enticement and incentive to gather at the tavern. The attraction to the foods he served allowed his tavern to become the city's social, cultural, and revolutionary hub, or, the rendezvous for rebels. The Stamp Act was discussed and attacked there, as well as the planning, in 1774, of a tea party by the Sons of Liberty, an affair similar to the one carried out in Boston. Samuel Fraunces, in maintaining a neverending friendship to the cause of the country, fed, without charge, those soldiers who had no money for food. In addition, he enlisted in George Washington's division when the Revolutionary War began, leaving his establishment in the hands of his wife. When Fraunces left the military in July of 1782, he received thanks from Congress, in the amount of two hundred pounds, as payment for distinctive service to American prisoners and to the secret service. Not surprisingly, Washington's farewell address to his officers on December 4,

1783, was made at Fraunces's Tavern. In 1789, however, when Washington was inaugurated in New York as the first President of the United States, Fraunces left his own establishment to become steward of Washington's household.

American history has yet to authenticate the story of Phoebe, Samuel Fraunces's daughter, who apparently "eclipsed her father's service to the country." A letter written by Dr. Solomon Drowne, who was a surgeon in the Continental Army, contained the details of Phoebe's heroic act. Phoebe, one of George Washington's maids, was made privy to a plan to assassinate the general. Thomas Hickey, who had been the chosen assassin, finagled his way into the ranks of Washington's bodyguards. He also managed to fall in love with Phoebe, confided in her, and enlisted her aid for the deadly deed. Fortunately for Washington, the plate of poisoned peas Phoebe served him was accompanied by her whispered message to him as to the contents of the dish. Washington tossed the peas out of the window, where chickens feeding on the grounds ate them and were later found dead. Hickey was hanged in the presence of twenty-thousand people. Fraunces's Tavern is still a historic landmark in 1999; however, there is still no plaque to Phoebe.

There may be no mention of Phoebe's saving the life of the slave-owning first president, but there have been more than one reference to the fare served at the famous tavern. The following peas are wonderful and are a must-have side dish with any meat, fish, or poultry entree. When you serve this dish, tell your diners the story behind it. If they trust you, they will eat them anyway.

Phoebe's Peas (without the Arsenic)

About ½ pound sugar snap peas
1 tsp. EACH lemon and lime juice
2 Tbs. butter
1 small carrot, cut into very thin rounds
⅓ cup plus 1 Tbs. chopped red onion
⅛ tsp. EACH basil, thyme, chili powder, and nutmeg
½ tsp. plus a generous pinch of sugar
Freshly ground black pepper, to taste
¼ tsp., or to taste, salt

Cook peas, covered, in a small amount of water with lemon and lime juices for about 15 minutes. Drain.

Melt butter in skillet. Add carrots and onion and cook and stir for 5 minutes. Add remaining ingredients and continue to cook and stir for 2–3 minutes more. Fold in peas. Taste for needed salt and pepper. Heat through and serve.

As steward of the household of the first president, Fraunces supervised the provisioning of food and drink. His business had always been food and many of Fraunces's culinary creations were presented on Washington's dining table. A hearty and sumptuous bowl of Washington Stew would very often hit the spot. This stew is enough to send any man, or woman, into battle, satiated. I can tell you, though, a big slice of Patriot Bread, made delectable by the addition of lots of sour cream, is the perfect choice to accompany this dish, or any other.

Washington Stew, After the Fashion of Sam Fraunces

2¹/₂–3 pounds of beef chuck, cut into very small chunks
1 ham hock
About 8 potatoes, peeled and cut into very small chunks
About 3 cabbage leaves, shredded
12 cups of beef stock
4 big onions, chopped
2 big green peppers, chopped
6 Tbs. Worcestershire sauce
1¹/₂ tsp. EACH celery seed and parsley flakes
Garlic salt and black pepper to taste
¹/₂ teaspoon, rounded, red pepper flakes
3 (6 oz.) cans tomato paste
4 heaping Tbs. sugar
2 (20 oz.) bags frozen sliced carrots
1 (16 oz.) bag frozen green peas

$^{1}/_{2}$ to $^{3}/_{4}$ of a 20-oz. bag of frozen corn
2 (20 oz.) bags frozen, cut green beans
2 (16 oz.) cans green lima beans

Combine first eight ingredients. Stir in all spices, tomato paste, and sugar. Simmer on low heat for 1 hour, 15 minutes. Remove ham hock. If you wish, cut meat from bone and return cut up meat to pot. Add all frozen vegetables and return to boil again, simmering until vegetables are tender. Stir in lima beans. Bring to boil again. Continue simmering for 2 or 3 minutes.

Light and delicious, this is the perfect accompaniment to Washington Stew. Would you say that this is just another corn bread recipe? Do not pass this one by. The aroma! The taste! The texture is like cake! Heaven!

Patriot Bread

1$^{1}/_{4}$ cups yellow corn meal
1$^{1}/_{4}$ cups flour
4 tsp. baking powder
1$^{1}/_{4}$ tsp. salt
3 heaping Tbs. sugar
2 eggs
$^{1}/_{2}$ cup oil
2 cups (16 oz. pint) sour cream
Several tablespoons of oil for greasing skillet

Combine first five ingredients and mix well. Make a well in the middle of mixture and add eggs and oil. Blend eggs and oil together and continue stirring as corn meal mixture starts to blend in. When mixture gets too thick to continue stirring, blend in sour cream. Stir just until well blended. Pour into a greased (use half of oil), preheated, nine-inch skillet. Make sure oil is hot before pouring batter in. Cover skillet and cook on medium-low heat till brown on bottom. Remove cover. Run a knife along the entire outside rim of crust to separate it from the skillet. Place a large dinner plate on top of skillet and holding the plate against the skillet with one hand, very carefully and quickly turn skillet upside down with the other so that cooked side is facing you when you lift skillet off. Wipe out brown crumbs and particles from skillet. Grease and preheat skillet again. Slide bread back into skillet, pushing uncooked batter under browned side as it goes in. Cover and cook until brown on bottom. Remove to platter.

⟨⟨⟨

One of the slaves Washington was said to eventually set free was "a most remarkable colored woman" by the name of Mary Simpson. After being freed, she made her living laundering clothes and selling her own pastries and sweetmeats, along with butter, eggs, and milk, from a tiny basement store. Her fondness for George Washington caused her to celebrate his birthday every year. She baked a *huge* cake, which she called "Washington cake," and prepared *large* pots of coffee and punch for patriotic visitors to her store. It is said that she continued this ritual until her death in the hope that Washington would never be forgotten. This attachment to the slave owner may be very touching to some. Ms. Simpson was a gentle and generous soul who loved to share in a big way.

I would like to share this fruitcake recipe with you. It is a mere fraction of the size that Mary Simpson would have baked. Trust me, it is thoroughly eatable. There is not one crumb of it that you would want to pick out and throw away. Serve this dazzling creation with pride to the general of your army.

𝄚𝄚

Mary Simpson's Fruitcake

Cake batter:
½ cup butter
½ cup dark brown sugar
¼ cup white sugar
3 jumbo eggs
1 tsp. vanilla
¼ cup Myers Dark Rum

¼ cup dark molasses

1¼ cups flour

½ tsp. EACH salt, baking powder, cinnamon, nutmeg, cloves

Combine the following fruits and nuts in a large bowl:

10–12 oz. package pitted dates, each one cut into halves or thirds, depending on size

2 (8 oz.) jars glacé pineapple (use most of it)

20 EACH green and red maraschino cherries, each one cut in half

10 oz. bag shelled walnuts, broken up or chopped

½ pint or more of Myers Dark Rum, for dousing

Preheat oven to the setting right between 300 and 325 degrees. Slightly grease and line with wax paper a 9 × 5 loaf pan.

Cream butter. Gradually blend in both sugars, a little at a time. Beat in eggs, one at a time. Combine dry ingredients. Gradually add dry ingredients to mixture alternately with vanilla, rum, and molasses, beginning with dry and ending with dry. Pour cake batter over prepared fruits. Gently fold and mix well. Pour mixture into prepared pan. Bake for 3½ hours. Cake will brown before it is done, so have aluminum foil ready to cover cake to keep it from baking too deep a brown (I should say, burning). When completely cool, remove from pan, place on aluminum foil and douse with about ⅓ cup of rum. Wrap tightly in a few layers of aluminum foil and then wrap in a plastic bag. In 48 hours douse again with ⅓ cup of rum. Rewrap and refrigerate. At the end of one week douse all over with ⅓ cup of rum. This goes on for two weeks, mind you. During the second week, douse twice more with a few Tbs. each time. The last douse should take place a full 48 to 72 hours before you cut it. Also, let cake sit out at room temperature for an hour or so (wrapped) after each dousing to let it soak up the rum.

A recipe called "George Washington Cake" was published in *Williamsburg Art of Cookery*, authored by Helen Bullock. The recipe is dated 1780. The origin of this recipe is stated as having come from an "Old Williamsburg Family Cook Book". It may be that the "Old Family Recipe" from Williamsburg is just another version and has no connection to Mary Simpson's (or, Mary Washington, as she came to be known), but I notice that there is no stated connection whatsoever with this recipe and any black cook.

George Washington *was* a slavemaster, and no "gentleman" in the Continental Army would be caught dead without his "negro" servants and cooks, if he had a choice. At Valley Forge, George Washington's forces were starving and ragged and began to desert in high numbers. It has been theorized that the dish known as Pepper Pot was created here. Washington is supposed to have commanded his head chef to come up with a great dish out of the scraps and odds and ends that were left over. Well, the chef simmered tripe together with ground peppercorns and a few stray beans and carrots. It was said that the resulting fragrance from this stew was enough in itself to comfort the men. When the stew was actually eaten, the troops were indeed fortified. Their spirits were revived. They were ready to take on the Redcoats again. General Washington considered this soup a dish for heroes. He was so pleased that he insisted that the dish be named "Philadelphia Pepper Pot," in honor of the home town of the chef.

I will call my version just plain "Pepper Pot" so Philadelphia will not get mad. By the way, pepperpot (made with casereep, a mixture of boiled cassava juice, brown sugar, and spices) and pepperpot soup (made with spinach and other greens and meat or fish) have always been staple dishes of Africans in the Caribbean Islands. Variations in ingredients occur in every pot. So, whatever first name you choose to give this dish, its bold spiciness challenges the taste buds. It is tasty enough to incite a riot. If you like peppers, this one is for you.

ꕬꕬꕬ

Pepper Pot

2 Tbs. EACH butter and vegetable oil
1½ large red bell peppers (or, 1 large red and ½ large green bell pepper), chopped
1 large onion, chopped
¾ tsp. EACH "hot, Mexican style" chili powder and parsley flakes and celery seed
½ tsp. EACH dill and crushed red pepper
¼ heaping tsp. cumin
1 tsp. garlic salt with parsley

½ pound cod or other boneless white fish, cut up
Freshly ground black pepper and a little salt
2 large cooked carrots, pureed
1 cup cooked and mashed calabash squash
1 EACH mustard green leaf (stem removed) and spinach leaf, finely chopped
1 cup beef stock
5 cups chicken stock

Combine butter and oil in a large pot over medium heat. When butter has melted add bell pepper and onion. Cook and stir for a few minutes. Add next seven spice ingredients. Continue cooking and stirring until onions are clear. Add fish, then black pepper and salt. Cook and stir for about 2 minutes, breaking up (flaking) chunks of fish as it cooks. Add carrots, squash, and greens, cooking and stirring for about 30 seconds more. Stir in both stocks. At this time, check for needed black pepper and salt. Bring to a boil. Lower heat and simmer, covered, for about 12 minutes.

Since the officers were usually treated to better food than the troops, a pudding, served as either a special dish or dessert, would sometimes highlight the meal. When these dishes were prepared, the cooks were relying on their African repertoire; various types of puddings have been served in Africa from time immemorial. One such flavorful pudding was made with fish and yams. This was and still is a particular favorite of those peoples of the coastal areas, as well as those who live near inland streams and rivers. Deliciously spiced with herbs native to the African continent, it can be seasoned with lemon juice or lemon extract stirred into the liquid ingredients. The tasty "Tigernut mold," as it is called in English, is a favorite dessert pudding of the Ghanaian people. Many different fruit puddings were made, such as pineapple, guava, banana, mango, coconut, apple, and orange, to mention a few. Puddings were made with vegetables and starches such as yams and sweet potatoes, beans, carrots, groundnuts, etc., in addition to many varieties of fruits and vegetables unknown in the Western world.

The following dessert is a creamy, rich, and delicate sweet, worthy of a place in your after-dinner repertoire.

Coconut Banana (Custard) Pudding

1 cup finely grated coconut, divided in half
2 cups milk
½ cup sugar
2 Tbs. flour
2 eggs
¼ tsp. salt
⅛ tsp. EACH cinnamon and nutmeg
1 whole clove, finely crushed
2 tsp. vanilla extract
2 ripe bananas (1 large, 1 medium-large), pureed
Butter
Sliced bananas

Under a broiler, toast half of the coconut by stirring frequently until most of it is golden brown.

Pour milk in a bowl and add sugar. Stir until dissolved. Stir in flour. Beat in eggs, then salt, cinnamon, nutmeg, and cloves. Add vanilla and mix well. Blend in bananas, then ALL of the coconut.

Pour into a buttered baking dish and bake in a preheated 350 degree oven for approximately 50 minutes. Cool completely.

Line serving dishes with thin banana slices. Spoon pudding on top of banana slices.

Fundamental bread articles included the corn dodger, ash cake, crackling bread, corn sticks, hush puppies, corn bread, and spoon bread. In fact, George Washington was in the habit of chomping down corn dodgers as part of his everyday diet. One of the "first essentials" of the corn dodger and other corn products was ground meal from the best white corn; and of course this is combined with water and salt and made into a dough. Now as far as what proportions of each ingredient go in, it all depends on the eye and judgment of the cook. African cooks in Virginia, "who make it perfectly every time, are never known to measure."

The heritage of these cooks primarily represented the culture of West Africa, although there was a small number of Central and Southwest Africans present in the colonies as well. Some slave owners chose Africans to work for them according to their regional origin. Apparently, whatever areas Africans specialized in at home was taken into account once they reached the colonies. Africans who were agriculturalists and cleared land for cultivation purposes in more country areas were familiar with growing rice, indigo, cotton, yams, maize, sorghum, okra, and sesame. The culture and civilization of urban Africans was based on trade and commerce, and they were used to strong centralized political authorities.

The fact that Africans brought to America so many useful skills enabled them to take over the performance of various tasks for slave owners, and due to the absolute segregation of Africans here in America, a great many aspects of African culture were retained. Various Africanisms from different societies in Africa were to converge on American soil. Joseph Holloway points out in *Africanisms in American Culture* that African groups of the field slave community shared and adopted these Africanisms, which evolved the various aspects of African American cooking, music, art, religion, philosophy, and language.

It was easy, therefore, for African cooks in America to come up with new and different ways to cook the same staples. They were simply doing what they had always done, what they had been trained to do, what generations for thousands of years had done in Africa. In Africa, cooks had always known how to fry chicken and other meats and by adding different spices and seasonings and dipping the pieces in various coatings and frying them in different oils, numerous unique flavors could be produced. The name variations are produced when you change the *method* of cooking. With African populations on plantations representing so many societies from Africa, and with their demonstrated superior knowledge of spices and other culinary creativity, chicken recipes were numerous. A chicken could be steamed in banana leaves, baked with nuts and corn, dipped in a groundnut (peanut) batter and fried in peanut or palm oil, stewed with yams and spinach, or roasted on a spit while being basted with a spiced banana sauce. African expertise in the area of cooking was one element of African culture that slave owners found useful. This aspect of African culture was, therefore, not destroyed. In fact, it was believed that "negroes" were born cooks. The Big House kitchen was said to be in safe hands with any number of male or female field slaves who had to fill a cook's shoes on a moment's notice.

If it is not on a moment's notice that you will have to fill the shoes of a cook, do plan to serve this creation. "A born cook" may be the label given to you.

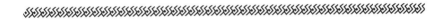

Roasted Hen Under Onion and Sour Cream Sauce with Bacon and Cream Tarts

1 large hen
White pepper, garlic salt, hot and spicy seasoned salt, freshly ground black pepper, paprika, and parsley flakes
4 bacon slices
Rendered oil from bacon
1 small, cooked link sausage
1 small onion, chopped
1/8 tsp. EACH thyme, tarragon, cumin, and cinnamon
1/4 tsp. EACH crushed red pepper and celery seed
1/4 rounded tsp. parsley flakes
Freshly ground black pepper and salt, to taste
2 slices bread, crumbed
1/4 cup finely crumbed corn flakes
4 Tbs. light cream
1 egg yolk

Season hen with white pepper, garlic salt, spicy salt, black pepper, paprika, and parsley. Place hen, covered with foil, in a preheated 450 degree oven. Immediately reduce oven temperature to 350 degrees and bake for 20 to 25 minutes per pound. Cut bird into serving pieces.

For the tarts*:
Fry bacon until brown and crisp. Brown sausage on all sides. Drain skillet, reserving rendered oil.

Over medium heat, return 2 Tbs. rendered oil to the same skillet bacon and sausage were cooked in. Add onion and cook and stir for a minute. Add thyme, terragon, cumin, cinnamon, crushed red pepper, celery seed, parsley flakes, and some black pepper and salt. Continue cooking and stirring until onion lightly browns. Add bread and corn flake crumbs. Remove from heat.

Crumble 2½ slices of the bacon and add to skillet. Finely chop sausage and add to skillet.

Combine cream and egg and mix well. Pour mixture into skillet and mix all ingredients well.

Line 4 "wells" of a cupcake pan with paper cups. Divide mixture among cups. Bake in a preheated 375 degree oven for about 15 to 20 minutes.

For the sauce*:
1 Tbs. EACH rendered bacon oil and butter
1 small onion, chopped
¼ of a small to medium red bell pepper, chopped
2 Tbs. white wine (white bordeaux or chardonnay)
½ cup beef or chicken bouillon
½ tsp. white pepper
Freshly ground black pepper, to taste
Salt, to taste
½ tsp. sugar
Remaining 1½ slices bacon, crumbled
¾ cup sour cream

DO NOT WASH SKILLET

In the same skillet, heat 1 Tbs. bacon fat over medium heat. Add butter and stir until melted. Add onion and bell pepper. Cook and stir until onion starts to brown. Add white wine and continue cook-

§§ §§ §§ §§ §§ §§ §§

*Recipe can be doubled, if desired.

ing and stirring for about 30 seconds. Add bouillon, then white pepper, black pepper, and salt. Cook and stir for a minute. Stir in sugar, then bacon. Continue cooking and stirring until mixture comes to a full boil. Add sour cream, lower heat, and continue cooking and stirring just until mixture comes to boil. Remove from heat. Taste for needed salt and pepper.

Place serving pieces of hen in serving plates (or on a serving platter).

Place one or two tarts upside down on each serving plate. Gently remove cupcake liners. Pour hot cream sauce over tarts and hen.

※※※

This belief that most Africans can be relied upon as competent cooks is all very noteworthy when you consider that most written information on American cooking states that it is carved out of layers of the past and then proceeds to name everyone's past except that of African people. Now and then, however, greens, chitlins, and corn bread are mentioned, as the "soul food" of "black people in America." The food staples and "primitive" cooking methods of "the Indians" are sometimes presented in the same breath with English settlers, in the context that the English settlers turned Native American foods into a much more sophisticated cuisine. So-called "soul food," it seems, was never worth emulating or placing on a high level of importance in "American" cuisine. But even soul food has been denied its African roots. Cookbooks that claim to deal with soul food or the cooking of African Americans emphasize that it is a mere "offshoot" or an "appropriation" or an "echo" of European cuisine. One volume emphasizes that soul food was not brought over from Africa. African contribution, this book continues, was in the area of ingenuity. *I* am emphasizing that Africans were totally familiar with corn, greens, and certainly the grilling or barbecuing of meats and fish before they were dragged here from their homeland. In addition, "soul food" may be the term given to the down-to-earth, simple fare African Americans have been known to cook and eat for economic reasons; but African American cooking itself encompasses numerous complex preparations that are considered to be standard "American" recipes in this country today. This neglect in giving credit where it is due reminds me of Vertamae

Smart-Grosvenor's comment in her book *Vibration Cooking*, when she remarked that white folks act like they invented food. Now, for sure, Africans ate much better on their own soil than they did on the plantations in this country. Once here, they were not given variety nor ample supply, to say the least. The meager offerings provided made ingenuity and skill responsible for making their rations edible. But Africans were already familiar with corn and maize. Making corn bread was not new to them. Africans were also known for cooking every part of an animal and turning these parts into delicacies. Cooking the feet or intestines of a pig, therefore, was not an insurmountable challenge.

It is not that I wish to enter into the E. Franklin Frazier/Melville Herskovits debate over whether Africans were so devastated by American slavery that all African cultural aspects were destroyed. Although I must say that I do not agree that African American culture began "without any African antecedents." For a discussion of the debate see *Africanisms in American Culture* (p. ix), edited by Joseph E. Holloway. In addition, *The Myth of the Negro Past* (1941), by Melville Herskovits and *The Negro Church in America* (1963), by E. Franklin Frazier, provide a great deal of fuel for this fire. The bottom line is that there are so many things African in American culture itself, it is inconceivable to try to separate the African from the African American.

Statements that attempt to deny Africa's connection with its sons and daughters here in America also seek to denigrate African experience and ability. These statements come off as saying that anything Africans have accomplished, they were only able to accomplish on the shores of America, under the influence of white people. Cooking was one of the first arts developed and evolved in Africa. But cooking "authorities" tell us that the African, after being brought to America, suddenly developed ingenuity even though, let them tell it, Africans possessed no prior culinary history. We are supposed to believe that Africans, the first people, never developed any cuisine. So I guess we should thank our lucky stars for being captured and dragged here, where we were allowed to learn to cook, for the first time, "with remarkable resourcefulness."

To state that soul food did not have origins in Africa is the same as saying that black music, African American music (gospel, jazz, ragtime, rhythm and blues, and the blues), has no roots in Africa either. In fact, one cookbook author has brazenly stated outright that jazz "has borrowed rhythmic influences from middle-European gypsy tempos." The same lies and distortions that credit anything good about Africa to outside sources, regarding its political, social, religious, cultural, and economic history, also permeate the pages of volumes written on African and African American cuisine. The same author suggests that emancipated slaves and their descendants learned frugality better than the Dutch in Pennsylvania. The African taste for beans and plain vegetables reminds him of German cooking in Virginia. I guess this accounts for the reason, according to this author, that soul food has merely echoed Central Europe's style and method with pig's feet and sauerkraut. Were the roaming Germanic cooks and Pennsylvania Dutch thrifty because they were rationed "leavings" and scraps by European slaveowners? I can frankly think of no connection whatsoever between Dutch and German immigrants and those persons dragged here in chains. I think this author is making fun of a very serious situation. At the very least we can say that this author trivializes slavery and its impact, not to mention that his lack of knowledge concerning the origins of certain dishes makes this entire discourse demeaning. If you notice, let Europeans tell it, black people still cannot be the originators of or own anything. Frankly, the only contribution Europeans have made to soul food has occurred when the ingredients have been obtained directly from them.

Some written material available on "soul food" conveys the message that it is a product of the South in general, so that the only role black folks played in it was to stir the pot, dish it up, and serve it when done. According to much literature there was no actual creativity nor invention involved on the part of the African. This accounts for the fact that old cookbooks on "bluegrass" and Virginia cookery will list some slave owner or her descendant as its author. These books are actually compilations of old recipes created by various black cooks who served the families of these authors, sometimes for generations. These old recipes were part of the repertoire of fine feasts served on plantations. After these dinners, the guests would corner the mistress and ask for her recipe for that marvelous poundcake and that beautiful red currant jelly. One guest at a Virginia banquet could be overheard to say,

> That ham! Mellow, aged, boiled in champagne, baked brown, spiced deeply, rosy pink within and of a flavor and fragrance to shatter the fast of a pope . . .

There are stories about visitors to Kentucky plantations who stopped to spend the night and stayed on for ten and twenty years. It is reputed that so many guests stayed for the rest of their lives and died on one plantation that a special cemetery was built for them. As the story goes, every meal was so good that the guest would weaken to stay on for another.

If it is not your intention to have your guests hanging around your house for ten or twenty years, prepare this pie only once. Then, on the other hand, they may hang around waiting for you to prepare it again. Either way, you may lose. One thing, however, is for certain: your guests' attachment to your table will make it plain that you have prepared a winning entree. Be prepared to lay in some extra toothbrushes and pillows.

Pork and Apple Pie

Two 9-inch unbaked pie crusts
2¼ pounds boneless pork shoulder steaks, cut into thin slices
About 1 tsp., or to taste, garlic salt mixed with parsley
Black pepper, to taste
1 medium-large onion, chopped
¼ tsp. ground cumin
8 whole allspice berries, finely crushed
¼ tsp. crushed red pepper
½ cup chicken broth
1 Tbs. light molasses
1¾ medium-small apples, peeled, cored, and sliced
Salt and black pepper, to taste

Line a 9-inch pie plate with one crust. Prick bottom and sides of crust with fork tines. Bake in preheated 450 degree oven for 10 minutes.

Cook pork in a large skillet over medium heat, covered, stirring frequently, for about 15 minutes. Drain oil from skillet. Add garlic salt and some black pepper. Mix well and continue cooking and stirring for a couple of minutes. Add onions. Stir in cumin and cook and stir for another couple of minutes. Add allspice and crushed red pepper one at a time, mixing well after each addition. Continue cooking and stirring for a minute or two more. Stir in chicken broth, then molasses, mixing well. Cover. Continue cooking and stirring occasionally, over medium-low heat, until meat is tender (about 25 minutes). Add apples and cook and stir for about 5–8 minutes more. Taste for needed salt and pepper.

Pour mixture into partially cooked pie shell. Cover with remaining pie crust. Cut slits across top of crust. Bake in preheated 450 degree oven until crust is golden brown, 15–20 minutes, depending on your oven.

Such attachment to the plantation table is evident in one introductory piece, in a book on Kentucky cooking. The writer gives credit to that autocratic black cook, the turbaned mistress of the Kentucky Kitchen, as he calls her. It seems that no matter where in the world he ate or what in the world he was eating, he would start to smell those waffles, spiced ham boiled in champagne, currant jelly and hot, buttered biscuits. According to him, as the social system of the South rested on the slave, the three pillars of the substructure were the overseer, the black mammy, and Aunt Dinah, the (black) cook. If it had not been for Aunt Dinah, master would not have had the desire for the type of hospitality he displayed and the guest would have found it less difficult to leave. He even credits (or blames) Aunt Dinah for the South's participation in the Civil War. The question he asks is whether Kentucky would have shelled out all of its money and manpower, sending forty thousand of her youth to fight in the army of the Confederacy, if it were not for those big cakes and pies. He takes off his hat to her, in spite of whatever "faults" she has (!?!), because the bottom line, he says, is that she is certainly held in loving remembrance. Frankly, I do not know whether to laugh or cry, for it is plain to see that the African cook in America has never been given serious credit nor a proper culinary pedestal for his or her culinary inventions, much less does he or she receive royalties from the books.

Have you ever been so fond of a dessert that you wish you could just wrap yourself up in it? Or maybe just jump in the cookie jar or the candy bag and take your time eating your way out? If you can stay away from these caramels long enough to give somebody else some, you are doing good. Make sure you eat lunch or dinner before you make these, or this will be all you will eat.

Peanut Butter Caramels

1 pound dark brown sugar
1 cup milk
1/8 tsp. salt
1 cup miniature marshmallows
1/3 cup plus 1 Tbs. creamy peanut butter
2 Tbs. butter
2 1/2 tsp. vanilla
4 Tbs. chopped nuts (optional)
1 tsp. benne (sesame) seeds (optional)

Combine sugar, milk, and salt and simmer over medium heat for 10 minutes. Remove from heat and immediately stir in marshmallows, peanut butter, and butter. Cool a little and beat in vanilla. Stir in nuts. Pour into a buttered, 9-inch square pan. Sprinkle the top with benne seeds, if desired. Cool completely. Refrigerate overnight. Cut into 20 squares. Lift out squares with a narrow spatula or cake cutter. Using a knife, slide each piece into a paper baking cup.

It was always common practice for whites to steal, claim, and rename culinary creations of black people. Aunt Jemima Pancake Mix, which I will discuss in a later chapter, is merely one example where enormous monetary profits were made by two white men from someone else's recipe. But it was also always taken for granted that preparing food was a simple task—just have the cook do it. In *Telling Memories Among Southern Women*, Susan Tucker presents a white mother who passed down to her daughter her recipe for corn relish. The daughter had asked her for the recipe, which was such a big hit every time her mother sent it over to the daughter's house. At any rate, Mae, the housekeeper and cook, drove them both to the market. Mother sat in the back seat of the car and had the fresh ingredients brought to her for inspection. When they arrived home they ate a huge lunch and afterward took a nap. When nap time ended they went downstairs to the kitchen, where a big pot of corn relish sat waiting. Mother walked over to the stove, stirred the pot and boasted to her daughter, "See, Anne, there's nothing to making corn relish."

Spicy, tangy, and delicious, this relish can be prepared and stored for serving at your most elegant dinners. Casual entertaining will most certainly find several spots for which it would be appropriate. You may, of course, add more hot pepper if your temperature needs rising.

Hot Corn and Pepper Relish

2 EACH red and green bell peppers
2 jalapeño chili peppers, stems and seeds removed
4 medium-small onions
2½ cups cooked corn
2 Tbs. plus 4 tsp. vinegar
1½ tsp. salt
1 tsp. celery seed
8 tsp. sugar
1 tsp. EACH whole cloves (finely crushed), ground ginger, and chili powder (Hot, Mexican style)

Grind bell peppers, jalapeños, onions, and corn. Transfer to a saucepan and pour 4⅔ cups boiling water over mixture. Allow to soak for 8 minutes. Drain. Add remaining ingredients, MINUS 2 tsp. vinegar and 2 tsp. sugar. Bring to a boil. Lower heat and simmer, covered, for 5 minutes. Cool. Add remaining vinegar and sugar. Mix well. Seal in jars. It makes a nice gift, too. Give a gift of Corn and Pepper Relish alongside with, or in place of, a fruitcake.

The dependence on and importance of the African cook to the South cannot be overemphasized. One present-day Georgia citizen, organizer of Savannah's restoration project, has remarked on how rapidly white Southerners' lives changed after Emancipation of the slaves; meaning, when the number of African house servants and cooks diminished. In many cases, she adds, when there is no African servant to make the decision on what to serve, to go and purchase what is needed, and then to actually cook the meal, the dining table becomes much more sparse than it used to be.

The southern states were not alone in their dependence on African labor. The large farms in colonial Connecticut and in the famous dairy section of the Narragansett country of Rhode Island were also worked by African slaves. Stock farming, it has been said, would have been impossible without them. Other slaves were assigned tobacco, vegetable, and sheep raising. In addition, the breeding of the famous horses known as the Narragansett pacers became a most profitable endeavor, mainly achieved by use of African labor. Africans who worked on the largest Rhode Island farms were responsible for the owners' dairies there, too. Robert Hazard, one of the richest slave owners in New England in 1730, owned twelve thousand acres, much of which was used to produce dairy products. Twenty-four African women were assigned to produce between twelve and twenty-four large cakes of cheese per day for his creamery. All throughout colonial New England, African males served as coachmen, attendants, butlers, valets, laborers, and also cooks.

New Englanders considered eggs another important dairy product. A common leavening in the eighteenth century was egg whites beaten to a froth and added to cakes and puddings. In the recipe below I have added beaten egg whites to sweet potatoes, a food I fell in love with as a child when my grandmother filled our house once a week with them in the form of a giant, velvety smooth pie. As a custard or pudding, sweet potatoes hit the spot just as well. Light, flavorful and not at all hard to prepare, you will come to consider Sweet Potato Custard a great-tasting way to end any meal.

Sweet Potato Custard (Soufflé)

4 big eggs, separated
2 big, cooked sweet potatoes
¼ cup butter, melted
2 Tbs. dark rum
4 tsp. vanilla extract

¹/₄ cup light molasses
¹/₂ cup sugar
¹/₂ tsp. salt
2 Tbs. flour
³/₄ cup crushed pineapple, well drained
2 Tbs. plus 2 tsp. sugar
¹/₄ tsp. salt
2 Tbs. chopped pecans or walnuts

In a bowl, beat egg yolks until thick and lemon colored. Add potatoes, then butter, beating until smooth. Add rum, vanilla, molasses, and ¹/₂ cup sugar and blend well. Mix in ¹/₂ tsp. salt and flour. Add pineapple and beat again, just until well blended.

In a separate bowl, beat egg whites until stiff, gradually adding remaining sugar and salt. Fold egg whites into sweet potatoes. Pour into a baking dish. Sprinkle nuts over the top. Bake in preheated, 350 degree oven for about 48 minutes.

The same duties, including those of cook, were performed by Africans who served the third president. Unfortunately, his most famous words did not refer to everyone:

> We hold these truths to be self-evident that all men are created equal, that they are endowed by their creator with inherent and inalienable rights . . .

Now, Thomas Jefferson took this statement seriously, insofar as white MEN were concerned. Africans were not really men (or women), as far as slave owners were concerned; Africans were chattel, property, and, therefore, not human. Consequently, anything that belonged to the slave master's property belonged to the slave master, including their culinary creations.

Jefferson is sometimes referred to as the first American gourmet. His culinary ventures have been written about in numerous books. However, one of his slaves, by the name of Isaac, stated that Jefferson "never went into the kitchen except to wind the clock." Reference is constantly made to his importation of French cooks to "train" his African cooks. The message conveyed is that the African cooks did not really become accomplished until the French had imparted all of their expertise upon the Africans. What is of more importance is the expertise imparted upon the French by the Africans. What innovations did the French take home? Slaveholders knew. One very chauvinistic Georgian has stated that he felt the French were completely outdistanced in the kitchen when it comes to the production of wholesome and appetizing cuisine; because, as far as he was concerned, the African female intellect has natural genius for cooking.

Jefferson sailed to France in 1784 to become Minister to the Court of Louis XVI. It is interesting that Jefferson left to go to France at a time when France was ruling what was then the richest colony in the world, Saint Domingue (Haiti). The wealth this colony produced was dependent upon slave labor and the plantation system. Furthermore, France's industrial climb during the eighteenth century was tied to a development of overseas trade; two-thirds of those trade goods were produced in Saint Domingue. Capital from the slave trade financed France's industries, which made its economy heavily dependent on the traffic in slaves. Saint Domingue grew and exported cotton, cocoa, indigo, and tobacco. But by far its chief crop was sugar. The enormous profits from the sugar mills were made literally on the backs of African men and women. Except for the sexual liaisons they forced upon African women, the planter class or slave owners hated life in the islands. This dislike for the islands sent the rich slaveholders packing off to spend their wealth in France as often as they could. Together with personal servants and cooks, the planter would arrive in France to show off his various "possessions." Whether hosting or attending parties, the planter took great pride in "show" or "tell" when it came to recipes normally prepared for him by his African cooks. And whether the situation was showing, as at a dinner party given by the planter, or telling, just by boasting verbally at dinner parties or social engagements attended by the planter, about what creations he was now used to, this new information became part of French culinary society. New standards were being set (new, that is, to France). After all, it is the rich who set the standards. Many fancy main and dessert dishes, containing sugar and vanilla obtained from their colony in Haiti, were now more readily available and served on the tables of the French elite. I find the paradox interesting: African cooks who served in kitchens here in America were "trained" by French cooks who received their training from African cooks who served the French in the kitchens of the French colonies.

Would it be paradoxical to suppose that preparing the following dish is preparation for a splendid meal which is in itself a magnificent preparation?

Tamarind Duck

One 5-pound duck
1½ cups "Sweet Tamarind Water" (see index)
1 inch piece cinnamon stick, toasted and ground
¼ tsp. EACH anise seeds (fennel) and allspice berries, both toasted and ground
Salt and freshly ground black pepper

Tamarind Sauce:
1 cup of the reserved "Sweet Tamarind Water"
2 Tbs. Myers Dark Rum
3 tsp. cornstarch
3 Tbs. rendered duck fat

Place duck in a baking pan or glass dish. Pour tamarind water over duck. Allow duck to soak, turning frequently, for 4 hours in refrigerator. Drain tamarind water and reserve. Combine cinnamon, anise, and allspice. Rub mixture over surface of duck. Season with salt and pepper. Roast duck, in a preheated, 350 degree oven, about 30 minutes for each pound.

Combine 1 cup of the cold, reserved tamarind water, rum, and cornstarch in a saucepan. Blend well. Add rendered duck fat. Bring to a boil. Lower heat and simmer for a minute or two. Ladle sauce over servings of duck.

When Jefferson was not paying attention to Sally Hemings (a slave who gave birth to at least four of Jefferson's children) he was paying wages to the free whites he employed at the White House, including the French cooks, Adrien Petit and Etienne Lemaire. It was said that Petit trained African cooks supposedly placed under him at Philadelphia and Monticello from 1791 to 1794. James Hemings (Sally's brother and tutor in the culinary arts), it was recorded, received wages during his stay with Jefferson in France, beginning in January 1788, in the amount of 24 francs a month, with an additional gift of 12 francs for the New Year's holiday.

The case of James Hemings was unusual because male and female bondsmen were rarely paid wages. In fact, when it came to basic needs, such as food, slave rations were usually inadequate and consisted of the least nutritious portions of the foods produced on the plantations. One way plantation owners could control dissident slaves was to ration out their food supply. Rations were given out once a week and usually consisted of one peck of cornmeal and two to four pounds of salt pork. However, those who were considered hard workers and who did not cause trouble received an extra pound of meat on Wednesday night (Whoopee!). Many farmers believed that an issue of four pounds of meat to a slave was going too far. One slave owner boasted about having Africans who were issued only one half pound per week for twenty years. At any rate, food rations changed with the season and in the warmer months even these meat allowances were severely cut. To compensate, after putting in a full day's work on the plantation, many slaves supplemented their diet by picking wild fruit, fishing, hunting, and sowing their own crops. A few slaves even raised their own livestock and poultry. Greens, sweet potatoes, and other yellow vegetables, and various dried beans were grown in some slaves' own gardens. Just how much of their own products the slaves consumed cannot be stated exactly, for they sold many of their goods to the slave master and to "the boats" where the sales were more profitable. It should also be noted that these off-duty duties were not performed to supplement the food supply. Rather, they were a crucial part of their dietary maintenance.

When Africans prepared some of their "home grown" fruits and vegetables in plantation kitchens, these simple staples turned up as delicious, fancy trimmings for main courses:

Brazen Tomatoes

1 Tbs. vegetable or peanut oil
1 large tomato, chopped
¼ tsp. EACH crushed basil leaves (dried) and crushed red pepper
¼ rounded tsp. hot, Mexican style chili powder
¼ heaping tsp. parsley flakes
½ tsp. garlic salt with parsley
About ¼ tsp. ground cumin
Freshly ground black pepper, to taste
2 tsp. EACH light molasses and Worcestershire sauce
½ cup beef broth
1 tsp. dark rum
Salt, to taste
3 large, firm tomatoes, sliced
1 whole green onion (tops included), chopped

Heat oil in skillet. Add chopped tomato. Cook and stir over medium heat for several minutes until tomato is quite soft. Add basil, red pepper, and chili powder. Cook and stir for 30 seconds. Add parsley, garlic salt, cumin, and continue stirring for another 30 seconds. Add black pepper and cook and stir constantly for a minute or two. Add molasses, Worcestershire sauce, broth, and rum. Blend well. Lower heat and simmer, stirring frequently, for a couple of minutes. Taste for needed salt. Remove from heat. Add sliced tomatoes and green onions. Fold tomatoes and onions until well coated with sauce. Over LOW flame, return tomatoes to heat and continue gently folding tomatoes occasionally until heated through. DO NOT ALLOW TO SIMMER OR BOIL.

Meats and game were added to African diets when Africans themselves obtained them. Partly as a supplement to the diet and partly at the behest of the slave owner for his own kitchen, Africans hunted small game. Quail were plentiful in New York and Africans were quite adept at trapping them. In addition, crows and other small animals could not escape African technique, which attracted the attention of younger white males across New England. White youth eagerly took notes from Africans, who showed them things their own fathers did not know, such as how to build snares and trap fish (Africans from coastal areas brought to America the art of handling and making nets for netcasting, a traditional method in the tidal waters of the Carolinas), as well as how to make whistles. From this catch, game was roasted as well as being made into many different sorts of stews and soups. Spices and herbs, when obtainable, were generously used by black cooks to season the meat. Africans, both back home and here in the United States, have traditionally loved to flavor roasted meats, stews, and sauces with red pepper and vinegar. On South Carolina's sea islands, the water's bounty in crabs and oysters was the favorite catch of bondsmen and bondswomen. Plantation owners there allotted them salt fish and salt beef. But whatever was cooking, three of the most favored ways of meat preparation were roasting, barbecuing, and braising.

Hunters' Blackbird Fricassee

Sometimes boys caught these birds with BB guns and air rifles or slingshots. Men would sometimes use a 22. caliber. You could get cats to catch both robins and rabbits. Female cats caught rabbits at night. They would bring rabbits in, lay them next to your bed and pull at the sheet to let you know that they were there.

Black folks in the South seasoned the birds with salt, pepper, and fat back, if they had it.—Mrs. Roberta Gayles

Adding a little wine will not hurt these delicately seasoned birds, either.

6 blackbirds
Salt (preferably, hot seasoned salt) and pepper
Flour
1/4 cup butter
1 pod garlic, crushed
1 cup sliced mushrooms
2 onions, sliced in thin rings
1/4 heaping tsp. red crushed pepper

Small piece of fatback
1 cup chicken broth
3 tsp. vinegar
½ cup white wine or sherry

Season birds with salt and pepper. Coat all over with flour. In a large skillet, brown birds in butter on both sides. With a slotted spoon, transfer birds to a dish and set aside.

Add garlic, mushrooms, onions, red pepper, and fatback to skillet and cook and stir for 2 minutes. Return birds to skillet. Combine broth, vinegar, and wine. Pour into skillet with birds. Cover and cook until meat falls from the bone. Baste birds from time to time with liquid. Add additional broth during cooking if liquid evaporates (If additional liquid is added, taste for needed seasoning).

Serve over rice that's wild or with mashed potatoes.

The capture and preparation of game placed a number of unforgettable delicacies on plantation dining tables. But game shared space with other meat, poultry, and pork delights. One Southerner, in reminiscing about the antebellum southern kitchen, wrote that he believed that Virginia cooks and cooking of that era were "the full realization of the dreams of epicures for centuries." This high praise must have certainly taken into consideration the most famous meat in all Virginia, the Smithfield ham.

The importance of the Virginia "hamcook," however, has hardly been recognized. In the days of slavery, the art of ham cooking reached its zenith under the guidance of the black cook. These hams, with their distinctive, nutty flavor, were regularly shipped directly to some of the noble families in England. Together with peanuts and tobacco, hams from Virginia soon became a major export to Europe. Mention is made in family memoirs of the bartering of Virginia hams for satins, laces, and other fabrics from the best shops in London.

This is a light splurge, wonderful for lunch but equally fine fare for dinner, especially if you prefer something not too heavy on the stomach. The buttery, crisp bread crumb topping gives this dish a pleasing flavor for which you will not be ashamed to reach for seconds.

⚇⚇⚇

Ham Casserole

2 cups uncooked macaroni
1¼ pounds Smithfield or other cooked ham, cut into small pieces
⅓ cup whole kernel corn, drained
1⅔ cups peas and carrots or mixed vegetables, drained
½ cup plus 2 Tbs. regular milk
1½ cups undiluted evaporated milk
2 Tbs. butter
10 slices American cheese, preferably yellow
2 chicken bouillon cubes
A sprinkle of salt
A heaping ½ tsp. EACH black pepper, parsley flakes, and celery seed
3 slices bread, torn into tiny pieces
Additional butter

Cook macaroni in salted water until tender. Drain. Transfer to a large (2½ quart) baking dish. Fold in ham and all vegetables.

Carefully heat milks in a saucepan over low heat. Add butter and 1 or 2 slices of cheese. Stir until each slice(s) has almost completely melted before adding another 1 or 2 slices. Repeat. When all slices have been stirred into and melted in milk, add bouillon cubes. Stir for a few minutes. Remove cubes with some of the hot cheese sauce and crush cubes with a fork. Return crushed cubes and sauce to pan. Blend in salt, black pepper, parsley flakes, and celery seed. Pour cheese sauce mixture over ham and macaroni and mix. Garnish with bread crumbs, then small squares of butter all over.

Bake in a preheated, 375 degree oven for 20 minutes.

I offer you and your guests another light and spicy dish, guaranteed to appeal to any hungry diner who is willing to share.

⚇ ⚇ ⚇ ⚇

Spicy Ham and Rice Skillet

3 Tbs. butter
1 large red bell pepper, chopped

1 medium-large onion, chopped
½ tsp. crushed red pepper
1⅓ to 1½ cups cut up cooked ham
Freshly ground black pepper (be generous)
1 large tomato, chopped
1 tsp. EACH sugar and Worcestershire sauce
2 cups cooked rice

Over medium heat, melt butter in skillet. Add bell pepper and onion. Cook and stir for a couple of minutes. Add crushed red pepper and some black pepper. Cook and stir for another couple of minutes. As onions become translucent, add ham and some more black pepper. Continue cooking and stirring for a couple of minutes. Add tomato and continue cooking and stirring for a few minutes. Add sugar and Worcestershire sauce. Cook and stir for a couple more minutes. Fold in rice and heat through.

The Smithfield ham was part of an ongoing procession of outstanding foods, and together with the financial success of cotton cultivation, made plantation mistresses queens at their dinner tables. The position would not have been possible without the African cook. Since "English cooking has never been competent," the first European women who settled on these shores brought with them nothing more than their lack of culinary expertise. Culinary practices in England did not include spices or the "spicing up" of meals. Spices stimulated the senses, that is, sensuality, according to English society's seventeenth century Puritan critics. This is ironic because later on it was spices that elevated Britain and Holland to important international trading centers. But during the first English migration to America, it was Native Americans who saved them from starvation and showed them what to do with herbs and spices and various crops; this, together with the Africans who ran their kitchens thereafter, helped Europeans do quite well in the way of eating.

Many European women spoke of being discouraged of ever learning to cook here. European methods sought to measure out everything in exact proportions. For this reason, they wanted to have written reference guides in order to pass along to their descendants what they had been taught by servants and by the Native peoples. A few cookbooks were published in the 1700s. One or two even included "receipts" or recipes for medicines for a vast assortment of illnesses. Africans did possess knowledge of herbal curatives, and many knew how to mix their own herbs to be used as needed. After all, Africans who knew the various uses of spices and herbs had compounded medicines in Africa since remote times. Very likely, the cookbook "receipts" were adapted from African methods.

Traditional African methods of herbal cures were transplanted and continued to be used by herbal specialists in African communities here in America. Black women, such as Doctress Phillis of Barrington, Rhode Island, were recognized locally for their ability and expertise in African traditional medicine. One African traditional medicinal art that was important to New England was the use of variolation against the outbreak of smallpox. An African servant of Cotton Mather taught him all about smallpox variolation, but was given no credit.

We are met with the same historical omission when it comes to the ability of the black cook. The more creative and important the dish turns out to be to the master or mistress of the house, the quicker it is defined away from the African cook and treated as one of the family's most prized possessions. When a reference or connection is made to the African cook, the cook's expert ability, developed as a result of practice and effort, is denigrated and reduced to magic and innate ability and no effort at all on her part. In the chapter on bread in *Housekeeping in Old Virginia*, there is a challenge to you to keep trying if at first you do not succeed, because if persons without brains can accomplish good bread, states the passage, you can, too! Those "persons without brains," of course, refers to the African cooks. These same cooks also created without standard measuring utensils. Almost never is any praise given to this unique ability of these culinary masters who sometimes created a new taste every time they baked or fried or roasted the same dish. Not measuring allows this to happen. However, as another cookbook sarcastically states regarding African cake baking, the African cook's "method is all a grave mistake"; meaning, even though the cake comes out right the African cook does not know what she is doing.

ⅢⅢⅢⅢⅢⅢⅢⅢⅢⅢⅢⅢⅢⅢⅢⅢⅢⅢⅢⅢⅢⅢⅢⅢⅢⅢⅢⅢ

Coconut Cake

In African American folklore the dance called the cakewalk "was a stylized caricature of whites minueting or waltzing." African bondsmen, who were mocking the manners of the plantation owners, originated the dance. The plantation owners, however, " 'who gathered around to watch the fun, missed the point.' " (*Africanisms in American Culture*, 217 and footnote #14, 223, 224)

Former slave, Eliza Diggs Johnson, in describing the cakewalk held on the plantation where she was born in Missouri, stated that white folks from the big house would come down to the clearing in the woods to watch their slaves do an elegant and poised dance-walk, to which was added a comical, exaggerated grace. Music was supplied by a violin, a drum, and a horn. The prize for the winning couple would be "a towering, extra sweet coconut cake."

The last time I had my paternal grandmother's coconut cake (she grew up in Little Rock, Arkansas) was in the 1950s. I can still smell and taste her cake to this day. The following recipe is slightly different from hers, but I will assure you that the finished product is quite worthy of your time. Trust me, you will be followed around and asked for the name of the bakery where you bought it. Yes, bought it, because anything that tastes this good, guests will hope they will be able to go right out and buy it whenever they want to instead of having to bake it themselves.

And yes, as you can see, I measured everything.

2½ cups all purpose flour (flour should be stirred many times before measuring)
3 tsp. baking powder
1 tsp. salt
1 cup (2 sticks) Parkay margarine (I think it works better than butter, but use butter if you prefer)
2½ cups sugar
5 eggs ("Jumbo")
7 ounces (about 2 cups) finely grated, fresh coconut (If you are faced with time constraints, frozen, finely grated coconut is available at some larger supermarkets and specialty food stores. Just

make sure you thaw it out completely.) OR 2²/₃ cups sweetened flake coconut, slightly packed (see below)
1¼ cups thick, unsweetened coconut milk (canned is fine) OR undiluted evaporated milk
1½ tsp. pure vanilla extract
1½ tsp. coconut extract
½ tsp. pure almond extract

Combine flour, baking powder, and salt in a bowl and set aside.

Cream butter until light and fluffy. Gradually add sugar and blend well. Add eggs one at a time, beating well, but briefly, after each addition.

(If using sweetened flake coconut, grind coconut together with the milk in food processor or blender at this time. Use as indicated below.)

Beginning with dry ingredients (flour mixture), add to butter mixture alternately with grated coconut, coconut milk, and extracts (the coconut, milk, and extracts should be considered as "the liquid ingredient," so that when they are added they should be added together, at the same time). Begin with dry ingredients, end with dry ingredients. There should be 4 dry ingredients additions, 3 liquid ingredients additions. After each addition, stir to blend, but do not beat or stir too much. After the very last addition, scrape down sides of bowl, mix well, but just until thoroughly blended.

Very lightly grease two 9-inch round cake pans. Line with wax paper. Divide batter between the two pans. Bake in a preheated, 350 degree oven for about 40 minutes, depending on your oven. When completely cool, frost and garnish with sweetened flake coconut.

$ $ $ $

Frosting

2 sticks butter (or Parkay margarine)
1 pound confectioners' sugar
1½ tsp. pure vanilla extract
1¼ to 1½ tsp. coconut extract
½ tsp. pure almond extract
5 tsp. thick coconut milk OR undiluted evaporated milk
Sweetened, flake coconut for garnishing (lots)

Cream butter. Gradually add sugar alternately with milk and extracts. After all ingredients have been added, scrape down sides of bowl and beat at highest speed of electric mixer until creamy smooth.

Frost top, sides, and between stacked layers. Garnish top and sides with coconut.

ss ss ss ss

Black Beauty Chocolate Coconut Cake

I have seen cookbooks and been to restaurants that boast of having a recipe for the "ultimate chocolate cake." Noticeably, the vast majority of these recipes are always connotated by such names as "Devil's Food," "Sin Cake," "Death By Chocolate," "Chocolate Beast," "Chocolate Death," "Chocolate Decadence," while an "Angel Food" cake recipe will, of course, usually turn out a white or pale colored cake. I have chosen the above name for my chocolate cake because it is, by physical definition, exactly what the name says. If I could define its taste I could surely call it *Angel Food*. All I can say is that you should try this one and compare it, for taste and moistness, to every other chocolate cake you know. This one is truly "a towering, extra sweet coconut cake," done in chocolate.

Fortunately, we are in an era when the praise of things dark in color is not against the law (theoretically). Remember when the book *Black Beauty* was banned in South Africa? The regime in power there at that time would not allow those two words to be seen together on a printed page, not to mention that they despised the theme of so much affection afforded to something so black in color. Well, like they say, the mind is a terrible thing to waste. Now me, I have nothing but affection for a chocolate cake that is almost black in color, so sometimes I use 9 tablespoons of cocoa with 3 tablespoons of vegetable shortening added to the butter, instead of the 3 squares of melted chocolate.

2½ cups all purpose flour (flour must be stirred many times before measuring)
3 tsp. baking powder
1¼ tsp. baking soda
1 tsp. salt
1 cup Parkay margarine, or butter
3 tablespoons vegetable shortening

2½ cups plus 2 Tbs. sugar
6 eggs ("extra large" or "jumbo")
9 tablespoons unsweetened cocoa OR 3 squares (3 ounces) unsweetened chocolate, melted and cooled (if using squares, *eliminate* vegetable shortening)
7 ounces (about 2 cups) finely grated, fresh coconut (If you are faced with time constraints, frozen, finely grated coconut is available at some larger supermarkets and specialty food stores. Just make sure that you thaw it out completely.) OR 2⅔ cups of sweetened flake coconut (see below)
1¼ cups plus 2 Tbs. ice water
1½ tsp. pure vanilla extract
1½ tsp. coconut extract
½ tsp. pure almond extract

Combine flour, baking powder, baking soda, and salt in a bowl and set aside.

Cream butter with shortening (if using cocoa) until light and fluffy. Gradually add sugar and blend well. Add eggs one at a time, beating well, but briefly, after each addition. Stir in cocoa or melted squares.

(If using flake coconut, grind coconut with the ice water in food processor or blender at this time. Use as indicated below in place of grated coconut.)

Beginning with flour mixture, add to chocolate mixture alternately with grated coconut, water, and extracts (the coconut, water, and extracts should be considered as "the liquid ingredient," so that when they are added they should be added together, at the same time). Begin with dry ingredients, end with dry ingredients. There should be 4 dry ingredient additions, 3 liquid ingredient additions. After each addition, stir to blend, but do not beat or stir too much. After the very last addition, scrape down sides of bowl, mix well, but just until thoroughly blended.

Very lightly grease three 9-inch round cake pans. Line with wax paper. Divide batter between the 3 pans. Bake 2 layers at a time (if using one oven) in a preheated 350 degree oven for 50 minutes.

When all 3 layers have completely cooled, frost and garnish with coconut.

§§ §§ §§ §§

Frosting

2 sticks butter (or Parkay margarine)
1 pound confectioners' sugar
¹/₂ cup unsweetened cocoa
1 tsp. coconut extract
1³/₄ tsp. pure vanilla extract
¹/₂ tsp. pure almond extract
Approximately 1¹/₂ Tbs. milk
Sweetened, flake coconut for garnishing (lots)

Cream butter. Gradually add sugar, cocoa, extracts, and milk to butter. When all ingredients have been added, scrape down sides of bowl and beat on highest speed of electric mixer until creamy smooth.

Frost all three layers in between, on top and sides. Garnish top and sides with coconut.

Black cooks' cake baking in the South certainly helped situate the plantation's reputation for hospitality on its dining room table. Hospitality (and cuisine) in the South reached its apex between 1750 and 1860. An endless variety of the best of foods, imported and native, passed through southern kitchens and were turned into sumptuous repasts, dedicated to capturing the taste buds and memories of any and all who dined at southern tables.

The dependence on the African cook was not felt merely in terms of being able to count on a good plate of food at mealtimes. This dependence on the part of slaveholders was emotional and psychological, to say the least. The African cook was a status symbol, one that provided an image of class and high station and allowed plantation owners to feign a "gentile" and "civilized" life-style, "respectable" in every way to slaveholding society. The African cook as status symbol was also the emblem, or image, of "good cooking" and remained important throughout every phase of development in this country wherever food was considered to be a major part of business, finance, and personal service.

Economics, War, and the Northern Migration of the Southern Black Cook

The African cook carried the mantle of "good cooking" throughout the plantation South and beyond. Black chefs were in demand among the Confederate fighting forces during the Civil War. The end of the war signaled the beginning of the migration of blacks out of the South and the disbursement and further enhancement of their reputation as great cooks. The end of the war also signaled the beginning of the redefining of southern white heritage. The "Lost Cause," or southern white elites' efforts to hold on to their old way of life, centered around food. Cooking and cuisine were remade to look uniquely southern. This effort to forge white southern nationalism resulted in an increase in the number of published cookbooks. Asserting that the recipes were "southern" made these cookbooks *exclusionary*, and therefore racist, because the cookbooks and recipes contained therein were heralded as the creations of the elite southern white women. In an attempt to promote southern white culture, therefore, the concept of "southern cooking," started out as *Whites Only Cuisine*.

This concept has remained influential with respect to why little has been written on the importance of black cooks in the development and economic expansion of America. From pig feet to teal ducks, from street vending and domestic service in the North to tableclothed dining rooms aboard southern steamboats, Africans contributed their culinary skills to the success of the very best kitchens, which claimed to serve the finest meals in the South.

Many kitchens making such claims were found in New Orleans and surrounding areas of Louisiana. The culinary foundation of these kitchens, the base on which New Orleans became a "recognized center of sophisticated culinary activity," was the African cook. The colony's first shipment of bondsmen and women arrived in 1720, and by 1860 the majority were in service, particularly in the city, as domestic servants. The extreme shortage of European females in the colony's early days made African women, slave and free, the targets of the white male population. In many cases the African women were taken on as mistresses, although there were a number of marriages as well. The fact remains that the foods and culinary skills of these women, and of African domestic servants brought with French and Spanish immigrants from Haiti and other Caribbean colonies, have had lasting effects upon the gastronomic preferences of New Orleans.

Such preferences in the city's private homes and commercial eateries have included numerous African-created dishes, such as gumbo, considered "the elixir of life," and jambalaya. They are two of New Orleans' most popular delicacies, and both are entrenched in the culture of the state of Louisiana. Jambalaya, it seems, is just as important in death as it is in life:

> As soon as a Creole enters into Heaven,
> it is said he waves a hand to Saint
> Peter: ... Then he turns to the nearest
> angel: "Where's the pot of jambalaya?"
> If he finds there is none of that strongly
> accented combination of shrimp, oysters,
> tomatoes, rice and other items, he rubs
> his chin, sidles over, and inquires about
> the food customs in the other place. . . .

(Harnett T. Kane, *Queen New Orleans, City By The River* [New York: Bonanza Books, 1949], 312)

Gumbo has become a permanent fixture as well and is often used to describe various aspects of Louisiana's art, music, language, architecture, and food. Cajun music, for example, has been called "a gumbo made of various ingredients and spices." Cajuns, or Acadians, who arrived in large groups in Louisiana between 1765 and 1785, are themselves very much aware that the most important stylistic influence on Cajun music was from African musicians. Africans contributed new rhythms and percussion techniques, improvisational singing and the blues. Zydeco music was developed by black musicians around the turn of the twentieth century, as these musicians continued to experiment with various sound and rhythm techniques. Experimentation with the accordion was carried on by both Acadian and African musicians, and during the nineteenth century Cajuns and Africans formed dance bands and performed together. Throughout the 1920s and 1930s Dennis McGee and Amede Ardoin, a black accordionist and singer of Cajun music, performed and recorded together on a regular basis. Ardoin has been called a "hero" of Cajun music, and many of his compositions are considered to be not only the foundation of the music but also responsible for its distinguished cultural standing.

Okra, hot peppers, and rice are among gumbo's main ingredients. Straight from the Motherland's west coast, gumbo is one of the most nourishing of all dishes, particularly when it is enhanced with a variety of ingredients from land and/or sea. I must say a few words about those ingredients. First, pork was not a part of the traditional African diet, so I have chosen not to include any sausage in the following recipe; although you can add about 1/2 pound of beef or pork sausage to this version, if you wish. Also, you will notice that I prepare a gravy first (known as roux in Louisiana). This is not a mandatory step. Also, in some West African kitchens, palm oil is added near the end of the cooking time.

⧢⧢⧢

Motherland Gumbo

Shells from 1 pound of medium shrimp
3 cups water
5 2/3 Tbs. butter
1/3 cup flour
1 large green pepper, chopped
1/2 of a *large* red onion, chopped

2 white onions, chopped and divided
¹/₂ of a medium carrot, sliced into thin rounds, then halved
8 EACH allspice berries and whole cloves, finely crushed
¹/₄ tsp. thyme
³/₄ tsp. cayenne (or malagueta or jalapeño chili peppers), divided
1 tsp. garlic salt with parsley
¹/₂ tsp. crushed basil leaves
2 bay leaves
Freshly ground black pepper to taste
2 large tomatoes, chopped
¹/₂ tsp. dried shrimp
4 chicken bouillon cubes
1 to 2 tsp. molasses
Salt and freshly ground black pepper, to taste
1¹/₂ cups sliced okra (sliced into rounds)
¹/₄ to ¹/₃ pound lump crabmeat
1 pound shelled medium shrimp

Bring shrimp shells to boil in water. Lower heat and simmer for 15 minutes. Strain and discard shells. Set aside, covered.

In a pot over medium heat, melt butter. Gradually add flour and cook and stir constantly until mixture becomes a deep medium brown color. Add next 4 ingredients, minus 1 onion. Cook and stir for a few minutes. Add all spices, minus ¹/₄ tsp. cayenne. Cook and stir for another few minutes. Stir in the tomatoes and dried shrimp. Add enough water to shrimp shell broth to make 3 cups. Heat, then dissolve bouillon in broth. Add broth and molasses to pot and mix well. Taste for needed salt and pepper. Bring to a boil. Lower heat and simmer, covered, for 20 minutes. Stir in okra, crab, shrimp, the ¹/₄ tsp. cayenne, and the 1 onion. Bring to boil again. Lower heat and simmer, covered, for about 9 or 10 minutes. Mound rice under or over servings of gumbo.

Many culinary compositions performed on a regular basis in New Orleans, and in Louisiana in general, had as their foundation corn. Acadians were only one of many immigrant groups who received help in acclimating themselves to the new culinary environment. Other newcomers to colonial Louisiana, such as French-Canadian Madame Langlois, cook and housekeeper to Jean Baptiste LeMoyne, Sieur de Bienville (brother of Pierre LeMoyne, Sieur d'Iberville, defender of France's American trade route to Saint Domingue), sought out Native American culinary expertise. Native Americans taught her and other new arrivals how to grind corn for bread, how to make hominy and grits with home-made lye, as well as how to prepare other local foods such as succotash, made with corn and an assortment of beans.

Another dish, made from preserved corn, and one of the oldest made in the Americas, was a plain cornmeal cereal sometimes called *sagamite.* The Acadians were said to have added milk and a sweetener to this same dish and renamed it *couche-couche,* "perhaps because of its resemblance to an African semolina-based steamed mush called cous-cous." It must be noted that sweet couscous, prepared with milk and sugar or molasses, raisins or dates, rosewater and spices, has been prepared since ancient times in many African countries. Obviously, Africans cooked a dish here in America very much like one served at home, which the Cajuns adopted and misspelled. This is another example of how quick people have been to assign Africa's culinary contributions to someone else.

Another treat for which Louisiana is well known is pralines. As with red beans and rice (Louis Armstrong's favorite dish), gumbo, jambalaya, shrimp, chicken, or any number of other dishes, every cook has his or her own rendition of this delicious candy. Whip up a batch of these sweet temptations for your snacking pleasure.

〽〽〽〽〽〽〽〽〽〽〽〽〽〽〽〽〽〽〽〽〽〽〽〽〽〽〽〽〽〽〽〽〽〽〽〽〽〽

Milk Chocolate Cream Pralines

6 Tbs. butter
³/₄ cup plus 3 tsp. light cream
³/₄ cup EACH light brown and white sugar
³/₄ cup milk chocolate chips
2¼ tsp. vanilla extract
³/₄ cup plus 3 tsp. chopped pecans (or walnuts)

In a saucepan, carefully melt butter (do not let it burn). Add cream, then sugar. Stir until sugar completely dissolves. Over medium heat bring to a boil, stirring constantly. Cook and stir constantly for five minutes. Remove from heat and *immediately* stir in chocolate. Stir until chocolate has completely melted. Stir in vanilla and mix well. Add nuts. Allow to rest for a minute. Line cookie sheet(s) with a double thickness of paper towels. Place spoonfuls of candy on towels (candy will spread so allow some space between spoonfuls). Allow to sit for several minutes before serving.

꽃꽃꽃꽃꽃꽃꽃꽃꽃꽃꽃꽃꽃꽃꽃꽃꽃꽃꽃꽃꽃꽃꽃꽃꽃꽃꽃꽃꽃꽃꽃꽃꽃꽃꽃꽃

African culinary contributions have always made food one of New Orleans strongest drawing points. Even as street hawkers, African women became "the most influential buyers and sellers of food in New Orleans." Thirty thousand dollars were spent to build a market house in 1813 which sold poultry of all kinds, including wild ducks, eggs, oysters and other seafood, oranges, bananas, apples, sweet and white potatoes, carrots, corn, sugarcane, roots, and various meats. African and Native American men and women sold foods at this market. However, the establishment in the city of permanent marketplaces did not deter primarily female hawkers (African, Native American, and a small number of whites) from remaining active. Years before, in 1797, they had been so successful that fifty-one shopkeepers, in an effort to protect their livelihood, had beseeched the city council to prohibit the commercial activities of an increasing number of bondswomen and free Africans who sold foods and other goods along New Orleans' streets and roads and on countryside plantations.

By the mid 1800s African culinary skill had permeated and effectively enhanced business and finance on every level in New Orleans. The steamboat had successfully ushered in a new era of commerce, one that would bring enormous wealth to the city. That wealth was intertwined with food. The cuisine, cooked and served by black chefs on the floating palaces, or steamboats, was heralded as one of the primary reasons for using that mode of travel.

The steamboat aided the economic expansion of America by opening up the West and South, both of which were thickly woven with streams and rivers. Approximately sixty of these "River Queens" cruised the Mississippi River and its tributaries by 1820. By 1860, one thousand set out. Steamboat kitchens, like plantation kitchens, featured gastronomic fare prepared by both African men and women, but mostly men. Culinary delight was often the SOLE purpose of passengers sailing from one river town to another aboard a steamship. Robins sauteed in wine and butter, teal ducks baked crisp, brightly colored and fruited ices and blancmange, and other fancy confections made with almonds and sugar, were but a small sample of the delicious offerings listed on the menu.

Salads were also part of the bill of fare. Apparently, they were in as much demand on board steamboats as the meats and vegetables. Actually, as you will soon see, all dishes served in steamboat dining rooms were in high demand. Salads frequently disappeared as quickly as the entrees and desserts. Serve the following salad as a first or second course. It also goes quite well as a healthy side dish to steaks, chicken, hamburgers, and hot dogs.

Slawed Red Cabbage with Red Raspberry Dressing

3 cups shredded red cabbage

2 Tbs. grated carrots

4 Tbs. red raspberry preserves

2 Tbs. EACH sour cream and mayonnaise

2 tsp. lemon juice

1/2 tsp. white pepper

1/4 tsp. EACH salt (or more to taste), garlic salt mixed with parsley, and crushed red pepper

Freshly ground black pepper, to taste

Place all cabbage and carrots in a bowl and mix well. In a separate bowl, combine remaining ingredients and mix well. Stir into cabbage mixture.

Delicacies such as this helped to soften the inconveniences of steamboat travel. After a few days and nights as a passenger aboard some of the steamboats, a little "Lubrication" was sorely needed. Do not let it fool you. It goes down like a fruity, tropical punch. Thing is, punch is exactly what it will do to you if you do not go slow and easy with this absolutely delicious drink.

When President Monroe was in Savannah in 1819 for the maiden voyage of the first steamship to cross the Atlantic, he was wined and dined on a river trip and was introduced to Chatham Artillery Punch, the origin of which is said to date back to colonial days. Chatham Artillery might boast of being the oldest military organization in Georgia, but "Lubrication" has the power.

Lubrication

1 cup gin
1 cup vodka
1 cup grain alcohol
1 cup 151 proof rum
2 cups whiskey sour mix
4 cups grape juice
4 cups orange juice
4 cups 7 Up or ginger ale
4 cups lemonade
2 cups Grenadine
Crushed ice, enough to fill each glass ³/₄ full
Red maraschino cherries

Combine all of the ingredients, except cherries and ice, in the above order. Stir and blend well. Pour into tall glasses, filled three quarters of the way with crushed ice. Garnish each glass with two maraschino cherries.

Before the Civil War, free Africans, as well as African bondsmen, were utilized as steamboat labor. African bondsmen were hired out to steamboats by plantation owners, chiefly as an additional source of revenue. They were employed as deckhands, the men who performed numerous chores all about the steamboat. They took care of wooding, manned capstan and pumps, handled cargo, served as firemen, and generally provided the brawn and muscle. Because of their use in all parts of the ship for the dirtiest jobs, often they were in the right place at the right time when the boilers blew up. Throughout the steamboat era cargo was moved by hand (carried on the backs of black and white "rousters"), mostly without the aid of machinery. In the late 1840s, however, the larger boats introduced hoisting engines, which were called "niggers" and "mickeys." These were used to stow and remove heavy freight from the hold, not for moving cargo between ship and shore.

Africans were also employed as part of the cabin crew, where they served as stewards, cooks, cabin boys, and chambermaids. In the kitchens and dining rooms they began as servants and waiters; as cooks they were considered to be even greater assets. Africans were to later make up more than half of the crew of the steamboats. For cabin passengers, steamboat cuisine set quite a pleasant table. The steward, who took care of all the needs of the first-class passengers, directed the purchase of staples and kitchen supplies at landings and the preparation and serving of the meals. Fruits, vegetables, lambs, pigs, and chickens were kept in supply on board for the cabin passenger's meals:

The animals were killed and dressed on board. The chickens lived until the menu called for a chicken dinner, whereupon three or four negroes in the starboard galley where the meats were prepared gathered around a barrel of hot water which had been filled from the boilers, broke the necks of the fowls over the edge of the barrel, scalded, picked and cut them— sometimes as many as a hundred and fifty in an hour. In the larboard galley were made the breads, cakes, pastries and desserts;.... (*Mississippi Steamboatin'*, 238).

Light, soft, and ready to melt in your mouth, I cannot get enough of these. You will find yourself heating them up, loading them with butter and eating these rolls as between-meal snacks. Roasted cornish hens, bacon and eggs, caesar or chef salads, spaghetti and meatballs, and everything else; all will crave the assistance of and will taste better going down with a couple of these rolls.

࿇࿇࿇࿇࿇࿇࿇࿇࿇࿇࿇࿇࿇࿇࿇࿇࿇࿇࿇࿇࿇࿇࿇࿇࿇࿇࿇࿇࿇࿇࿇࿇࿇࿇࿇࿇࿇࿇࿇

Dinner Rolls

1/4 cup warm water
1 ounce cake yeast or yeast granules
1 cup milk

⅓ cup shortening
1 egg
¼ cup sugar
1½ tsp. salt
Between 3 and 3½ cups flour
Butter or shortening

Combine water and yeast. Let yeast dissolve in water and stir slightly into a mixture.

Scald milk and pour into very large bowl. Place shortening in milk and stir until dissolved. Let mixture cool.

Stir in egg, then sugar and salt. Blend well. Stir in yeast mixture.

Start stirring in flour about ½ cup at a time. Cover with wax paper. Let dough rise for 1 hour.

While dough is rising, preheat oven at 350 degrees. Grease baking pans. Heavily flour counter surface.

To make rolls: with heavily floured hands (dough will be sticky) take small handfuls of dough and drop onto floured counter. Roll in flour a bit and form into a ball in your hands. Pat out air bubbles by holding ball in one hand and gently slapping (in a clapping fashion) dough with the other hand. Continue to flour hands as needed to offset stickiness. Shape into round rolls and place ½ inch apart in greased pans. Allow rolls to rise again for 45 minutes.

Bake until golden brown, about 15 minutes. As soon as you take rolls out of the oven, generously grease the tops with butter or shortening. This last step is actually essential to producing a totally soft bread.

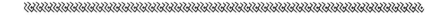

In the early decades of steamboat travel, when even the fastest boats took several weeks to complete a trip, it was important to travelers to select boats with reputations for a good table. There was competition among the boats to acquire that reputation by serving cabin travelers the most elaborate meals. On one of the boats thirteen different desserts were offered: Six custards, jelly and cream, served in tall glasses; seven pies, puddings, and ice creams. It was said that some of the northern line ships served what was called a foundering meal at the start of each run, which was so heavy that the passengers were left feeling squeamish about food for the remainder of the trip.

Game was added to the menu by members of the crew who were expert hunters and trappers. I have already mentioned the skill with which African men trapped squirrel and quail and other small animals. For those persons who could afford to travel by cabin it was said that steamboat fare

> delighted the palate and overwhelmed the digestion with a cuisine which in quantity and variety at least demonstrated the peaks to which civilization could rise above the hog-and-hominy of the pioneers. (*Steamboats on the Western Rivers*, 391)

Some steamers boasted breakfasts offering a choice of pigeon, fowl, steaks, ragout, ham, coffee and tea, chicken fricassee, and other meats. Dinner offerings included baked pork and turkey, huge platters of steaks, small platters of duck, chicken, other fowl and game, potatoes, rice, corn, other platters of sliced meats. In addition, a selection of tarts and rice pudding, and coffee and tea and rum, was available.

Even if you are not a superb hunter and prefer to order your game from the market, you will enjoy the following preparation. It is a tasty combination of flavors.

〰〰〰〰〰〰〰〰〰〰〰〰〰〰〰〰〰〰〰〰〰〰〰〰〰〰〰〰〰

Rabbit Smothered with Sausage

2½ to 3 pounds rabbit meat, cut into serving size pieces
Garlic salt, seasoned salt, black pepper, and paprika
Flour
Several Tbs. of vegetable oil
One 16-ounce roll of hot sausage
1 large onion, chopped
1 large tomato, chopped
¼ (rounded) cup black raisins (preferably, organically grown, from the refrigerated section of a health food store; the taste is substantially better)

⅛ tsp. crushed red pepper
½ tsp. "hot, Mexican style" chili powder
¾ tsp. celery seed
1 tsp. parsley flakes
½ to 1 tsp. garlic salt; OR, a fresh, small garlic pod, crushed
2 tsp. molasses
1 cup chicken broth
2 Tbs. dark rum

Season rabbit with garlic salt, seasoned salt, black pepper, and paprika. Coat rabbit with flour. Brown pieces on both sides in hot oil in a large skillet or pot. Transfer rabbit to a covered dish and set aside. Drain oil from pot. In the same skillet or pot, break sausage apart with a fork and very lightly brown. Drain all oil, then crumble into bite size pieces (if using your hands, wait until sausage is cool enough to handle). Add next 8 ingredients to sausage in pot. Mix well. Combine molasses, chicken broth, and rum in a small bowl. Mix well. Pour chicken broth mixture into pot. Mix well. Bring to a boil over medium heat. Continue cooking and stirring for 20 to 30 seconds. Add rabbit meat to pot and, using a spoon, cover rabbit with portions of the sausage mixture. Simmer, covered, for about 45 minutes, over medium-low heat. Serve immediately. WAH LAH!

On a trip from St. Louis to Louisville in 1833 it was reported that a single meal consisted of thirty-one different dishes, available to twenty-two passengers. Another steamboat's table was noted as being covered from end to end with different dishes, all of them wedged together like a "battalion of infantry in solid square." On one special occasion aboard the *Telegraph No. 1* in January 1849, a feast was served consisting of one soup, five kinds of fish, six kinds of boiled meats with accompanying sauces, eleven entrees consisting of meats and baked dishes such as fricasseed kidneys and spiced pig's head, nine roasts, five kinds of game, which included squirrel, wild turkey, and venison, fifteen kinds of pastry and dessert, and fruits and nuts to top it off.

In the 1850s it was customary for passengers traveling on upper Mississippi steamboats to receive one special treat on each trip upstream. This special treat took the form of thirteen desserts arranged in a circle around each passenger's plate. Passengers could taste, eat or throw away any or all of it. The food on many of the less luxurious steamboats was considered plentiful but greasy. However, the more luxury carriers were said to have offerings that were quite pleasing.

Though the kitchen quarters were lacking in a number of conveniences, this handicap did not keep the cooks and stewards from presenting, aboard the larger and more luxurious boats, a praiseworthy bill of fare. The haste and immoderate indulgence with which meals were consumed must have had something to do with passenger approval of the food. Quality must have been involved there somewhere. On the other hand, table manners aboard steamboats were a shame and a disgrace. "Bestial feeding" was one term used to describe mealtime. Passengers had apparently never been exposed to such quantity and elaborateness of food. Apparently, they felt that since they had paid full passage, as one Cincinnati editor later related in print, they were entitled to get their money's worth. The same editor related how the passengers ate extravagantly, excessively, and promiscuously, and how they devoured everything they could get their hands on, choosing the closest dishes first and working their way across both ends of the table. One man began dinner by swallowing a whole moulded blancmange. Others snatched the tarts, pies, jellies, raisins, and almonds, not because they really wanted them, but because the stuff was sitting there and they were too greedy to wait for dinner to be served.

Bishop Henry Benjamin Whipple recorded his mealtime experience with fellow passengers in 1844 on board the *Goddess of Liberty:*

When the supper bell rang with a rush, one grand race, and woe to the luckless wight who should stop in his course, he might as well expect to be crushed to death—and then such a clatter of knives and forks and tableware, such screaming for waiters, ... and such exhibitions of muscle and nerve as men entered with all their powers into the game of knife and fork. It was worse than a second Babel. As a Missouri "puke" who stood next to me said, "it looked for all the world like one great scrummage." The table was cleared in an amazing short space of time and food was bolted as I have never seen before. (*Steamboats On the Western Rivers,* 402, 403)

You think perhaps hunger made them do it? Maybe Bishop Whipple just did not understand the power of a growling stomach. You will know for sure when you prepare the following recipe. Set the table and stand back. After all, you do not want to be knocked down and crushed to death. Find out how this irresistible dish fares in the game of knife and fork.

Steak Smothered in Tomatoes and Sauce

Two 2½ pound top round steaks
Garlic salt, seasoned salt, black pepper, parsley flakes, paprika, and flour
3 or 4 Tbs. oil, and more as needed
5 large plum tomatoes, sliced
¼ tsp. EACH crushed basil leaves and crushed red pepper
½ tsp. garlic salt with parsley
Freshly ground black pepper and a little salt
2 tsp. EACH light molasses and Worcestershire sauce
½ cup beef broth
1 large plum tomato, sliced
1 large onion, sliced into rings

Season meat with garlic and seasoned salts, black pepper, parsley, and paprika. Coat with flour.

Heat oil in a skillet. Brown both sides of meat. Transfer to a baking pan, one layer deep.

Cook 5 sliced tomatoes in same skillet (do not clean) over medium heat by gently folding, for about a minute. Add basil, red pepper, garlic salt, black pepper, and salt. Continue cooking by gently folding tomatoes for another minute. Add molasses, Worcestershire sauce, and beef broth. Cook and fold for another couple of minutes. Taste for needed salt and pepper. Add the remaining sliced tomato and remove from heat. Pour tomatoes and sauce over steaks. Cover steaks with onion slices. Cover with aluminum foil. Bake in a 350 degree preheated oven for 2 hours.

In 1846, there were two seatings at meals on northern steamboats. Officers and passengers were first, then the servants. Southern steamboats had five seatings, in this order: cabin passengers, white nurses, children, officers; white deck passengers; white waiters; colored passengers, free or slaves; and colored waiters. After the Big Liberation, by way of Lincoln, the "freedmen's bureau" was added to some larger steamboats. The "freedmen's bureau" was the "Negro cabin" and was located on what was called the Texas or hurricane deck. There was one period when the hurricane deck had only tarpaulin or canvas awning for cover. I have no idea whether they ever changed it. Anyway, with the depravity that went on during mealtime, can you imagine what could possibly be left by the time the "coloreds" were allowed a seating?

In addition to providing good food, Africans provided song singing for the passengers' entertainment. Many tunes made reference to the kitchen and culinary creations, such as "corn starch pudding" and "tapioca pie." Many of their rhymes were simply tunes they sang while working. The dining rooms and kitchens were totally staffed by black people and were excellent. It was little wonder then that veteran rivermen, who were still trying to brag about their wives' cooking, had to admit that meals served on board the steamboats were often much better than what they ate at home with their families.

Duck is wonderful spiced just right and moistened with a good sauce or gravy. Serve this riverboat favorite for your most auspicious occasion. Problem: How will you stop people from inviting themselves to your house for dinner?

Duck Braised in Spiced Tomato Sauce

A piece of duck fat from duck below
One 6-pound duck, cut into 8 serving pieces
Garlic salt mixed with parsley, seasoned salt, cinnamon, cumin, black pepper, and paprika
Flour
½ of a small green pepper, chopped
1 medium onion, chopped
1½ large tomatoes, chopped
Rounded ½ cup sliced mushrooms

One 6-ounce can tomato paste
2 tomato paste cans of water
2 tsp. Worcestershire sauce
2 chicken bouillon cubes
½ cup boiling water
2 Tbs. EACH dark rum and light molasses
¼ heaping tsp. EACH crushed red pepper and ground cumin
½ heaping tsp. EACH parsley flakes and celery seed
¼ rounded tsp. ground cinnamon
A few shakes of garlic salt mixed with parsley
Freshly ground black pepper, to taste
Salt, to taste

Melt duck fat in large skillet or pot. While fat is melting, season both sides of duck with garlic salt with parsley, seasoned salt, cinnamon, cumin, black pepper, and paprika. Coat with flour and brown on both sides in rendered fat in a large skillet or pot. Transfer duck to a covered platter. Drain all oil from skillet or pot. Over medium heat add green pepper and onion to pot. Cook and stir for a minute or so. Add tomatoes and mushrooms and continue cooking and stirring for another minute. Add tomato paste and water and mix well. Stir in Worcestershire sauce. Dissolve bouillon in boiling water. Add bouillon water to pot and mix well. Stir in rum, then molasses, and bring to a boil over medium heat. Stir in next 6 ingredients, two at a time, cooking and stirring for about a minute after each addition. Add black pepper and salt, to taste. Return duck pieces to pot, covering pieces with sauce as you do so. Simmer, covered, over low to medium-low heat for 1 hour and 45 minutes to 2 hours.

⊰⊱

African men served in much the same capacity on board the steamers used by the Confederate Navy during the Civil War. One additional service African slaves provided during the war was as pilots of these vessels. Robert Smalls was one such slave pilot. However, on May 13, 1862, he sailed his family out of Charleston Harbor aboard *The Planter,* an armed Confederate steamer, to a Union squadron that was blockading the harbor.

During the Civil War, verses and songs were composed to express various sentiments of soldiers, Confederate and Union alike.

One southern war song, "Goober Peas," became very popular during this time. Its words were the sentiments of soldiers who wanted the war to end so that they could go home and "gobble goober peas." The terms "goober" and "pindar" are extractions of a Congolese term (*zinguba* or *nguba* and *mpinda*) for "ground pea," or "groundnut," or the more popular term, peanut.

Since soldiers could not wait to get home to gobble peanuts, I am sure that the officers in the Confederate army in particular missed the various ways that blacks in southern kitchens had prepared them. Some of peanuts' finest moments were spent in spreads, or what are now referred to as pâtes. Peanut Chicken Spread is very tasty and I highly recommend serving it during any of those critical discussions on saving the union (assuming that there *is* one that you would like to save).

Peanut Chicken Spread (Pâte)

Two 5-ounce cans "Mixin' Chicken," well drained
2 Tbs. Braunsweiger (liverwurst)
2 tsp. creamy peanut butter
4 Tbs. mayonnaise
2 Tbs. light cream
4 tsp. dark rum
6 tsp. Worcestershire sauce
1½ tsp. garlic salt with parsley
¼ tsp. EACH ground cinnamon and poultry seasoning
Several shakes of crushed red pepper
Freshly ground black pepper and a little salt, to taste
2 whole green onions with tops, finely chopped
4 Tbs. plus 2 tsp. finely chopped cucumber (you do not have to remove outer skin)
⅔ cup finely crushed peanuts or walnuts
2 Tbs. fine bread crumbs

Combine chicken and Braunsweiger and mix well. Add next five ingredients and mix well. Mix in spices, then remaining ingredients. Taste for needed black pepper and salt. Chill thoroughly. Serve chilled spread inside of hot biscuits or on top of crackers.

The soldiers who sang songs about the peanut were more concerned about getting home to eat them than in their source. However, it is interesting to note that information on the origin of the peanut brings us to much racist literature. *The Origin of Cultivated Plants,* in its outline of gene centers of the world, lists South America, specifically Peru, as the country that first grew peanuts. It is very noticeable that the places designated as being the areas of origin were the same, exact areas where there was strong, influential African presence in remote times. When one does find written discourse on the peanut and how Africa came to know it, it is put in the context of Europeans bringing it to Africa and then Africans accompanying the crop to America on board slave ships.

In *Africa and the Discovery of America* the author discusses the various Italian names for a plant that was confused with the peanut. The Italian names dolcichino, *dolzolino, bacicci babbagigi* are merely translations of Arabic terms for the peanut. It is the author's contention that the original term for the peanut is derived from Arabic but that all other forms are derived from the Mandingo.

As early as the 1300s the Mandingo peoples of Mali were observed using the peanut. They sometimes fried them and ate them like a snack. They also ground them and added them to bread doughs and tiny cakes which they baked and fried. The oil from the peanut was used in their culinary preparations as well as furnishing light for lamps and as oil to lubricate the skin. Mixed with a particular type of clay and earth it helped to make plaster for their houses.

Snacks were the most common use of the peanut. Here is a wonderful anytime peanut snack that some people choose to eat with beer. Of course, no chasers are necessary. Just have your appetite ready.

§§

Spicy Peanut Crunch

³/₄ cup chopped peanuts OR walnuts OR pecans

¹/₄ cup EACH finely grated coconut and fine corn flake crumbs

¹/₈ tsp. EACH salt, cinnamon, and nutmeg

¹/₈ to ¹/₄ tsp. cayenne

3 Tbs. butter

6 Tbs. dark brown sugar

6 tsp. water

Combine first 7 ingredients and mix well.

In a saucepan, melt butter. Add water, then sugar, and stir until sugar melts. Over medium heat bring mixture to a FULL ROLLING BOIL. Cook and stir frequently and vigorously for a little over 3 minutes. IMMEDIATELY (syrup hardens quickly) POUR HOT SYRUP INTO NUT MIXTURE, STIRRING AND MIXING RAPIDLY to completely coat nut mixture. When well coated, place spoonfuls (using your hands to scoop mixture up in balls is easier) of mixture on wax paper-lined cookie sheet. When completely cooled, store in covered container.

In spite of Africans' early use of the peanut, some writers try to avoid acknowledging the fact, offering a make-your-own-judgment type of explanation. At other times downright lies are offered. An article titled "Peanut Butter: It's Not Only For Sandwiches" (*The Hartford Courant,* Wednesday, September 28, 1983) states that there is some confusion as to where the peanut originated. The same writer is also confused regarding the creator of peanut butter. The article contends that peanut butter was created by a St. Louis physician in 1890, who was responsible for its becoming marketed as an easily digested, high quality protein health food. It is beyond comprehension how such lies and misinformation are allowed in print. It is ironic and quite fitting that one of Africa's most versatile crops should become one of America's most versatile crops, thanks to the "Wizard of Tuskegee," Dr. George Washington Carver.

Another extremely significant aspect of the *Hartford Courant* article is that recognition is given to peanut butter as a flavor enhancer for a variety of other foods including meat marinades, salad dressings, ice cream, and layer cake. The article implies not only that the varied use of the peanut is something new but also that its uses were invented or concocted by "someone" here in America. This, of course, is a slap in the face to the genius of Dr. Carver, as well as all African cooks. Mention of a skewered meat dish using a peanut marinade is credited to Indonesia, but only in the sense that the peanut marinade is a Western idea. Apparently some Western cooks have finally "discovered" the versatility of peanut butter. But its acceptance is viewed as a new culinary discovery by "gourmet" cooks.

Peanuts and peanut butter, which held a common place in the culinary lives of Africans in the Mother Country for centuries before European invasion, are used in various food preparations of chicken, vegetable, and beef stews and soups; breads, snacks, desserts, sauces, and condiments. The following aromatic peanut condiment is a tasty accompaniment to salmon (or crab) cakes.

§§

Groundnut Carrot Relish

3 medium carrots
3 green onions, with tops
½ cup chopped peanuts or walnuts
½ tsp. EACH coriander seeds and anise seeds
¼ tsp. EACH cumin seeds and crushed red pepper
½ tsp. garlic salt with parsley
1¼ tsp. sugar
1 tsp. EACH lemon and lime juice
2½ tsp. vinegar
Freshly ground black pepper and a little salt, to taste

In a food processor, *grate* carrots and onions, then nuts. Transfer mixture to a bowl.

In a skillet, toast together coriander, anise, and cumin by shaking skillet back and forth frequently, for a few minutes. DO NOT ALLOW SEEDS TO BURN. Cool completely, then grind. Stir ground spices into carrot mixture. Add remaining ingredients and stir until well blended. Serve chilled.

§§

Peanuts and peanut butter also found their way into a number of dishes prepared by Africans in the United States during the era of slavery. However, it was George Washington Carver's scientific research and creations that revolutionized the economy of the South, and propelled the use of the peanut, sweet potato, and other plants to astronomical heights well into the twentieth century. From peanuts he created more than three hundred products including milk, cream, buttermilk, cheese condiments, coffee, plastics, paper stains, insulating boards, and flour, to name just a few things. From sweet potatoes he produced 118 products such as starch, tapioca, mock coconut, syrup, breakfast food, stains, and flour.

One of the products he created from the peanut was ice cream powder. Mixed with water it was said to produce a rich and delicious ice cream, with a taste like that made with real cream. Thirty different dyes were extracted from the skin of the peanut. They held their colors, were harmless to the skin, and were a substitute for quinine. He also made pickles, Worcestershire sauce, and buttermilk from the peanut. In addition, the peanut served as food for livestock. Fed on peanuts, cattle thrived, showing a marked increase in milk production.

From sweet potatoes he produced crystallized ginger, vinegar, mucilage, ink, relishes, pomade, and later synthetic rubber. During World War I, it was Carver's genius that allowed at least two pounds of wheat a day to be saved by mixing sweet potato flour with wheat flour. Better bread products resulted from this mixture. Immediately adapted to food products, it fed millions of American soldiers and their allies.

Dr. Carver is also known for his food recipes. One such recipe was for Strawberry or Peach Leather. Another was for a dish he called Sweet Potato Peanuts.

Dr. Carver's Strawberry or Peach Leather

"Take thoroughly ripe strawberries, mash to a pulp, spread on platters and dry in the sun or oven; when dry, dust with powdered sugar, and roll up like a jelly cake, cut into suitable sized pieces and pack away in jars. Peaches may be treated exactly in the same manner." They can "be eaten as confection or soaked in water and used for pies, shortcake, sauce, tarts, etc." Powdered sugar can be left out.

(*Dr. George Washington Carver, Scientist,* 207, 208).

⅟⅟ ⅟⅟ ⅟⅟ ⅟⅟

Dr. Carver's Sweet Potato Peanuts

1 pint EACH cooked and mashed sweet potatoes, toasted bread crumbs, and finely chopped mixed nut meats. Spice with a little salt, pepper, sage, and mace. Beat together 2 egg yolks and 2 tsp. of baking powder. Stir this mixture into potato mixture. Form mixture into small cakes. Dip each cake in egg white, then shredded coconut. Brown on both sides in a little pork fat. Drain. Serve hot or cold.

(The Integrated Cookbook, 97)

He also developed his own recipes for peanut sausage, sweet potato biscuits, peanut salad, peanut cake, as well as numerous dishes made from cowpeas.

When the boys finally got to go home and gobble goobers, that is, after the Civil War ended, Northerners and Southerners alike continued to view the newly freed slaves as childlike and incapable of taking care of themselves. By the end of 1867 it was decided that freed slaves represented a difficulty that could only be solved through proper education, that is, industrial schooling—the educational philosophy of schools such as Hampton and Tuskegee Institutes. Hampton Institute's founder and principal, General Samuel Chapman Armstrong, made it quite clear that by *design* this educational institution was established to prepare the "Negro" for the more productive exploitation of his and her labor, thus allowing the "Negro" to be fitted into his and her place. Armstrong stated in 1874 that the goal of the school was not to produce scholars, but rather, to allow Hampton to function as a direct source for northern employers who wanted black labor.

Black labor was needed in the North in the area of industry and domestic service. The Irish had begun to abandon domestic service in cities such as Boston and New York for jobs in the expanding factory system. Hampton provided black women with the necessary training in dusting, making beds, and cooking that made them perfect as domestic servants. So, thanks to Armstrong and schools such as Hampton, many white northern households could boast of their specially trained, "imported" black cooks from down South.

Migrating to the North was a dream shared by many black folks living in the South. During the 1890s, Africans left the South by the thousands each year. This fostered great concern in Armstrong, who realized the South was losing much of its wealth in terms of black labor. The Great Accommodator, Booker T. Washington, principal of Tuskegee Institute from 1881 until his death in 1915, was very much aware of the dependence of the South upon African labor:

> It is sometimes said that the destiny of the Negro is in the hands of the white people of the South. I say that the destiny of the white people of the South is, to a large degree, in the hands of the Negro cook! The majority of our prosperous Southern white people have their food prepared and served three times a day by a Negro woman or girl.

"Fried Chicken, Booker T. Washington Jr. Style"

Booker T.'s son, Booker Jr., had a gala going-away party hosted for him by the faculty men at Tuskegee. Extravagant preparations were made that included an orchestra and seating arrangements imitating those of the Cabinet Room of the White House. The main event was dinner: "Fried Chicken, Booker T. Washington Jr. Style."

Any night of the week, any occasion that comes up, is the right one for this dish. Captivating is the word that will come to mind when you inhale the aroma. Captured is how you will feel after you take the first bite.

3/4 cup milk
2 eggs, well beaten
1 tsp. EACH white pepper, black pepper and salt
1 whole chicken, cut into serving pieces
Hot and spicy seasoned salt, black pepper, and paprika
Flour
1/3 to 1/2 cup rendered chicken fat or peanut oil
2 onions, chopped

2 tsp. flour
¼ cup white wine

Combine milk, eggs, the 1 tsp. each of the white pepper, black pepper, and salt. Pour over chicken pieces and marinate, refrigerated, for 2 to 4 hours, turning pieces occasionally.

Remove chicken from marinade and season with spicy salt, black pepper, and paprika. Coat with flour.

Heat oil in a skillet and add chicken pieces, browning on both sides. Transfer chicken (one layer deep) to a baking pan.

Drain all but 2 or 3 Tbs. of oil from skillet. Cook and stir onions for a few minutes in oil in skillet. Combine flour and wine and blend until smooth. Add remaining marinade and wine mixture to onions and stir well, stirring crumbs and all into mixture. Pour onion mixture over chicken and bake, covered, in a preheated 350 degree oven for about 1 hour, or until chicken is tender. As you have discovered, this is really oven fried chicken. As you will also discover, it is finger lickin' good, too.

Before the South began losing its wealth to the North, in terms of black labor, there was an African presence already established in one particular city in the North that was responsible for setting lavish tables in prosperous households. Dining tables in this city were making incomparable marks in the hands of the "Negro" cook. These cooks' accomplishments were particularly important when you consider that as long as Africans worked for free, or for next to nothing, they were assured full-scale employment. In the farm areas, Africans were house servants or field hands, but as city life grew, Africans dominated large portions of certain types of skilled trades. The expressions of jealousy and outrage by whites who wanted these positions were ignored by the slaveholders. Such was the case in Philadelphia between 1790 and 1820. During this time, most of Philadelphia's artisans were African. Twenty years later, and for thirty years after that, Africans would dominate another trade in Philadelphia; one that raised these same Africans to prominence and affluence; one that, as W. E. B. DuBois points out in *The Philadelphia Negro,*

> transformed the Negro cook and waiter into the public caterer and restaurateur, and raised a crowd of underpaid menials to become a set of self-reliant, original businessmen, who amassed fortunes for themselves and won general respect for their people.

This new economic development, known as the guild of the caterers, boasted six masters, two of whom it was said held reign over Philadelphia's social world through its stomach. It was black folks who made Philadelphia famous as a city of good food through their monopoly on the catering business. This business had been an integral part of Philadelphia's history from before the Civil War. Robert Bogle, who practically invented the catering business in Philadelphia, was the first successful African caterer in the city. Peter Augustin, an immigrant from the West Indies, gained nation-wide fame for that city's catering services. Augustin's customers were distinguished foreign visitors, as well as the so-called best families of the city. His fame was worldwide, and his terrapin soups and stews often wound up in Paris. The father and son team by the name of Prosser are credited with perfecting restaurant catering and for creating much in "American" cuisine that is now famous.

To be honest, unless it is lettuce and cucumbers, I have a real problem trying to stick a knife and fork into green things, especially green meat. However, terrapin and turtle are low in fat, with green turtle meat having 0.5 percent. If consuming meat that is low in fat interests you, even if it is green, Terrapin Soup is right for you. I am sure you can request from your grocer turtle meat that has been cleaned and prepared for cooking. Otherwise, if you are like me, by the time you finish cutting off turtle heads and toes and nailing them on their backs while disarticulating tails and removing gall bladders oh so carefully, you might not feel up to eating any of it.

I guess some people do not mind cleaning turtles. The Marine Society of Salem hired a black chef to oversee the preparation of their important turtle feast. I hope he had someone to assist in cleaning all those turtles.

Terrapin Soup

About 2 pounds terrapin or turtle meat
About ⅓ cup rendered bacon fat
½ tsp. EACH dried thyme and basil
½ tsp. ground allspice
2 onions, chopped
2 tomatoes, chopped
2 carrots, sliced into rounds
1 stalk celery, chopped
2 tsp. finely chopped garlic
1 jalapeño chili pepper (stem and seeds removed), finely chopped
3 bay leaves, crumbled
1 tsp., or to taste, freshly ground black pepper
Salt, to taste
4 to 5 cups EACH chicken and beef broth
⅓ cup sherry or dark rum
2 tsp. lime juice
Whole, boiled turtle eggs or slices of boiled chicken eggs (you choose), and lemon and/or lime slices for garnish

Cut meat into cubes and set aside.

Heat fat in a pot and add thyme, basil, and allspice and cook and stir for 20 seconds. Add next 9 ingredients and cook and stir until onions are clear. Add meat and continue cooking and stirring for a couple of minutes more. Stir in broths. Taste for needed salt and pepper. Bring to a boil. Lower heat and simmer, covered, for about 1½ hours. Add wine and lime juice. Simmer for 1 hour more, or until meat is tender.

Garnish servings with whole, boiled turtle egg or slices of boiled chicken egg and lemon and lime slices.

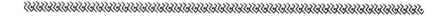

Terrapin, lobster salad, chicken croquettes, and deviled crab were served at every major Philadelphia function by either Thomas J. Dorsey, Henry Jones, or Henry Minton, the household names in catering. From 1845 to 1875, none of these delicacies were accepted as fine dining unless Dorsey, Jones, or Minton had prepared them.

These influential African men took part in the Abolitionist movement and made concerted efforts to help in the uplift of their fellow brethren. In addition, The success of these men paved the way for numerous Africans to open other businesses in the city. One such African was a wealthy lumber merchant who used his money to later endow an African convalescent home. Other Africans were coal merchants and in the furniture business. There were also artists, composers, and band leaders, who were in constant demand. A trumpet, from Queen Victoria, was given to one such band leader.

Having a cocktail party? Pass these with the drinks. They make a delightful and excellent appetizer. If you serve them before dinner, the only problem is preventing family or guests from filling up on them and not leaving room for your other courses.

〽〽〽

Tipsy Salmon Cakes

⅓ cup dark rum
½ cup chopped red bell pepper
1 small onion, chopped
2 Tbs. finely chopped celery
Two 6½-ounce cans salmon (preferably chinook), drained
About ½ tsp. crushed red pepper
¾ tsp. parsley flakes
½ tsp. celery seed
Rounded ½ tsp. hot, Mexican style chili powder
½ tsp. garlic salt with parsley
Salt and black pepper, to taste
4 tsp. Worcestershire sauce
2 Tbs. plus 1 tsp. light molasses
2 eggs, well beaten
2 Tbs. light cream
2 slices wheat bread, broken into small crumbs
Fine bread crumbs
Butter for browning—about 1 Tbs. for every 5 or 6 cakes

Pour sherry into a saucepan. Stir in red bell pepper and onion. Bring sherry mixture just to a rolling boil. Remove from heat and cool.

Combine remaining ingredients (except fine bread crumbs and butter) one or two at a time, mixing well after each addition. Pour cooled sherry mixture into salmon mixture and mix well. Cover and refrigerate overnight.

Add butter to skillet over medium heat. On a sheet of wax paper, pour out a thick layer of fine bread crumbs. Take tablespoonfuls of mixture (mixture will be soft) and lay on top of bread crumbs. Top mixture with a generous coating of crumbs, flattening mixture a bit into a circle or oblong shape as you do so (I usually do these one at at time). Using a spoon or spatula, carefully transfer coated mixture to hot skillet (you may have to reshape cake a bit with spatula at this time). Brown on both sides. I recommend allowing them to become a little dark brown. The crusty, or charred flavor makes them particularly irresistible. Between batches (brown 5 or 6 at a time in a 9-inch skillet), clean skillet with paper towels.

If you are hostessing a luncheon, prepare this one a bit in advance. Here is another taste-filled item that may be of particular interest to guests who happen to be fond of shellfish.

Oyster Pie

Two 9-inch pie crusts
2 Tbs. butter
2 small onions, chopped
½ of a medium-large red bell pepper, chopped
⅛ tsp. crushed red pepper
¼ tsp. chili powder
½ heaping tsp. parsley flakes
½ tsp. dill weed
¼ heaping tsp. ground cumin
6 allspice berries, finely crushed
Salt and lots of freshly ground black pepper
¾ of a large tomato
½ cup cooked kernel corn
Two 12-ounce containers of fresh oysters, rinsed and chopped

½ cup light cream
1 egg
1 tsp. EACH lime and lemon juice
1 Tbs. EACH all purpose flour and corn meal

Line a 9-inch deep dish pie plate with 1 crust. Prick bottom and sides with fork tines. Bake in preheated 450 degree oven for 10 minutes.

In a skillet over medium heat, melt butter. Add onion and bell pepper and cook and stir for a minute or two. Add next six ingredients. Mix in some salt and black pepper. Continue cooking and stirring for a couple of minutes. Add tomato, corn, and oysters. Cook and stir for a few minutes more. Remove skillet from heat.

Beat cream and egg together in a bowl. Add remaining ingredients and mix until thoroughly blended.

Return skillet to medium heat. Pour cream mixture over oysters. Bring to a boil. Reduce heat and simmer a minute or so. Taste for needed salt and pepper.

Transfer mixture to partially baked pie crust. Place second crust on top of mixture. Cut slits in top crust. Bake in preheated 450 degree oven for 20–22 minutes. Cover with aluminum foil after it becomes golden brown (after approximately 12 minutes), so that it does not burn. After pie is removed from oven, allow to rest for 1½ to 2 hours. Serve warm or room temperature. Can also be reheated, if preferred.

Desserts were of course a large part of catering services. One could not have a party and not include two or three dessert items on the menu. Ice cream was always a must. In fact, Philadelphia became the hub of ice cream production in the United States, and the birthplace of the ice cream soda, in 1874. However, various people and places have been credited as the "first" to produce this dessert. It has been said that upon Thomas Jefferson's return from France he brought with him the absolute first recipe for ice cream. American reference books present varied histories of ice cream. *Encyclopedia International,* published in 1980, claims that Emperor Nero (37–68 A.D.) had prepared for him the very first ice cream, made with snow and fruit juice. Upon his return from China, Marco Polo reintroduced the dessert to Europe. Milk was suddenly a favored ingredient, so that it was now fit for royalty. By the close of the eighteenth century, ice cream had become popular in the United States, particularly New York. George Washington, the entry adds, served it often at Mount Vernon.

A White House tradition was said to have been established by Dolly Madison when she served, on one occasion, a tall mound of pink ice cream on a silver platter. Soon the entire country was able to follow suit, for making ice cream at home was made easy after Nancy Johnson invented the hand-cranked freezer in 1846. It was William Young, however, who patented her machine and thereby received credit for it.

The *Merit Students Encyclopedia* adds to this that the American colonies were introduced to ice cream in the late 1600s. Its popularity, however, increased in 1904 after the introduction of the ice cream cone at the Louisiana Purchase Exposition, held in St. Louis, Missouri. The *World Book Encyclopedia,* however, carries the most interesting of all historical notes on ice cream, in which it states that no one knows when ice cream was originated. That is usually a pseudonym for, "Black people originated it, but we ain't tellin.' "

Philadelphia, Pennsylvania (Pennsylvania being the first state to emancipate Africans by legislative action, in 1780), as mentioned earlier, was home to Africans of various occupations who owned businesses. By 1838 there were eight bakers of African descent recorded in Philadelphia. There were also five black confectioners. One of these confectioners was a man named Augustus Jackson. It is believed by many that Mr. Jackson created a more modern version of ice cream, comparable to that consumed today. He had an establishment in the city, on Goodwater Street, between 7th and 8th, where he monopolized the sale of the dessert for a dollar a quart. His daughter continued his tradition on Walnut Street for several years following his death. Sarah Ann Gordon is also listed as an ice cream maker and seller.

Follow this recipe precisely and you will no longer have need for Baskin-Robbins nor Haagen Daz (if you're not pressed for time, that is). Set aside a block of time for this recipe. When making the custard on the stove, each step must be made in one, continuous flow. Have everything ready at hand. I promise, you will be flanked by compliment after compliment.

Vanilla Ice Cream

1½ cups plus 2 Tbs. sugar
¼ tsp. salt
2 Tbs. all purpose flour
2 cups milk
4 whole eggs plus 5 egg yolks (use "jumbo" eggs, please), well beaten
1 pint plus 1¼ cups *whipping* cream, Medium is best (DO NOT USE "heavy," and especially NOT "ultra-pasteurized")
1 Tbs. plus 1½ tsp. pure vanilla extract
3¾-ounce package instant French Vanilla (preferably) pudding or instant regular vanilla pudding

Combine sugar, salt, and flour.

Scald milk. Add some of the hot milk to the sugar mixture to make a thin paste. Stir paste into hot milk. Cook over low heat, stirring constantly (without stopping) for exactly 15 minutes. Gradually add some of this hot mixture to the eggs and stir well. Quickly add egg mixture to hot milk and cook over low heat, stirring constantly (again without stopping) for 2 minutes (absolutely no longer than 2 minutes or eggs will begin to cook). Cool quickly but *completely* in freezer. Watch the cooling process to make sure custard does not develop ice crystals. Wipe away ice crystals that form, as they collect inside container, just above the custard.

Remove custard from freezer and stir in cream, vanilla extract, and pudding. Blend with electric mixer for about 3 minutes, or until there are no lumps of undissolved pudding left.

Pour custard into ice cream freezer can and freeze according to directions for electric freezers (which is the only kind I personally use).

Age this ice cream 48 to 72 hours before serving. You will notice that it turns quite yellow (from the eggs and pudding) during the aging process.

VARIATIONS:

Chocolate Ice Cream
Increase sugar to 2¹/₄ cups plus 2 Tbs. Add 4 squares unsweetened chocolate to milk before scalding. After scalding, use a rotary beater to make flecks of chocolate disappear. Continue according to directions. Increase vanilla extract to 3 Tbs, and add one 4¹/₈-ounce package of instant chocolate pudding. Continue according to directions. Age 2 to 3 days before serving.

Banana Ice Cream
Decrease sugar to 1¹/₄ cups. Cream together 2 medium plus 3 small bananas and 2 Tbs. sugar. After cooking custard for the 15 minutes, add a little of the hot custard mixture to the bananas. Quickly add bananas to hot mixture and cook and stir for 2 minutes. Decrease eggs to 3 whole eggs plus 2 egg yolks ("jumbo"). Continue according to directions. Decrease vanilla to 1 Tbs. plus ¹/₂ tsp. Decrease cream to 1 pint plus 1 cup, and add half (¹/₄ cup plus 2 tsp.) of a 3¹/₂ ounce package of instant banana pudding. Continue according to directions. Age 2 to 3 days before serving.

Now, for those northern black folks who could not afford the services of the Philadelphia caterers, necessity could indeed be the mother of invention. Both my paternal and maternal grandparents, and black folks in midwestern and eastern cities everywhere, made Snow Ice Cream as a fast, inexpensive, fun (unless you fall off the roof collecting the snow), and tasty treat. The proportion of ingredients used depended on the desired amount made and the condition of the snow.

Snow Ice Cream

Ice cold evaporated milk, (start off with) 2 to 3 cans
Vanilla, about 2 tsp. per can of milk
Sugar, ¹/₂ cup or more per can of milk
Freshly fallen snow collected from the roof and/or window ledges of your house or apartment building

Combine all ingredients except snow. Blend well. When ready, re-trieve a pile of freshly fallen snow. Quickly stir 2 to 3 cups of snow at a time into milk mixture. Keep stirring and adding snow until mixture becomes a smooth, thick slush.

Freeze any remaining ice cream.

Cakes were simply an essential of the Philadelphia caterers. Pound cakes, layer cakes, all kinds of cakes for all types of occa-sions. So, what is ice cream without a little cake to go with it? This pound cake is always a hit. You simply will not lose if you take the time to prepare this one. Cut yourself a big piece and spoon some of my vanilla ice cream à la mode or on the side. Diet tomorrow!

Lemon Pound Cake

1¼ cups butter
3 cups sugar
6 egg yolks plus 3 whole eggs (use "jumbo" if possible)
1 tsp. salt
3 tsp. baking powder
3 cups all purpose flour (flour should be stirred many times before measuring)
1 Tbs. pure vanilla extract
1 Tbs. pure lemon extract
1¼ cups milk

Cream butter until light and fluffy. Gradually add sugar and blend well. Add eggs, one at a time, beating well after each addition.

Combine salt, baking powder, and flour in a bowl.

Beginning with flour mixture, add to butter mixture alternately with extracts and milk. Begin with dry ingredients, end with dry ingredients. There should be 4 additions of dry ingredients, 3 of liquid ingredients. (After each addition, stir to blend, but do not beat or stir too much).

Very lightly grease a tube pan and line with wax paper. Pour batter in pan. Bake in preheated oven at 350 degrees for 1 hour and 10 minutes. When completely cool, frost with Crunch Glaze.

⚏ ⚏ ⚏ ⚏

Crunch Glaze

1 cup sweetened flake coconut (slightly rounded and not packed)
½ cup (slightly rounded) pecan halves
Confectioners' sugar, enough to make a stiff, yet spreadable glaze
4 Tbs. milk
½ tsp. pure lemon extract
¾ tsp. pure vanilla extract

Turn food processor on. Pour coconut in through opening and let processor run until coconut is ground up. Empty bowl and turn on again. Pour pecans in through opening and grind. Combine pecans with coconut in a bowl. Add sugar and milk alternately. When moist, add extracts and mix well. Allow to sit for a few minutes to stiffen a bit. But watch closely. Do not allow it to sit too long because it will harden.

Spread all over cake.

The black woman also provided food and good cooking in the North. One penniless African whose cooking southern whites had to do without was Lillian Harris. Ms. Harris typified those blacks who migrated North and turned to food and cooking to survive. Pig Foot Mary, as she was soon to be called, left the Mississippi delta in 1901 and migrated to New York to make her fortune. She earned five dollars as a domestic at the end of her first week there. Although unable to read or write, Pig Foot Mary became one of Harlem's wisest businesswomen.

Three of her first five dollars went for the purchase of a beaten-up baby carriage and a wash boiler. The other two dollars she used to purchase pigs' feet. She somehow persuaded the owner of a saloon near 61st Street on Amsterdam Avenue into allowing her to use his stove for cooking her pigs' feet. When done she would set the tub of cooked feet on the baby carriage and set up shop on the sidewalk, right in front of the saloon. She became a hit operating in front of "Rudolphs" saloon, and with her profits she added hog maws, chitterlings, and corn on the cob to her menu. She could now afford a license and a steam table, which she designed, and which she worked over from early in the morning until late at night. Even after she opened a bank account, she continued to live in her small furnished room. As for clothes, her wardrobe consisted of two dresses.

Sixteen years passed before Pig Foot Mary would move to Harlem. She rented a tiny space or booth, connected to a shoe shine parlor at Lenox Avenue and 135th Street. Three weeks later she married John Dean, the owner of the booth. Pig Foot Mary ventured into purchasing real estate in Harlem. Her first purchase was a $44,000 Seventh Avenue apartment house, which she sold six years later to Adolph Howell, a black undertaker, for $72,000. Her additional ventures in real estate were so successful that at one point her total holdings were estimated at $375,000.

When I was a child, the thought of a foot, any foot, sitting in my plate was a total turnoff. It took a while for my eyes, senses, and taste buds to adjust to this object that used to trot along on the ground, occupying a place in my stomach. I got used to it finally, and I am glad I did because there was no debate about this horrid thing being my dinner. Just do not think about where they have been and you will come to the conclusion that pig feet can be quite tasty, as you will recognize after trying the following recipe.

Pig Foot Mary's Feet

4 pig feet
About 2 to 4 Tbs. apple cider vinegar
1/2 tsp. lemon juice
Salt (to taste)
Black pepper (to taste)
1/2 tsp. red pepper flakes
1 medium-large onion, chopped

Place feet in a large pot. Fill with enough water to cover feet. Add remaining ingredients. Cover and simmer for 2½ to 3 hours. Add additional water as needed. Adjust seasoning. Pass hot sauce.

Black folk in the North and Northeast and in bondage on southern plantations, or hired out to work in the kitchens on board steamboats, continued to captivate dining audiences with their culinary creations. With the end of formal slavery, southern blacks would fill northern cities in record numbers and bring with them the knowledge and art of cooking and food preparation that generations before them had handed down. In the decades to follow, war and especially economics would still be an issue of concern for the entire country. As for blacks, whether their economics were tied to jobs as cooks and domestics or in the ever-expanding factories, they would assume yet another position: that of an exploitable culinary role model.

Flapjacks and Blue Notes

Cake used to be my life. I could never get enough. I had to be there waiting for my piece as soon as the last bare spot was covered with frosting. I could not wait for the cake to dry or "set." My friends hated me coming to their houses sometimes, because if they were trying to save the last slices of cake for a next day treat for themselves, my presence ruined it. Their mothers always extended hospitality and that meant that even the last piece of cake would be offered to me. I always accepted. I paid my friends back, however, by sharing Twinkies and cupcakes with them from time to time. We ate cake while I played selections from my 45 rhythm and blues record collection. The best tunes of the '60s were not simply played over and over on a turntable; they were used by us to develop "creative composing skills." For example:

DEAR LOVER,
    "WITH EVERY BEAT OF MY HEART" you can be assured that this letter is "DEDICATED TO THE ONE I LOVE." And as we "TURN BACK THE HANDS OF TIME" I can remember when you was just a "RUN AWAY CHILD RUNNING WILD" in "THE GHETTO." "BUT IF MY HEART COULD SPEAK" it would have told you how I wanted to be your "GYPSY WOMAN." "THE WAY YOU DO THE THINGS YOU DO" tells me you'll always "STAY IN MY CORNER," even though I've been a "BAD GIRL." "YOU ARE THE SUNSHINE OF MY LIFE" which is why I'm "NEVER GONNA GIVE YOU UP."

Those "creative composing skills" were quite popular when I was growing up in Chicago. It was fun for me and my friends, particularly since we did not have much else to do during the summer (Mom and Dad sending us to Fort Lauderdale for a few weeks just was not quite in the cards). We did not have funds for any type of real travel, so we would walk to various places and just have a look-see. We lived right off Roosevelt Road and Ashland and in the summer we walked to Grant Park. It was a wonderful park with its Museum of Natural History, Planetarium, Shedd Aquarium (which were all free back then), and 12th Street Beach, all right on Lake Michigan. We walked from there to the Art Institute. Then, too, there was the glorious window-shopping on Michigan Avenue. Most of the time that was the only kind of shopping we did. But once school was back in session, we walked to school and skipped lunch and saved our bus fare and lunch money so we could go shopping or buy more rhythm and blues recordings.

With my shopping completed, I came home to the smell (stench to me) of chitlins, or the aroma of fried chicken or lamb chops or some other entree. Usually, however, it was chicken. Preparation was often completed while my mother sang along with Dinah Washington and Sarah Vaughan recordings. When my father came home from work, he went into the kitchen, looked in the pots and then yelled out his familiar: "Your mother is serving 'dead birds' again!" With my father in the house, the record player was graced with Miles Davis or Sonny Stitt or Gene Ammons. My father said he needed musical sustenance before trying to tackle another one of my mother's "dead birds." I would sometimes have to beg to play tunes from my collection of rhythm and blues 45s, which I could boast was the best collection in the neighborhood. My mother played my 45s, too; but whatever was on the turntable you could always hear it blasting a block away.

In the following recipe I have substituted shoulder lamb chops for the "dead birds" my mother used. You may, of course, do it her way. If you have a taste for chicken, six breasts will produce a stunning entree as well.

⁄⁄

Lamb Chops with Thyme and Mushrooms

6 shoulder lamb chops
Seasoned salt, black pepper, and paprika
Flour

1/4 to 1/3 cup peanut OR vegetable oil
1/2 tsp. thyme
8-ounce can tomato sauce
1 Tbs. Worcestershire sauce
2 tsp. sugar
1/4 tsp. red pepper flakes
3/4 tsp. parsley flakes
1 1/4 to 1 1/2 cups sliced, mushrooms

Season chops on both sides with seasoned salt, black pepper to taste, and generously with paprika. Dredge chops in flour and brown on both sides in hot oil.

Combine remaining ingredients and mix well. Pour mixture over chops in skillet. Simmer, covered, for about 45 minutes.

Note: Mixture may be poured over browned chops (or chicken breasts) in a baking pan and baked in preheated 350 degree oven for about 50–60 minutes.

Those lamb chop and chicken entrees and rhythm and blues tunes were part of an evolution of tastes and sounds in the African American culinary and music experience. From plantation minstrel shows to Charlie Parker and Aretha Franklin, from Beaten Biscuits to Maryland Crab Cakes and fried oysters, African Americans set the standards for food and music from this country's inception well into modern times and were the major contributors to what euphemistically became "American cuisine" and "American music." But those accomplishments were on numerous occasions denied. Just as important, they were copied by white America and then defined away from their source. By act this is racism; by definition it is cultural imperialism.

Cultural imperialism of black folks' cooking occurred, for example, every time the culinary skill and expertise of African cooks were compiled by non-African Americans into collections and handed down as heirlooms or presented as part of a new bride's dowry. Part or all of these collections were sometimes published as cookbooks. The collections were now considered to be *the owner's version* of the recipes. Add to that, "the owner's version" was then "established" as *the version* for those particular dishes, and were defined as such.

What was happening to African American cooking was also happening to black music.

African American music was regularly termed by the majority society as "coon," "jungle," and "nigger" music, well into the 1950s. It was so defined and characterized until some whites learned how to play it. Once they did, the music became "sweet" and "swing." It became "jazz" and "rock n' roll." It became another "new" form of "American" music, and its authentic creators, African Americans, were relegated increasingly to the periphery. As Ortiz M. Walton points out in his book, *Music: Black, White and Blue*:

> Once the definitive Afro-American musical models have been studied and copied, with novelty effects added, the best imitators become white models and are then promoted nationally and internationally. The antecedents of cultural parasitism occurred well before the formal establishment of "Tin Pan Alley."

Such cultural exploitation has situated itself just as deeply into the African American culinary heritage. As the phonograph record, or "canned" music, allowed white musicians to hear over and over and eventually imitate the external aspects of African American music, certain "instant" or packaged "ready mix" foods, based on recipes of African Americans, enabled the larger society to replicate the originals. One could now "perfectly" imitate the pancake and the poundcake. Without a black woman physically in the kitchen to prepare these things, a box or a jar was the next best thing. Packaged mixes were heralded as emancipating the American housewife from the drudgery of virtual slavery in her kitchen. The irony is that those American housewives, who have always had cooks and house servants, have never had to suffer said drudgery.

Times have changed. There was a time when only a miniscule number of black folks dared touch a box of cake mix. For the vast majority of black people a cake was made "from scratch" or there would be no cake. If you even *looked* as though you were suggesting that they consider using a cake mix, your life was in jeopardy. Pride went into every slice of a cake baked by people I knew. That meant, therefore, that you went into the kitchen and carefully thought out every step, each and every ingredient. Your finished creation was a work of art, hopefully, a masterpiece. These days, however, everybody is too busy to cook, especially "from scratch." Now, to show you what a box can do, with a few embellishments, I offer you a Carrot Cake recipe. I have followed it with what I feel is a superior "from scratch" version.

Carrot Cake (Partly from a Box)

1 package carrot cake mix
Eggs and oil according to box directions
Water and reserved pineapple juice, combined to make same amount of water called for on box
³/₄ tsp. cinnamon
8-ounce can crushed pineapple, drained and juice reserved
³/₄ tsp. EACH vanilla, sherry, brandy, and coconut extracts
1 cup sweetened flake coconut, chopped in blender or food processor
¹/₂ cup finely chopped nuts

Combine cake mix, eggs, oil, water, and reserved juice and mix with electric mixer until moistened. Add remaining ingredients and mix on high speed for about 3 minutes.

Pour batter into 2 slightly greased, wax paper–lined 9-inch cake pans. Bake in a preheated 350 degree oven for about 40 minutes, or until knife inserted in center of layer comes out clean (a crumb or two stuck to the knife does not matter).

Frost however you please.

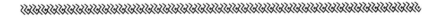

If you are concerned about how you will be remembered after your time is up, create the fondest, most delicious "hereafter" memories possible to leave your loved ones. Bake the following cake and you may have doubts about a box taking your place in the kitchen.

Carrot-Walnut Cake Imperial

1 cup butter
2 cups light brown sugar (1 pound box)
½ cup white sugar
5 eggs
2½ cups flour
1 tsp. EACH salt and baking soda
3 tsp. baking powder
1½ tsp. cinnamon
8 ounce can crushed pineapple, drained
2 tsp. vanilla
1 tsp. EACH coconut, sherry, and brandy extracts
1 Tbs. dark rum
1⅔ cups sweetened flake coconut
8-ounce package *shredded* carrots, ground in food processor
1 slightly rounded cup of finely chopped walnuts

Cream butter until light and fluffy. Add brown and white sugars about a half cup at a time, mixing well after each addition. Beat in eggs, one at a time. Combine flour, salt, baking soda, baking powder, and cinnamon in a bowl. Add dry ingredients alternately with pineapple, extracts, and rum. Begin with dry ingredients, end with dry ingredients. Blend well. By hand stir in coconut, carrots, and nuts. Mix well.

Pour into 2 slightly greased, wax paper-lined, 9-inch cake pans. Bake in a preheated 350 degree oven for 40 to 50 minutes (depending on your oven).

✍ ✍ ✍ ✍

Cream Cheese Frosting Imperial

One 8-ounce package cream cheese, softened
1 stick butter (½ cup), softened
1 pound confectioners' sugar
1 tsp. EACH coconut, brandy, and sherry extracts
2 tsp. vanilla extract

Cream together cream cheese and butter. Gradually add remaining ingredients. Mix thoroughly.

This frosting must rest for approximately 50 minutes before using. In its just-finished form it is very soft and "loose." Keep an eye on it by stirring occasionally. It will gradually stiffen. When a spoonful turned sideways does not fall off the spoon, it is time to frost the cake. Do not rush in frosting the sides of the cake. Proceed slowly. It takes a bit more time but your end product will be *well worth the wait.*

§§ §§ §§ §§

Topping for Cream Cheese Frosting Imperial

½ cup sweetened flake coconut
½ cup walnut pieces

Turn on food processor. Pour coconut and walnuts through top hole and grind together until they resemble meal. Use as a garnish for top of cake. For a fluffier look, you can combine 1 or 2 Tbs. of ground nuts with ¾ cup or more flake coconut (do not grind), toss well and garnish top of cake.

I am not a culinary snob. Sometimes a jar can be a friend as well. So, to show you what a jar can do, prepare the following as a side dish to your most elegant meat dishes. No one will ever know you were not in the kitchen all day.

Potatoes in Cream Sauce

8 potatoes
1 large jar of the commercial "Simmer Sauces," preferably a white one
1½ cups of milk
About 6 Tbs. butter
1½ tsp. (or to taste) white pepper
Salt to taste

Cook potatoes in the microwave or regular oven. Cool and remove skins. Place potatoes in saucepan over medium heat. Stir in milk and butter, breaking up potatoes as you do so. Stir in salt and white pepper, continuing to break up potatoes. Lower heat, if necessary, to keep mixture from scorching on the bottom. Cook and stir until mixture boils. Simmer for only 1 or 2 minutes, stirring often.

Before my long pregnant pause I was saying that there is a connection between the various forms of African American music and African American cooking, and it is an important one. This connection represents a system that can be traced back to African languages. A characteristic of African languages is that the same word can have many different meanings depending on the tone or pitch of the word. Africans were always taught, early in childhood, to develop acuity in pitch. One of those persons who specialized in this acuity was the Griot. In Africa, the Griot was the most honored of professional musicians; he was a performer of folktales, poetry, and verse. Music, whether performed on the flute or *baulafo* (African xylophone), or performed as song, was an important part of the Griot's performance. The Griot's music was history in song. It contained the sounds of years long ago, events mostly forgotten by the clan or society. To listen to the Griot was to learn about the recent past or ancient history. The various developments in African American music (work songs, field hollers, gospel, blues, ragtime, jazz, rhythm and blues) have proven that slavery was incapable of destroying the African heritage that evolved that system of language in song.

African language in song was showcased in the black minstrel performances. It was one of the most common shows in which black musicians participated in the early eighteenth century in the South. At the end of the Civil War, hundreds of black minstrel companies were formed. The minstrel show was, among other things, another vehicle to showcase black professional musicianship, and like other forms of African American culture, it was copied by white America. Well, on one autumn evening in 1889, Chris L. Rutt, editor-in-chief, and later, manager of the Saint Joseph, Missouri, *Gazette,* visited the local vaudeville house. The bill featured Baker & Farrell, "blackface" entertainers. Their principal act was a song called "Aunt Jemima," for which one of the white men donned an apron and red bandanna headband such as the traditional southern cook wore.

Now, as for Chris L. Rutt, he could not have spent a more profitable evening. You see, he and his friend, Charles G. Underwood, who was in the milling business, had been looking for a trademark, a symbol, you might say, for the self-rising pancake flour they had just packaged under a generic label. The symbol they wanted was one that would identify with the best tradition of southern cooking. And here it was in the form of the ultimate expert of the culinary art, the genius of the southern kitchen—the Negro cook. Chris Rutt named his pancake flour after the song's title and emblazoned the likeness of a wide-eyed, grinning, southern "mammy" on a one-pound sack as a trademark. He was now, as they say, in business.

Aunt Jemima Pancake Mix, the first ready mix of any kind ever developed, and the company that bore its name, were the experiment of Chris L. Rutt and Charles G. Underwood, two men who admitted that they knew nothing at all about cooking. Obviously, the one thing they did know was that if they wanted to sell their product they needed to associate it with those known for their ability in the kitchen.

Well, whose recipe was it? Whose concoction was it with which they were experimenting? Saint Joseph, Missouri, had been in earlier times a frontier town. It had served as the eastern regional office for the Pony Express, which offered an eight-day mail run to California. Cattle barons made their homesteads there. Saint Joseph also witnessed the passage of covered wagon trains to the west over the Santa Fe, Oregon, and Mormon trails. Because Saint Joseph was a rich and very important milling town, goods such as breads and pancakes traveled west with the pioneers. They soon became an indispensable food to farmers, ranchers, cowboys, miners, and lumberjacks alike.

Here is an old recipe invented out of the belief that food should never be wasted, even though the milk is about to spoil (or already has), or the bread crumbs are old and stale. I hate to waste food, too, but I have used fresh ingredients for this one. The next time you go camping and decide to "rough it," try the following concoction for a different pancake breakfast.

ⵣⵣⵣⵣⵣⵣⵣⵣⵣⵣⵣⵣⵣⵣⵣⵣⵣⵣⵣⵣⵣⵣⵣⵣⵣⵣⵣⵣⵣⵣⵣⵣⵣⵣⵣⵣⵣⵣⵣ

Bread Crumb Flapjacks

1½ cups buttermilk
¼ tsp. EACH salt and baking soda
4 Tbs. flour
2½ tsp. baking powder
3 tsp. sugar
2 eggs

2 Tbs. oil

1½ cups corn bread crumbs

1½ cups wheat bread crumbs

Place buttermilk in a bowl. Stir in salt, baking soda, flour, baking powder, and sugar. Add eggs and oil and blend well. Stir in corn bread crumbs, then wheat bread crumbs. Allow batter to rest for a few minutes.

Pour batter in circles into a well greased, preheated skillet, browning on both sides.

Serve with syrup or honey.

How did such an indispensable food become the product of two men who knew nothing about cooking? Are we supposed to believe that a newspaper editor and a businessman came up with a formula, a recipe, on their own out of the blue, for self-rising pancake flour? It was concocted in Rutt's kitchen, one history on the subject reports. Was it formulated without their having any knowledge whatsoever of what went into its making? A look at Saint Joseph's history tells us that Missouri had been a slave state. Consequently, a very large African population remained. They comprised the majority of the household servant population and worked at the hotels and restaurants. Both Rutt and Underwood held positions that allowed them to employ servants. More than likely one or both of these men employed a black cook or ate at some establishment or someone's home where the cook was an African, one of whose specialties was pancakes. They probably got the cook to tell them what went into the recipe. I am suggesting to you that someone *was* in the kitchen with Dinah, and on this occasion it was Chris L. Rutt. It is inconceivable that either Rutt or Underwood could have avoided coming into contact with African cooks.

Aunt Jemima Manufacturing Company was sold around 1890 to R. T. Davis, who owned the largest and oldest milling company in Saint Joseph at that time. He was also quite adept at advertising. His concept was to bring the Aunt Jemima symbol to life. He wanted a living, breathing representative of the face on the package who could tour the major cities and towns, visiting fairs, expositions, and festivals demonstrating his mix.

The first of three African women chosen to personify Aunt Jemima was Nancy Green. She was a *magnificent cook* who worked for a Chicago judge. Green was fifty-nine years old and had been born, ironically enough, into slavery on a plantation in Montgomery County, Kentucky. For thirty years, until her death in 1923, she was under exclusive contract with the company. She was more than just a trademark, which her debut at the Columbian Exposition of the Chicago World's Fair of 1893 proved. During the Exposition she prepared pancake demonstrations while singing songs and telling stories of her old plantation days. Much of her dialogue was said to be from her imagination. Her tales must have been clever enough to capture audiences, since R. T. Davis had a pamphlet printed after the 1893 Fair titled "The Life of Aunt Jemima, the Most Famous Colored Woman in the World." The pamphlet, put together by Purd Wright, was a narrative of plantation life in the Old South as remembered by Nancy Green. According to her biographer, she made up much of its contents. In other words, she also wrote her own scripts. One of her stories explains how her pancakes kept her master from having his mustache snatched from his lip by Yankee villains. One forkful of her delicious cakes and the Blue Coats forgot all about him, which enabled him to get away.

She was mobbed by visitors to the Fair wherever she went. Merchants worldwide placed more than fifty thousand orders for Aunt Jemima's mix. The big city grocery stores also hosted Nancy Green and her live pancake demonstrations. In addition, R. T. Davis decided to change the Aunt Jemima pancake recipe. He felt that improving the flavor would not hurt sales either. No doubt Nancy Green's ability as a cook helped in making that improvement.

The success of Aunt Jemima at the 1893 Fair inspired R. T. Davis to develop another promotional project that would make merchandising history: the Aunt Jemima Rag Doll. The doll could be puchased for twenty-five cents plus one trademark off the pancake mix carton. An earlier promotion in 1895 inspired the Rag Doll. The flour was packaged in cartons instead of paper sacks. To gain favorable responses and higher sales from the new packaging, Davis had it printed with a cutout paper doll of Aunt Jemima. Ten years later, this tremendously successful idea reemerged as the

Aunt Jemima Rag Doll and helped to pull the company out of bankruptcy. An entire family of rag dolls was soon created, including Uncle Mose and twin moppets Diana and Wade. The Quaker Oats Company acquired Aunt Jemima right after the rag doll was again advertised in a women's magazine. The response was overwhelming. The requests were from women who said they had been raised with Aunt Jemima dolls and now wanted them for their daughters.

Nancy Green's success inspired advertisers all over the country to use living trademarks for their products. Such was the decision of the Clifford family of Minneapolis, who owned Cream of Wheat. The man who appears on the Cream of Wheat package, "primed to offer health through food and cheeriness," was the cook in the Clifford house. Uncle Ben was, and still is, another famous smiling face, poised to skyrocket sales of a long grain rice. Skyrocketing sales was exactly what these faces accomplished. Just prior to World War I, Aunt Jemima Pancake Mix sales were the highest in history. During the war it was used overseas, prepared for breakfast meals for U.S. troops.

Hot pancakes are just the ticket to start off your day with that well-fed feeling. Scramble some eggs, brown some sausage, and prepare a stack of Spicy Rice Flapjacks for that special Sunday, breakfast-in-bed spread you have been promising someone for months now. He, or she, will beg for more—pancakes that is.

Spicy Rice Flapjacks

1 cup yellow corn meal
$1/4$ plus $1/8$ tsp. salt
1 tsp. baking powder
$1/4$ tsp. EACH cayenne, cinnamon, nutmeg, and baking soda
$1/3$ cup cold, cooked rice
1 cup buttermilk
1 egg
$3^{1}/2$ tsp. sugar
3 Tbs vegetable oil

Combine dry ingredients (first 7) in mixing bowl.

Grind rice with milk in food processor.

In a separate bowl, beat egg. Stir in ground rice and milk, then sugar, then oil. Mix well. Add liquid ingredients to dry ingredients, stirring just until thoroughly blended. Allow batter to rest for a few minutes.

Pour batter in circles in a well greased skillet and brown on both sides.

Dates are always a welcome addition to cake and bread products, and you may save a little time by using buttermilk pancake mix:

🎵 🎵 🎵 🎵

Quick Spicy Date Flapjacks

3/4 cup buttermilk
1 Tbs. melted butter
1/8 tsp. EACH cinnamon and nutmeg
1/2 cup buttermilk pancake mix
4 whole dates, very finely chopped

Combine buttermilk and butter and mix well. Add cinnamon, nutmeg, then pancake mix. Stir just until thoroughly blended. Stir in dates. Allow batter to rest for a minute.

Pour batter in circles in a greased skillet, browning on both sides.

As sales in pancake mix soared, the war raged on. Many black men had taken jobs in city factories, such as Chicago's South Side Stockyards. After the war ended, these men were fired due to industry cutbacks. Wives of these men sold sweet potato and other pies to make extra money. It is true. My grandparents purchased a great number of pies from friends and relatives who became victims of the cutbacks of the era. Most of the time, my grandmother donated the pies to churches for raffles and weekend socials. At other times, my grandfather had the knack of making them magically disappear in the middle of the night.

> One Potato! Two Potato! Three Potato! Four!
> Run and See Who's At The Door!

Every time I make a sweet potato pie, I find myself singing this rhyme, the way we used to do as kids while playing. It was a dessert staple in many homes then, as it is now. If you have never had sweet potato pie, I am sure the following recipe will convince you that you have really been missing something.

§§§

Sweet Potato Pie

2 sweet potatoes, 1 very large, 1 large
½ cup butter, melted
1 cup plus 1 Tbs. white sugar
½ cup dark brown sugar
3 eggs
¾ tsp. EACH nutmeg and cinnamon
½ tsp. cloves
1 Tbs. plus 1 tsp. pure vanilla extract
½ tsp. salt
1 cup evaporated milk, undiluted
3 Tbs. flour
3 unbaked pie crusts, *two* fitted into a 9-inch pie plate

Cook potatoes in skins. Cool and peel. Add potatoes to butter in large bowl. Gradually mix in white sugar, then brown sugar. Beat in eggs, one at a time. Stir in nutmeg, cinnamon, cloves, vanilla, salt, milk, and flour. Blend on medium speed of electric mixer until smooth.

Pour into unbaked 9-inch double crust. (You will probably have some leftover filling which you can bake separately, like pudding, in a small baking dish, for 40 minutes. It will have a cake-like crust on the bottom and sides.) Bake in a preheated 400 degree oven for 30 minutes. Cut third crust into strips (you may not need to use all of third crust for strips). Place strips in a criss cross fashion over top of pie. Bake for another 15 to 20 minutes.

§§§

Another favorite pie baked in northern and southern black kitchens before, during and after the war was, of course, apple, which many people consider to be the pie of pies. To each his own, but personally I prefer to use Delicious apples, which I cook before baking because I can better control the texture of the apple slices. This is a great pie. Sweet and juicy, you will prepare it constantly.

Apple Pie

3 unbaked pie crusts
One 3-pound bag Delicious apples
4 Tbs. apple juice
6¹/₃ Tbs. butter
Approximately ³/₄ cup sugar
1 Tbs. vanilla extract
³/₄ tsp. EACH nutmeg and cinnamon
4 Tbs. plus 4 tsp. cornstarch

Place two pie crusts in a 9-inch pie plate. With a fork, perforate bottom and sides of crust. Bake in a preheated 450 degree oven for 10 minutes.

Peel and slice apples. Transfer to large saucepan or pot. Sprinkle juice over apples. Cook apples until soft enough to stick a knife or fork into without any resistance. Apples should still be a bit firm, but not hard; soft, but not mushy.

Drain all juice from the pot into a small bowl. Return 1 Tbs. of juice to apples. Add butter and let hot apples melt it. Gently fold in sugar, vanilla, and spices and mix well.

Mix the cornstarch with 4¹/₂ Tbs. of the reserved juice. Mix well. Pour over apples and fold in to mix well. Pour into partially baked pie shell. Top with third unbaked pie crust. Cut slits in crust. Bake for 11 to 13 minutes or until top crust is brown. Cool for at least 2 hours before cutting.

The close of World War I did little to alter the economic plight of black people. In fact, during the 1920s racism in America provided a double whammy for blacks. In Harlem, as elsewhere, not only were blacks relegated to jobs as "pot rasslers," "kitchen mechanics," "sud busters," and "ham heavers" but they were also paid wages that did not allow any splurging for nightly entertainment. The Thursday and Saturday night "House-Rent Parties," therefore, were a welcome addition to Harlem entertainment. The so-called ballroom was an empty room, except for a piano, with a red glow for light. Between "Bumping" and doing the "Mess

Around" to the harmonies of the piano man or lady, you could quench your thirst on corn liquor, satiate your hunger with hot pig feet and chitlins. It was a very down-to-earth affair. Folks would party all night and the host would have rent money the next day.

When black folks did go out on the town in Harlem, places such as Ed Small's Sugar Cane Club at 135th and Fifth Avenue was at the top of the list. Typical of the many "jump joints" of the day, it was down in a basement and was known for its dancing and singing waiters. After having worked up an appetite on the dance floor, or, if you wanted to eat first to build up your energy before dancing, you could visit one of the chitlin' joints in the area for some home cooking. The menu would usually offer a variety of entrees such as "poke" chops smothered in onions, chicken fricassee served with rice, and side dishes such as stewed okra, corn, and peas. Dessert would include coconut pie.

If tonight is your night out on the town, eat first and party later. On the other hand, you could have these pork chops waiting for you when you get back. This is an entree for which you will not mind cutting short other activities.

"Poke" Chops Smothered in Onions

12 centercuts, or whatever cut you like
Hot and spicy salt, garlic salt, black pepper, and paprika
Flour
Approximately ⅓ cup of vegetable oil
1 cup boiling water
1 chicken bouillon cube
1 tsp. EACH parsley flakes and celery seed
4 big onions, sliced into rings

Season chops with all spices, but only on one side. Coat with flour on BOTH sides. Brown chops in hot oil in a large skillet or pot.

Dissolve cube in water. Add parsley flakes and celery seed to bouillon.

When all chops have been browned, "smother" each chop with lots of onion rings in skillet. Carefully pour bouillon over and around chops. Bring skillet to a boil. Cover, simmer for 1 hour. Round out your work with wild rice and/or mashed potatoes.

After that repast, make dessert not only the grand finale but an unforgettable experience. This may not be coconut pie, but a slice of Banana Coconut Pound Cake will definitely hit the spot. It is, without question, the most flavorful banana cake you have ever tasted.

Banana Coconut Pound Cake

1½ cups butter, or Parkay margarine (3 sticks)
3 cups sugar
6 eggs
1 tsp. salt
3 tsp. baking powder
3 cups all purpose flour
1½ cups (very loosely packed) sweetened, flake coconut
¼ cup plus 2 Tbs. milk
3 very large, very ripe bananas
1 Tbs. pure vanilla extract
1 Tbs. coconut extract

Cream butter until light and fluffy. Gradually blend in sugar and mix well. Add eggs one at a time, beating well after each addition. Combine salt, baking powder, and flour in a bowl.

In food processor or blender, puree coconut in milk. Add bananas to coconut mixture and process until bananas are also pureed.

Beginning with dry ingredients (flour mixture), add flour mixture to butter mixture alternately with coconut puree and extracts. Begin with dry ingredients, end with dry ingredients. There should be 4 additions of dry ingredients, 3 additions of liquid ingredients. Mix well but do not beat or stir too much.

Very lightly grease a tube pan. Line with wax paper. Pour batter into pan. Bake in a preheated 350 degree oven for 1 hour and 19 minutes. Cool thoroughly before removing from baking pan.

You have just created a piece of heaven.

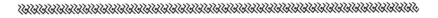

The Harlem menus became famous even in the literary world. *Home to Harlem*'s Jake knew. Jake could not wait. He could not wait to catch that subway train for Harlem. One of the first things he did when he got there was to eat at a place where he had a big Maryland fried chicken dinner, candied sweet potatoes and all.

Maryland is, after all, a part of the South. It stands to reason, therefore, that some of the best recipes would have been created there. One Maryland recipe for small game calls for quail. Irresistible sauces and glazes are the driving force in presenting game meats. Here are two that are waiting to be discovered.

Baked Quail with Drunken Red Currant Glaze

4 quail
White pepper, hot and spicy seasoned salt, black pepper, parsley flakes, and paprika
2 or 3 Tbs. of fat rendered from bacon
2 Tbs. EACH dark rum and chardonnay
1 tsp. EACH lemon juice and cornstarch
1/8 tsp. "hot, Mexican style" chili powder
4 Tbs. of prepared chicken broth (dissolve 1 chicken bouillon cube in 1/2 cup boiling water—use only 4 Tbs.)
3 Tbs. red currant jelly

Season quail all over with spices. Brown quail in hot fat. Transfer to baking pan. Bake, covered, in a preheated 450 degree oven for 5 minutes. Reduce heat to 350 degrees and bake for 15 to 20 minutes.

Combine next 5 ingredients in a saucepan. Blend until smooth. Over medium heat, add broth and jelly. Stir until jelly melts. Bring to a full rolling boil and simmer for 30 seconds. Ladle glaze over quail.

Carrots and Sauce
(Actually, It Is More an Accompaniment)

6 cherry tomatoes
1/2 cup chicken bouillon
1 1/2 Tbs. peanut, corn, or sunflower oil
1 small onion, chopped
6 Tbs. honey
1/2 tsp. thyme

Salt and pepper
½ pound baby carrots, cooked and drained
2 or 3 Tbs. brown sugar (optional)

Puree tomatoes with bouillon. Heat oil in skillet. Add onion and cook and stir for a few minutes. Transfer puree to skillet. Add honey and thyme. Cook and stir for a few more minutes. If too thick add a little more broth. Season with pepper to taste. Stir in carrots and heat through. Arrange quail surrounded by carrots and sauce. Sprinkle carrots with brown sugar before serving, if desired.

Crab is another Maryland specialty, seasoned hot and spicy and served steamed or as crab cakes. Soft shell crabs are fried and eaten with tartar sauce or prepared stuffed. There are crabmeat omelets, soups, croquettes, salads, burgers, loafs, and casseroles. In addition, deviled, creamed, and au gratin crab is served in abundance in numerous homes. Crab used as stuffing for avocado and in deviled eggs is also popular. The following is a very simple to prepare, yet elegant, concoction, spiked with rum and loaded with crabmeat:

Crab Soup

3 Tbs. butter
1 large onion, chopped
¼ of a large red bell pepper, chopped
1 large tomato, chopped
2 serrano chili peppers OR half of a jalapeño pepper (no seeds from jalapeño, unless you prefer soup extra hot), chopped
½ tsp. EACH "hot, Mexican style" chili powder, celery seed, ground cumin, and dill weed
1 tsp. parsley flakes
About ½ tsp. freshly ground black pepper, or to taste
Two 6-ounce cans lump crabmeat, juice and all
1 cup chopped mushrooms
One 15-ounce can creamed corn
5 cups chicken broth

2 Tbs. dark rum
2 tsp. light molasses
1 slice wheat bread, crumbed
1 Tbs. finely crushed corn flakes
$^{1}/_{2}$ tsp. sesame seeds

Melt butter in a pot. Add onions and tomatoes and cook and stir for a minute or two. Add next seven ingredients and continue cooking and stirring until onions become clear. Stir in crabmeat, then mushrooms, then creamed corn. Add broth, rum, and molasses and mix well. Bring to a boil. Lower heat and simmer, covered, for about 12 minutes, stirring occasionally. Taste for needed salt.

Combine bread, corn flakes, and sesame seeds. Mix well. Spread mixture on a cookie sheet or metal baking pan. Place under a broiler until toasted brown. Sprinkle toasted mixture on top of individual servings of soup.

Now, the traditional accompaniment for all meat dishes, whether crab, ham, chicken, or terrapin stew, is Beaten Biscuits. It was conceded, even in the year 1776, that this particular hot bread would never have been served if it were not for the South's black cooks. One of the earliest recipes for Beaten Biscuits calls for 1 quart of flour, lard the size of a hen's egg, one teaspoon of salt, and sweet milk—enough to turn the mixture into a stiff dough. It then suggests that the dough be beaten on a smooth flat surface of a tree stump with the side of a hatchet until the dough forms little blisters of air and is smooth and shiny. The dough is formed into round flat balls and the balls are stuck with a fork once or twice. In order to achieve just the right texture and lightness in the finished product, the dough must be beaten hard. For everyday eating, three hundred whacks are said to suffice; however, if the biscuits are being served to dinner guests, then five hundred strokes, no less, are appropriate. Incidentally, a colored boy about twelve years old is the best beater, and he should really spend close to an hour on the beating process.

Why the "colored boy" could not be nine or thirteen I do not know, but people of European ancestry and tradition seem to hold that when it comes to music and cooking and other aspects of their lives it is best to proceed by the numbers. Well, rest assured, after the end of formal slavery, Beaten Biscuits were seen less and less on dining room tables in white households. Left to be prepared by the mistresses of these households, they were considered to be burdensome and time consuming.

It is interesting that such an important hot bread was dropped from the menus of these homes, since a substantial number of people of European ancestry felt that "they had nothing to draw on from the mother country" in the way of cuisine. Perhaps they felt they had little to draw on in the way of music as well. Employing nuances that would allow variations or augment the European style of music was virtually unheard of and almost always unacceptable. Likewise, here in America, chord changes were few in the compositions of the so-called standard tunes of the '40s. White bands and orchestras adhered to prearranged compositions for the most part. Jazz musicians, on the other hand, employed changes and substitutions within these compositions, and with the addition of improvisation, produced various innovative concepts. Infinite harmonic combinations were created by jazz musicians, leaving merely a melodic resemblance to these standard tunes. Black musicians' use of these standard tunes reversed the game, whereby they used what had been defined as "white" elements of music, which whites had actually stolen from black music.

In the same way that creative skill enabled the African slave to improvise her family's meals on the piss-poor rations provided, those same artistic values enabled the same African, in her slave master's kitchen, to use, once in a while, a few European basics and employ changes and substitutions. These changes usually left no resemblance to the blandness of the European style. These cooks could make, at random, infinite variations "on a theme."

Culinary "themes" were varied on the slave's own table even though rations consisted of the fatty, low-end cuts or portions and the discards of the pig, chicken, or cow. Pork was never a food voluntarily eaten by Africans during slavery, many of whom had practiced strict dietary rules in their homeland. However, turning scraps into something eatable was often accomplished by simply altering seasonings or the method of preparation. In the following dish, beef or chicken variations can be made on the pork theme.

Variations can also be made on the seasonings as well. Wonderful for lunch or dinner, its winning flavors are sure to keep you coming back for more.

℘℘

Gingered Pork

About 1³/₄ to 2 pounds boneless pork shoulder steak, cut into thin strips
2 medium carrots, cut into very thin rounds
1 medium-large and 1 medium-small onion, cut into quarters, then sliced
³/₄ tsp. ground ginger
¼ tsp. crushed red pepper
Salt, to taste
Freshly ground black pepper, to taste
1 cup beef broth
2 Tbs. dark rum
1 tsp. Worcestershire sauce
1 Tbs. light molasses
Salt and black pepper, to taste

In a large skillet, cook pork, covered, over medium heat, stirring occasionally, for 15–20 minutes. Drain oil from skillet. Stir in carrots, onions, ginger, red pepper, and some salt and black pepper. Stir in next four ingredients, one at a time, mixing well after each addition. Simmer, covered, over medium-low heat for another 15–20 minutes, stirring occasionally. Five minutes before end of cooking time, taste again for needed salt and pepper.

Serve over buttered and seasoned noodles, or rice.

℘℘

I wonder if the reason Africans developed so many different recipe styles, so many different, elegant dishes was not only because they could but also to make themselves indispensable to the slave master. Cooks saw other slaves being born and growing up on a plantation, marrying and having children, only to have their families split up and sold away to some other plantation. I think many cooks believed that the better they were, the better recipes they produced, the more compliments on "her" table the white mistresses would receive, the more bows this cook was asked to come out and take, the more likely she or he would be kept on that particular plantation. It did not always work, however.

Perhaps an African cook would hear of another African cook's performance and feel threatened if his or her master and/or mistress raved over it. This cook would then have to either reproduce it or come up with something just as good or better. I guess it could have simply been a matter of personal pride and honor; however, it is possible that jealousies between African cooks were a part of their existence. Maybe African cooks would not give their secrets to *each other*. After all, they may have felt that they were only protecting themselves and possibly family. Slavery and racism, the very nature of its bestialities, seems to have imposed a sense of competition (if only implied) in many aspects in a slave's life. This sense of rivalry and competition, it seems to me, is partly responsible for what has been a poor African American self-image.

Fear of being sold may also partly explain why African cooks would always tell the mistress that they never knew how much of this or that they were using. After all, once the white mistress had the cook's recipes, *that* cook was dispensable. The mistress still needed someone to actually do the work, and she could always get another cook. Every time new slaves were brought onto the plantation, in came new culinary talent. African cooks passed down to their daughters their secrets from memory. Daughters learned by watching what their mothers did from memory. Just as early jazz trumpet greats in New Orleans placed handkerchiefs around the trumpet valves to try to keep interlopers from copying their fingering techniques, African cooks during slavery tried to keep their recipes secret from the mistress of the plantation. Being *owned* by someone, however, meant that even the slave's secrets ultimately belonged to the slave master.

Because everything the slave possessed actually belonged to the slave master, Africans could not arbitrate their own lives on any level. Even as a free people, they held little to no control over their dispensability. I am reminded that the King of Ragtime, Scott Joplin, and other black musicians, attended the 1893 World's Fair. A number of these musicians found employment and thereby further exposed

Americans to the ragtime sound. By the time the Fair had ended ragtime had taken center stage in the popular music culture in America. It was during this era in America that both a ready mix for reproducing pancakes and a more efficient model for mechanical sound reproduction of music were being marketed. There would be little need to go to the source (black musicians) if that source could be imitated and then reproduced mechanically, outside of its place of origin.

The dynamics of racism and cultural imperialism warrant attention. When Rutt and Underwood decided on a version of pancake mix that they packaged and marketed all over the world, *their version became the model, the original pancake mix.* We see every day in modern times that African Americans are being defined out of their own music, just as surely as they have been defined out of their own culinary creations since arriving on these shores.

Africans, during the slave trade, were defined out of Egypt as well; or Egypt was defined out of Africa, whichever you prefer. That means, as well, that they were defined away from the first keyboard instrument, which was created in Egypt in the third century B.C. It was a water organ, made by putting together flutes of various sizes in a frame and directing air from a bellows by way of a keyboard. It is quite natural that its invention took place in Africa. An organ is a instrument designed to blend chords; pianos, on the other hand, are single note instruments. The organ works on the principal of continuous sound. When you push your finger down on one key, it continues to play. A piano cannot do this. When you play an organ, you blend extended chords to produce a full-bodied and lasting sound. Just listen to Jimmy Smith, Brother Jack McDuff, Jimmy McGriff, Alice Coltrane, Groove Holmes, Charles Earland, and Trudie Pitts. They bring this point home constantly.

Another organist, Larry Young, a leading pioneer in successfully incorporating the Hammond B-3 organ into a jazz group, defined the instrument. In a February 5, 1992, replay of an interview broadcast on National Public Radio, he said that the Hammond B-3 "has the spirituosity of the church and the flavor of down home cooking." He said that many musicians never wanted to play with the organ as part of the group because it was so overpowering. So, he continued, when you play the organ you have to know how to mix with the group, how to accent, how to blend. Knowing how to mix, he said, was everything.

Knowing how to mix, how to combine different flavors together to create a recipe can sometimes be a tricky task. But black people, both here and in Africa, have always been able to blend spices, herbs, and seasonings to develop so many different recipes because our cooking is inextricably linked to other aspects of our cultural heritage. It is for this reason that African cooking, both in Africa and in America, has had deep cultural influences on African American music and, therefore, on America in general. Cooking has always been a necessity and thus a much older craft than music making. But there is a definite relationship between the African American musical artist and the African American culinary artist. Gospel, blues, ragtime, jazz, as well as rhythm and blues, have all been influenced by African American cuisine. It is in the harmonics, the limitless blends. It is in the rags of Scott Joplin—the playing of two distinct melodies on the piano at the same time. It is in the song stylings of Al Green in "I Can't Get Next to You" and "Let's Stay Together," whose one elongated syllable embraces a flurry of different notes. It is in Miss Sarah Vaughan, who gives you the entire musical scale, from bass to soprano, in one sung word. It is in the guitar of Wes Montgomery and his "Bumpin' On the Sunset." It is in the perfect harmony of Shep and the Limelights in "Daddy's Home," and in "I Only Have Eyes For You" by the Flamingos. Cooking, likewise, is the blending of groups of ingredients to produce a harmony of flavors. One way the connection between cooking and music is made by music (and food) lovers is that culinary expressions, no less, were used in the '40s, '50s and '60s to describe jazz artists: "Ah, man, Brother McDuff was cookin' on that organ, Jack!" Or, "Dexter is really smokin', tonight." And, "Miles is sizzlin', ain't he?" Or, "Wow! That solo was hot!"

Well, jazz is composed and performed on the same principle as cooking. There is no playing by the numbers. There are no prescribed, prearranged, unalterable limits to which the musician must adhere. Watch and listen to a big orchestra with a conductor. The conductor tries to "blend" all the sections of the orchestra together as they play. His job is to try to keep the group in unison. The individual musicians are not blending notes, not creating on their own. They merely play the notes *written down in front of them.* There is limited creative expression.

In jazz, there is definitive form and content. The difference between it and European orchestrations is that in jazz there is vision and creative expression; versatility is born from that vision. Let us cook, for instance, a simple pot of greens:

a pound of spinach
a half pound of mustard greens
a half pound of collards
approximately 6 ounces of salt pork
water, to which has been added a few tablespoons of vinegar
black pepper

Each green has its own taste and flavor and can be cooked, seasoned, and eaten individually. When the three greens are cooked together, a new taste is created, each green seasoning or accenting the other. That is like John Coltrane, playing three notes at the same time on tenor sax, doing his thing with Wilbur Hardin on trumpet in "I'll Get By." The salt pork—the salt pork is another accent. All you need is one or two small pieces—a lick here, a lick there. It is a four-piece combo with Elvin Jones doing drum solo in "Summertime" with Coltrane. He plays the melody. Everybody else plays rhythm and accents. When the solo is done, he accents. Not too much accent. He leaves a lot of space. The greens are both the melody and the accent. The salt pork and pepper accent and season. The rhythm might belong to the method of cooking the ingredients. What started out as an economical and plain affair turns out to be a pretty tasty dish. Those few ingredients are all you need to turn a simple dish into a completely nourishing meal.

§§

"Summertime"

Take a four-piece combo:
4 tablespoons of Paul Chambers on bass
A pinch of McCoy Tyner on piano
$1/2$ pint of John Coltrane on sax
$3/4$ cup of Miles Davis on trumpet

Come to think of it, I think King Curtis used those exact, same proportions for his "Memphis Soul Stew," which "tasted" mighty good, too.

Now bring to a boil, and, with Elvin Jones on drums, beat—well.

Speaking of drums, the tap dance, also invented by African Americans, influenced drum playing. During the early days, when drummers were developing their licks, they accented only certain beats. They did not play as full. They left more space. As we approach the modern era, the beat becomes more intense. Tap dance led the way in helping drummers hear the beat and rhythm differently. It is also interesting that one of the cymbals jazz drummers like to use is a "sizzle" cymbal. It is called that because it gives a sound like something frying in the skillet.

When that next culinary creation is taking shape in the skillet or coming to life in the oven, let us remember the contributions of African Americans to music and cuisine. After all, the glorious sounds and tastes created by black hands have enriched the culinary experience and cultural heritage not only of blacks but of all Americans and much of the world; a world that dances and pats its feet to music that blacks have created, and satiates itself on foods that have long been part of the African culinary repertoire.

The distorted picture, however, is that Africans and people of African descent have no connection to history when it comes to cooking, or, for that matter, on any other front, that is worth knowing, much less celebrating. I am repeating here that Africa's tremendous population growth was a result of Africa's ability and stability in agricultural production. A varied cuisine developed as a result of this production of cultivated crops. Numerous aspects of African culture, such as methods of food preparation, migrated, mostly by way of Africans themselves, to every distant shore. These facts have traditionally been ignored or cloaked between the pages of books that have *other people's* names in them. That tradition has been passed down like recipes. I have tried to bring some light and attention to what has been the failure of both scholars and laypersons who write history and/or cookbooks, persons who use the cloaking device but claim that they are presenting unbiased and factual information on the cuisines and cultures of people all over the globe. That globe, I contend, is tied racially, culturally, and certainly by way of the kitchen, to the African continent.

Glossary

ACHIOTE SEEDS: Also known as *annatto*. A red vegetable coloring in seed form. It comes in bottles of granules that can be dissolved in hot corn oil to give food a delicate flavor and a reddish orange color. Available in stores specializing in foods from Latin America and India.

AGUSI SEEDS: See EGUSI SEEDS.

ALLSPICE BERRIES: Sold whole or ground, allspice is a pepperlike berry. Used in a variety of spice mixtures, dessert and main dish preparations, it is also known as Jamaica pepper.

ANCHO CHILI PEPPERS: A dried pepper and member of the cayenne family, anchos are deep mahogany in color, somewhat heart shaped, and are three to five inches long. *Mulato* and *pasilla* are other names for the dried ancho. The fresh variety is known as *poblano*. Anchos are sometimes roasted first (to concentrate flavor), but almost always soaked, then ground to a paste before further cooking. Used to make sauces, salsas, and moles for chicken, beef, fish, and vegetable dishes, it has a mild flavor and is available in Latin American markets and some health food stores.

ANNATTO: See ACHIOTE.

ARROWROOT: A starchy substance obtained from the roots of a plant found in tropical America. Ground into a powder, it is used as a flavorless thickening agent for glazes and sauces.

ASAFETIDA (or Asafoetida): A favored spice of vegetarians in India because of its onionlike smell when exposed to heat. It is the dried gum resin from several species of the *Ferula* plant. Available in lump or powdered form, it is sometimes said to be an "acquired taste." If you purchase the powdered form, sometimes it is necessary to double the amount called for in the recipe. However, the amounts called for in the recipes I have presented seem to work well.

BEAN CURD (Tofu): Resembles custard. It has no real flavor of its own but absorbs the flavors of foods with which it is cooked. Made from soybeans, it is an important source of protein. Available in all Asian food stores.

BERBERE: This is one of the hot pepper seasonings of the Motherland. Ethiopian and many East African dishes REQUIRE Berbere to add that special flavor, as well as fire, to the dish. Every cook has his or her own preference, as far as proportions, of the ingredients. In the selection of spices blended and the specific uses for Berbere, it can certainly be compared to the spice blends *sambaar podi,* or other *masalas,* prepared in India. There are powdered Berberes made with dry, ground spices and Berbere pastes, made by grinding spices and other ingredients into an almost thick puree. They are blended according to the food being prepared. The following is but one example:

1½ tsp. ground ginger
¾ tsp. EACH ground coriander, ground fenugreek seeds, cardamom, and nutmeg
½ tsp. EACH cloves, cinnamon, and allspice
¼ of a small onion, finely chopped
½ cup Ethiopian Spiced Oil (See index)
1 cup EACH cayenne powder and paprika
1½ tsp. black pepper, preferably freshly ground
3 Tbs. salt

Toast the first 8 ingredients together in a saucepan over low heat. Shake and stir constantly for a few minutes.

Combine toasted spices, onion, and oil in a blender or food processor. Blend until the mixture is a smooth paste. Combine the cayenne, paprika, black pepper, and salt in the saucepan and toast them the same way, shaking and stirring constantly, for 10 minutes. Add toasted spices to spice paste. Thin, if necessary, with water, adding a tablespoon at a time, until the desired consistency is reached. Cool and store, covered, in the refrigerator.

BERBERE SEASONINGS, DRY:
All spices must be toasted in a dry skillet over medium heat, then cooled, before grinding to a powder. Cayenne powder can be added to spices before grinding (in the traditional way), if you prefer. I have chosen to add the "heat," in most cases, separately, to enable you to subtract or add the "fire" to suit your own taste.

(A) ¼ tsp. EACH coriander seeds, yellow fenugreek seeds, cardamom pods, whole cloves, allspice berries, and a small piece of cinnamon stick

(B) ½ tsp. EACH coriander seeds, crushed red pepper, and whole cloves, 13 allspice berries, 11 cardamom pods, ¼ tsp. EACH cumin (geera), black fenugreek seeds, yellow fenugreek, 2 small pieces of cinnamon stick, ⅛ tsp. anise seed

(C) Same as A above, plus ¼ tsp. EACH black fenugreek, anise seed, cumin seed

(D) ¼ tsp. EACH whole cloves, allspice berries, anise seed, coriander seed, yellow fenugreek, *ground* ginger

BIRD CHILI PEPPERS: Small, elongated chilies, available fresh in red, green, purple, and orange from specialty food grocers.

CACTUS: See NOPAL CACTUS, below.

CANELA: Also known as true cinnamon or Ceylon cinnamon, imported directly from Sri Lanka. Softer and different in flavor from cinnamon sold at your grocer's, it is available in powdered and stick form from specialty spice and herb dealers. Do not confuse with the sticks of powdered spice labeled "canela," available in Cuban markets. This, too, is cassia, a substitute.

CARAMEL SUGAR: Used in various recipes in Southeast Asian cooking. To make, you will need:

1 cup of sugar
1⅓ cups water

2 teaspoons lime juice
1 teaspoon lemon juice

Place sugar in a saucepan over high heat. As it starts to brown, stir constantly. When completely browned, remove from heat and add water (sugar will crystallize instantly). Return to high heat, stirring frequently, for 4 to 5 minutes. Remove from heat. Add juices, then cool. Store in a covered jar in the refrigerator.

CARDAMOM PODS: They are about the size of a pea. Cardamoms are the dried fruit of a plant in the ginger family. The small aromatic black seeds found inside the pods have a lemonlike flavor (the green cardamom is the most pungent). One-fourth teaspoon ground cardamom is equal to the seeds of four whole pods. Always toast (brown) pods in a dry skillet, over medium heat, before grinding. They are available in Indian, Middle Eastern, and specialty stores.

CASSAVA: Part of the diet of many African peoples on the continent and in the diaspora. Cassava's tuberous roots are edible, and may be cooked whole or pulverized and used in a number of different dishes. Of the two varieties, bitter and sweet, the bitter one is poisonous until cooked. Also called *yuca* and manioc, some larger and specialty food stores carry it fresh and/or frozen.

CASSAVA FLOUR (MEAL): The dried and ground form of cassava, it is used to make bread and as a thickening agent for sauces, soups, and stews. By far cassava's most popular form and is sometimes called *gari* in West Africa, *farinhe de mandioca,* or manioc, in Brazil, and tapioca in Western societies. It is considered nutritious and is also prepared as a side dish, taking the place of rice or couscous.

CELLOPHANE NOODLES: These dried noodles must be soaked before cooking. Made from mung beans, they are available in two-, four-, and eight-ounce packages. Available in Asian markets and groceries.

CHICHA: Native wine from Peru, Ecuador, Colombia and also Central America. In some locales in Central America it is made from fruits such as peaches, apples, quinces, etc. But the ancients of all these areas grew a special variety of sweet corn for fermentation. When fermentation reached a certain point, "they added . . . a meal made from ground toasted sweet corn to increase the sugar content and give the chicha its extra kick." (Edgar Anderson, *Plants, Man and Life,* [Boston: Little, Brown & Co., 1952], 112, 113). The ears of this special corn "are nearly as wide as they are high, as big as an orange, with a thick heavy cob, numerous irregular rows of kernels, . . . They may be pale lemon yellow, orange yellow, and various shades of orange red, . . ." (*Plants, Man and Life,* 113). These days, brown sugar is used.

CHICHARRONES: The outer fat of the pig is twice fried in boiling fat. They are very crisp and make a good appetizer to serve with drinks. Chopped or ground, they can be softened by adding to sauces or other preparations. Available in bags at a numerous supermarkets.

CHILI PEPPER (AJÍ): Ají is the generic name for chilies in Peru, and includes such varieties as panca, cereza, limo, amarillo (one of the most common grown in Peru), ayucllo, norteño, and charapa. They may vary in lengths from two to five inches, and in pungency and heat from mild to extreme.

CHILI PEPPER LEAVES: Available at specialty stores.

CHIPOTLE CHILI PEPPER: A favorite among the ancients of Mexico, the chipotle is produced by drying and smoking the jalapeño pepper. Can be used whole in simmering soups and stews until flavor permeates. Remove before serving. It may also be soaked in hot water for about 1½ hours to rehydrate. Remove skin, seeds, and inner ribs and chop before adding to your recipes.

CILANTRO: See CORIANDER, below.

CINNAMON STICK: Available usually in four-inch lengths, they are the dried, reddish-brown bark from the cassia tree (evergreen family). Ground cinnamon has a less aromatic flavor than the stick.

COCONUT, FINELY GRATED: Available, sweetened or unsweetened, in seven- or fourteen-ounce packages in the frozen food section of larger groceries or specialty food stores.

COCONUT MILK: Not to be confused with coconut cream, canned coconut milk is used for these recipes. It turns out to be a pretty good substitute for fresh. Available unsweetened in cans. However, purists may prefer to crack open fresh coconuts, pouring the liquid into a container and removing the coconut meat. You can add water to the coconut liquid, placing it and coconut meat into a blender or food processor and then puree. With about a cup of water, strain two to three times, using your hands to extract as much liquid as possible. To make your own: Grated, fresh coconut, packed in measuring container is combined with boiling water (in equal proportions). Allow mixture to rest for thirty minutes or so. The mixture is then pureed in a blender or food processor. Strain mixture through a double layer of cheesecloth, squeezing as much juice out of the pulp as you can. It freezes well.

CORIANDER: Also known as cilantro. The seeds are the primary ingredient in curry powder. This white pepper–like spice is sometimes ground and fried in hot oil before adding to vegetables and bean and pea dishes. The leaves are highly aromatic and are used mainly the same way as parsley. It is available in Indian, Asian, and Mexican groceries.

CORNHUSKS: Usually dried. Keeps indefinitely. Parchment paper can be substituted. Available in Latin American food stores.

CUMIN: Also known as *geera*. The white or green seeds resemble caraway seeds and are eaten in appetizers, main dishes, and snacks. The black seeds are a rare variety, and have a mellow, sweet taste. Sold in specialty food stores.

CURRY POWDER: Curry powder is said to be "the classic masala of southern India." But the word *kari* is the correct spelling and represents the aromatic leaves of the kari plant used in the cuisine of southern and southwestern India. It also defines a particular cooking style of the south. A blend of coriander seeds, red chili pods, cumin seeds, mustard seeds, fenugreek seeds, black peppercorns, kari leaves, and turmeric powder, *kari podi* (powder) can also be combined with ground cinnamon and ground cloves. The southern Brahmins from Bangalore add fresh, flaked unsweetened coconut to their blend.

DENDE OIL: A variety of palm oil, REQUIRED in a great many African dishes on the continent and in Brazil. See PALM OIL below.

DHAL: There are a number of types, but the recipes here include dhal, a flour made of yellow split peas (sometimes called *channa dal*), a legume from the pod of the *Cicer arietinum* plant. An integral ingredient in many Indian cooks' spice blends, dhal is a thickening agent as well.

DILL: Sometimes used in making soups, stews, and sauces. Complements fish and seafood dishes very nicely.

DORO WAT: The Ethiopian national dish, consisting of chicken stewed in red pepper sauce (berbere).

EGUSI SEEDS: From the egusi melon, the seeds are ground and used as a soup and stew ingredient in West Africa, Brazil, and the Caribbean. Available from specialty grocers. May be difficult to find. Sold in ground meal and whole seeds.

EPAZOTE: Fresh or dried herb leaves, used for medicinal purposes, as well as in food preparations such as soups and stews. Somewhat bitter in taste, it is sold in ⅛-ounce packages in Latin American and some American food markets.

FENNEL: Also known as anise, or aniseed, the sometimes greenish yellow, sometimes yellowish brown seeds have a licorice flavor. From the parsley family and shaped like a tiny watermelon, it is used sometimes in cooking okra and other vegetables, as well as to flavor beverages and desserts. Coated with syrup, it is often served as an after-dinner mint in homes and restaurants in India.

FENUGREEK: Brownish yellow and reddish brown varieties exist. It has a bitter flavor, and is therefore used sparingly. It is often fried or toasted before adding to the dish. Used extensively in vegetarian cooking, it is available in Indian and Middle Eastern groceries.

GARAM MASALA: A spice blend used in Indian dishes, sometimes consisting of coriander, cumin, black pepper, cinnamon, fennel, and nutmeg. Available at Indian and specialty food stores. Also see MASALA below.

GARI: See CASSAVA FLOUR (MEAL) above.

GEERA: See CUMIN above.

GHEE: Clarified butter, made by heating or cooking butter until all of the moisture evaporates. To make, put 1 cup of butter in a saucepan and melt over low heat. Stirring occasionally, simmer until solids at the bottom brown. Remove from heat and allow residue to settle to the bottom. Strain off the clear fat and bottle. Note that it is very similar to Ethiopian Spiced Oil, but without the spices. It is sold in Indian groceries.

GINGER ROOT: Brown root with a lemony flavor. Much more pungent in flavor than the dry variety. It is used in various cuisines, including Indian, Asian, and African.

GREEN CHILI PEPPER: See BIRD and SERRANO CHILI PEPPERS.

GUAJILLO CHILI PEPPER: Guajillo chilies are four- to six-inches long, tapering to a point. Dark red to reddish-brown in color, they are considered to be very mild and sweet and are used in sauces, soups, stews, meat, and corn dishes. Soak dried guajillos in boiling or scalding hot water to soften before use. Available in some larger grocery stores and specialty food markets.

JAGGERY: Occasionally made from the juice of certain kinds of palm trees. It is a brownish, maple or molasses flavored, unrefined lump sugar. Considered a delicacy, and used as an ingredient in candies made in southern India. It is also served as a syrup to accompany different kinds of thin pancakes.

JUNIPER BERRIES: Used to flavor fish, game, and other preparations. One teaspoon of these berries simmered for a good while, say, in a soup or stew flavors the dish with an equivalent to ½ cup gin.

LEMON GRASS: Or Citronella root, resembles the white part of a scallion on its lower end. A tropical grass extensively used in Southeast Asian cooking. The lower part, up to where the leaves begin to branch out, is the portion used in cooking. Use dried variety, not powdered, as a substitute, which you have to soak in hot water for two hours and chop fine before using. Sold in Asian markets. Fresh lemon grass, which remains somewhat fibrous after cooking, is sold in many major supermarkets.

MALAGUETA CHILI PEPPER: A "main ingredient" chili, particularly for Africans in Brazil. Available bottled, in some specialty grocery stores and from one or two mail order houses.

MANIOC MEAL: A flourlike meal, ground fine. Made from the bitter cassava, it is used extensively as a thickener. Common to African, West Indian, and South American cooking, it is available at African and Latin American markets.

MASA HARINA: A very finely ground corn flour. Not to be confused with cornmeal. Sold in Latin American groceries, and some supermarkets sell Quaker brand.

MASALA (GARAM MASALA): A special blend of spices added to a dish to impart a particular flavor distinguishing it from other dishes or to identify regional cuisines. Also see SAMBAAR PODI, below.

MINT LEAVES: A weedlike herb available at most supermarkets.

MIRASOL CHILI PEPPERS: Extremely hot. The word *aji* is sometimes the word Peruvians use interchangeably with mirasol. It grows with the fruit erect, or pointing up, which gives it the name "looking, or gazing at the sun."

MUSTARD SEEDS (Black, Green): A spice yielded from the mustard green plant. The black seeds are smaller than the yellow mustard seeds, and less pungent in flavor.

ÑAME: White yam.

NOPAL CACTUS (Nopales): Flat-jointed paddles of the prickly pear or nopal cactus. Thorns must be cut off by the "bumps." Remove the base and trim edges. Rinse and cut into small pieces. Boil in salted water with scallions for ten minutes. Drain and rinse sticky substance from cactus. Prized for food and is now available in Mexican and Latin American markets.

NUOC MAM: Fish sauce that is an essential ingredient in Southeast Asian cooking. It is the equivalent to salt in American diets. Available at all Asian groceries.

NUTMEG (Fresh): Often used in combination with cardamom, it is the aromatic nut of the *Myristica fragrans* tree.

OYSTER SAUCE: Sold in Asian food stores, it is a thick brown sauce made of oysters and soy sauce. Used to flavor various dishes, including beef, seafood, and chicken.

PALM OIL: Dende is one of its varieties. Used extensively in African cuisine to color and impart characteristic flavors to certain preparations. Available at African and a few specialty food stores.

PAPAYA: A tropical fruit of many varieties, some of which reach a length of twelve inches. It is cooked in many preparations, including salads, when green. When yellow, it is eaten as fruit.

PASILLA CHILI PEPPER: Known also as *Chile Negro* because of its dark, rich color, the pasilla has a fruity flavor. It is mildly hot so that it combines well with other chili peppers. Use to flavor sauces, stews, soups, and moles.

PILONCILLO: Also called *panela* or Mexican sugar. Brown sugar sold at your grocer's is the closest substitute. The hard cones or large flat cakes of unrefined sugar can be softened in water (small pieces at a time), grated, or ground in a food processor.

PLANTAIN: Green in color and a member of the banana family. They should be cooked for a long time when green. When black (ripe), it is sometimes prepared by slicing and frying. Can stain hands. Peel under running water, or wear gloves.

POBLANO CHILI PEPPERS: A fairly mild chili, dark green, almost black in color. It is the fresh variety of the ancho chili pepper.

It is a widely used pepper, heart shaped, and about the size of a bell pepper (the smaller ones are hotter).

PUMPKIN SEEDS: Usually shelled, toasted in oil and salted. Available in West Indian and Mexican markets. Also sold in health food stores, other specialty stores and gourmet foods section of supermarkets. Squash seeds can be substituted.

RICE FLOUR: Rice that has been ground into a very fine powder. Sold at Asian markets.

RICE PAPERS (Dried): They are tissue thin, made of rice, salt, and water. They are dried in the sun on bamboo mats after being made. Rice papers must be dampened and softened before using. Available in 6- and $8^{1}/_{4}$-inch diameter rounds at Asian and specialty food stores.

ROSE WATER: Distilled from fresh rose petals, this liquid flavoring is available in pharmacies, as well as Asian, Middle Eastern, and Indian specialty food stores.

SAFFRON THREADS, GROUND SAFFRON: The threads are orange red dried stigmas of a flower of the *crocus sativus*. It is used to impart a golden yellow color to the food. It is reported to be the most expensive spice in the world. In southern and southwestern India all religious festival desserts are laced with saffron. It has a mildly, somewhat sweet-bitter flavor, and in addition to the golden color adds a wonderful aroma. Ground saffron, which may be substituted in half the quantity, and the threads, are available in Middle Eastern and specialty food stores.

SAMBAAR PODI (Masala of Southern India): Spice blend of varying proportions added to Indian cuisine. It requires many of the same ingredients as Berbere seasoning, and is prepared in much the same way. Some of the ingredients for a blend include coriander seeds, cumin seeds, fenugreek seeds (yellow and black), dry red chili pods, black peppercorns, turmeric, black salt, yellow mung beans, white split gram beans, and yellow split peas. As with African cooks, Indian cooks themselves decide how much of each ingredient goes into the blend.

Two sample blends would include:

A) 1 tsp. fenugreek seeds
$3/4$ tsp. mustard seeds
1 Tbs. coriander seeds
1 Tbs. cumin seeds
$1^1/_2$ tsp. turmeric
2 tsp. freshly ground black pepper
$1/2$ cup red pepper (cayenne)
$3/4$ tsp. freshly grated cinnamon
$1/2$ tsp. ground cloves
1 Tbs. salt

B) $1/2$ tsp. black mustard seeds
$1/4$ tsp. black peppercorns
$1/4$ tsp. coriander seeds
$1/4$ tsp. cumin seeds
$1/4$ tsp. yellow fenugreek seeds
$1/2$ tsp. red pepper (cayenne)

All of the seeds are first roasted in a preheated skillet by stirring and shaking the pan constantly. Brown but do not burn seeds. When cool, grind in a spice mill or blender or coffee grinder (not a food processor). Combine with remaining spices.

SERRANO CHILI PEPPERS: Bright green in color and one- to two-inches long. Only mildly hot. Sold fresh as well as packed in cans in Latin American markets and some major supermarkets.

SESAME SEED OIL: Sometimes called Gingelly oil and is used extensively in Indian, Asian, and some African dishes. Salad dressings and condiments utilize this oil. In addition, braised dishes, as well as soups and stews, are flavored with it.

SESAME SEEDS: Very rich in protein and therefore a mainstay in vegetarian diets. Used in many southern and southwestern Indian dishes, as well as being extensively used in African cooking.

SHRIMP (Dried, ground): Contains a strong, or sharp, salty flavor. Africans on the continent and in Brazil use it extensively in their cuisine. It is also used in Caribbean and Southeast Asian dishes. Can be soaked in water before using. Available in one-ounce packaging in Asian and Latin American food stores.

SUNFLOWER SEEDS: Available fresh at health food stores.

TAMARIND: Native to Africa and grown throughout tropical regions, the dried pulp of the seed pod is brittle and cinnamon colored. Juice is produced by soaking the fruit in boiling water. The pulp is valued for its somewhat acid sweet taste. Some varieties taste like sour prunes. It is prepared sun dried and also preserved in syrup. The peeled, pitted, and compressed pulp is more herbal and is available in one-pound cakes in Latin American, Caribbean, Indian, Middle Eastern, and Indonesian specialty food stores.

TOMATILLO: Also known in Mexico as *tomate verde, tomate de cascara,* and *miltomate.* Bright green in color, it is a relative of the Cape gooseberry and the American ground cherry. Note that it is a fruit, not a green tomato. It is surrounded on the outside by a thin, paperlike outer husk that must be removed before cooking. Sold fresh in large supermarkets and at specialty grocers. They are also available in cans, husks removed, in Latin American and gourmet and specialty shops.

TURMERIC: Ground turmeric is responsible for the yellow color of curry powder. From the ginger family, the young shoots are cooked as a vegetable. Considered a delicacy in southern Indian cooking, it is the chief spice in vegetarian cooking. Turmeric shoots, which look similar to ginger root, as well as the ground powder, are sold in Indian and specialty, gourmet food stores.

WATERMELON SEEDS: Available at larger health food stores. Used in the preparation of tea and other drinks, and in soups and stews (finely ground).

YAM: Available in the white (also known as ñame) and yellow varieties, fresh and frozen from regular and specialty grocers.

YUCA: See CASSAVA.

Sources for Specialty Foods

Mo Hotta Mo Betta
P.O. Box 4136
San Luis Obispo, California 93403
1 (800) 462-3220
(805) 544-4051
www.mohotta.com

Monterrey Food Products
3939 East Cesar East Chavez Avenue
Los Angeles, California 90063
(323) 262-2143: Phone
(323) 263-2545: Fax

The Spice House
1941 Central Street
Evanston, Illinois 60201
(847) 328-3711: Phone
(847) 328-3631: Fax

The Spice House
1031 North Old World Third Street
Milwaukee, Wisconsin 53202
(414) 272-0977: Phone
(414) 272-1271: Fax

Penzeys, Ltd. Spices and Seasonings
P.O. Box 933
Muskego, Wisconsin 53150
(414) 679-7207: Phone
(414) 679-7878: Fax
www.penzeys.com

Sutton Place Gourmet Shops (Hay Day Markets):

1385 Post Road East
Westport, Connecticut 06880
(203) 254-5200: Phone
(203) 254-5216: Fax

21 Governor Street
Ridgefield, Connecticut 06877
(203) 431-4400

1050 East Putnam Avenue
Riverside, Connecticut 06878
(203) 637-7600

15 Palmer Road
Scarsdale, New York 10583
(914) 722-0200

Alliant Food Service
Boca Raton, Florida
(561) 994-8500
1 (800) 275-5723
1 (800) 331-6569

Guyana Market Place
18653 S. Dixie Highway
Miami, Florida 33157
(305) 256-4122: Phone
(305) 256-3712: Fax

Jamaica Groceries and Spices Imports, Inc.
9587 S. W. 160th Street
Miami, Florida 33157
(305) 252-1197

Asia Market
9531 S. W. 160th Street
Miami, Florida 33157
(305) 232-2728

Rajo African Products
5356 Crenshaw Boulevard
Los Angeles, California 90043
(323) 299-1989

African Produce Central Market
4564 West Washington Boulevard
Los Angeles, California 90016
(323) 932-1722: Phone
(323) 954-0701: Fax

Pacific Spice Company ($100 minimum order)
722 Stanford Avenue
Los Angeles, California 90021
(213) 626-2302

The Green House (Fine Herbs)
Encinitas, California 92023-1069
(760) 942-5371: Fax

Dowel Quality Products, Inc.
91 1st Avenue
New York, New York 10003
(212) 979-6045

Foods of India
121 Lexington Avenue
New York, New York
(212) 683-4419: Phone
(212) 251-0946: Fax

Subzi Mandi
72-30 37th Avenue
Jackson Heights Queens, New York
(718) 457-1848

Buzzeos
11 West 46th Street, 2nd Floor
New York, New York 10036
(212) 869-6552

Rafal Spice Company
2521 Russell Street
Detroit, Michigan 48207
(313) 259-6373

Bengal Spices
11435 Joseph Campau Street
Hamtramck, Michigan 48212
(313) 365-7090

Sidney's Spices
1300 Booth Avenue Northwest
Atlanta Georgia 30318
(404) 352-8465

Bibliographical Notes

The following references were most useful in identifying the African culinary collage and tracing its migration. I also consulted sources that I found problematic but contained bits and pieces of information that helped to construct this culinary tapestry. The selective list of sources that follow is also intended to give the reader an indication of the research at the foundation of the study.

Chapter One. Feasting among the "Eastern Ethiopians"

African Glory (Baltimore, MD: Black Classic Press, 1986; 1954) by J. C. deGraft-Johnson, offers one of many accounts of vanished African civilizations. One segment of the text deals with the life of "a non-Christian African personage—Septimus Severus," who, in 193 A.D., became the emperor of Rome.

Africa's wealth in terms of food and its East Coast cities is discussed in E. Jefferson Murphy, *History of African Civilization* (New York, NY: Thomas Y. Crowell Company, 1972); and Margaret Shinnie, *Ancient African Kingdoms* (New York, NY: St. Martin's Press, 1965). Numerous sources provide insight into East African trading ports and its trade network. For example, see Basil Davidson, *The African Slave Trade* [originally, *Black Mother*] (Boston, MA: Little, Brown and Co., 1961); and his *A History of East and Central Africa* (New York, NY: Doubleday, 1969); and his *The African Past: Chronicles from Antiquity to Modern Times* (Boston, MA: Little, Brown, and Co., 1964). Also see John Jackson, *Introduction to African Civilization* (Secaucus, NJ: The Citadel Press, 1970); Lester Brooks, *Great Civilizations of Ancient Africa* (New York, NY: Four Winds Press, 1971); and

Murphy's, *History of African Civilization*. A detailed description of the people and the plentitude and opulence of East African foodstuffs during the fourteenth century is recounted by the famous traveller Ibn Battuta in Said Hamdun and Noel King, eds., *Ibn Battuta in Black Africa* (London, Eng.: Rex Collings, 1975). Also see Shinnie's *Ancient African Kingdoms*; Murphy's, *History of African Civilization*; and Richard W. Hull, *African Cities and Towns before the European Conquest* (New York, NY: W. W. Norton and Co., Inc., 1976). Duarte Barbosa, Portuguese royal commercial agent, was another witness to the beauty and economic viability and commercial importance of Africa's East Coast cities. He is quoted in Shinnie's *Ancient African Kingdoms* and Davidson's *A History of East and Central Africa*.

The origin of humankind in Africa and the development of DNA studies are very ably expressed by Louis S. B. Leakey in *The Progress and Evolution of Man in Africa* (London, Eng.: Oxford University Press, 1961); and in his *White African* (London, Eng.: Hodder and Stoughton, 1937). His wife, Mary Leakey, offers additional insight into the origins of some edible plants and of the human species in *Disclosing the Past: An Autobiography* (New York, NY: Doubleday and Co., Inc., 1984). The African "mother" of humankind, "Lucy," and the beginnings of civilization receive extensive treatment from Donald Johanson and Blake Edgar, *From Lucy to Language* (New York, NY: Simon and Schuster, 1996); Johanson and James Shreeve, *Lucy's Child: The Discovery of a Human Ancestor* (New York, NY: William Morrow, 1989); Johanson, Lenora Johanson, and Blake Edgar, *Ancestors: In Search of Human Origins* (New York, NY: Villard Books, 1994); Johanson and Maitland Edey, *Lucy: The Beginnings of Humankind* (New York, NY: Simon and Schuster, 1981); and Johanson and Kevin O'Farrell, *Journey from the Dawn: Life with the World's First Family* (New York, NY: Villard Books, 1990). See also Cheikh Anta Diop, *The African Origin of Civilization: Myth or Reality* (Westport, CT: Lawrence Hill, 1974); and the documentary, "Children of Eve," NOVA, program orginally broadcast on PBS on January 27, 1987 (Boston, 1987). Philip S. Foner's *History of Black Americans*, Vol. I (Westport, CT: Greenwood Press, 1975) contains material on the Sahara and its green, fertile region, eight thousand years ago.

Readers interested in mining activity in Africa and its impact on internal commerce and trade can consult William E. B. Du Bois, *The World and Africa* (New York, NY: International Publishers, Co., Inc., 1965, 1946); Chancellor Williams, *The Destruction of Black Civilization* (Dubuque, IA: Kendall/Hunt Publishing Co., 1971); and Franz Boas, *Race and Democratic Society* (New York, NY: J. J. Augustin, 1945). Articles and essays on the antiquity of mining in Africa include Tendai Mutunhu's "Africa: The Birthplace of Iron Mining," *Negro History Bulletin* (Jan.-Feb.-March 1981); R. A. Dart and P. Beaumont's "Amazing Antiquity of Mining in Southern Africa," *Nature Magazine* (October 28, 1967); Debra Shore's "Steel-Making in Ancient Africa," in Ivan Van Sertima, ed., *Blacks in Science: Ancient and Modern* (New Brunswick, NJ: Transaction Books, 1983); and Nino Del Grande's "Prehistoric Iron Smelting in Africa," *Natural History* (Sept.-Oct. 1932). There is also a section on metallurgy in Africa in Cheikh Anta Diop's *Precolonial Black Africa*(Brooklyn, NY: Lawrence Hill Books, 1987). Diop's work looks at the prevalence and antiquity of gold mining in Africa, that is, "from antiquity to modern times, from the Indian Ocean to the Atlantic, i.e., from the Nubia of Herodotus and Diodorus Siculus to the Ghana of Bakri and the Mali of Ibn Battuta and Khaldun and the Songhai of Sadi and Kati." The passage continues, "Historically, Nubia was the country from which Egypt acquired all her gold." The use of iron implements in Africa for crop production is discussed in Franz Boas, *Race and Democratic Society* (New York, NY: J. J. Augustin, 1945). For a discussion of Swaziland's Lion Cavern see Mutunhu, "Africa: The Birthplace of Iron Mining," and Dart and Beaumont, "Amazing Antiquity of Mining in Southern Africa." In addition, Mutunhu's piece makes reference to the commonplace role of the African female in the mining process. Gary B. Nash, *Red, White, and Black* (Englewood Cliffs, NJ: Prentice Hall, 1974, 1982, 1992) and Williams's *The Destruction of Black Civilization* both shed light on Africa's skill in iron production, which made possible industrial achievements that impacted on agriculture and cooking.

Material on the plunder and aggression against South Africa's people can be found in Thomas Pakenham, *The Scramble for Africa* (New York, NY: Avon Books, 1991); Walter Rodney, *How Europe Underdeveloped Africa* (Washington, DC: Howard University Press, 1974); Peter Abrahams, *Wild Conquest: A Novel of Boer Aggression and African Resistance in South Africa* (New York, NY: Doubleday, 1971); and J. P. R. Wallis, *The Matabele Journals of Robert Moffat 1829–1860* Vol. 1 (London, Eng.: Chatto and Windus, 1945; 1965). See also Robert I Rotberg and Ali A. Mazrui, eds., *Rebellion in Black Africa* (London, Eng., New York, NY: Oxford University Press, 1971, 1970).

Terrace farming and irrigation were the agricultural way of life in many African communities. Williams's *The Destruction of Black Civilization* gives us a look into this system. Discourse on Africa's sharp increase in population, technical improvements, specialization of services, sophistication in agricultural methods, and other advances made in African culture are treated in the following: Hull, *African Cities and Towns before the European Conquest*; Molefi Asante and Kariamu Asante, "Great Zimbabwe: An Ancient African City-State," in Ivan Van Sertima, ed., *Blacks in Science: Ancient and Modern* (New Brunswick, NJ: Transaction Books, 1983). Also see Basil Davidson, *The Lost Cities of Africa* (Boston, MA: Atlantic-Little Brown, 1959) and his *The African Past: Chronicles from Antiquity to Modern Times*.

For discussions that shed light on the "city-empire" of Kilwa and other East Coast cities, as well as the Zanj and their inland and coastal neighbors, see *Zamani: A Survey of East African History* (London, Eng.: Longman, 1968), edited by B. A. Ogot; Davidson, *A History of East and Central Africa*; Jackson, *Introduction to African Civilization*; Brooks, *Great Civilizations of Ancient Africa*. See also Davidson, *The African Slave Trade* (originally, *Black Mother*); and his *The African Past: Chronicles from Antiquity to Modern Times*; and Murphy, *History of African Civilization*. J. C. deGraft-Johnson's *African Glory* can also be consulted for descriptions of East and Central African wealth. The literary prominence of Kilwa's native peoples is treated in Brooks, *Great Civilizations of Ancient Africa*, and in *The African Slave Trade* by Davidson.

European jealousy and plots to take over African trade in spices and minerals is discussed in Vincent B. Thompson, *The Making of the African Diaspora in the Americas, 1441–1900* (London, Eng.: Longman, 1987); Walter Rodney, *How Europe Underdeveloped Africa* (Washington, DC: Howard University Press, 1974); Eric Williams, *Capitalism and Slavery* (London, Eng.: Andre Deutsch, 1964, 1944); Jackson, *Introduction to African Civilization*; and Davidson, *The African Slave Trade*. Also see Thomas Pakenham, *The Scramble for Africa* (New York, NY: Avon Books, 1991), for discourse on European rivalry subsequent to Portuguese invasion. The Christian Church as participant and partner in the rape and destruction of Africa has been well documented. Among the many volumes that furnish specific accounts are Jackson's *Introduction to African Civilization*; Davidson's *The African Slave Trade*, and his *The African Past: Chronicles from Antiquity to Modern Times*.

A number of volumes take on the subject of African primacy in the area of medicine and philosophy. See for example, George G. M. James, *Stolen Legacy* (San Francisco, CA: Julian Richardson Associates, 1976; 1988 reprint; New York, NY: Philosophical Library, 1954); W. E. B. Du Bois, *The World and Africa* (New York, NY: International Publishers Co., Inc., 1965 reprint; 1946; 1947); Jackson, *Introduction to African Civilization*; Davidson, *The African Slave Trade*; Yosef ben-Jochannan, *Africa: Mother of Western Civilization* (New York, NY: Alkebu-Lan Books, 1971); and Martin Bernal, *Black Athena: The Fabrication of Ancient Greece* (New Brunswick, NJ: Rutgers University Press, 1987).

The African-Indian connection made for a people, culture, and way of cooking that shares much in common. Even the Greeks understood the racial affinity of Indians and Africans. In the *Iliad,* composed during the dawn of Greek literature, mention is made of the activities of the gods, which included their feasting among the "blameless" and "righteous" Ethiopians. The Greek poet Homer called the people of India "eastern Ethiopians." These "eastern Ethiopians," or Dravidians, were the primeval and aboriginal race of India, and have been described as "negro black in color," with "fuzzy" hair and having thick lips and wide, flat noses. Homer's likening of the people of India with those of Africa can be found in Akshoy Kumar Mazumdar's *The Hindu History,* second ed. (Allahabad, India: R. S. Publishing House, 1979 reprint; Dacca, Bangladesh: Nagendra Kumar Roy, 1920). The physical similarities between the two peoples are discussed in this volume, as well as in Wilfried Noelle's *Dravidian Studies— A Review* (Delhi, India: Jain Brothers, 1965); and in Gilbert Slater's *The Dravidian Element in Indian Culture* (New Delhi, India: Ess Ess Publications, 1976). Dravidian and Egyptian origins are ably handled in Joseph P. Widney, *Race Life of the Aryan Peoples* Vol. II (New York, NY: Funk and Wagnalls, 1907); Edward G. Balfour, ed., "Negro Races," in *Cyclopaedia of India* Vol. II, third ed. (London, Eng.: Quaritch, 1885); Theodore Celenko, ed., *Egypt in Africa* (Indianapolis, IN: Indianapolis Museum of Art, 1996); Mazumdar, *The Hindu History,* second ed.; and Du Bois, *The World and Africa.* You may also want to take a look at P. T. Srinivasa Iyengar's two volumes, *Pre-Aryan Tamil Culture* (Madras, India: Asian Educational Services, 1985; 1930) and *History of the Tamils* (Madras, India: Asian Educational Services, 1983, 1900; Madras: 1929). Also see K. P. Aravaanan, *Anthropological Studies on the Dravido-Africans* (Madras, India: Tamil Koottam, 1980). Material on the subject of close affinities between plants and animals in Africa and India in prehistoric times, and the land bridge believed to have once connected Africa and India can be found in Noelle's *Dravidian Studies—A Review,* and Du Bois's *The World and Africa.* See also T. R. Sesha Iyengar, *Dravidian India* Vol. I (Madras, India: The India Printing Works, 1925).

The manufacture of goods in India and the Far East from African raw materials such as ivory is discussed in Davidson, *The African Past: Chronicles from Antiquity to Modern Times,* and Jackson, *Introduction to African Civilization.* There are a number of volumes that deal with African explorers, diplomatic missions and trade expeditions to India, Ceylon, Indonesia, Southeast Asia, China, and the rest of the Far East, including Stanley Burstein, ed., *Ancient African Civilizations, Kush and Axum* (Princeton, NJ: Markus Wiener, 1998); G. F. Hourani, *Arab Seafaring in the Indian Ocean in Ancient and Early Medieval Times* (Princeton, NJ: Princeton University Press, 1951); Charles Tauber, whose work *Seafarers and Hieroglyphs* (American Documentation Institute, Washington) also lists the blacks of Melanesia as the inventors of one of the world's first written languages; Jackson, *Introduction to African Civilization;* and Davidson, *The African Slave Trade.* The *Journal of African History* VI, no. 2 (1965) also offers Yu. M. Kobishchanow's article, "On the Problem of Sea Voyages of Ancient Africans in the Indian Ocean." African cowries were used as money in many societies outside of Africa. Their use in India is mentioned in Haldhar Pathak, *Cultural History of the Gupta Period* (Delhi, India: Bharatiya Publishing House, 1978); and Iyengar, *Dravidian India* Vol. I. African commodities were certainly commonplace in India. For more on the subject, see Jackson, *Introduction to African Civilization*; and Davidson, *A History of East and Central Africa.*

The African origin of western India's alphabet, and its incorporation into the language of Tamil is cited in Mazumdar, *The Hindu History*; Slater, *The Dravidian Element in Indian Culture*; and Davidson, *A History of East and Central Africa*. There are two other studies that offer a comparative analysis of African and Dravidian languages. See U. Padmanabha Upadhyaya's *Dravidian and Negro African: Ethno-Linguistic Study on Their Origin, Diffusion, and Prehistoric Contacts, and Common Cultural and Linguistic Heritage* (Udupi, Karnataka, India: Samshodhana Prakashana, 1983); and *Dravidians and Africans*, published by Tamil Koottam in Madras in 1977.

Ballads and songs were important in both Africa and India. Suniti Kumar Chatterji explains elements and characteristics of Dravidian songs in *Dravidian: A Course of Three Lectures on Dravidian Origins and on Modern Dravidian Literature* (Annamalainagar, Madras India: Annamalai University Publications in Linguistics, 1965). *Hymns of the Tamil Saivite Saints* (Calcutta, India: Association Press, 1921; London, Eng.: Oxford University Press, 1921), edited by F. Kingsbury and G. E. Phillips, expounds the beauty of composition of Tamil lyrics. Also see *Carnatic Music and the Tamils* (Delhi, India: Kalinga Publications, 1992), by T. V. Kuppuswani; and International Institute of Tamil Studies' *Literary Heritage of the Tamils* (Adayaru, Madras: 1981), which is a series of papers first presented at the "Heritage of the Tamils" seminars in 1978.

Festivals were an integral part of Dravidian life. The activities prevalent during these festivals are presented in Santha Rama Rau, *The Cooking of India* (Alexandria, VA: Time-Life Books, 1969, 1975); Iyengar, *Dravidian India* Vol. I; Noelle, *Dravidian Studies—A Review*; and Chatterji, *Dravidian: A Course of Three Lectures on Dravidian Origins and on Modern Dravidian Literature*. The festival of Diwali, or Divali, is showcased in Rau's *The Cooking of India*. The same festival is celebrated (under different names) in many other cultures as well. See, for instance, Jomo Kenyatta, *Facing Mount Kenya* (New York, NY: Vintage Books, 1965); John S. Mbiti, *African Religions and Philosophy* (New York, NY: Anchor Books, 1970). Discourse on Boosketau is available in Lucien Carr's "The Food of Certain American Indians and Their Methods of Preparing It," *American Antiquarian Society* (Worcester, MA: Proceedings, 1896). Shops selling wines and other beverages were commonplace, as indicated in Pathak, *Cultural History of the Gupta Period*. The city of Madura and its similarity to cities in East Africa is a focal point in Slater's *The Dravidian Element in Indian*

Culture; Iyengar's *Dravidian India* Vol. I; Davidson's *The African Slave Trade* and his *A History of East and Central Africa*; and Shinnie's *Ancient African Kingdoms*.

A description of the royal hairstyle is contained in Haldhar Pathak, *Cultural History of the Gupta Period* (Delhi, India: Bharatiya Publishing House, 1978); and Noelle, *Dravidian Studies—A Review*. Leo Wiener, in volume I of his *Africa and the Discovery of America* (Philadelphia, PA: Innes and Sons, 1920), provides material and photographs of the favored hairstyles of African females.

The same hairstyles were favored by Southeast Asian men and women alike. See the numerous photographs, including cornrowed ladies and soldiers in Madeleine Giteau's, *The Civilization of Angkor* (New York, NY: Rizzoli, 1976).

For discourse on the organization of agricultural activity and the committment of village officials to equal distribution of land and successful farming in ancient times, see T. R. Sesha Iyengar, *Dravidian India* Vol. I; Pathak, *Cultural History of the Gupta Period*; Mazumdar, *The Hindu History*; and Chatterji, *Dravidian: A Course of Three Lectures on Dravidian Origins and on Modern Dravidian Literature*. Also see Noelle, *Dravidian Studies—A Review*. The concept of supporting those in the community who are unable to produce their own food is expressed in T. R. Sesha Iyengar's *Dravidian India* Vol. I. *Dravidian India* Vol. I also contains literary work that extols the importance of agriculture. Iyengar's work holds that farming, as an occupation, was ranked at the top of ancient Dravidian society. Other works on the subject of Tamil literature include the International Institute of Tamil Studies's *Literary Heritage of the Tamils* (Adayaru, Madras, India: 1981), which is a series of papers first presented at the "Heritage of the Tamils" seminars in 1978; and S. Ratnaswami, *A Short History of the Ancient Tamils and Their Literature* (Annamalainagar, New Delhi, India: Thaiyalnayaki Veliyeedu, 1979). Dieties worshipped by the different pastoral, hunting, or fishing societies are also mentioned in Iyengar's *Dravidian India* Vol. I. James Hornell, who has written numerous articles on various aspects of Indian and African culture, authored "The Ancient Village Gods of South India," published in June 1944 (Gloucester, England) in *Antiquity Publications* (Vol. 18).

The Dravidians' solar calendar and their ancient academies established for the study of astronomy are discussed in Iyengar, *Dravidian India* Vol. I; and Chatterji, *Dravidian: A Course of Three Lectures on Dravidian Origins and on Modern Dravidian Literature*. Another focus of Iyengar's *Dravidian India* Vol. I is the female-ruled Pandya Kingdom of southern India.

Several texts provide information on the creed of Jainism. Among them are John R. Hinnells, ed., *A Handbook of Living Religions* (Harmondsworth, Eng.: Viking, 1984), with an article titled "Jainism," by Kendall W. Folkert. See also

Myrtle Langley's article, "Respect for All Life: Jainism," contained in *Eerdmans' Handbook to the World's Religions* (Grand Rapids, MI: W. B. Eerdmans Publishing Co., 1982); and Iyengar, *Dravidian India* Vol. I.

The generosity bestowed on contending armies by kings is discussed in Iyengar, *Dravidian India* Vol. I. The soldiers consumption of the rare black *Nelli*, or black gooseberry, and drum communication to signal the advent of war are also under discussion in Iyengar's piece.

Consult Iyengar, *Dravidian India* Vol. I; and Mazumdar, *The Hindu History*, for material on the rich port town of Puhar. *The Hindu History* is also a good source on the Dravidian Cholas and their relations with China. The expansion of Dravidian traditions (such as the Kaundinya), language, and culture into Asia and the South Pacific is treated in Noelle, *Dravidian Studies—A Review*; and T. K. Krishna Menon, *Dravidian Culture and Its Diffusion* (Ernakulam, India: The Viswanath Press, 1937; 1934).

Several volumes help to round out research on the subjects of culture and cuisine in Africa and India. See Mbiti, *African Religions and Philosophy*, for a look at the Didinga and other societies of the Sudan. Gerald Massey's, *A Book of the Beginnings* (Baltimore, MD: Black Classic Press, 1995; London, Eng.: Williams and Norgate, 1881) offers discourse on the "Black Buddha of India" imaged "in the Negroid type," and Buddhism carried to China by, among others, ten black apostles. Also see K. P. Aravaanan, *The Serpent Cult in Africa and Dravidian India* (Madras, India: Paari Nilayam, 1977) for a comparative view of African and Dravidian serpent worship. Jomo Kenyatta's *Facing Mount Kenya* looks at African religious beliefs.

Slater's *The Dravidian Element in Indian Culture* and Iyengar's *Dravidian India* Vol. I, offer insight on the varieties and importance of rice to the people of India. For culinary views of the two continents see Tami Hultman, ed., *The Africa News Cookbook* (New York, NY: Penguin Books, 1985); Madhur Jaffrey, *Flavors of India* (New York, NY: Carol Southern Books, 1995). The Time-Life volume *African Cooking* by Laurens van der Post (New York, NY: Time-Life Books, 1970) is one of a number of books on African cuisine that led the way in promoting lies and distortions regarding what it claims is a lack of African culinary traditions. One of the first books to acknowledge the connection between African and African American cuisine was Helen Mendes's classic, *The African Heritage Cookbook* (New York, NY: Macmillan, 1971). Her work points out that the essence of African cuisine is its sauces and stews. See Santha Rama Rau's *The Cooking of India* for a look at special Indian feasts, as well as different food preparations, including methods of marinating meats. As with most cookbooks on the subject, Rau's *The Cooking of India* credits Indian cuisine to Europe and parts of the Middle East. A discussion of the importance of ghee in the diet of the Brahmans, as well as the general Indian population, is explained in Julie Sahni's *Classic Indian Cooking* (New York, NY: William Morrow and Co., Inc., 1980). The characteristics of the pippali, or long pepper, is a topic of discussion in Iyengar's *Dravidian India* Vol. I. Also see Julie Sahni, *Classic Indian Vegetarian and Grain Cooking* (New York, NY: William Morrow and Co., Inc., 1985).

Works expressing varying opinions on Dravidian origins and/or culture include Edward James Rapson, *Ancient India, from the Earliest Times to the First Century* A.D. (Cambridge, Eng.: Cambridge University Press, 1914); K. A. Nilakanta Sastri, *The Culture and History of the Tamils* (Calcutta, India: K. L. Mukhopadhyay, 1964, 1963); Po Cankarappillai, *Nam Tamilar: A Short History of the Tamils* (Kolumpu, India: Vijayalatcumi Puttakacalai, 1979); Raju Kalidos, *History and Culture of the Tamils: From Prehistoric Times to the President's Rule* (Dindigul, India: Vijay Publications, 1976); E. L. Tambimuttu, *Dravida, A History of the Tamil From Pre-historic Times to* A.D. *1800* (Colombo, Sri Lanka: General Publishers, 1945); and Kolappa Pillay K. Pillay, *A Social History of the Tamils* (Madras, India: University of Madras, 1969). James Hornell's article, "The Origins and the Ethnological Significance of Indian Boat Designs," published in the *Memoirs of the Asiatic Society of Bengal* Vol. VII, Number 1 (1918); Lynn Thorndike, *Short History of Civilization* (New York, NY: F. S. Crofts, 1930, 1926); Sir John Hammerton, ed., *Wonders of the Past* Vol. II (New York, NY: Wise and Co., 1937; London, Eng.: The Amalgamated Press, 1923, 1924); Will Durant, *Our Oriental Heritage* (New York, NY: MJF Books, 1992, 1935); Paulinus Tambimuttu, *Europe and the Dravidians* (London, Eng.: P. Tambimuttu, 1980); Nicolas Margioris, *Dravidians: The Pre-Hellenic Greeks* (Athens, Greece: Omakoion Anthinon, 1979); and K. A. Nilakanta Sastri's book containing four lectures delivered in 1964 at the department of history at Patna University, titled, *Aryans and Dravidians* (Ajmer, India: Sachin Publications, 1979).

Chapter Two. Catfish, Harvest, and Celebration among the Sons and Daughters of Kambu

Excavated bas reliefs in Cambodia yield the relationship between Khmer myths and legends and food in their daily lives. See, for example, I. G. Edmonds, *The Khmers of Cambodia* (Indianapolis, IN: Bobbs-Merrill, 1970). Other bas reliefs, such as those discussed in Christopher Pym's *The Ancient Civilization of Angkor* (New York, NY: Mentor Books, New American Library, 1968), show the importance of food even in death.

The story of the development of Khmer civilization, the Indian influence, and the territories that became part of its empire is told, for example, in

Lawrence P. Briggs, *The Ancient Khmer Empire* (Philadelphia, PA: American Philosophical Society, 1951); Martin F. Herz, *A Short History of Cambodia* (New York, NY: F. A. Praeger, 1958); Malcolm MacDonald, *Angkor* (London, Eng.: J. Cape, 1958); Bernard P. Groslier, *Indochina* (London, Eng.: Muller, 1967, 1966); Madeleine Giteau's *The Civilization of Angkor* (New York, NY: Rizzoli, 1976); and I. G. Edmonds's *The Khmers of Cambodia*. Also see George Coedes, *Angkor An Introduction* (Hong Kong, London, New York, NY: Oxford University Press, 1966; 1963); and Horace G. Q. Wales, *The Indianization of China and of South East Asia* (London, Eng.: Quaritch, 1967).

The ancient Khmer empire was a merging of the peoples of Funan and Chenla (or Tchenla) in Southeast Asia. Both peoples were described as being black. A physical description of the Khmers can be found in Malcolm MacDonald's *Angkor*. MacDonald quotes a Chinese visitor to the court of King Isanavarman (seventh century, A.D.): "The men are small and black." *The Ancient Civilization of Angkor*, by Christopher Pym, reports that the "common people were very dark, sometimes nearly black-brown, . . ." A very extensive treatise, *The Ancient Khmer Empire*, by Lawrence P. Briggs, quotes earlier Chinese historical documents: "The men are all ugly and black. Their hair is curly . . ." Briggs goes on to say that "the statement about curly hair may indicate a negrito element." Briggs's work also quotes the same visitor to King Isanavarman's court. In addition, see Robert Silverberg's *Lost Cities and Vanished Civilizations* (New York, NY: Bantam, 1963).

There are a number of works containing discourse on the African presence in the early periods of Southeast Asian, Chinese, and Japanese history. Cheikh Anta Diop mentions in the footnote section of chapter three, in his *The African Origin of Civilization: Myth or Reality* (Chicago, IL: Lawrence Hill Books, 1974), various black groups in Asia, such as the Negritos and Ainus of Japan, and records a Japanese proverb: "For a Samurai to be brave, he must have a bit of black blood." Also see Edward G. Balfour, ed., "Negro Races," *Cyclopaedia of India* Vol. II, third ed. (London, Eng.: Quaritch, 1885); Neil Gordon Munro, *Prehistoric Japan* (New York, NY: Johnson Reprint Co., 1971 reprint; Yokohama, Japan: [s.n.], 1911); Henri Imbert, *Les Negritos de la Chine* (Hanoi Haiphong, Vietnam: Imprimerie d' Extreme Orient, 1923); W. E. B. Du Bois, *The World and Africa* (New York, NY: International Publishers, 1965 reprint, 1946, 1947); John G. Jackson, *Introduction to African Civilizations* (Secaucus, NJ: The Citadel Press, 1970); and Joseph Harris, *The African Presence in Asia* (Evanston, IL: Northwestern University Press, 1971). In the area of Chinese religion, Buddhism brought into China by, among others, ten black apostles, and the African features and hair of Buddha are discussed in Gerald Massey, *A Book of the Beginnings* Vol. I (London, Eng.: Williams,

1881). J. A. Roger's text, *Sex and Race* Vol. I (New York, NY: H. M. Rogers, 1942-1944), contains an article by Professor Chang Hsing-land on an early population to the south of Lin-yi that had "woolly hair and black skin." He also mentions Li, an empress of China (373–397 A.D.) and consort of Emperor Hsiao Wu Wen, "who is spoken of as being a Negro."

The "splendor and high civilization" of the Khmers between 800 and 1500 A.D. has been the focus of much controversy and debate among archaeologists and anthropologists regarding Khmer origins. For the traditional views that either ignore or deny any African contribution, see, for example, Robert J. Casey, *Four Faces of Siva* (Indianapolis, IN: Bobbs-Merrill, 1929); and I. G. Edmonds, *The Khmers of Cambodia*. George Coedes's *Angkor An Introduction* offers Pierre Loti's (*Pelerin d' Angkor*) opinion that "The Khmer people were a detached branch of the great Aryan race . . ." Coedes does not disagree with the theory of an Aryan origin; however, he does disagree that the Khmers "came in a solid block from India."

The complex irrigation system of ancient Cambodia was constructed as part of a dual program: economic and religious. Pym's *The Ancient Civilization of Angkor* and *The Civilization of Angkor* by Madeleine Giteau provide many details. Pym's *The Ancient Civilization of Angkor* looks at the king's religious duty, the multiple harvests each year, made possible by the construction of the irrigation system, and the free kitchen run for the workers. Rituals and festivals are among the many aspects of ancient Khmer life discussed in Pym's work.

See John S. Mbiti, *African Religions and Philosophy* (New York, NY: Praeger Publishers, 1969; Anchor Books, 1970), for data on African beliefs regarding the intertwining of people and the fertility of the land. Also, Mbiti's work gives an in-depth look into many of Africa's societies, such as the Lugbara and the Akamba. Edmonds's *The Khmers of Cambodia* mentions religious festivals, including those intended to celebrate the fertility of the soil. A number of works deal with the subject of African rites and rituals. They include J. Middleton, *The Kikuyu and Kamba of Kenya* (London, Eng.: International African Institute, 1965; 1953) and *Lugbara Religion* (Oxford, Eng.: Published for International African Institute by Oxford University Press, 1960); Mbiti's *African Religions and Philosophy*; Kenyatta's *Facing Mount Kenya*; O. Lucas, *The Religion of the Yoruba* (Lagos, Nigeria: C. M. S. Bookshop, 1948); J. B. Danquah, *The Akan Doctrine of God* (London, Eng.: Lutterworth Press, 1944); M. Banton, ed., *Anthropological Approaches to the Study of Religion* (London, Eng.: Tavistock, 1969, 1966); C. Cagnolo, *The Akikuyu* (Nyeri, Kenya: Mission Printing School, 1933); M. M. Edel, *The Chiga of Western Uganda* (Oxford, Eng.: Oxford University Press, 1957); C. Dundas, *Kilimanjaro and Its People* (London, Eng.: Witherby, 1924); S. Yokoo, *Death Among the Abaluyia,*

Dissertation (Kampala, Uganda: Makerere University, 1966); M. Wilson, *Rituals of Kinship among the Nyakyusa* (London, Eng., New York, NY: International African Institute, 1956) and *Communal Rituals of the Nyakyusa* (London, Eng., New York, NY: International African Institute, 1959); and George P. Murdock, *Africa: Its Peoples and Their Culture History* (New York, NY and London, Eng.: McGraw-Hill, 1959). For more information on the culture of the Abaluyia of Kenya see Yokoo's, *Death Among the Abaluyia* and Mbiti's *African Religions and Philosophy. Peoples of South-West Ethiopia and Its Borderland* (London, Eng.: International African Institute, 1956), by E. Cerulli, sheds additional light on the Koma and other peoples of Ethiopia.

The two hundred ways of describing rice and details of its harvest is surveyed in *The Ancient Civilization of Angkor,* by Christopher Pym, and Edmonds's *The Khmers of Cambodia.* Rice planting and the ceremonies surrounding this event are treated in Edmonds's *The Khmers of Cambodia.* Ceremonies also surrounded the advent of sports activities, and were an important part of Khmer life. Pym's *The Ancient Civilization of Angkor* looks at these activities. Another look at Khmer life is in the area of the phenomenal fishing harvests that took place. In addition to Pym's volume, also see Edmonds's *The Khmers of Cambodia*; Briggs, *The Ancient Khmer Empire*; and Herz, *A Short History of Cambodia.*

Khmer burial practices and the philosophy of reincarnation are under discussion in Giteau's *The Civilization of Angkor*; MacDonald's *Angkor*; Pym's *The Ancient Civilization of Angkor.* The African philosophy of reincarnation is a topic followed in a number of books and articles. Among them are Okot p'Bitek, "The concept of Jok among the Acholi and Lango," *The Uganda Journal* XXVII, No. 1 (March 1963); J. R. Goody, *Death, Property, and the Ancestors* (London, Eng., Stanford, CA: Stanford University Press, 1962); S. Yokoo, *Death Among the Abaluyia*; and Mbiti's *African Religions and Philosophy.* "Burial parties" and cultural aspects of the Ndebele of southern Africa are the study of an edited volume titled *African Ideas of God* 2nd revised edition (London, Eng.: Edinburgh House Press, 1961), by E. W. Smith. In addition, see A. J. B. Hughes, J. Van Velsen, and H. Kuper, *The Shona and Ndebele of Southern Rhodesia* (London, Eng.: International African Institute, 1954); and Mbiti, *African Religions and Philosophy.*

The Ancient Civilization of Angkor by Christopher Pym carries details of the "Churning of the Sea of Milk" legend, and its relation to marriage and family. See also Edmonds's *The Khmers of Cambodia.* The African family, and the diet of expectant mothers is the focus of "Birth and Childhood," a chapter in Mbiti's *African Religions and Philosophy.*

Chou Ta-Kuan (Zhou Daguan) was a Chinese ambassador to Cambodia for about a year (1296 to 1297 A.D.) during the height of its splendor. Much of the discourse on Khmer life and culture comes from him and other Chinese visitors. See Chou Ta-Kuan, *Notes on the Customs of Cambodia* (Bangkok, Thailand: The Siam Society, 1987; 1967), J. Gilman D'Arcy Paul's translation of Paul Pelliot's French version. Also see a partial account by Chou Ta-Kuan of his travels to the city of Angkor in 1296 A.D. in Asia House Gallery's *Khmer Sculpture* (New York, NY: Asia House Gallery, 1961). Chou's version of the *ch'en-tan* (or *tch'en-tan*) is totally unsubstantiated, yet a number of books quote him. See for example, Herz, *A Short History of Cambodia*; Pym, *The Ancient Civilization of Angkor*; and Briggs, *The Ancient Khmer Empire*. Briggs states that Chou Ta-kuan is wrong in claiming that the ceremony was carried out by Taoist priests, because Briggs says, "Taoist here apparently means Brahman. There were no (Chinese) Taoists in Cambodia." For a description of the character of the Buddhist monk, see H. L. Seneviratne, *Rituals of the Kandyan State* (Cambridge, Eng.: Cambridge University Press, 1978).

"Rites of passage" practiced by East Africans is under discussion in A. Van Gennep, *The Rites of Passage* (London, Eng.: Routledge and Paul, 1960); Kenyatta, *Facing Mount Kenya*; and S. Cherotich, "The Nandi Female Initiation and Marriage and Christian Impact upon It" *Dini na Mila* 2, No. 2/3 (Kampala, Uganda, December 1967). There are also a few works that deal with African Judaism (the Agao people of Ethiopia, and the Bayudaya, or Jews of Judah, in eastern Uganda) and the clitoridectomy they perform on girls. See E. Ullendorf, "Hebraic-Jewish elements in Abyssinian (Monophysite) Christianity," *Journal of Semitic Studies* I (1956); J. S. Trimingham, *Islam in Ethiopia* (London, Eng.: Frank Cass, 1952; Oxford, Eng.: Oxford University Press, 1952); E. Dammann, *Die Religionen Afrikas* (1963); and A. Oded, "A Congregation of African Jews in the Heart of Uganda," *Dini na Mila* III, No. 1, (Kampala, Uganda: Makerere University, 1968).

The business acumen of Khmer women, their importance to the economy, and the foods and other goods sold at market are detailed in Briggs, *The Ancient Khmer Empire*; Pym, *The Ancient Civilization of Angkor*; Giteau, *The Civilization of Angkor*; and Casey, *Four Faces of Siva*. In addition, *The Myth of the Negro Past* (Boston, MA: Beacon Press, 1958; 1941), by Melville J. Herskovits, gives us a look at the empowerment of West African women, as the result of their being able to hold "their economic destinies in their own hands." African trade with Southeast Asia is documented in Stanley Burstein, ed., *Ancient African Civilizations Kush and Axum* (Princeton, NJ: Markus Wiener, 1998). He states that "Kush and its Medieval successors played a central role in an international trading system that extended from Southeast Asia to the Mediterranean." The fact that many Cambodian bas reliefs depict ivory-tusked elephants, such as the ones from the story related in Pym's *The Ancient Civilization of Angkor*, is certainly an indication of African-Southeast Asian trade contact.

Leo Wiener, in volume I of his *Africa and the Discovery of America* (Philadelphia, PA: Innes and Sons, 1920), provides material and photographs of the favored hairstyles of African females. The same hairstyles were favored by Southeast Asian men and women. See the numerous photographs, including those of cornrowed ladies and soldiers in Madeleine Giteau's, *The Civilization of Angkor*. Ancient Khmer hairstyles are also discussed in Briggs, *The Ancient Khmer Empire*; Pym, *The Ancient Civilization of Angkor*; and MacDonald, *Angkor*.

Details on the collection of honey and the different types of wine manufactured in ancient Cambodia are contained in Pym's volume, *The Ancient Civilization of Angkor*. The collection of sap from the styrax tree for the production of perfume is also detailed in Pym's work. For discourse on Khmer agriculture, food, and food products see Briggs, *The Ancient Khmer Empire*; Herz, *A Short History of Cambodia*; and MacDonald, *Angkor*. Also, Edmonds, in his *The Khmers of Cambodia*, mentions the agricultural product cardamom, grown by the Khmers and the "Hill People" of Kambujadesa. Cardamom (and its use as a curative) and pepper are discussed in Giteau's *The Civilization of Angkor*.

The 1990s has seen a flurry of books, articles, and audiovisual productions on the African American celebration known as Kwanzaa. *Kwanzaa: A Celebration of Family, Community, and Culture* (Los Angeles, CA: University of Sankore Press, 1997), by Maulana Karenga; and *Seven Days of Kwanzaa* (New York, NY: Viking, 1997), by Ella Grier, are two such works.

An interesting political perspective on imperialism and the Cambodians can be found in Jan Myrdal and Gun Kessle, *Angkor: An Essay on Art and Imperialism* (New York, NY: Random House, 1970). Christopher Pym's *The Road to Angkor* (London, Eng.: R. Hale, 1959), is also somewhat political in its focus; however, do check out "Tree-Bark Soup" on pages 123 and 124.

W. J. Perry, in his *The Growth of Civilization* 2nd Edition (Harmondsworth, Eng.: Penguin Books, Ltd., 1937), and other writers have made the same observation: "Many features of the pyramids and rituals of Maya people conform so closely to those found in Cambodia."

Volumes on the cuisine of Southeast Asia include P'eng-chan Li Tseng, *Tung-Nan-Ya Mei Shih South-east Asian Cuisine* (Hsiang-kang, China: Po i ch'u pan chi t'uan: Fa hsing Hsiang-kang tien shih ch'u pan yu hsien Kung, 1988); Huynh Quan Chieu, *Les meilleures recettes de la cuisine sino-vietnamienne* (Paris, France: J.-P. Delarge, 1976; Strasbourg, Germany: Les Fils du dragon, 1973); Lan Thi Nguyen, *The Best of Vietnamese Cooking* (Vancouver, Canada: Friedman Investments, 1992); *Myanmar Cuisine* (Yangon, Myanmar (Burma): AV Media, 1994), an audiovisual presentation; and Thi Huong Nguyen, *Nghe Thuat Nau An: Gom 180 Mon Man Va Chay* (Ha Noi, Vietnam: Phu nu, 1990). Bach Ngo and Gloria Zimmerman prepare succulent recipes in their book *The Classic Cuisine of Vietnam*

(New York, NY: Barron's, 1979). Much use is made from the indispensable sauce called nuoc mam.

For those interested in other volumes dealing with the ancient Khmers of Kambujadesa, see for example: Thierry Zephir, *Khmer, The Lost Empire of Cambodia* (New York, NY: Abrams, 1998); Ian W. Mabbett, *The Khmers* (Oxford, United Kingdom, Cambridge, MA: Blackwell Publishers, 1996, 1995); Andre Migot, *Les Khmers des Origines d'Angkor au Cambodge d' Aujourd'hui* (Paris, France: LeLivre Contemporain, 1960); Donatella Mazzeo, *Civilizacion Khmer* (Valencia, Spain: Mas-Ivars, 1972); John Audric, *Angkor and the Khmer Empire* (London, Eng.: R. Hale, 1972); Guy Poree, *Traditions and Customs of the Khmer* (New Haven, CT: Human Relations Area Files, 1970, 1976); Horace G. Q. Wales, *The Mountain of God: A Study in Early Religion and Kingship* (London, Eng.: Quaritch, 1953), and his *Towards Angkor in the Footsteps of the Indian Invaders* (London, Eng.: G. G. Harrap and Co., Ltd., 1937); Madeleine Giteau, *Khmer Sculpture and the Angkor Civilization* (New York, NY: H. N. Abrams, 1966, 1965); Joan Lebold Cohen, *Angkor: Monuments of the God-Kings* (London, Eng.: Thames and Hudson, 1975); Hermann Kulke, *The Devaraja Cult* (Ithaca, NY: Southeast Asia Program, Cornell University, 1978); Deane H. Dickason, *Wondrous Angkor* (Shanghai, China: Kelly and Walsh, 1937); and Geoffrey Gorer, *Bali and Angkor, Or, Looking at Life and Death* (Boston, MA: Little, Brown and Co., 1936).

Chapter Three. Peppers, Cracklings, and Knots of Wool

Studies done on sexuality and the "G Spot" can be consulted in Alice Kahn Ladas, Beverly Whipple, and John D. Perry, *The G Spot and Other Recent Discoveries About Human Sexuality* (New York, NY: Holt, Rinehart and Winston, 1982); William H. Masters, Virginia E. Johnson, and Robert C. Kolodny, *Masters and Johnson on Sex and Human Loving* (Boston, MA: Little, Brown and Co., 1988).

There are a number of books, as well as articles, that record Columbus's encounter with Africans already residing in the Americas upon his arrival. See, for example, Ivan Van Sertima, *They Came before Columbus* (New York, NY: Random House, 1976); Leo Wiener, *Africa and the Discovery of America* Vol. III (Philadelphia, PA: Innes and Sons, 1922); Peter DeRoo, *History of America before Columbus* Vols. I and II (Philadelphia, PA and London, Eng.: J. B. Lippincott Co., 1900); John G. Jackson, *Introduction to African Civilizations* (Secaucus, NJ: The Citadel Press, 1970); Floyd W. Hayes, "The African Presence in America before Columbus," *Black World* (July 1973); and Harold G. Lawrence, "African Explorers of the New World," *The Crisis* (June-July 1962).

The opulent empires of West Africa's Golden Age are under discussion in Basil Davidson, *African Civilization Revisited* (Trenton, NJ: Africa World Press, 1991), and his *The Lost Cities of Africa* (Boston, MA and Toronto, Canada: Atlantic-Little Brown, 1959), and Davidson together with F. K. Buah, *A History of West Africa to the Nineteenth Century* (Garden City, NY: Doubleday, 1966); Harry H. Johnston, *A History of the Colonization of Africa* (London, Eng.: Cambridge University Press, 1899); Daniel Chu and Elliott Skinner, *A Glorious Age in Africa* (Garden City, NY: Doubleday, 1965); John G. Jackson, *Introduction to African Civilizations*; Lady Flora Shaw Lugard, *A Tropical Dependency* (New York, NY: Cass, 1964); Winwood Reade, *The Martyrdom of Man* (London, Eng.: Pemberton, with Barrie and Rockliff, 1968); Chancellor Williams, *The Destruction of Black Civilization* (Dubuque, IA: Kendall/Hunt Publishing Co., 1971); J. D. Fage, *A History of West Africa* (Cambridge, Eng.: Cambridge University Press, 1969); T. A. Osae, S. N. Nwabara, and A. T. O. Odunsi, *A Short History of West Africa* A.D. *1000 to the Present* (New York, NY: Hill and Wang, 1968, 1973); J. F. Ade Ajayi and Ian Espie, eds., *A Thousand Years of West African History* (New York, NY: Humanities Press, 1972); W. E. B. Du Bois, *The World and Africa* (New York, NY: International Publishers Co., Inc., 1965; 1946, 1947); Cheikh Anta Diop, *Precolonial Black Africa* (Brooklyn, NY: Lawrence Hill Books, 1987); and Walter Rodney, *How Europe Underdeveloped Africa* (London, Eng., Dar es Salaam, Tanzania: Bogle-L'Ouverture Publications, 1972). *The Voice of Africa* Vol. I and II (London, Eng.: 1913; New York, NY and London, Eng.: Benjamin Blom, Inc., 1968), by Leo Frobenius, chronicles the political systems and other aspects of culture (including culinary), as well as commerce and trade routes of West Africa that had remained open "from time immemorial" until "missionaries of civilization" destroyed them."

An array of discourse is available on the Olmecs of Mexico. Discussion as well as pictorial evidence of the African presence in ancient America is available in Alexander Von Wuthenau's, *Unexpected Faces in Ancient America* (New York, NY: Crown Publishers, 1975) and his *The Art of Terracotta Pottery in Pre-Columbian Central and South America* (New York, NY: Crown Publishers, 1965; 1969). There are a number of publications that offer compelling evidence of an African presence and of transmission of African culture to the Americas. See, for example, R. A. Jairazbhoy, *Rameses III: Father of Ancient America* (London, Eng.: Karnak House, 1992). A philological approach to the subject is found in Leo Wiener, *Mayan and Mexican Origins* (Cambridge, MA: privately printed, 1926), and in his three volume treatise *Africa and the Discovery of America* (Volume I: Philadelphia, PA: Innes and Sons, 1920; Volumes II and III: Philadelphia, PA: Innes and Sons, 1922). See also Ivan Van Sertima, *They Came Before Columbus* (New York, NY: Random House, 1976), and his edited volume *African Presence in Early America* (New Brunswick, NJ: Transaction Publishers, 1992); John G. Jackson, *Introduction to African Civilization;* J. A. Rogers, *Africa's Gift to America* (New York, NY: Futuro Press, 1961); Sir Harry Johnston, *The Negro in the New World* (1969; London, Eng.: Methuen, 1910); University of California at Berkeley, Archaeological Research Facility, *Colossal Heads of the Olmec Culture* (Berkeley, CA: University of California, Berkeley, 1980, 1967); and Alexandre Braghine, *The Shadow of Atlantis* (New York, NY: E. P. Dutton and Co., 1940). African transatlantic voyages and presence in ancient America is the subject of a number of articles, including M. D. W. Jeffreys, "Pre-Columbian Negroes in America," *Scientia* XIIC (1953); Floyd W. Hayes, "The African Presence in America Before Columbus," *Black World* (July 1973); Harold G. Lawrence, "African Explorers of the New World," *The Crisis* (June–July 1962); Roberto Rodriguez, "The Columbus 1492–1992 Quincentennial Debate, Part I, African American Scholars Respond," *Black Issues in Higher Education* (September 26, 1991); Jose Maria Melgar y Serrano, "Estudio sobre la antiguedad y el origen de la cabeza colosal de tipo etiopico que existe en Hueyapan del canton de los Tuxtlas," *Sociedad Mexicana de Geografia y Estadistica* Boletin 3, no. 2a (1871), as well as his "Antiguedades Mexicanas," *Sociedad Mexicana de Geografia y Estadistica* Boletin I, no. 2a (1869). Also see Rudolph Bershadsky, "Atlantis," *On the Track of Discovery*, Series 2 (Moscow: 1964). On audiovisual cassette see "The Black Heritage of Ancient Mexico" (Los Angeles, CA: Golden Legacy, 1990).

For standard, more traditionally held views, which omit, reject, or minimize any connection between Africa and ancient America, see, for example, Jacques Soustelle, *The Olmecs: The Oldest Civilization in Mexico* (Garden City, NY: Doubleday, 1984); Roman Piña Chan, *The Olmec: Mother Culture of Mesoamerica* (New York, NY: Rizzoli, 1989); Michael D. Coe, *America's First Civilization* (New York, NY: Heritage Publishers, 1968); Robert J. Sharer and David C. Grove, eds., *Regional Perspectives on the Olmec* (Cambridge, Eng.: Cambridge University Press, 1989). Also see the multi-essayed *The Olmec and Their Neighbors* (Washington, DC: Dumbarton Oaks Research Library and Collections, 1981). Two articles conveying the traditional school of thought are Jeanne Reinert, "Secrets of the People of the Jaguar," *Science Digest* (September 1967), and John Spizzirri, "Unearthing the Treasures of Copan," *Illinois Quarterly* 5, Issue 4 (January–February 1993).

Other works offering varied perspectives on Olmec and ancient American culture include, Rafael Girard, *La Misteriosa Cultura Olmeca* Third ed. (Guatemala: 1969); Ignacio Bernal's *The Olmec World* (Berkeley, CA: University of California Press, 1969); Nigel Davies, *The Ancient Kingdoms of Mexico* (New York, NY: Penguin Books, 1990); Thomas Dickey, Vance Muse, and Henry Wiencek, *God Kings of Mexico* (Chicago, IL: Stonehenge Press, 1982); Philip Drucker, Robert F. Heizer, and Robert J. Squier, "Excavations at La Venta, Tabasco, 1955," *Smithsonian Institution Bureau of American Ethnology* Bulletin 170 (Washington, DC: 1959); Pierre Ivanoff, *Mayan Enigma* (New York, NY: Delacorte Press, 1971); Thomas W. Killion, ed., *Gardens of Prehistory: The Archaeology of Settlement Agriculture in Greater Mesoamerica* (Tuscaloosa, AL: University of Alabama Press, 1992); A. Hyatt Verrill, *Old Civilizations of the New World* (New York, NY: Tudor, 1938); Victor W. Von Hagen, *The Ancient Sun Kingdoms of the Americas* (New York, NY: The World Publishing Co., 1957), and his *The Aztec: Man and Tribe* (New York, NY: New American Library, 1961); Charles R. Wicke, *Olmec, An Early Art Style of Precolumbian Mexico* (Tucson, AZ: The University of Arizona Press, 1971); Juan Schobinger, *The First Americans* (Grand Rapids, MI: Eerdmans, 1994); Alfredo Chavero, *The Jaguar's Children: Pre-Classic Central Mexico* (New York, NY: Museum of Primitive Art, 1965), and his *America's First Civilization: Discovering the Olmec* (New York, NY: American Heritage, 1968). Chavero also produced "Historia Antigua," *Mexico A Traves De Los Siglos* Vol. I (1887). Also see Mike H. Xu, *Origin of the Olmec Civilization* (Edmond, OK: University of Central Oklahoma Press, 1996), Robert Silverberg, *Lost Cities and Vanished Civilizations* (New York, NY: Bantam, 1963); Alphonse de Quatrefages, *The Human Species* (New York, NY: Appleton, 1905); James C. Gruener, *The Olmec Riddle: An Inquiry into the Origin of Pre-Columbian Civilization* (Rancho Santa Fe, CA: Vengreen Publications, 1987); Barry Fel, *Saga America* (New York, NY: Times Books, 1980); O. L. Gonzalez Calderon, *The Jade Lords* (Coatzacoalcos, Veracruz, Mexico: O. L. Gonzalez Calderon, 1991); *Los Olmecas En Mesoamerica* (Mexico, D. F.: Citibank, 1994); and Andrzej Wiercinski's anthropomorphic treatise, *An Anthropological Study on the Origin of "Olmecs"* (Warsaw, Poland: Swiatowit, 1972). For discussions regarding Olmec astronomy and trade see the University of California at Berkeley, Department of Anthropology's *Papers on Olmec and Maya Archaeology* (Berkeley, CA: 1971).

Numerous sources were consulted on plant and agricultural origins. For an enlightened and engaging point of view see George P. Murdock, *Africa Its People and Their Culture History* (New York, NY: McGraw-Hill, 1959). Also see W. B. Morgan, "The Forest and Agriculture in West Africa," *Journal of African History* III, No. 2 (1962); P. A. Allison, "Historical Inferences to be Drawn from the Effect of Human Settlement on the Vegetation of Africa," *Journal of African History* III, No. 2 (1962); and H. G. Baker, "Comments on the Thesis That There Was a Major Centre of Plant Domestication Near the Headwaters of the River Niger," *Journal of African History* III, No. 2 (1962). Baker's article lists specific species of pumpkin, groundnut (peanuts), and other crops indigenous to West Africa. Also, look for the forthcoming *Cambridge Encyclopedia of Human Nutrition* as part of *The Cambridge History and Culture of Food and Nutrition Project,* edited by

Kenneth F. Kiple and Kriemhild Conee Ornelas (Cambridge University Press, however, publication date has not been set). Among those promoting the standard interpretation that Africa has played no role as an agricultural center are Alphonse de Candolle, *Origin of Cultivated Plants* (New York, NY: Hafner, 1967), and Franz Schwanitz *The Origin of Cultivated Plants* (Cambridge, MA: Harvard University Press, 1967). The introduction into Africa of maize and other crops is an area of debate. For the traditional view see Sophie D. Coe, *America's First Cuisines* (Austin, TX: University of Texas Press, 1994). Also see P. C. Mangelsdorf and R. G. Reeves, "The Origin of Maize: Present Status of the Problem," *American Anthropologist* 47, No. 1 (January-March 1945). Marvin P. Miracle's article, "The Introduction and Spread of Maize in Africa," in *Journal of African History,* vi, I (1965), examines the "problem" chiefly through early travel accounts. A far more plausible and compelling treatment of maize introduction into Africa can be found in Frank Willett, "The Introduction of Maize into West Africa: An Assessment of Recent Evidence," *Africa* XXXII, No. 1 (January, 1962); M. D. W. Jeffreys, "How Ancient Is West African Maize?" *Africa* (January 1963).

In preparing the material dealing with food, several books and articles were very helpful. They include Helen Mendes, *The African Heritage Cookbook* (New York, NY: Macmillan, 1971); Ana Benitez, *Pre-Hispanic Cooking* (Mexico, Ediciones Euroamericanas, 1991); Beatriz Cadena, *Cocina Mexicana Mexican Cooking* (Mexico, D.F.: Monclem Ediciones, 1996); Aida Gabilondo, *Mexican Family Cooking* (New York, NY: Fawcett Columbine, 1986); Elena Zelayeta, *Elena's Secrets of Mexican Cooking* (Garden City, NY: Dolphin/Doubleday, 1968, 1958); Dolores Latorre, *Cooking and Curing with Mexican Herbs* (Austin, TX: Encino Press, 1977); Alice Dede, *Ghanaian Favourite Dishes* (Accra, Ghana: Anowuo Educational Publications, 1969); Jessica Kuper, ed., *The Anthropologists Cookbook* (New York, NY: Universe Books, 1977); Zarela Martinez, *Food From My Heart, Cuisines of Mexico Remembered and Reimagined* (New York, NY: Macmillan Publishing Co., 1992); Blanche McNeil and Edna V. McNeil, *First Foods of America* (Los Angeles, CA: Suttonhouse Ltd., 1936); E. Chapman Nyaho, E. Amarteifio, and J. Asare, *Ghana Recipe Book* (Accra, Ghana: Ghana Publishing Corp., 1970); Cherry Hamman, *Mayan Cooking: Classic Recipes from the Sun Kingdoms of the Yucatan* (New York, NY: Hippocrene Books, 1997); Copeland Marks, *False Tongues and Sunday Bread* (New York, NY: M. Evans and Co., Inc., 1985); and *Cooking in Cazuelas,* published in Mexico City by The Circle in the 1950s. Also, see Sara Rimer, "For the Determined, the Search for a Rare Taste of Senegal," *The New York Times* (Living Section, Wednesday, August 26, 1992); John G. Bourke, "The Folk-Foods of the Rio Grande Valley and of Northern Mexico," *Journal of American Folklore* (January-April 1895).

Information on the last descendants of the Maya, the Lacandones, is available in Wolfgang Cordan, *Secret of the Forest* (Garden City, NY: Doubleday and Co., Inc., 1964); Victor Perera and Robert D. Bruce, *The Last Lords of Palenque, The Lacandon Mayas of the Mexican Rain Forest* (Boston, MA: Little, Brown and Co., 1982). Also see Sophie D. Coe, *America's First Cuisines*.

Chapter Four. Zancu, Sweet Potatoes, and Beer

Numerous volumes record various aspects of ancient Peruvian culture as it related to the Chavin, Chimu, and Chibcha peoples, including its likeness and connection to the ancient Olmecs; the ingenious irrigation system, and the development of a complex agricultural society; the trade network established between the valley, highlands, and Mexico and Central America; and religious ideologies. See, for example: George Bankes, *Peru Before Pizarro* (Oxford, Eng.: Phaidon Press, 1977); Elizabeth P. Benson ed., *Dumbarton Oaks Conference on Chavin* (Washington, DC: Dumbarton Oaks Research Library and Collection, 1971); John Bierhorst, ed., *Black Rainbow Legends of the Incas and Myths of Ancient Peru* (Toronto, Canada: McGraw-Hill Ryerson, Ltd., 1976); Wm. Bollaert, *Antiquarian, Ethnological, and Other Researches in New Granada, Equador, Peru, and Chili, With Observations on the Pre-Incarial, Incarial, and Other Monuments of Peruvian Nations* (London, Eng.: Trubner and Co., 1860); Burr Cartwright Brundage, *Lords of Cuzco* (Norman, OK: University of Oklahoma Press, 1967); Richard L. Burger, *Chavin and the Origins of Andean Civilization* (London, Eng.: Thames and Hudson, 1992); G. H. S. Bushnell, *Peru Ancient Peoples and Places* (New York, NY: Praeger, 1957; London, Eng.: Burns and MacEachern, 1957); George Earl Church (Clements R. Markham KCB, ed.), *Aborigines of South America* (London, Eng.: Chapman and Hall Ltd., 1912); Henry F. Dobyns and Paul L. Doughty, *Peru A Cultural History* (New York, NY: Oxford University Press, 1976); C. B. Donnan, *Early Ceremonial Architecture in the Andes: A Conference at Dumbarton Oaks, 8–10 October, 1982* (Washington, DC: Dumbarton Oaks Research Library and Collection, 1985); Jonathan Haas, Shelia Pozorski, and Thomas Pozorski eds., *The Origins and Development of the Andean State* (Cambridge, Eng.: Cambridge University Press, 1987); Evan Hadingham, *Lines to the Mountain Gods* (New York, NY: Random House, 1987); Christine A. Hastorf, *Agriculture and the Onset of Political Inequality before the Inka* (Cambridge, Eng.: Cambridge University Press, 1993); Edgar Lee Hewett, *Ancient Andean Life* (Indianapolis, IN; New York, NY: The Bobbs-Merrill Co., 1939); Richard W. Keatinge, ed., *Peruvian Prehistory* (Cambridge, Eng.:

Cambridge University Press, 1988); A. L. Kroeber, *The Chibcha* (1946); Hermann Leicht (translanted from German by Mervyn Savill), *Pre-Inca Art and Culture* (Zurich, Switzerland: Orell Fussli Verlag, 1944; New York, NY: The Orion Press, 1960); L. Leland Locke, *The Ancient Quipu or Peruvian Knot Record* (New York, NY: The American Museum of Natural History, 1923); Thomas F. Lynch, *Guitarrero Cave Early Man in the Andes* (New York, NY: Academic Press, Inc., 1980); J. Alden Mason, *The Ancient Civilizations of Peru* (Baltimore, MD: Penguin Books, 1957; Revised, 1964); Charles W. Mead, *Old Civilizations of Inca Land* (New York, NY: American Museum Press, 1924; New York, NY: Cooper Square Publishers, 1972, 1935); P. Ainsworth Means, *Ancient Civilizations of the Andes* (New York, NY: Gordian Press, 1931, 1964; New York, NY: Scribner, 1936); Michael Edward Moseley, *The Maritime Foundations of Andean Civilization* (Menlo Park, CA: Cummings Publishing Co., 1975); George P. Murdock, *Outline of South American Cultures, Behavior Science Outlines* Vol. II (New Haven, CT: Human Relations Area Files, 1951); William H. Prescott, *World of the Incas* (Geneva, Switzerland: Editions Minerva, 1970); V. Restrepo, *Los Chichas antes de la Conquista Española* (1895); John W. Rick, *Prehistoric Hunters of the High Andes* (New York, NY: Academic Press Inc., 1980); Mariano Edward Rivero and John James Von Tschudi, *Peruvian Antiquities* (New York, NY: A. S. Barnes and Co., 1854; Cincinnati, OH: H. W. Derby, 1854; New York, NY: Kraus Reprint Co., 1971); E. George Squier, *Incidents of Travel and Exploration in the Land of the Incas* (New York, NY: Harper and Brothers, 1877); H. Trimborn, *Das Recht der Chibcha in Colombien* (Leipzig, Germany: E. Wiegandt, 1930); Victor W. Von Hagen, *The Desert Kingdoms of Peru* (London, Eng.: George Widenfeld and Nicolson Ltd., 1964; Greenwich, CT: New York Graphic Society Publishers, 1965); Ferdinand Anton, *The Art of Ancient Peru* (New York, NY: G. P. Putnam's Sons, 1972); and an M.A. thesis by Joelyn Miller Heslep, titled *The Relationship Between the Olmec Art of Mesoamerica and the Chavin Art of Peru* (University of Georgia, 1971). Also see articles by Charles R. Ortloff, "Canal Builders of Pre-Inca Peru," *Scientific American* (December 1988); and William K. Stevens, "Andean Culture Found to Be As Old As The Great Pyramids," *The New York Times*, Science Times (October 3, 1989).

    C. J. van Riet Lowe, in an article titled, "Mapungubwe," in a September 1936 issue of *Antiquity* magazine; Debra Shore's article, "Steel Making in Ancient Africa," in Ivan Van Sertima's edited volume *Blacks in Science* (New Brunswick, NJ: Transaction Books, 1983); and John S. Mbiti, in his *African Religions and Philosophy* (New York, NY: Praeger, 1969; Garden City, NY: Anchor, 1970), deal with aspects of ancient African culture. Other works explore the cultural and/or agricultural connection between Africa and Peru and other areas in the Americas: Rudolph Bershadsky, "Atlantis,"

On the Track of Discovery, Series 2 (Moscow, USSR: Progress Publishers, 1964); Alexandre Braghine, *The Shadow of Atlantis* (New York, NY: E. P. Dutton and Co., 1940); W. J. Perry, *The Growth of Civilization* second ed. (Harmondsworth, Eng.: Penguin Books, Ltd., 1937); John G. Jackson, *Introduction to African Civilizations* (Secaucus, NJ: The Citadel Press, 1970); Leo Wiener, *Africa and the Discovery of America* Vol. II (Philadelphia, PA: Innes and Sons, 1922); Ivan Van Sertima, *They Came before Columbus* (New York, NY: Random House, 1976); and George P. Murdock, *Africa Its Peoples and Their Culture History* (New York, NY: McGraw-Hill, 1959).

Agriculture, crop origin, and various foods are the subjects of Report of an Ad Hoc Panel of the Advisory Committee on Technology Innovation Board on Science and Technology for International Development National Research Council, *Lost Crops of the Incas* (Washington, DC: National Academy Press, 1989); Edgar Anderson, *Plants, Man, and Life* (Boston, MA: Little Brown, 1952, 1983; Berkeley, CA: University of California Press, 1971); and Leo Wiener, *Africa and the Discovery of America* Vol. II. See also C. B. Heiser, "Contributions of the Indians of America to Agriculture"; M. L. Fowler, "The Origins of Indian Corn," *Principal Papers Delivered at the Tenth Annual Pan American Festival, April 8–11, 1963* (Carbondale, IL: Southern Illinois University, Latin American Institute, 1963); and Hortensia Maes, "Notes on Diet and Food Habits in Columbia," U.S. Office of Indian Affairs, Division of Inter-American Cooperation (Washington, DC: 1941).

Other volumes that focus on food and cuisine are A. Stanbury, *Great Peruvian Recipes: Pre-Columbian* (Lima, Peru: Peru Reporting, 1997); Roelie Lenten, *Cooking under the Volcanoes: Communal Kitchens in the Southern Peruvian City of Arequipa* (Amsterdam, Netherlands: CEDLA, 1993); Josefina Brusco de Liberti, *Arte Culinario Peruano Peruvian Cooking Art* (Lima, Peru: Tip. Santa Rosa, 1961); Wilma Hays and R. Vernon Hays, *Foods the Indians Gave Us* (New York, NY: Ives Washburn, Inc., 1973); Lupe Camino, *Chicha de Maíz: Bebida y Vida del Pueblo Catacaos* (Piura-Peru: Centro de Investigacion y Promocion del Campesinado, 1987); Jessica Kuper, ed., *The Anthropologists Cookbook* (New York, NY: Universe Books, 1977); E. Chapman Nyaho, E. Amarteifio, and J. Asare, *Ghana Recipe Book* (Accra, Ghana: Ghana Publishing Corp., 1970); Bill Odarty, *A Safari of African Cooking* (Detroit, MI: Broadside Press, 1971); and Felipe Rojas-Lombardi, *The Art of South American Cooking* (New York, NY: Harper Collins Publishers, 1991). See also Sara Rimer, "For the Determined, the Search for a Rare Taste of Senegal," *The New York Times*, Living Section (August 26, 1992); and, although its views are quite traditional, *Latin American Cooking* (Alexandria, VA: Time-Life Books, 1968), by Jonathan N. Leonard.

Chapter Five. Body and Soul

There is an exceptionally large number of works on the history and culture of Brazil. Volumes dealing with slavery and sugar and coffee production during the colonial period, and various aspects of the African contribution and influence during this era, for instance, are the focus of three of Leslie Bethell's books: *Colonial Brazil* (Cambridge, Eng.: Cambridge University Press, 1987); *The Abolition of the Brazilian Slave Trade* (Cambridge, Eng.: Cambridge University Press, 1970); and his *World of Sorrow* (Baton Rouge, LA: Louisiana State University Press, 1986). See also C. R. Boxer, *The Golden Age of Brazil* (Berkeley and Los Angeles, CA: University of California Press, 1962); Katia M. de Queiros Mattoso, *To Be a Slave in Brazil* (New Brunswick, NJ: Rutgers University Press, 1986); Carl Degler, *Neither Black nor White* (New York, NY: The Macmillan Co., 1971); Gilberto Freyre, *The Masters and the Slaves* (New York, NY: Alfred A. Knopf, 1946); and his *The Mansions and the Shanties* (New York, NY: Alfred A. Knopf, 1963; reprint 1966); Joseph E. Harris, *Global Dimensions of the African Diaspora* (Washington, DC: Howard University Press, 1982); Joseph C. Miller, *Way of Death* (Madison, WI: University of Wisconsin Press, 1988); Abdias do Nascimento, *Africans in Brazil* (Trenton, NJ: Africa World Press, 1992); Jose H. Rodriques, *Brazil and Africa* (Berkeley and Los Angeles, CA: University of California Press, 1965); Vincent Thompson, *The Making of the African Diaspora* (England: Longman, 1987); Felix Reichmann, *Sugar, Gold, and Coffee* (Ithaca, NY: Cornell University Press, 1959); Eric Drysdale, *The Afro-Brazilian Touch: The Meaning of its Artistic and Historic Contribution* (Tenenge, Brazil: Tecnica Nacional de Engenharia S. A., 1988); Bert J. Barickman, *A Bahian Counterpoint: Sugar, Tobacco, Cassava, and Slavery in the Reconcavo, 1780–1860* (Stanford, CA: Stanford University Press, 1998); Robert W. Slenes, *Malungu, Ngoma Vem!: Africa Encoberta E Descoberta No Brasil* (Luanda, Angola: Museu Nacional da Escravatura, I. N. P. C., 1995); Raymond T. Smith, ed., *Kinship Ideology and Practice in Latin America* (Chapel Hill, NC: University of North Carolina Press, 1984); Miriam Joel, *African Tradition in Latin America* (Cuernavaca, Mexico: Centro Intercultural de Documentacíon, 1972); and Karen A. Yarbrough's M.A. thesis for Northeastern Illinois University, *Slavery, Colonization, and Oppression of Africans in Brazil* (1996).

Slave resistance and insurrection, and the resulting maroon communities that arose in Brazil are under discussion in many of the aforementioned works. Those dealing primarily with this subject include Jose Joao Reis, *Islam and Slave Resistance in Bahia, Brazil* (Paris, France: 1989); and his *Slave Rebellion in Brazil: The Muslim Uprising of 1835 in Bahia* (Baltimore, MD: Johns Hopkins University Press, 1995, 1993); R. K. Kent's article, "Palmares An African State in Brazil," *Journal of African History* 1, No. 2 (1965); Howard M. Prince's thesis for Columbia University, *Slave Rebellion in Bahia, 1807–1835* (New York, NY: 1972, 1975); Dalva Lazaroni de. Moraes, *Quilombos e Tiradentes na Baixada Fluminense* (Rio de Janeiro, Brazil: Editora Codpoe, 1991); and Richard Price, ed., *Maroon Societies: Rebel Slave Communities in the Americas* second ed. (Baltimore, MD: Johns Hopkins University Press, 1987). Also see Selma Vasconcelos's book of poems, *Zumbi Dos Palmares* (Recife, Brazil: Governo do Estado de Pernambuco, Secretaria da Cultura, Fundcao do Patrimonio Historico e Artistico de Pernambuco—FUNDARPE, 1995).

Candomble and the religious practices of Africans in Brazil, as they relate to the Baiana, are treated in Zeca Ligiero's article, "Candomble Is Religion-Life-Art," in Phyllis Galembo's edited volume, *Divine Inspiration* (Albuquerque, NM: University of New Mexico Press, 1993); and in Zeca Ligiero's forthcoming book, *Carmen Miranda: An Afro-Brazilian Paradox*, in which he cites the Baiana's fame "for her skills as pastry cook, greengrocer, and fruit vendor." Other aspects of Candomble are the subject of Ruth Landes, *The City of Women* (Albuquerque, NM: University of New Mexico Press, 1947); Sandra T. Barnes, *Africa's Ogun* (Bloomington, IN: Indiana University Press, 1989); and James W. Wafer, *The Taste of Blood* (Philadelphia, PA: University of Pennsylvania Press, 1991); and his article, "Africa in Brazil: Cultural Politics, and the Candomble Religion," in Hedonimo Rodrigues Santana, ed., *Folk Religions of the African Diaspora* (Bloomington, IN: Folklore Publications Group, 1990). See also Roger Bastide, *The African Religions in Brazil: Toward a Sociology of the Interpenetration of Civilizations* (Baltimore, MD, London, Eng.: Johns Hopkins University Press, 1978); Jose Joao Reis, *Islam and Slave Resistance in Bahia, Brazil;* Michael A. Nicklas, "Mythology, Knowledge, and Power: An Examination of Social Forces in Brazil and the Emergence of Umbanda," *Folk Religions of the African Diaspora* (Bloomington, IN: Folklore Publications Group, 1990); and Rachel E. Harding's Ph.D. Thesis, *Candomble and the Alternative Spaces of Black Being in Nineteenth Century Bahia, Brazil: A Study of Historical Context and Religious Meaning* (University of Colorado, 1997).

Santeria, and the religious practices of Africans in Cuba, is the main focus of such works as Amparo Lopez Pujol, "African Religion in Cuba as a Way of Self-Affirmation and a Way of Resistance," *Survivors of the Middle Passage: Affirmation and Change* (Barbados: 1992,1995); Judith Gleason, *Oya, In Praise Of An African Goddess* (San Francisco, CA: HarperCollins, 1992); George Brandon, *Santeria from Africa to the New World: The Dead Sell Memories* (Bloomington, IN: Indiana University Press, 1997, 1993); Joseph Murphy, *Santeria, African Spirits in America* (Boston, MA: Beacon Press, 1993); Migene Gonzalez-Wippler's two volumes, *Legends of Santeria*

(St. Paul, MN: Llewellyn Publications, 1994) and *Santeria: African Magic in Latin America* second revised ed. (New York, NY: Original Products, 1992); Oba Ecun, *Ita: Mythology of the Yoruba Religion* (Miami, FL: ObaEcun Books, 1996); Agun Efunde, *Los Secretos de la Santeria* (Miami, FL: Universal, 1996); Petra Codina, *Ancient Recipes of Power* (S.l., P. Codina, 1993); John DuMoulin, "The Participative Art of the Afrocuban Religions," *Abhandlungen und Berichte des Staatlichen Museums für Volkerkunde Dresden* 21 (Berlin, Germany: Akademie-Verlag, 1962); and Jesse G. Kulp's senior history thesis for Colorado College, *Santeria and the African Cabildo in Nineteenth-Century Cuba* (1997).

Among the many texts that offer insight on slavery's brutality, the growth of sugar production, and the Africanization of Cuba are Louis Perez, *Slaves, Sugar, and Colonial Society* (Wilmington, DE: Scholarly Resources, 1992); the astounding work of Juan Francisco Manzano in Edward Mullen, ed., *The Life and Poems of a Cuban Slave* (Hamden, CT: Archon Books, 1981); Herbert S. Klein, *African Slavery in Latin America and the Caribbean* (New York, NY: Oxford University Press, 1986); L. Foner and E. Genovese, *Slavery in the New World* (Englewood Cliffs, NJ: Prentice-Hall, Inc., 1969); Robert L. Paquette, *Sugar Is Made with Blood* (Middletown, CT: Wesleyan University Press, 1988); African-Caribbean Institute of Jamaica, *Salute to Afro-Cuba* (Kingston, Jamaica: African-Caribbean Institute, 1975); Rebecca J. Scott, *Slave Emancipation in Cuba* (Princeton, NJ: Princeton University Press, 1985); Vincent Thompson, *The Making of the African Diaspora;* Leslie B. Rout, *The African Experience in Spanish America, 1502 to the Present* (Cambridge, Eng., New York, NY: Cambridge University Press, 1976); Kenneth Franklin Kiple's Ph.D. Dissertation for the University of Florida (1970), *The Cuban Slave Trade, 1820–1862: The Demographic Implications For Comparative Studies* (Ann Arbor, MI: Xerox University Microfilms, 1975); and his text, *Blacks in Colonial Cuba, 1774–1899* (Gainesville, FL: University Press of Florida, 1996, 1976); Ann Pescatello, *The African in Latin America* (New York, NY: Knopf, 1975); Robert Brent Toplin, *Slavery and Race Relations in Latin America* (Westport, CT: Greenwood Press, 1974); Franklin W. Knight, *The African Dimension in Latin American Societies* (New York, NY: Macmillan, 1974); David A. Sartorius's M.A. thesis for the University of North Carolina, *Slavery, Conucos, and the Local Economy: Ingenio Santa Rosalia, Cienfuegos, Cuba, 1860–1886* (Chapel Hill, NC: 1997); Antonio C. Gallenga, *The Pearl of the Antilles* (London, Eng.: Chapman and Hall, 1873); Gwendolyn Hall, *Social Control in Slave Plantation Societies: A Comparison of St. Domingue and Cuba* (Baton Rouge, LA: Louisiana State University Press, 1996, 1971); Jose Aniceto Iznaga, *Cuba and Africa* (Paris, France: Blondeau, 1853); Jose Antonio Saco, *La Supresion Del Trafico De Esclavos Africanos En La Isla De Cuba Examinada Con Relacion A Su Agricultura*

Y A Su Seguridad (Paris, France: Imprs. de Panckoucke, 1845); Hubert Hillary Suffern Aimes, *A History of Slavery in Cuba, 1511 to 1868* (New York, NY, London, Eng.: G. P. Putnam's Sons, 1907); Esteban Montejo, *The Autobiography of a Runaway Slave* (London, Eng.: Macmillan Caribbean, 1993); Chester S. Urban, *El Temor A La Africanizacion De Cuba, 1853–55* (Habana, Cuba: Cardenas y cia., 1957); and his *Slavocracy and Empire: New Orleans and the Attempted Expansion of Slavery, 1845–1861* (based on his thesis submitted at Park College, Parkville, Missouri, 1976), which has a segment on Cuban history and insurrection there between 1849 and 1851; Ines Roldan de Montaud, *Origen, Evolucion Y Supresion Del Grupo De Negros "Emancipados" En Cuba (1817–1870)* (Madrid, Spain: Consejo Superior de Investigaciones Cientificas, 1982); and James J. O'Kelly, *La Tierra Del Mambi* (La Habana, Cuba: Editorial de Ciencias Sociales, 1990). See also the Library of Congress's YA Pamphlet Collection for a published letter addressed to Secretary of State Theo. F. Frelinghuysen, and signed by Nathaniel Paige, *Property in Slaves and Proceeds of Slave Labor in Cuba* (Washington, DC: Thomas McGill and Co., 1881, 1885); and Fernando Ortiz, *Cuban Counterpoint, Tobacco and Sugar* (Durham, NC: Duke University Press, 1995).

Other volumes that explore the life and culture of Africans in Brazil, Cuba, and the West Indies include Abdias do Nascimento, *Brazil, Mixture or Massacre* (Dover, MA: The Majority Press, 1979, 1989); Robert M. Levine and Jose Carlos Sebe Bom Meihy, *The Life and Death of Carolina Maria de Jesus* (Albuquerque, NM: University of New Mexico Press, 1995); P. Sarduy and J. Stubbs, *AfroCuba* (New York, NY: Ocean Press, 1993); Vernon Boggs, *Salsiology: Afro-Cuban Music and the Evolution of Salsa in New York City* (Westport, CT: Greenwood Press, 1992, 1991); Ann Pescatello, *Old Roots in New Lands: Historical and Anthropological Perspectives on Black Experiences in the Americas* (Westport, CT: Greenwood Press, 1977); Anani Dzidzienyo, *The Position of Blacks in Brazilian and Cuban Society* (London, Eng.: Minority Rights Group, 1979); Carlos Moore, *Castro, The Blacks, and Africa* (Los Angeles, CA: Center for Afro-American Studies, U.C.L.A., 1988); and Lucille Mathurin, *The Rebel Woman in the British West Indies during Slavery* (Kingston, Jamaica: African Caribbean Institute of Jamaica, 1975). Also see Verena Stolcke, *Coffee, Planters, Workers, and Wives: Class Conflict and Gender Relations on Sao Paulo Plantations, 1850–1980* (New York, NY: St. Martin's Press, 1988).

The African origin of coffee and much additional information on this plant is explored in Joel Schapira, David Schapira, and Karl Schapira, *The Book of Coffee and Tea* (New York, NY: St. Martin's Press, 1975, 1982); Frederick L. Wellman, *Coffee: Botany, Cultivation, and Utilization* (New York, NY: Interscience Publishers, Inc.; London, Eng.: Leonard Hill Ltd., 1961), which offers discourse on "blood brother" ceremonies; Francis B.

Thurber, *Coffee: From Plantation to Cup* (New York, NY: American Grocer Publishing Association, 1881). Also, a good sampling of Brazilian and/or Cuban cuisine can be found in Jessica B. Harris, *Tasting Brazil* (New York, NY: Macmillan Publishing Co., 1992); and her *Iron Pots and Wooden Spoons* (New York, NY: Atheneum, 1989); Antonio Houaiss, *Magia Da Cozinha Brasileira: For Gods and Mortals* (Rio De Janeiro, Brazil: Primor, 1979); Felipe Rojas-Lombardi, *The Art of South American Cooking* (New York, NY: HarperCollins Publishers, 1991); Joyce LaFray, *Cuba Cocina* (New York, NY: Hearst Books, 1994); and Philip Bellber, *Cook, Eat, Cha Cha Cha: Festive New World Recipes* (San Francisco, CA: Chronicle Books, 1997). There is also an audiovisual program, *Brazil: A Bahian Menu,* published in Deerfield, Illinois, by MTI Teleprograms (1980). Jonathan N. Leonard's *Latin American Cooking* (Alexandria, VA: Time-Life Books, 1968), by Time-Life Books, contains some information, although much of its discourse reflects traditional views.

William C. Willoughby's *The Soul of the Bantu* (Garden City, NY: Doubleday, Doran and Co., Inc., 1928), provided information on the burial practices of cattle herders of the Baila society.

Chapter Six. Without Rival, Anywhere

For discourse on Bartolome de Las Casas and his proposal of importing Africans as slaves into the Americas, see Luis Riviere (Rivera?), "Las Casas and Slavery," in Harcourt Blackett, ed., *Survivors of the Middle Passage: Affirmation and Change* (St. John, Barbados: Lectures delivered at the Quincentennial Consultation sponsored by Caribbean/African American Dialogue and the Caribbean Conference of Churches from April 30th to May 3, 1992, at the Catholic Retreat Centre, Verdun, St. John, Barbados, 1992, 1995).

Among the literature offering discourse on Haiti's life and culture during the colonial period, as well as its revolution, are C. L. R. James, *A History of Pan-African Revolt* (Washington, DC: Drum and Spear Press, 1969); and his *The Black Jacobins* (New York, NY: Vintage Books, 1963); Herbert S. Klein, *African Slavery in Latin America and the Caribbean* (New York, NY: Oxford University Press, 1986); James G. Leyburn, *The Haitian People* (New Haven, CT: Yale University Press, 1966, 1941); Blair Niles, *Black Haiti* (New York, NY: Knickerbocker Press—G. P. Putnam and Sons, 1926); Vincent Thompson, *The Making of the African Diaspora in the Americas 1441–1900* (London, Eng.: Longman, 1987); Hilary Beckles, " 'A Dangerous and Unnatural Independence': The Haitian Revolution and Black Liberation in the Caribbean," in Harcourt Blackett, ed., *Survivors of the*

Middle Passage: Affirmation and Change (St. John, Barbados: Lectures delivered at the Quincentennial Consultation sponsored by Caribbean/ African American Dialogue and the Caribbean Conference of Churches from April 30th to May 3, 1992, at the Catholic Retreat Centre, Verdun, St. John, Barbados, 1992, 1995); Jose Morales's Ph.D. dissertation for the University of Connecticut, *The Hispaniola Diaspora, 1791-1850: Puerto Rico, Cuba, Louisiana, and Other Host Societies* (1986); Henock Trouillot, *La Condition Des Negres Domestiques A Saint-Domingue* (Port-au-Prince, Haiti: Impr. de l'Etat, 1955); Jean Fouchard, *The Haitian Maroons: Liberty or Death* (New York, NY: E. W. Blyden Press, 1981); *An Inquiry into the Causes of the Insurrection of the Negroes in the Island of St. Domingo to Which Are Added, Observations of M. Garran-Coulon on the Same Subject, Read in His Absence by M. Guadet, Before the National Assembly, 29th Feb. 1792* (London, Eng.: J. Johnson, 1792); Carolyn E. Fick, *The Making of Haiti: The Saint Domingue Revolution from Below* (Knoxville, TN: University of Tennessee Press, 1990); Prince Saunders, *Haytian Papers: A Collection of the Very Interesting Proclamations and Other Official Documents; Together with Some Account of the Rise, Progress, and Present State of the Kingdom of Hayti* (Wilmington, DE: Scholarly Resources, 1972, 1818); Thomas Clarkson, *The True State of the Case, Respecting the Insurrection at St. Domingo* (Ipswich, Eng.: J. Bush, 1792); Michel Laguerre's M.A. thesis for Roosevelt University, *Nativism in Haiti (1625–1803): The Politics of Voodoo* (Chicago, IL: 1973); Robert Forster, *A Sugar Plantation on Saint-Domingue* (Mona, Jamaica: U. W. I., Department of History, 1988); Richard D. E. Burton, *Afro-Creole: Power, Opposition, and Play in the Caribbean* (Ithaca, NY: Cornell University Press, 1997); David Patrick Geggus, *Slave Society in the Sugar Plantation Zones of Saint Domingue and the Revolution of 1791–1793* (Universite Antilles Guyane, Groupe de Recherche AIP-CARDH, 1997); and Gwendolyn Hall, *Social Control in Slave Plantation Societies: A Comparison of St. Domingue and Cuba* (Baton Rouge, LA: Louisiana State University Press, 1996, 1971).

Africans in slavery on the island of Barbados are treated in, for example, Hilary Beckles's article, "An Economic Life of their Own: Slaves as Commodity Producers and Distributors in Barbados," in Ira Berlin and Philip D. Morgan, eds., *The Slaves' Economy: Independent Production by Slaves in the Americas* (London, Eng.; Portland, OR: Frank Cass, 1991); and her two volumes, *Black Rebellion in Barbados: The Struggle against Slavery, 1627–1838* (Bridgetown, Barbados: Antilles Publications, 1984), and *White Servitude and Black Slavery in Barbados, 1627-1715* (Knoxville, TN: University of Tennessee Press, 1989); Claude Levy, *Emancipation, Sugar, and Federalism: Barbados and the West Indies, 1833–1876* (Gainesville, FL: University Press of Florida, 1980); Jerome S. Handler, *Plantation Slavery in Barbados: An Archaeological and Historical Investigation* (Cambridge, MA: Harvard

University Press, 1978); Harry J. Bennett, *Bondsmen and Bishops* (Berkeley, CA: University of California Press, 1958); and Gary A. Puckrein, *Little England: Plantation Society and Anglo-Barbadian Politics, 1627–1700* (New York, NY: New York University Press, 1984).

The Bahamas, during the colonial period, is a focal point of Howard Johnson, *The Bahamas from Slavery to Servitude, 1783–1933* (Gainesville, FL: University Press of Florida, 1996); and his *The Bahamas in Slavery and Freedom* (Kingston, Jamaica: Ian Randle Publishers, London, Eng.: James Currey Publishers, 1991); Gail Saunders, *Slavery in the Bahamas, 1648–1838* (Nassau, Bahamas: D. G. Saunders, 1985); and her *Bahamian Loyalists and Their Slaves* (London, Eng.: Macmillan Caribbean, 1983). Also see B. W. Higman, *Slave Populations of the British Caribbean, 1807–1834* (Baltimore, MD: Johns Hopkins University Press, 1984); and the diaries of Charles Farquharson in *A Relic of Slavery: Farquharson's Journal for 1831–32* (Nassau, Bahamas: Deans, Peggs Research Fund, 1957).

The commercial enterprise of slavery, as practiced in Puerto Rico, can be viewed in Francisco A. Scarano, *Sugar and Slavery in Puerto Rico: The Plantation Economy of Ponce, 1800–1850* (Madison, WI: University of Wisconsin Press, 1984); Jalil Sued Badillo, *Puerto Rico Negro* (Rio Piedras, Puerto Rico: Editorial Cultural, 1986); Pedro San Miguel, *El Mundo Que Creo El Azucar: Las Haciendas En Vega Baja, 1800–1873* (Rio Piedras, Puerto Rico: Ediciones Huracan, 1989); Guillermo A. Baralt, *El Machete de Ogun: Las Luchas De Los Esclavos En Puerto Rico* (Rio Piedras, Puerto Rico: CEREP, Proyecto de Divulgacion Popular, 1989, 1990); and George D. Flinter, *View of the Present Condition of the Slave Population in the Island of Puerto Rico* second ed. (San Juan, Puerto Rico: Instituto de Cultura Puertorriquena, 1976).

The structure of slave society in Jamaica is the subject of Lucille Mathurin Mair, "Women Field Workers in Jamaica During Slavery," in Rosalyn Terborg-Penn and Andrea Benton Rushing, eds., *Women in Africa and the African Diaspora: A Reader* second ed. (Washington, DC: Howard University Press, 1996); B. W. Higman, "Domestic Service in Jamaica, Since 1750," in B. W. Higman, ed., *Trade, Government, and Society in Caribbean History, 1700–1920: Essays Presented to Douglas Hall* (Kingston, Jamaica: Heinemann Educational Books Caribbean, 1983); Orlando Patterson, *The Sociology of Slavery: An Analysis of the Origins, Development, and Structure of Negro Slave Society in Jamaica* (London, Eng.: MacGibbon and Kee, 1967); Richard Hart, *Slaves Who Abolished Slavery* (Kingston, Jamaica: U. W. I., Institute of Social and Economic Research, 1980); and his *Black Jamaicans' Struggle Against Slavery* (Kingston, Jamaica: Institute of Jamaica, 1977); Roderick A. McDonald, *The Economy and Material Culture of Slaves: Goods and Chattels on the Sugar Plantations of Jamaica and Louisiana* (Baton Rouge, LA: Louisiana State University Press, 1993); Carey Robinson, *Fight for Freedom* (Kingston, Jamaica:

Kingston Publishers, 1987); Mavis Christine Campbell, *The Maroons of Jamaica, 1655–1796: A History of Resistance, Collaboration, and Betrayal* (Granby, MA: Bergin and Garvey, 1988); Michael Craton, *Searching for the Invisible Man: Slaves and Plantation Life in Jamaica* (Cambridge, MA: Harvard University Press, 1978); and John Stewart, *A View of the Past and Present State of the Island of Jamaica; With Remarks on the Moral and Physical Condition of the Slaves and on the Abolition of Slavery in the Colonies* (Edinburgh, Scotland: Oliver and Boyd, 1823). See also Bryan Edwards's *The History, Civil and Commercial, of the British West Indies* 5th ed. (London, Eng.: Baldwin, Cradock, and Joy [etc], 1818, 1819), for information on agriculture, "exotic plants," and the "Maroon Negroes" in Jamaica.

There are a number of works that explore slave and plantation society in Trinidad and Tobago: K. O. Laurence, "Tobago and British Imperial Authority, 1793–1802," in B. W. Higman, ed., *Trade, Government, and Society in Caribbean History, 1700–1920: Essays Presented to Douglas Hall* (Kingston, Jamaica: Heinemann Educational Books Caribbean, 1983); Carl C. Campbell, "The Opposition to Crown Colony Government in Trinidad before and after Emancipation, 1813–46," in B. W. Higman, ed., *Trade, Government, and Society in Caribbean History, 1700–1920: Essays Presented to Douglas Hall* (Kingston, Jamaica: Heinemann Educational Books Caribbean, 1983); Richard D. E. Burton, *Afro-Creole: Power, Opposition, and Play in the Caribbean* (Ithaca, NY: Cornell University Press, 1997); A. Meredith John, *The Plantation Slaves of Trinidad, 1783–1816: A Mathematical and Demographic Enquiry* (Cambridge, Eng.; New York, NY: Cambridge University Press, 1988); Carlton Robert Ottley, *Slavery Days in Trinidad: A Social History of the Island from 1797–1838* (Trinidad: Ottley, 1974); A. B. Huggins, *The Saga of the Companies* (Princes Town, Trinidad: Twinluck Printing Works, 1978); William H. Burnley, *Observations on the Present Condition of the Island of Trinidad, and the Actual State of the Experiment of Negro Emancipation* (London, Eng.: Longman, Brown, Green, and Longmans, 1842); and James Millette, *Socialism and Slavery* (Curepe, Trinidad and Tobago: Moko Enterprises, 1978).

Black and Native Carib history is examined in Nancie L. Gonzalez, *Sojourners of the Caribbean* (Urbana and Chicago, IL: University of Illinois Press, 1988); Ruy Coelho, *The Significance of the Couvade among the Black Caribs* (London, Eng.: Royal Anthropological Institute, 1949); Peter Hulme and Neil L. Whitehead, eds., *Wild Majesty: Encounters with the Caribs from Columbus to the Present Day* (Oxford, Eng.: Clarendon Press, 1992); C. J. M. R. Gullick, *Myths of a Minority: The Changing Traditions of the Vincentian Caribs* (Assen, Netherlands: Van Gorcum, 1985); I. Lester Firschein, *Population Dynamics of the Sickle-Cell Trait in the Black Caribs of British Honduras, Central America* (reprinted from American Journal of

Human Genetics, XIII, No. 2, June, 1961); Woodville K. Marshall, " 'Vox Populi': The St. Vincent Riots and Disturbances of 1862," in B. W. Higman, ed., *Trade, Government, and Society in Caribbean History, 1700–1920: Essays Presented to Douglas Hall* (Kingston, Jamaica: Heinemann Educational Books Caribbean, 1983); Michael H. Crawford, *Black Caribs: A Case Study in Biocultural Adaptation* (New York, NY; London, Eng.: Plenum, 1984); I. E. Kirby, *The Rise and Fall of the Black Caribs* (Caracas, Venezuela: 1985; Kingstown, St. Vincent: St. Vincent and the Grenadines National Trust, 1972); Kent D. Myrick, *The Black Caribs of Honduras* (Tegucigalpa, Honduras: 1964); Peter Kloos, *The Maroni River Caribs of Surinam* (Assen, Netherlands: Van Gorcum, 1971); and Richard S. Dunn, *Sugar and Slaves* (New York, NY: Norton, 1973). Also see what is called "an impartial view of slavery," as well as discourse on the Caribs (authored by a "Mrs. Flannigan," or "Lanaghan") in *Antigua and the Antiguans: A Full Account of the Colony and Its Inhabitants from the Time of the Caribs to the Present Day, Interspersed with Anecdotes and Legends* (London, Eng.: Spottiswoode, Ballantyne, 1967; London, Eng.: Saunders and Otley, 1844).

Among other articles and volumes offering discourse on slavery in the Caribbean are Colin A. Palmer, "The Slave Trade, African Slavers, and the Demography of the Caribbean to 1750," in Franklin W. Knight, ed., *The Slave Societies of the Caribbean* (London, Eng.: UNESCO Pub.: Macmillan Education, Ltd., 1997); Rosalyn Terborg-Penn, "Slavery and Women in Africa and the Diaspora," in Rosalyn Terborg-Penn and Andrea Benton Rushing, eds., *Women in Africa and the African Diaspora: A Reader* second ed. (Washington, DC: Howard University Press, 1996); Bernice Johnson Reagon, "African Diaspora Women: The Making of Cultural Workers," in Rosalyn Terborg-Penn and Andrea Benton Rushing, eds., *Women in Africa and the African Diaspora: A Reader* second ed. (Washington, DC: Howard University Press, 1996); Darien J. Davis, ed., *Slavery and Beyond: The African Impact on Latin America and the Caribbean* (Wilmington, DE: SR Books, 1995); Ira Berlin and Philip D. Morgan, *Cultivation and Culture: Labor and the Shaping of Slave Life in the Americas* (Charlottesville, VA: University Press of Virginia, 1993); Richard S. Dunn, *Sugar and Slaves;* Sidney W. Mintz's article, "Slave Life on Caribbean Sugar Plantations: Some Unanswered Questions," in Stephan Palmie, ed., *Slave Cultures and the Cultures of Slavery* (Knoxville, TN: University of Tennessee Press, 1995); and his two volumes, *The Birth of African-American Culture: An Anthropological Perspective* (Boston, MA: Beacon Press, 1992), co-authored with Richard Price; and *Caribbean Transformations* (New York, NY; Oxford, Eng.: Columbia University Press, 1989, 1974); Magnus Morner, *Race Mixture in the History of Latin America* (Boston, MA: Little, Brown and Co., 1967); Alan Gregor Cobley and Alvin Thompson, eds., *The African-Caribbean Connection: Historical and Cultural Perspectives* (Bridgetown,

Barbados: Natural Cultural Foundation U. W. I., 1990); Richard Price, "Subsistence on the Plantation Periphery: Crops, Cooking, and Labour among Eighteenth-Century Suriname Maroons," in Ira Berlin and Philip D. Morgan, eds., *The Slaves' Economy: Independent Production by Slaves in the Americas* (London, Eng.; Portland, OR: Frank Class, 1991); David Eltis, "The Slave Economies of the Caribbean: Structure, Performance, Evolution, and Significance," in Franklin W. Knight, ed., *The Slave Societies of the Caribbean* (London, Eng.: UNESCO Pub.: Macmillan Education Ltd., 1997); Gad Heuman, "The Social Structure of the Slave Societies in the Caribbean," Franklin W. Knight (Ed.), *The Slave Societies of the Caribbean* (London, Eng.: UNESCO Pub.: Macmillan Education Ltd., 1997); and Hilary Beckles, "Social and Political Control in the Slave Society," in Franklin W. Knight, ed., *The Slave Societies of the Caribbean* (London, Eng.: UNESCO Pub.: Macmillan Education Ltd., 1997).

For works offering insight into insurrection, resistance, and maroon life, see, for example, Gary Y. Okihiro, ed., *In Resistance: Studies in African, Caribbean, and Afro-American History* (Amherst, MA: University of Massachusetts Press, 1986); Michael Mullin, *Africa in America: Slave Acculturation and Resistance in the American South and the British Caribbean, 1736–1831* (Urbana, IL: University of Illinois Press, 1992); Gad Heuman, *Out of the House of Bondage: Runaways, Resistance, and Marronage in Africa and the New World* (London, Eng.; Totowa, NJ: Cass, 1986); Silvia W. de Groot, Catherine A. Christen, and Franklin W. Knight's article, "Maroon Communities in the Circum-Caribbean," in Franklin W. Knight, ed., *The Slave Societies of the Caribbean* (London, Eng.: UNESCO Pub.: Macmillan Education Ltd., 1997); and Michael Craton, "Forms of Resistance to Slavery," in Franklin W. Knight, ed., *The Slave Societies of the Caribbean* (London, Eng.: UNESCO Pub.: Macmillan Education Ltd., 1997).

The life of George Washington is under discussion in W. E. Woodward, *George Washington* (New York, NY: Boni and Liveright, Inc., 1926, 1946; paperbound, 1972); Walter H. Mazyck, *George Washington and the Negro* (Washington, DC: The Associated Publishers, Inc., 1932); Nigel Cawthorne, *Sex Lives of the U.S. Presidents* (London, Eng.: Prion, 1996); Washington Irving, *Life of George Washington* (New York, NY: G. P. Putnam and Co., 1856, 1859); Matthew Spalding, *A Sacred Union of Citizens: George Washington's Farewell Address and the American Character* (Lanham, MD; London, Eng.: Rowman and Littlefield, 1996); and John Corry, *The Life of George Washington* (Philadelphia, PA: Joseph Charless for James Rice and Co., 1801).

The African, free and slave, during the colonial period in mainland America, is the subject of John Hope Franklin, *From Slavery to Freedom: A History of Negro Americans* sixth ed. (New York, NY: Alfred A. Knopf, 1988); Winthrop D. Jordan, *White Over Black* (Baltimore, MD: Penguin Books Inc., 1969); Lerone Bennett, *Before the Mayflower: A History of*

Black America (New York, NY: Penguin, 1984, 1961); Lorenzo Johnston Greene, *The Negro in Colonial New England* (New York, NY: Atheneum, 1969, 1942); Roi Ottley and William J. Weatherby, eds., *The Negro in New York* (New York, NY: Praeger Publishers, 1969); William R. Riddell, "The Slave in Early New York," *Journal of Negro History* XIII (January 1928); Samuel McKee, *Labor in Colonial New York, 1664–1776* (New York, NY: Columbia University Press, 1935); Edwin V. Morgan, *Slavery in New York* (Washington, DC: American Historical Association Papers, V, Part 4, 1891); James C. Ballagh, *A History of Slavery in Virginia* (Baltimore, MD: The Johns Hopkins Press, 1902); Thad W. Tate Jr., *The Negro in Eighteenth-Century Williamsburg* (Williamsburg, VA: The Colonial Williamsburg Foundation, 1965); T. H. Breen, *Myne Owne Ground: Race and Freedom on Virginia's Eastern Shore, 1640–1676* (New York, NY: Oxford University Press, 1980); Matthew T. Mellon, *Early American Views on Negro Slavery* (New York, NY: New American Library, 1969; Boston, MA: Meador Publishing Co., 1934); Peter Wood, *Black Majority: Negroes in Colonial South Carolina From 1670 through the Stono Rebellion* (New York, NY: W. W. Norton and Co., 1974); Daniel F. Littlefield, *Rice and Slaves: Ethnicity and the Slave Trade in Colonial South Carolina* (Baton Rouge, LA: Louisiana State University Press, 1981); Edward Channing, *The Narragansett Planters* (Baltimore, MD: Johns Hopkins Press, 1886, reprinted 1973); Bernard C. Steiner, *History of Slavery in Connecticut* (Baltimore, MD: Johns Hopkins Press, 1893); William D. Piersen, *Black Yankees: The Development of an Afro-American Subculture in Eighteenth-Century New England* (Amherst, MA: University of Massachusetts Press, 1988); William Johnston, *Slavery in Rhode Island, 1755–1776* (Providence, RI: In, Publication of the Rhode Island Historical Society, 1894; New York, NY; Negro Universities Press, 1969); Betty Wood, *Slavery in Colonial Georgia, 1730–1775* (Athens, GA: University of Georgia Press, 1984); Ralph B. Flanders, *Plantation Slavery in Georgia* (Chapel Hill, NC: University of North Carolina Press, 1933); Edgar A. Toppin, *A Biographical History of Blacks in America Since 1528* (New York, NY: McKay, 1971); John B. Boles, *Black Southerners, 1619–1869* (Lexington, KY: University Press of Kentucky, 1984); Leon F. Litwack, *North of Slavery: The Negro in the Free States, 1790–1860* (Chicago, IL: The University of Chicago Press, 1961); and Joe Gray Taylor, "Blacks in Colonial America," *Early American Life* 11, No. 1 (Feb. 1980). Also see Carl N. Degler, "Slavery and the Genesis of American Race Prejudice"; M. Cantor, "The Colonial Image of the Negro"; and Winthrop D. Jordan, "Initial English Attitudes toward Africans," all in *Race, Prejudice, and the Origins of Slavery in America* (Rochester, VT: Schenkman Books, 1990). *The Origins of American Slavery and Racism* (Columbus, OH: Merrill, 1972), edited by Donald L. Noel, contains *"Red, White, and Black: The Origins of Racism in Colonial America,"* by G. B. Nash; *"Slavery and the Rise of Racism,"* by

D. L. Noel; and "*Race Relations in Seventeenth-Century America: The Problem of the Origins of Negro Slavery,*" by J. Boskin. Works covering African participation in the War for Independence include Philip S. Foner, *Blacks in the American Revolution* (Westport, CT: Greenwood Press, 1975); and his *History of Black Americans* Vols. I–III (Westport, CT: Greenwood Press, 1975–1981); Benjamin Quarles, *The Negro in the American Revolution* (Chapel Hill, NC: University of North Carolina Press, 1961); David Brion Davis, *The Problem of Slavery in the Age of Revolution, 1770–1823* (Ithaca, NY: Cornell University Press, 1975); and his *Slavery in the Colonial Chesapeake* (Williamsburg, VA: Colonial Williamsburg Foundation, 1986); Walter H. Mazyck, *George Washington and the Negro;* George H. Moore, *Historical Notes on the Employment of Negroes in the American Army of the Revolution* (New York, NY: C. T. Evans, 1862); Duncan J. MacLeod, *Slavery, Race, and the American Revolution* (Cambridge, England: Cambridge University Press, 1974, 1975); William C. Nell, *The Colored Patriots of the American Revolution* (Boston, MA: R. F. Wallcut, 1855); Luther P. Jackson, "Virginia Negro Soldiers and Seamen in the American Revolution," *Journal of Negro History* XXVII (July 1942); and Sidney Kaplan, *The Black Presence in the Era of the American Revolution, 1770–1800* (Boston: 1973).

The life of Thomas Jefferson is considered in Annette Gordon-Reed, *Thomas Jefferson and Sally Hemings: An American Controversy* (Charlottesville, VA: University Press of Virginia, 1997); Fawn M. Brodie, *Thomas Jefferson, An Intimate History* (New York, NY: W. W. Norton and Co. Inc., 1974); Nigel Cawthorne, *Sex Lives of the U.S. Presidents: An Irreverent Exposé of the Chief Executive From George Washington to the Present Day;* James A. Bear, Jr., ed., *Jefferson at Monticello, Memoirs of a Monticello Slave* (Charlottesville, VA: University Press of Virginia, 1967); Sarah N. Randolph, *The Domestic Life of Thomas Jefferson,* also known as *Jefferson's Domestic Life* (Charlottesville, VA: University Press of Virginia, 1985); Edwin M. Betts, ed., *Thomas Jefferson's Farm Book* (Charlottesville, VA: University Press of Virginia, 1976, 1977); and, although it is a cookbook, *Thomas Jefferson's Cook Book* (Charlottesville, VA: University Press of Virginia, 1976), by Marie Kimball, contains information on food and drink served in Jefferson's household, as well as on the brother of Jefferson's African slave mistress. See also Thomas Jefferson, *Notes on the State of Virginia* (New York, NY: Norton, 1972; reprint).

Numerous accounts of slavery and race in America include Leslie Howard Owens, *This Species of Property* (New York, NY: Oxford University Press, 1976); Benjamin Quarles, *The Negro in the Making of America* (New York, NY: Collier Books, 1964); Eugene D. Genovese, *Roll Jordan Roll, The World the Slaves Made* (New York, NY: Random House, 1974); Elizabeth Fox-Genovese, *Within the Plantation Household* (Chapel Hill, NC: University of North Carolina Press, 1988); George M. Fredrickson, *The Black Image in the White Mind: The Debate on Afro-American Character and Destiny, 1817–1914* (New York, NY: Harper and Row, 1971); Eugene D. Genovese, *The World the Slaveholders Made* (New York, NY: Vintage, 1971); Georgia Writers' Project, *Drums and Shadows: Survival Studies among the Georgia Coastal Negroes* (Athens, GA: University of Georgia Press, 1986; reprint, 1940); Margaret W. Creel, *A Peculiar People: Slave Religion and Community-Culture Among the Gullahs* (New York, NY: New York University Press, 1988); Nathan Irvin Huggins, *Black Odyssey: The Afro-American Ordeal in Slavery* (New York, NY: Vintage, 1977); and Harriet A. Jacobs, *Life of a Slave Girl* (Cambridge, MA: Harvard University Press, 1987; reprint). Joseph E. Holloway's *Africanisms in American Culture* (Bloomington and Indianapolis, IN: Indiana University Press, 1990), offers numerous insights into the transfer of African culture onto American soil, and presents a discussion of the debate between E. Franklin Frazier (*The Negro Church in America*, New York, NY: Schocken, 1964) and Melville J. Herskovits (*The Myth of the Negro Past* (Boston, MA: Beacon Press, 1958), concerning the level of destruction of African culture as the result of the slave trade. The introductory pages, as well as other material in John G. Jackson's *Introduction to African Civilizations* (Secaucus, NJ: Citadel, 1974), provide insight into the African origin of African American literature, history, and art. For a discussion of the food rations for African bondsmen, see Sam Bowers Hillard, *Hog Meat and Hoe Cake: Food Supply in the Old South, 1840–1860* (Carbondale, IL: Southern Illinois University Press, 1972); and Owens's *This Species of Property*. Piersen's *Black Yankees*, and an article titled "The Scar on the African's Arm," in *Hippocrates The Magazine of Health and Medicine* (March/April 1989), offer discourse on the smallpox epidemics in Boston and the African method of variolation. See also Thomas Bailey, *The American Pageant* (Lexington, MA: D.C. Heath and Co., 1975).

Although the time period of their books reaches beyond formal slavery, see Susan Tucker, *Telling Memories Among Southern Women* (Baton Rouge, LA: Louisiana State University Press, 1988) for stories by and about black women and their employers in the segregated South; and Cynthia Neverdon-Morton, *Afro-American Women of the South and the Advancement of the Race, 1895–1925* (Knoxville, TN: University of Tennessee Press, 1989).

"Traditional Medicine," practiced by African Americans, is the focus of Loudell F. Snow, *Walkin' Over Medicine* (Detroit, MI: Wayne State University Press, 1998; Boulder, Co.: Westview Press, 1993). General accounts of "Traditional Medicine" in Egypt, Nigeria, and other parts of Africa are given in Charles Finch, "The African Background of Medical Science," in *African Background to Medical Science: Essays on African History, Science, and Civilizations* (London, Eng.: Karnak House, 1990); C. A. Dime,

African Traditional Medicine: Peculiarities (Ekpoma, Nigeria: Edo State University Publishing House, 1995); Ismail Hussein Abdalla, *Islam, Medicine, and Practitioners in Northern Nigeria* (Lewiston, NY, E. Mellen Press, 1997); Olukayode Olowe's Ph.D. dissertation for the University of Chicago, *Culture and Medical Practice, the Nigerian Example A Study in the Sociology of Medicine* (1976); and Zacharys Anger Gundu, "Healing Technology: The African Perspective," *Humanitas* No. 2 (1984, 1985). See the therapeutic use of herbs and medicinal plants in Nigeria in *African Traditional Medicine: A Case Study of Hausa Medicinal Plants and Therapy* (Zaria, Nigeria: M. H. Jinju, 1990), by Muhammadu Hambali Jinju.

Food and cooking in the Caribbean is the subject of Geoffrey Holder, *Geoffrey Holder's Caribbean Cookbook* (New York, NY: The Viking Press, 1973); Elsa Miller and Leonard Henry, *Creative Bahamian Cooking and Menus* (Kingston, Jamaica: Kingston Publishers, 1982, 1984, 1991, 1994); Cindy Williams, *Cindy's Treasures* (Nassau, Bahamas: The Nassau Guardian Ltd., 1986); Marie Mendelson and Marguerite Sawyer, *Gourmet Bahamian Cooking* (Iowa City, IA: Best-Way Publishing Ltd., 1995; Abaco, Bahamas, 1979); Linda Wolfe, *The Cooking of the Caribbean Islands* (Alexandria, VA: Time-Life Books, 1970); Elsa Miller, *Caribbean Cookbook, Using the Foods We Grow* (Kingston, Jamaica: Kingston Publishers Ltd., 1979); Virginie F. Elbert and George A. Elbert, *Down-Island Caribbean Cookery* (New York, NY: Simon and Schuster, 1991); Leila Brandon, *A Merry Go Round of Recipes from Jamaica* (Kingston, Jamaica: Novelty Trading Co., Ltd., 1963); Helen Willinsky, *Jerk Barbecue from Jamaica* (Freedom, CA: The Crossing Press, 1990); and Elisabeth Lambert Ortiz, *The Complete Book of Caribbean Cooking* (New York, NY: M. Evans and Co., Inc., 1973). Also, see a contemporary presentation of Caribbean vegetarian cuisine, this time from Rastafarians, titled *The Rasta Cookbook* (Trenton, NJ: Africa World Press, Inc., 1992; 1988), by Laura Osborne; and Yvonne John's *Guyanese Seed of Soul* (Holly Hill, SC: R and M Publishing Co., Inc., 1980).

The United States has published a plethora of works on cuisine. Many of the earliest works offered advice on "good housekeeping" and "cures" as well. Be forewarned that a number of these contain racist discourse, common for the times. See, the "first cookbook compiled by an American Black," *The House Servant's Directory* (Waltham, MA: Gore Place Society, 1977; Boston, MA: Munroe and Francis, 1827), by Robert Roberts, butler to Governor Gore of Massachusetts in 1809. This facsimile edition, first published in Boston and New York in 1827, contains a few recipes but primarily tips on cleaning. Another extremely interesting cookbook, *What Mrs. Fisher Knows about Old Southern Cooking* (San Francisco, CA: Women's Cooperative Printing Office, 1881; Bedford, MA: Applewood Books, 1995), is a collection of recipes by Mrs. Abby Fisher, a black woman believed to have been born into slavery. This volume is said to be the first true cookbook by a black person. The 1995 facsimile edition contains afterword remarks titled "African Women Cooks in the Southern Kitchen". Also see *The University of Virginia Hospital Circle, The Monticello Cookbook* (Richmond, VA: The Dietz Press, Inc., 1950); Olive Bailey, *Christmas with the Washingtons* (Richmond, VA: The Dietz Press, Inc., 1948), which contains what are referred to as Martha Washington's fruit cake and eggnog recipes; Polly Graham Latane and Joyce Graham, eds., *The Old Washington Recipes* (Mount Vernon, or Oak Grove, Virginia, 1931); Mary Randolph, *The Virginia Housewife* (Philadelphia, PA: E. H. Butler and Co., 1860; Baltimore, MD: Plaskitt and Cugle, 1824); Sarah Rutledge *The Carolina Housewife* (Columbia, SC: University of South Carolina Press, 1979), a facsimile of the 1847 work; Mary Stuart Smith, *Virginia Cookery-Book* (New York, NY: Harper and Bros., 1885); Marion Cabell Tyree, ed., *Housekeeping in Old Virginia* (Louisville, KY: John P. Morton and Co., 1879); The Virginia Federation of Home Demonstration Clubs, *Recipes From Old Virginia* (Richmond, VA: The Dietz Press, 1958); Helen Bullock, *Williamsburg Art of Cookery* second ed. (Richmond, VA: Dietz Press, 1939); and her edited volume, *Recipes of Ante Bellum America* (New York, NY: Heirloom, 1967); Marie Kimball, *Thomas Jefferson's Cook Book* (Charlottesville, VA: University Press of Virginia, 1976). I might add that Bullock's *Williamsburg Art of Cookery* has garnered a bit of criticism regarding the authenticity of the time period the book claims to represent. Questions have also been raised concerning the authencity of some material contained in Kimball's *Thomas Jefferson's Cook Book*. Others include Marion Flexner, *Out of Kentucky Kitchens* (New York, NY: Franklin Watts, Inc. 1949); Minnie C. Fox, ed., *The Blue Grass Cookbook* (New York, NY: Fox, Duffield and Co., 1904); F. Meredith Dietz, *De Virginia Hambook by De Ol' Virginia Hamcook* (Richmond, VA: The Dietz Press, Inc., 1946); Mary Vereen Huguenin and Anne Montague Stoney, eds., *Charleston Receipts* (Charleston, SC: Junior League of Charleston, 1950); Caroline Darden Hurt and Joan Hundley Powell, eds., *The Smithfield Cookbook* (Smithfield, Virginia: Junior Women's Club of Smithfield, VA, 1978); Mrs. Walter Husted, ed., *Virginia Cookery Past and Present* (Franconia, Virginia: Woman's Auxiliary of Olivet Episcopal Church, 1957); Junior League of New Orleans, *The Plantation Cookbook* (Garden City, NY: Doubleday and Co., 1972); and Betty Benton Patterson, *Mammy Lou's Cook Book* (New York, NY: Robert M. McBride Co., 1931).

There are a number of books on African American cooking that form linkages to the Motherland. Two important treatises on the African contribution to food and cuisine in America include Helen Mendes, *The African Heritage Cookbook* (New York, NY: Macmillan, 1971); and Karen Hess, *The Carolina Rice Kitchen: The African Connection* (Columbia, SC: University of South Carolina Press, 1992), which deals primarily with South Carolina. John Egerton's *Southern Food* (New York, NY: Alfred A. Knopf, 1987) offers important comments on the role of Africans in southern kitchens. For African recipes straight from the Motherland, see Dinah Ameley Ayensu, *The Art of West African Cooking* (Garden City, NY: Doubleday, 1972); and *Ghana Recipe Book* (Accra, Ghana: Ghana Publishing Corp., 1970), by E. Nyaho, E. Amarteifio, and J. Asare.

American Food The Gastronomic Story (New York, NY: Random House, 1974, 1975, 1981), by Evan Jones, contains a chapter on African American cooking, in which he credits the origin of jazz to "gypsy rhythm tempos." The Time-Life cookbook series includes Eugene Walter, *American Cooking: Southern Style* (New York, NY: Time-Life Books, 1971; reprint 1975), in which he disconnects the roots of so-called "soul food" from Africa; Dale Brown, *American Cooking* (New York, NY: Time-Life Books, 1968); and Peter S. Feibleman, *American Cooking: Creole and Acadian* (New York, NY: Time-Life Books, 1971; reprint 1975), all of which offer little to no treatment of the African contribution.

Interviews were obtained from Mrs. Roberta Gayles on May 7, 1980, and from Mrs. Rader Glenn on June 4, 1979. An 8:00 P.M. public television program broadcast in August 1987, titled "Ancient Lives," offered commentary on ancient Egyptian shopkeepers who kept jars of fried cracklings on their shelves.

Chapter Seven. Economics, War, and the Northern Migration of the Southern Black Cook

Like Brazil, the history of Louisiana, and particularly New Orleans, has generated numerous volumes. For example, see Barry Jean Ancelet, Jay D. Edwards and Glen Pitre, *Cajun Country* (Jackson, MS and London, Eng.: University Press of Mississippi, 1991), in which attention is given to the Africanization of aspects of Louisiana culture through cuisine, and the African (the authors refer to it as Black Creole) influence on Cajun music. Also, see John W. Blassingame, *Black New Orleans, 1860–1880* (Chicago, IL, London, Eng.: The University of Chicago Press, 1973); George W. Cable, *The Creoles of Louisiana* (New York, NY: Garrett Press, Inc., 1970); Hodding Carter, *The Past as Prelude: New Orleans 1718–1968* (New Orleans, LA: Tulane University, 1968); Edna B. Freiberg, *Bayou St. John in Colonial Louisiana 1699–1803* (New Orleans, LA: Harvey Press, 1980); Nelson George, *The Death of Rhythm and Blues* (New York, NY: Pantheon Books, 1988), in which he writes that rhythm and blues became, "along with gumbo, the city's most popular local delicacy"; Kimberly S. Hanger, *Bounded*

Lives Bounded Places, Free Black Society in Colonial New Orleans, 1769–1803 (Durham, NC, London, Eng.: Duke University Press, 1997); M. H. Herrin, *The Creole Aristocracy* (New York, NY: Exposition Press, 1952); Leonard V. Huber, *The Battle of New Orleans, New Orleans as It Was in 1814–1815* (New Orleans, LA [?]: Battle of New Orleans Anniversary Committee, 1965); Harnett T. Kane, *Queen New Orleans, City by the River* (New York, NY: Bonanza Books, 1949); Eliza Ripley, *Social Life in Old New Orleans* (New York, NY, London, Eng.: D. Appleton and Co., 1912); and Lura Robinson, *It's an Old New Orleans Custom* (New York, NY: The Vanguard Press, Inc., 1948).

Steamboat folklore and culinary and commercial history are covered in, for example, Thomas Hamilton, *Men and Manners in America* second ed. (Edinburgh, Scotland: W. Blackwood, 1834, 1843; second American ed., Philadelphia, PA: Carey, Lea and Blanchard, 1833); Stephen H. Hayes, "Letters From the West in 1845," *Iowa Journal of History and Politics* XX (1922); Ralph Nading Hill, *Sidewheeler Saga* (New York, NY: Rinehart and Co., Inc., 1953); Louis C. Hunter, *Steamboats on the Western Rivers* (Cambridge, MA: Harvard University Press, 1949; New York, NY: Octagon Books, 1969); William E. Lass, *A History of Steamboating on the Upper Missouri River* (Lincoln, NE: University of Nebraska Press, 1962); George Merrick, *Old Times on the Upper Mississippi* (Cleveland, OH: A. H. Clark Co., 1909; New York, NY: Dover Publications, 1993, 1949); Wm. J. Petersen, *Steamboating on the Upper Mississippi, the Water Way to Iowa* (Iowa City, IA: The State Historical Society of Iowa, 1937); Herbert Quick and Edward Quick, *Mississippi Steamboatin'* (New York, NY: Henry Holt and Co., 1926), which contains some examples of lyrics sung by African workers as they entertained passengers; Patrick Shirreff, *A Tour Through North America* (New York, NY: B. Blom, 1971, 1835); and Ben Wattenberg, *Busy Waterways: The Story of America's Inland Water Transportation* (New York, NY: The John Day Co., 1964). See also Donald C. Ringwald, *Steamboats for Rondout: Passenger Service between New York and Rondout Creek, 1829 through 1863* (Providence, RI: Steamship Historical Society of America, 1981); Harry Sinclair Drago, *The Steamboaters, from the Early Side-Wheelers to the Big Packets* (New York, NY: Bramhall House, 1967); and Harry P. Owens, *Steamboats and the Cotton Economy: River Trade in the Yazoo, Mississippi Delta* (Jackson, MS: University Press of Mississippi, 1990).

The condition of Africans under the Confederacy during the Civil War is the focus of James H. Brewer, *The Confederate Negro: Virginia's Craftsmen and Military Laborers, 1861–1865* (Durham, NC: Duke University Press, 1969); and Brainerd Dyer, "The Treatment of Colored Union Troops by the Confederates, 1861–1865," *Journal of Negro History* XX (July 1935). African participation in the Civil War in general is dealt with in James M. McPherson, *The Negro's Civil War* (New York, NY: Vintage Books, 1965).

Also see McPherson's *Battle Cry of Freedom: The Civil War Era* (New York, NY: Oxford University Press, 1988); Clarence L. Mohr, *On the Threshold of Freedom: Masters and Slaves in Civil War Georgia* (Athens, GA: University of Georgia Press, 1985); Benjamin Quarles, *The Negro in the Civil War* (Boston, MA: Little, Brown, 1953); and his two other works, *Lincoln and the Negro* (New York, NY: Da Capo Press, 1991, 1962); and *The Negro in the Making of America* (New York, NY: Collier Books, 1964); Herbert Aptheker, *The Negro in the Civil War* (New York, NY: International Publishers, 1938); Joseph T. Glatthaar, *Forged in Battle: The Civil War Alliance of Black Soldiers* (New York, NY: Meridian, 1990, 1991); Thomas Wentworth Higginson, *Army Life in a Black Regiment* (New York, NY: Collier, 1962 reprint; Boston, MA: Fields, Osgood and Co., 1870); John Hope Franklin, *From Slavery to Freedom: A History of Negro Americans* sixth ed. (New York, NY: Alfred A. Knopf, 1988); Lerone Bennett, *Before the Mayflower: A History of Black America* (New York, NY: Penguin, 1984, 1961); George W. Williams, *A History of the Negro Troops in the War of the Rebellion* (New York, NY: Harper and Brothers, 1888); Joseph T. Wilson, *The Black Phalanx* (Hartford, CT: American Publishing Co., 1888); and Dudley T. Cornish, *The Sable Arm: Negro Troops in the Union Army, 1861–1865* (New York, NY: Longmans, Green, 1956).

Even discussions of the peanut and its origins lead to controversy. See, for example, Leo Wiener, *Africa and the Discovery of America* Vol. I (Philadelphia, PA: Innes and Sons, 1920); Mary T. Wilson, "Peaceful Integration: The Owner's Adoption of His Slaves' Food," *The Journal of Negro History* XLIX, No. 2 (Washington, D.C. April 1964); Samuel Purchas, *Hakluytus Posthumus, Or Purchas His Pilgrimes: Contayning A History of the World in Sea Voyages and Lande Travells By Englishmen and Others* VI (London, Eng.: H. Fetherstone, 1625); Lisanne Renner, "Peanut Butter Goes Upscale," *The Hartford Courant* (July 29, 1987); and "Peanut Butter: It's Not Only for Sandwiches," *The Hartford Courant* (September 28, 1983). The life of George Washington Carver and his many accomplishments is the subject of Shirley Graham and George D. Lipscomb, *Dr. George Washington Carver, Scientist* (New York, NY: Julian Messner, Inc., 1944), which also cites some Carver recipes; Augusta Stevenson, *George Carver Boy Scientist* (Indianapolis, IN: Bobbs-Merrill Co., 1944); David Smallwood, *Profiles of Great African Americans* (Lincolnwood, IL: Publications International, 1998); and Harry James Albus, *The Peanut Man; The Life of George Washington Carver in Story Form* 3rd printing (Grand Rapids, MI: W. B. Eerdmans Publishing Co., 1948, 1950). Also, see Mary Jackson and Lelia Wishart, *The Integrated Cookbook or the Soul of Good Cooking* (Chicago, IL: Johnson Publishing Co., Inc., 1971) for a few of George Washington Carver's recipes.

The role of Booker T. Washington and Hampton and Tuskegee Institutes in dispensing Industrial Education to blacks is very ably handled in

Donald Spivey, *Schooling for the New Slavery: Black Industrial Education, 1868–1915* (Westport, CT: Greenwood Press, 1978). Louis Harlan offers an opposing view in his article, "Booker T. Washington and the Politics of Accommodation," in John Hope Franklin and August Meier, eds., *Black Leaders of the Twentieth Century* (Champaign-Urbana, IL: University of Illinois Press, 1982). Spivey's and Harlan's arguments are presented in a separate volume, titled, *Taking Sides: Clashing Views on Controversial Issues in American History* Vol. II (Guilford, Connecticut: Dushkin Publishing Group, 1997), edited by Larry Madaras and James M. SoRelle. See also W. E. B. Du Bois, *The Souls of Black Folk* (Greenwich, CT: Fawcett Publications, 1961); and Carter G. Woodson, *The Miseducation of the Negro* (New York, NY: Associated Pubs., 1933).

W. E. B. Du Bois's *The Philadelphia Negro* (1899; New York, NY: B. Blom, 1967) contains discourse on the Guild of the Philadelphia Caterers. See also Henry M. Minton, "Early History of Negroes in Business in Philadelphia," read Before The American Historical Society (March 1913). Whittington B. Johnson's *Black Savannah 1788–1864* (Fayetteville, AR: University of Arkansas Press, 1996) contains interesting information on property and businesses, such as bakeries, owned by free blacks in Savannah, Georgia. *Black Yankees* (Amherst, MA: University of Massachusetts Press, 1988), by William D. Piersen, mentions the black chef who oversaw the turtle feast for the Marine Society of Salem. Abolition is the focus of *Black Abolitionists* (New York, NY: Oxford University Press, 1969), by Benjamin Quarles; and James M. McPherson's *The Abolitionist Legacy* (Princeton, NJ: Princeton University Press, 1975). "Pig Foot Mary" is presented in Roi Ottley and William J. Weatherby, eds., *The Negro in New York* (New York, NY: Praeger Publishers, 1969). Works covering the black exodus and urban North include David Gordon Nielson, *Black Ethos: Northern Urban Negro Life and Thought, 1890–1930* (Westport, CT: Greenwood Press, 1977); St. Clair Drake and Horace R. Cayton, *Black Metropolis: A Study of Negro Life in a Northern City* Vol. I and II (New York, NY: Harcourt, Brace and Co., 1945); Florette Henri, *Black Migration: Movement North, 1900–1920* (Garden City, NY: Anchor Books, 1976); Richard B. Sherman, ed., *The Negro and the City* (Englewood Cliffs, NJ: Prentice-Hall, 1970); Gilbert Osofsky's thesis presented at Columbia University, *Harlem: The Making of a Negro Ghetto* (New York, NY: 1963); Herman D. Bloch, *The Circle of Discrimination: An Economic and Social Study of the Black Man in New York* (New York, NY: New York University Press, 1969); Charles Keil, *Urban Blues* (Chicago, IL: University of Chicago Press, 1966); John Henrik Clarke, ed., *Harlem: A Community in Transition* (New York, NY: Citadel Press, 1964); and David M. Katzman, *Before the Ghetto: Black Detroit in the Nineteenth Century* (Urbana, IL: University of Illinois Press, 1975).

Encyclopedia International (1980); *Merit Students Encyclopedia* (New York, NY; Toronto, Canada: Macmillan Educational Co., Collier Macmillan Canada, 1991; 1982); *The New Encyclopedia Britannica* fifteenth ed. (Chicago, IL: Encyclopedia Britannica Educational Corp., 1998, 1986); and *The World Book Encyclopedia* (1983; Chicago, IL: World Book Inc., 1999) were consulted on the question of ice cream.

See New Orleans' classic, *The Original Picayune Creole Cook Book* (New Orleans, LA: Times-Picayune Publishing Co., 1936, 1901), which states that the old recipes, passed down through the generations, "from the old time 'Mammy,' who could work all kinds of magic . . . was such cookery . . . that won the hearts of beruffled gentlemen and crinolined ladies in the early nineteenth century and made them declare that never were there such cooks as in New Orleans." See also Paul Prudhomme, *Louisiana Kitchen* (New York, NY: William Morrow and Co., Inc., 1984); Emma Allen Hayes, *Kentucky Cook Book, "By a Colored Woman"—Mrs. W. T. Hayes* (St. Louis, MO: J. R. Tomkins Printing Co., 1912); Jackson and Wishart's *The Integrated Cookbook, Or the Soul of Good Cooking;* Betty Benton Patterson, *Mammy Lou's Cook Book* (New York, NY: Robert M. McBride Co., 1931); Mary D. Pretlow, *Old Southern Receipts* (New York, NY: Robert M. McBride Co., 1930); and Harriet Ross Colquitt, ed., *The Savannah Cook Book* (Charleston, SC: Colonial Publishers, 1933). Edna Lewis's *The Taste of Country Cooking* (New York, NY: Knopf, 1976), contains many good recipes and insight into African American methods of cooking, including her discourse on ice cream, snow ice cream and on "lovely cakes and breads that rose by the power of beaten egg whites . . . " Nancy Johnson is mentioned as the inventor of the hand-cranked ice cream freezer in Dale Brown's *American Cooking* (New York, NY: Time-Life Books, 1968). Also see Bea Moten, *Two Hundred Years of Black Cookery* (Indianapolis, IN: Leonbea Corp., 1976); Consumer Division, Reynolds Metals Company, *The Way Mama Cooked It* (Richmond, VA: Reynolds Metal Company, Consumer Division, 1981); Eugene Walter, *American Cooking: Southern Style* (New York, NY: Time-Life Books, 1971); and Christine Terhune Herrick, *Like Mother Used to Make* (Boston, MA: D. Estes and Co., 1912).

Chapter Eight. Flapjacks and Blue Notes

Some important discussions on African American music can be found in Ortiz M. Walton's *Music: Black, White, and Blue* (New York, NY: William Morrow, 1972); Samuel A. Floyd, *The Power of Black Music* (New York, NY: Oxford University Press, 1995); and two articles by Wynton Marsalis, "Why We Must Preserve Our Jazz Heritage," *Ebony*, XLI, No. 4 (February 1986), and "What

Jazz Is—and Isn't," *The New York Times* (July 31, 1988). For other sources on black music see Francis Bebey, *African Music* (Westport, CT: Lawrence Hill, 1975); J. H. Kwabena Nketia, *The Music of Africa* (New York, NY: Norton, 1974); Nelson George, *The Death of Rhythm and Blues* (New York, NY: Pantheon, 1988); Donald Spivey, *Union and the Black Musician, The Narrative of William Everett Samuels and Chicago Local 208* (Lanham, MD: University Press of America, 1984); Susan Curtis, *Dancing to a Black Man's Tune* (Columbia, MO and London, Eng.: University of Missouri Press, 1994); Joachim Berendt, *The Jazz Book* (Westport, CT: Lawrence Hill, 1975); Eileen Southern, *The Music of Black Americans* (New York, NY: Norton, 1971); Jack V. Buerkle and Danny Barker, *Bourbon Street Black: The New Orleans Black Jazzman* (New York, NY: Oxford University Press, 1973); Winthrop Sargeant, *Jazz, Hot and Hybrid* (New York, NY: Da Capo, 1975); Frank Tirro, *Jazz: A History* (New York, NY: Norton, 1977); Bessie Jones et al., *Step It Down: Games, Plays, Songs, and Stories from the Afro-American Heritage* (Athens, GA: University of Georgia Press, 1987); and John Litweiler, *The Freedom Principle: Jazz After 1958* (New York, NY: Da Capo, 1984).

Minstrel performances are the subject of *Blacking Up: The Minstrel Show in Nineteenth-Century America* (New York, NY: Oxford University Press, 1974), by Robert C. Toll; and Joseph Boskin's *Sambo: The Rise and Demise of an American Jester* (New York, NY: Oxford University Press, 1986). For a look at other works on this subject see Lynne F. Emery, *Black Dance in the United States From 1619 to 1970* (Palo Alto, CA: National Press Books, 1972); Carl Wittke, *Tambo and Bones: A History of the American Minstrel Show* (Durham, NC: Duke University Press, 1930); Ralph Keeler, "Three Years as a Negro Minstrel," *Atlantic Monthly* (July 1869); Hugh F. Rankin, *The Theatre in Colonial America* (Chapel Hill, NC: University of North Carolina Press, 1965); Hans Nathan, *Dan Emmett and the Rise of Early Negro Minstrelsy* (Norman, OK: University of Oklahoma Press, 1962); and Brander Matthews, "The Rise and Fall of Negro Minstrelsy," *Scribner's Magazine* (June 1915).

For discourse on the creation of Aunt Jemima Pancake Mix, its living symbols, and the early days of the Quaker Oats Company, see Arthur F. Marquette, *Brands, Trademarks, and Good Will: The Story of the Quaker Oats Company* (New York, NY: McGraw-Hill, 1967); and Mildred Grenier, "World's First Ready-Mix Food Was Made in Missouri," *Kansas City Star* (January 25, 1976). Also, see a 1927 Chamber of Commerce publication, *St. Joseph, Missouri Today*, which offers information on the Aunt Jemima Mills Branch of the Quaker Oats Company. Biographical information on Chris L. Rutt is contained in *Centennial History of Missouri—The Center State, 1820–1921* (St. Louis, MO: S. J. Clarke Publishing Co., 1921); *The Daily News' History of Buchanan Co. and St. Joseph, Missouri* (St. Joseph, MO: St. Joseph Publishing Co., 1898); *History of Buchanan County and*

St. Joseph, Missouri (St. Joseph, MO: Midland Printing Co., 1915); Christian Ludwig Rutt, ed., *History of Buchanan County and the City of St. Joseph and Representative Citizens* (Chicago, IL: Biographical Publishing Co., 1904); and *Missouri Historical Review* Vol. 31. There are a few treatises that explore African-American women as they relate to cooking, and to the stereotypical aspects of advertising in the United States. These works include Doris Smith Witt's Ph.D. Thesis for the University of Virginia, *What Ever Happened to Aunt Jemima?: Black Women and Food in American Culture* (1995); Maurice M. Manring, *Slave in a Box: The Strange Career of Aunt Jemima* (Charlottesville, VA: University Press of Virginia, 1998); and Marilyn Kern-Foxworth, *Aunt Jemima, Uncle Ben, and Rastus: Blacks in Advertising, Yesterday, Today, and Tomorrow* (Westport, CT: Praeger, 1994).

Works that shed light on black existence in Chicago and other urban areas include Sterling D. Spero and Abram L. Harris, *The Black Worker* (New York, NY: Atheneum, 1968; Kennikat Press, 1931); David Gordon Nielson, *Black Ethos: Northern Urban Negro Life and Thought, 1890–1930* (Westport, CT: Greenwood Press, 1977); Allan H. Spear, *Black Chicago: The Making of a Negro Ghetto, 1890–1920* (Chicago, IL: Chicago University Press, 1967); Thomas Lee Philpott, *The Slum and the Ghetto: Neighborhood Deterioration and Middle-Class Reform, Chicago, 1880–1930* (New York, NY: Oxford University Press, 1978); Raymond Wolters, *Negroes and the Great Depression* (Westport, CT: Greenwood Publishing Corp., 1970); and Richard B. Sherman, ed., *The Negro and the City* (Englewood Cliffs, NJ: Prentice-Hall, 1970). Black life in Harlem in the early part of the century is considered in Roi Ottley and William J. Weatherby, *The Negro in New York* (New York, NY: Praeger Publishers, 1969). Also, see Herman D. Bloch, *The Circle of Discrimination: An Economic and Social Study of the Black Man in New York* (New York, NY: New York University Press, 1969). Harlem, as seen through the eyes of the Harlem Renaissance and black literature, is written about in Claude McKay, *Home to Harlem* (New York, NY: Pocket Books, 1969 reprint); Jervis Anderson, *This Was Harlem, 1900–1950* (New York, NY: Farrar, Straus, Giroux, 1981); Langston Hughes, *The Best of Simple* (New York, NY: Noonday Press, 1961); and James Weldon Johnson, *Black Manhattan* (New York, NY: Atheneum, 1968; 1930).

Other works that shed light on African-American life include William H. Harris, *The Harder We Run: Black Workers Since the Civil War* (New York, NY: Oxford University Press, 1982); Jacqueline Jones, *Labor of Love, Labor of Sorrow: Black Women, Work, and the Family, From Slavery to the Present* (New York, NY: Vintage Books, 1986). See also Benjamin Quarles, *The Negro in the Making of America* (New York, NY: Collier Books, 1964). Adelbert H. Jenkins's *Psychology and African-Americans* (Needham Heights, MA: Allyn and Bacon, 1995, 1982); and Daryl Michael Scott's *Contempt and Pity, Social Policy and the Image of the Damaged Black Psyche 1880–*

1996 (Chapel Hill, NC: University of North Carolina Press, 1997), offer insight into perceived self-esteem of African Americans. Also, see Robert V. Guthrie's edited volume, *Being Black: Psychological-Sociological Dilemmas* (San Francisco, CA: Canfield Press, 1970); Julia A. Conyers Boyd, *In the Company of My Sisters: Black Women and Self-Esteem* (New York, NY: Dutton, 1993); James Davison, *Prisoners of Our Past: A Critical Look at Self-Defeating Attitudes within the Black Community* (Secaucus, NJ: Carol Publishing Group, 1993); and William H. Grier and Price M. Cobbs, *Black Rage* (New York, NY: Basic Books, 1968). Ali A. Mazrui's treatise, *The African Diaspora: African Origins and New World Identities* (Bloomington, IN: Indiana University Press, 1999), offers insight on African American history and African cultural influences on America.

Numerous works have emerged in the modern era, offering culinary lore, as well as updated versions of classic recipes. Among them are Norma Jean Darden and Carole Darden, *Spoonbread and Strawberry Wine* (Garden City, NY: Anchor Press/Doubleday, 1978); LaMont Burns, *Down Home Southern Cooking* (Garden City, NY: Doubleday and Co., 1987); Edna Lewis, *The Taste of Country Cooking* (New York, NY: Alfred A. Knopf, 1976); Jessica B. Harris, *Iron Pots and Wooden Spoons* (New York, NY: Atheneum, 1989), which establishes the important link between Africans at home and in the Caribbean, Brazil, and the southern United States; Cleora Butler, *Cleora's Kitchen: The Memoir of a Cook and Eight Decades of Great American Food* (Tulsa, OK: Council Oak Books, 1985); Joseph Stafford, *The Black Gourmet* (Detroit, MI: Harlo Printing Co., 1984); Alice McGill, Mary Carter Smith, and Elmira M. Washington, *The Griots' Cookbook, Rare and Well-Done* (Columbia, MD: C. H. Fairfax Co., 1985); *The Black Family Reunion Cookbook* (Memphis, TN: Tradery House, 1991; New York, NY: Fireside-Simon and Schuster, 1993) and *The Historical Cookbook of the American Negro* (Washington, DC: Corporate Press, 1958), both by The National Council of Negro Women; Bea Moten, *Two Hundred Years of Black Cookery* (Indianapolis, IN: Leonbea Corp., Inc., 1976); and John Egerton, *Southern Food* (Chapel Hill, NC: University of North Carolina Press, 1993; New York, NY: Knopf, 1987). Other sources include Julianne Belote, *The Compleat American Housewife 1776* (Concord, CA: Nitty Gritty Productions, 1974); Marion Brown, *Marion Brown's Southern Cook Book* (Chapel Hill, NC: University of North Carolina Press, 1951); Mrs. Clyde X. Copeland, ed., *Southern Sideboards* (Jackson, MS: The Junior League of Jackson, Mississippi, 1978); and Charleen McClain, ed., *Hollands's Southern Cookbook* (Atlanta, GA: Tupper and Love, Inc., 1952). Also, see *The Hartford Courant* article, "Giving Thanks to English for Breakfast Tradition," (May 30, 1984); and Jolene Worthington's article, "In Praise of Pancakes," *Cuisine* (February 1983).

Replay of interview with Larry Young was broadcast on National Public Radio on February 5, 1992. Interview was obtained from Dr. Donald Spivey in December, 1984, on the subject of "Jazz Drummers and Tap Dance."

Index

391